This book's critical examination of crossing boundaries – organizational, juris-dictional, sectoral, international – is vital reading for those unsatisfied with typical discussions of collaboration and network management. The questions addressed in this volume demonstrate that overcoming such boundaries is the signature governing issue of our time.

Michael McGuire, Indiana University, USA

A rich and satisfying collection that rewards the continuing policy and scholarly interest in the theory and practice of cross boundary working by drawing on international experiences, detailed cases and innovative methods to offer new insights on fundamental questions.

Helen Sullivan, University of Melbourne, Australia

This book assembles a diverse and inter-disciplinary set of contributions high-lighting the importance of 'boundaries' as sites of ambiguity, conflict and poten-tial in the theory and practice of international public policy and management. It represents a valuable and thought-provoking addition to the existing literature on this important subject.

Paul Williams, Cardiff Metropolitan University, UK

T0382830

Crossing Boundaries in Public Management and Policy

In the twenty-first century governments are increasingly focusing on designing ways and means of connecting across boundaries in order to achieve goals. Whether issues are complex and challenging – climate change, international terrorism, intergenerational poverty – or more straightforward – provision of a single point of entry to government or delivering integrated public services – practitioners and scholars increasingly advocate the use of approaches which require connections across various boundaries, be they organizational, jurisdictional or sectorial.

Governments around the world continue to experiment with various approaches but still confront barriers, leading to the general view that there is considerable promise in cross-boundary working, but that this promise is often unfulfilled. This book explores a variety of topics in order to create a rich survey of the international experience of cross-boundary working. The book asks fundamental questions such as:

- What do we mean by the notion of crossing boundaries?
- Why has this emerged?
- What does cross-boundary working involve?
- What are the critical enablers and barriers?

By scrutinizing these questions, the contributing authors examine the promise, the barriers, the enablers, the enduring tensions, and the potential solutions to cross-boundary working. As such, this will be an essential read for all those involved with public administration, management and policy.

Janine O'Flynn is Professor of Public Management at the University of Melbourne, Australia and an adjunct at The Australian and New Zealand School of Government. She examines Public Sector Reform and Relationships and recently published *Rethinking Public Services: Managing with External Providers* (2012, Palgrave Macmillan) with John Alford.

Deborah Blackman is Professor of Human Resources Management in the Faculty of Business, Government and Law, and the Director of the Graduate Research Office, both at the University of Canberra, Australia. She publishes in the areas of Performance Management, Organizational Learning, Knowledge Management and Organizational Effectiveness in both the private and public sectors.

John Halligan is Professor of Public Administration at the ANZSOG Institute for Governance, University of Canberra, Australia. His recently published books include *Public Sector Governance in Australia* (2012, ANU Press) and *Performance Management in the Public Sector* (2010, Routledge). He is currently working on a comparative analysis of public management reform in four Anglophone countries.

Routledge critical studies in public management
Edited by Stephen Osborne

The study and practice of public management has undergone profound changes across the world. Over the last quarter century, we have seen

- increasing criticism of public administration as the over-arching framework for the provision of public services,
- the rise (and critical appraisal) of the 'New Public Management' as an emergent paradigm for the provision of public services,
- the transformation of the 'public sector' into the cross-sectoral provision of public services, and
- the growth of the governance of inter-organizational relationships as an essential element in the provision of public services.

In reality these trends have not so much replaced each other as elided or co-existed together – the public policy process has not gone away as a legitimate topic of study, intra-organizational management continues to be essential to the efficient provision of public services, whilst the governance of inter-organizational and inter-sectoral relationships is now essential to the effective provision of these services.

Further, whilst the study of public management has been enriched by the contribution of a range of insights from the 'mainstream' management literature it has also contributed to this literature in such areas as networks and inter-organizational collaboration, innovation and stakeholder theory.

This series is dedicated to presenting and critiquing this important body of theory and empirical study. It will publish books that both explore and evaluate the emergent and developing nature of public administration, management and governance (in theory and practice) and examine the relationship with and contribution to the over-arching disciplines of management and organizational sociology.

Books in the series will be of interest to academics and researchers in this field, students undertaking advanced studies of it as part of their undergraduate or postgraduate degree, and reflective policy makers and practitioners.

Crossing Boundaries in Public Management and Policy

The international experience

**Edited by Janine O'Flynn,
Deborah Blackman and
John Halligan**

Routledge
Taylor & Francis Group

LONDON AND NEW YORK

First published in paperback 2024

First published 2014
by Routledge
4 Park Square, Milton Park, Abingdon, Oxon OX14 4RN

and by Routledge
605 Third Avenue, New York, NY 10158

Routledge is an imprint of the Taylor & Francis Group, an informa business

British Library Cataloguing in Publication Data
A catalogue record for this book is available from the British Library

Library of Congress Cataloging in Publication Data
A catalog record has been requested for this book

ISBN: 978-0-415-67824-7 (hbk)
ISBN: 978-1-03-292237-9 (pbk)
ISBN: 978-0-203-10690-7 (ebk)

DOI: 10.4324/9780203106907

Typeset in Times New Roman
by Wearset Ltd, Boldon, Tyne and Wear

Contents

Figures and tables

Figures

Tables

Contributors

Fiona Buick is an early career academic in the Faculty of Business, Government and Law at the University of Canberra.

Deborah Blackman is Professor of Human Resources Management in the Faculty of Business, Government and Law and the Director of the Graduate Research Office, both at the University of Canberra.

Kate Blatchford is a researcher at the Institute for Government in London, a think tank that seeks to improve the effectiveness of government in the UK.

Dag Arne Christensen is a senior researcher at Stein Rokkan Center for Social Studies, Bergen.

Tom Christensen is Professor of Public Administration and Policy in the Department of Political Science, University of Oslo, and Adjunct Professor at the University of Bergen and the City University of Hong Kong.

John Diamond is Professor of Urban Policy Studies and Director of Research in the Business School at Edge Hill University, UK, and joint editor of the Sage journal *Teaching Public Administration.*

Timothy Donnet is a lecturer in the fields of management, negotiation and operational risk management at QUT Business School, with a research focus on inter-organizational decision making, particularly in the governance of infrastructure projects.

Elizabeth Eppel is Senior Research Fellow in the School of Government, Victoria University of Wellington, with a research interest in complex policy processes and collaborative governance.

Derek Gill is Principal Economist at the New Zealand Institute of Economic Research and Research Associate at the Institute for Governance and Policy at Victoria University of Wellington.

John Halligan is Professor of Public Administration, ANZSOG Institute for Governance, University of Canberra. His recent books include *Public Sector Governance in Australia* (ANU Press 2012) and *Performance Management* *in the Public Sector* (Routledge 2010). He is working on a comparative analysis of public management reform in four Anglophone countries.

Brian W. Head is Professor of Policy Analysis in the Institute for Social Science Research at the University of Queensland and a board member of several international journals.

Owen E. Hughes is Dean of Students at RMIT University. Until late 2011 he was Deputy Dean (Education) in the Faculty of Business and Economics at Monash University, with a fractional appointment as Professor of Public Management with the Australia and New Zealand School of Government.

Robyn Keast is Professor in the Southern Cross University Business School and an adjunct professor in the school of management, QUT Business School, Queensland University of Technology.

Esther Klaster works as a consultant in the public sector and is finishing her PhD thesis, which is on collaborative networks in education and employment, at the University of Twente.

Sanja Korac is Assistant Professor at the Department of Public, Nonprofit and Health Management, Alpen-Adria Universitaet Klagenfurt, Austria. Her main research and teaching fields are collaborative delivery of public services, public performance management, and integrated health care.

Per Lægreid is Professor at the Department of Administration and Organization Theory, University of Bergen, and an adjunct senior researcher at Stein Rokkan Center for Social Studies, Bergen.

Kelly LeRoux is Assistant Professor in the Department of Public Administration at the University of Illinois, Chicago. Her current research focuses on issues of performance and accountability in multi-sector networks and partnerships.

Joyce Liddle is Professor of Public Leadership and Head of the Centre for Strategy and Leadership at Teesside University Business School, UK. She is also a visiting professor at Paul Cezanne University, France, and the University of Eastern Finland.

Evert A. Lindquist is Professor and Director of the School of Public Administration at the University of Victoria, British Columbia, and editor of the journal *Canadian Public Administration*.

Miriam Lips is Professor of e-Government at the School of Government, Victoria University of Wellington. Her Chair is sponsored by Datacom Systems Limited, Department of Internal Affairs, State Services Commission, FX Networks Limited and Microsoft New Zealand Ltd.

Tore Midtbø is Professor in the Department of Comparative Politics, University of Bergen.

Dennis R. Muntslag is Professor of Business Transformation at the University of Twente in the Netherlands. He is also a partner at PwC Advisory. He advises multinational clients on optimizing their value chain from a business, tax and legal perspective.

Janine O'Flynn is Professor of Public Management in the School of Social and Political Sciences at The University of Melbourne, Australia.

Akash Paun is a senior researcher at the Institute for Government in London, a think tank that seeks to improve the effectiveness of government in the UK. Akash formerly worked as a researcher in the Constitution Unit, University College London.

Bill Ryan is Associate Professor in the School of Government, Victoria University of Wellington, a member of the Institute of Governance and Policy Studies, and co-editor of *Policy Quarterly*.

Iris Saliterer is Senior Assistant Professor at the Department of Public, Non-profit and Health Management, Alpen-Adria Universitaet Klagenfurt, Austria, and an active member in various international public management associations. Her research focuses on public performance management, public budgeting and accounting, and public innovation.

Carole Talbot is Lecturer in Public Policy and Management at Manchester Business School.

Colin R. Talbot is Professor of Government at the University of Manchester, Director of Policy@Manchester, author of the influential WhitehallWatch blog, and a Fellow of the Royal Society of Arts.

Celeste P. M. Wilderom, chair 'Change Management and Organizational Behavior,' University of Twente, the Netherlands, examines how human talent is led toward highly-performing organizations and their stakeholders. This includes change effectiveness predictors; participation modes; and effective consulting and leadership. For instance, she video-tapes and analyzes leaders and followers at meetings.

Acknowledgements

In drawing together this group of authors, we sought to explore the international experience of crossing boundaries in public management and policy. In and of itself, the book is an example of the benefits of working in this way. The genesis of the book came from a very successful panel session held at the XIV International Research Society for Public Management Conference in Berne in 2010, where many of the authors of these chapters presented the first drafts of their work. It was an outstanding panel, with emerging and experienced scholars from across the world coming together to explore the potential, but also the puzzles and paradoxes, of working across boundaries. In addition to several presenters from the panel, we sought contributions from others and, together, these authors have enabled us to consider a range of issues related to crossing boundaries.

Jacqueline Curthoys from Routledge encouraged us to consider bringing these together in a book and worked with us throughout the long process of bringing that to fruition.

For the editors, this collection connects to a large-scale project, funded by the Australian Research Council, which explored the Australian experiment with 'whole-of-government' or joined-up approaches. Bringing aspects of that together with the research of our colleagues from different systems, all facing similar challenges, enables us to deliver added value to the project.

We express our thanks to all of the authors who have contributed to this collection, for their hard work in putting together their chapters and for their continued commitment to the overall project.

We reserve our biggest thanks for Rosemary Lohmann, who took on the role of Editorial Assistant. Without Rosemary this would not be the coherent and well-presented collection that it is. She worked extensively with all of the authors on their chapters, offering suggestions for improvements, and ensuring that our work was presented to the best possible standard, exercising her charm and persistence in equal measure. She meticulously managed the process of drafts, revisions, and corrections to produce the manuscript and managed every stage of the production process with patience and attention to detail. The end product owes much to her considerable efforts.

Janine O'Flynn

Abbreviations

ACIR	Advisory Commission Intergovernmental Relations
ADM	Assistant Deputy Minister
AGRAGA	Advisory Group on Reform of Australian Government Administration
ANAO	Australian National Audit Office
APS	Australian Public Service
BIS	Department for Business Innovation and Skills
CCDM	Continuing Committee of Deputy Ministers
CCMD	Canadian Centre for Management Development
CCT	Compulsory Competitive Tendering
CDRP	Crime and Disorder Reduction Partnership
CE	Customs and Excise
CJB	Criminal Justice Board
CLG	Department for Communities and Local Government
COAG	Council of Australian Governments
COSO	Committee of Senior Officials
CPA	Comprehensive Performance Assessment
CPRN	Canadian Policy Research Networks
CSA	Common Services Agreement
CSP	Community Safety Partnership
CSPS	Canada School of Public Service
CSR	Comprehensive Spending Review
CT	Children's Trusts
CYPP	Children and Young People's Plan
DCS	Directors for Children's Services
DCSF	Department for Children, Schools and Families
DECC	Department of Energy and Climate Change
Defra	Department for Environment, Food and Rural Affairs
DFES	Department for Education and Schools
DG	Director General
DH	Department of Health
DIMIA	Department of Immigration and Multicultural and Indigenous Affairs

DIUS	Department for Innovation, Universities and Skills
DWP	Department for Work and Pensions
ECM	Every Child Matters (UK Green Paper published 2003)
EMIS	Expenditure Management Information System
FaCS	Department of Family and Community Services
FaHCSIA	Department of Families, Housing, Community Services and Indigenous Affairs
GEO	Government Equalities Office
GO	Government Office
GUEDO	Government Urban and Economic Development Office
HMO	Health Maintenance Organizations
HMRC	Her Majesty's Revenue and Customs
HMS	Horizontal Management Secretariat
HRM	Human Resource Management
HUD	Housing and Urban Development
ICC	Indigenous Coordination Centre
ICT	Information and Communications Technology
IMP	Industrial [originally International] Marketing and Purchasing
IR	Inland Revenue
JUG	Joined-Up Government
LA	Local Authority
LAA	Local Area Agreements
LCJB	Local Criminal Justice Board
LSCB	Local Safeguarding Children's Boards
LSP	Local Strategic Partnerships
MAC	Management Advisory Committee
MECS	Ministry of Education, Culture and Science
MOU	Memorandum of Understanding
MRRS	Management Resources and Results Structure
MSAE	Ministry of Social Affairs and Employment
NADCP	National Association of Drug Court Professionals
NGO	Non-Government Organization
NHS	National Health Service
NMCC	National Maritime Coordination Centre
NOMS	National Offender Management Service
NPM	New Public Management
NZ	New Zealand
OAG	Office of the Auditor General
OECD	Organisation for Economic Cooperation and Development
OFSTED	Office for Standards in Education
OIPC	Office of Indigenous Policy Coordination
PCO	Privy Council Office
PCSD	Police and Crime Standards Directorate
PG	Performance Group
PMDU	Prime Minister's Delivery Unit

PRI	Policy Research Initiative
PSA	Public Service Agreement
RCC	Rescue Coordination Centre
RSE	Recognised Seasonal Employer
S&T	Science and Technology
SCR	Serious Case Review
SEMO	Strengthening Education in Mangere and Otara
SIP	Service Integration Project
SRO	Senior Responsible Owner
SSC	State Services Commission
TBS	Treasury Board of Canada Secretariat
UK	United Kingdom
US	United States
UN	United Nations
WG	Whole-of-Government

Part I

Introduction and the fundamental questions

1 Crossing boundaries in public management and policy

An introduction

Janine O'Flynn

Introduction

In this volume we draw together the work of scholars from across the world, all of them experts in various aspects of crossing boundaries in public management and policy. We explore different contexts through a range of studies in different countries and policy domains and draw broader lessons of relevance to scholars and practitioners alike. We do this in order to address what are considered to be the key challenges in both the theory and the practice of public management and policy.

The challenge

Fifteen years ago, Frederickson set out three important features of contemporary public administration, which had created what he referred to as 'the fragmented and disarticulated state' (1999: 702). First, jurisdictions were losing their borders and boundaries through economic, social and technological transformation; second, the state was becoming disarticulated in that its capacity to deal with complex issues had eroded over time, in part due to his first point; and third, what was meant by 'public' was changing and being redefined as more and more actors became involved in the practice of governing, creating fuzziness around boundaries. Kelman has noted that questions of how to work across governments and sectors are the 'most-discussed questions involving the performance of public institutions and achievement of public purpose' (2007: 45). Many have written on topics related to boundary-crossing, from various perspectives, and in the post-New Public Management era considerable attention has been given to a more relational approach to governing. Whether we are interested in how governments work together, how public organizations work together, how public organizations work with those from the non-profit or private sector, how professionals cross knowledge boundaries, or various other iterations, we are focused on boundary-crossing activity.

But crossing these boundaries creates a range of dilemmas which have occupied scholars and practitioners seeking to understand or operationalize such modes of working. What types of boundaries exist? Are they movable, permeable, constructed or concrete? What are the driving forces for boundary-crossing, and how do these take hold in different contexts? How are boundaries traversed, and what forms of bridge-building are appropriate, effective, efficient; when, and how do we know? What factors can catalyze change, enabling cross-boundary activity? Is it people, culture, structures, money and/or power? What are the embedded barriers built into our models of governing, and can these be removed? Such questions and puzzles confront policy-makers and scholars, and are explored by the contributors here.

We must also recognize that governments across the world have always faced the challenge of cross-boundary working. Put simply, they have always needed to work with others in order to get things done. What has changed, however, is that as the role and nature of government has changed, they have become increasingly focused on this as a core mode of operating. The drivers vary across nations, as do the forms and configurations that this cross-boundary activity takes. In different nations and policy contexts there are factors that enable or undermine attempts to cross boundaries and these provide a multitude of stories of success and failure. Making sense of these diverse experiences is never easy, and comparative work in real world settings is a challenge to scholars interested in these topics. But determining what works and in what circumstances is part of the challenge for scholars and policy-makers; we seek to advance this under-standing through the contributions in this book.

The purpose

This volume aims to bring together a fragmented field of study through the development of a set of fundamental questions which are then explored in the contributions in various ways. It is more than a book about collaboration, net-works or joined-up government; it explores what we mean by boundaries, the imperatives for cross-boundary working, the various forms and configurations that this can take, and the plethora of enablers and barriers that facilitate or block this in practice. In doing so, we are well placed to identify enduring tensions and puzzles, draw lessons, and move our thinking forward by connecting to a range of literatures that inform theory and practice in this area.

The book is divided into three main parts. Part I introduces the book and sets out the fundamental questions. Part II explores 'solutions' to cross-boundary dilemmas, and Part III explores specific policy domains. Part IV returns us to the fundamental questions and provides the concluding remarks.

The fundamental questions

The study of crossing boundaries is explored in a diverse set of literatures. Each has its own perspective, but offers something to the public management and policy scholars and practitioners who are increasingly interested in this topic. Rarely, however, do these disciplines speak to each other or draw lessons that are shared across these boundaries (see O'Flynn 2009 for a discussion). In this volume we bring together ideas from these literatures in order to set out the fundamental questions that cut across them. This has enabled us to impose some order upon a diffuse and multi-disciplinary set of literatures.

In Part I of this volume, four framing questions are distilled and positioned as central to the study and practice of boundary crossing. Reviewing the relevant literatures showed us that various fragments of these are explored in different ways, but there had not yet been an attempt to synthesize these ideas. Such a synthesis is valuable for many reasons, but in our case it enables us to clearly set out what has been done in this area and how we might make sense of the various threads and strands of work. From here, we can not only order the past somewhat, but can also push forward in trying to address these questions in theory and practice.

Each of these questions is seemingly simplistic, yet each reflects a complex array of factors which bring together various ideas from different disciplines and literatures. These questions run through the various contributions in this collection, showing that they are common to the practice and study of these phenomena. The four questions are explored in detail in Chapter 2, but are set out briefly here to provide the overarching framework for the book.

Question 1: What do we mean by the notion of crossing boundaries?

This question invites us to discuss what we actually mean by boundaries. In Chapter 2, various forms and issues are identified and explored: are boundaries symbolic or social? Are they objective or constructed? Are they knowledge-based, organizational, jurisdictional, sectoral, or policy-based? Are they fixed, malleable, permeable? Or do various combinations of these exist in our particular setting? From here we can also consider what is meant by crossing boundaries. The mere existence of these various forms drives us to attempt to traverse them, for various reasons (explored further in Question 2). Many variants and terms which address this question have emerged in the literature, and a menu of forms and configurations have developed (explored further in Question 3).

Question 2: Why has this emerged?

Across the world there have been diverse imperatives for the focus upon crossing boundaries in public management and policy. We distil these imperatives into six dominant 'stories': the twenty-first century modus operandi story; the coordination story; the disaggregation and fragmentation story; the complexity story; the strategic management story; and the better value story. These manifest in different settings, and sometimes in combination, as the driving rationale for boundary crossing.

Question 3: What does cross-boundary working involve?

This question enables us to explore the various forms and configurations that crossing boundaries takes. A broad range of typologies, continua and individual forms are identified to showcase the various means that are in play. Boundary crossing, we note, is not just about collaboration, or just about networks, but is a much more diverse and differentiated set of mechanisms employed in attempts to traverse boundaries.

Question 4: What are the critical enablers and barriers?

The final question allows for an exploration of a substantial literature, from various disciplines, about how boundary-crossing activity works, or does not work. The main focus is on which factors allow us to do this effectively, and those that block cross-boundary activity. Distilling key ideas from an expansive literature we set out the seemingly critical ones: formal structures; commonality and complexity; people, culture and leadership; power and politics; performance, accountability and budgets; and boundary objects. Again, these barriers are context-specific, with some dominating in certain settings, but not others; we also know that, in practice, these come not as single factors, but often as bundles.

Whilst there has been much written on working across boundaries generally, and more recently in the area of public management and policy, these four questions provide a means of ordering these various literatures and distilling them into what we consider to be the fundamental questions. As noted, each is inherently complex, opening up myriad sub-questions, and the contributors to this book take them in various directions.

The contributions

Our contributors address these fundamental questions in a variety of ways. One group focuses on exploring what might be considered 'solutions' to cross-boundary dilemmas, and another on specific policy domain cases. We have contributions from around the world, spanning different political and administrative traditions, which provide a unique opportunity to explore these fundamental questions in very different settings.

Solutions to cross-boundary dilemmas?

In Part II of this collection, the contributors explore potential 'solutions' to cross-boundary dilemmas. They do not necessarily advocate these as solutions, but rather investigate, critique and question the various means that have been set forth for addressing cross-boundary dilemmas. They consider specific phenomena, mostly in a specific country, and help us to understand the challenges, tensions and puzzles of crossing boundaries in public management and policy.

In their chapter, Eppel *et al.* examine the cross-organizational collaboration solution, presenting findings on conditions, roles and dynamics as they have played out in the New Zealand context. Exploring the experience of front-line officials across several areas of government activity, they show us how those carrying out boundary-crossing behavior understood their work, and how they enacted collaborative action. From their study, the authors articulate some of the preconditions for collaboration, the relationships and roles required, and the phases and dynamics of the work that relates to these particular roles.

From a different perspective, LeRoux explores the increasing use of horizontal networks and boundary spanning in the United States, pointing to a more collaborative era in which government works with various actors to deliver goods and services. She explores how the imperatives have emerged, the dominant forms of cross-boundary activity, and the enablers and barriers to the success of such approaches. Whilst boundary spanning has become routine in the United States, she argues this has created a new set of challenges for public agencies, which must provide high performing programs that are, in reality, delivered by other parties.

The culture solution is one that is often promulgated as a panacea to dilemmas of cross-boundary working. In her chapter, Buick investigates this and presents findings from Australian experiments with joining-up that show us that the culture 'solution' is much more complex than many advocates grasp. She finds that it is the interaction between common purpose and culture that provides a mutually reinforcing basis for successfully operationalizing joined-up government approaches. This shows us that whilst culture *may* be a solution to cross-boundary dilemmas, in practice it is the coupling of cultural compatibility with common purpose that increases the likelihood of success.

Structural factors are examined by Talbot and Talbot, who explore whether mergers between government organizations provide an effective solution to cross-boundary dilemmas. Mergers, they note, are often part of government restructuring, and can therefore be viewed as a common 'solution' to cross-boundary dilemmas. Applying the notion of task structures to three cases in the United Kingdom, they explain that public sector mergers have had mixed success, often under-delivering on promised improvements. One reason for this, they argue, is that the pre-merger organizations had incompatible task structures and, therefore, were poor merger candidates in an organizational sense.

Christensen *et al.* bring together the notions of people and structures in order to examine collegial models of administration in Norway. Drawing on a large-scale longitudinal study of civil servants, they show us that, in fact, collegial models are nothing new in Norway. Rather, such approaches of cross-boundary working are embedded in the Norwegian model. What they do find, however, is that structural and demographic factors are important at the individual and organization level in explaining how and why this works. Rather than cross-boundary working supplanting hierarchy, their study finds that it supplements it, providing a counterweight to the strong 'siloization' tendency within government.

Formal agreements have often been seen as a means of connecting across boundaries, whether that is through legal contracts, memoranda of understanding, or various other forms. In their chapter, Paun and Blatchford examine whether the experience of cross-cutting inter-organizational public service agreements in the United Kingdom addressed the challenges of joining-up within government. They argue that whilst the 'agreements solution' did deliver meaningful working and some improvements, its effectiveness was hampered by embedded structural constraints which privileged and incentivized departmental rather than cross-cutting concerns.

Collaboration has been seen by many as *the* solution to cross-boundary dilemmas, although others have questioned this notion (see Alford and O'Flynn 2012; O'Flynn 2009). In his chapter, Head takes us through a rich analysis of the effectiveness of collaboration, setting out various process and outcome factors that underpin successful approaches and then raises the question of whether, in the final evaluation, collaboration delivers better/different outcomes. He shows us that, in the end, collaboration is a solution only some of the time; it is not necessarily the panacea that advocates suggest it to be.

Hughes explores how, with increasingly complex governing arrangements and changing notions of authority, public managers can manage across boundaries. He explains that as models of governing have changed, formal authority has diminished, demanding new approaches to leadership and a different set of managerial skills. He argues that 'soft power' is becoming increasingly important as a solution to cross-boundary dilemmas.

Blackman explores the notion of readiness for cross-boundary working. She argues that organizations commonly adopt practices that they do not have the internal capabilities to enact, and that this may explain why cross-boundary working is often unsuccessful. Drawing on a large-scale project examining whole-of-government working in Australia, she develops an approach for identifying readiness that acts as a means of diagnosing areas of strengths to be exploited and weaknesses to be addressed. In doing so, she challenges our current thinking on enablers and barriers.

Finally, Lindquist examines how horizontal governance has gone from being a dominant issue to being embedded in the everyday practice of governing in Canada. He explores how and why this happened, and how, alongside this, discussion of horizontal governance has seemingly disappeared from the *lingua franca* of civil servants. The solution to cross-boundary dilemmas, it seems, has been to simply make working across boundaries part of everyday life in government.

Together, the contributions to Part II present studies of the four fundamental questions in various ways. They consider different types of boundaries, explain the imperatives for crossing boundaries in different contexts, and explore the forms of cross-boundary working, with many of them examining in detail the various enablers and barriers to working across boundaries. By exploring these issues within different countries we can see the importance of context, and bringing them together allows us to draw lessons for theory and practice that are explored in more detail in the final chapter of this volume.

Cases of crossing boundaries in public management and policy

Part III of this volume comprises five chapters in which the contributors explore specific areas of public policy. They examine the complexities of operating across various boundaries, using a range of forms, and detail the factors that facilitate or frustrate attempts to do this; in a sense, they consider the 'solutions' outlined in Part II *in situ*.

Service integration is a popular means of delivering increased value and tackling complex challenges. In her chapter, Talbot explores experiments with service integration in children's services in England. Catalyzed by a seeming inability to protect vulnerable children, as highlighted in several scandals, considerable pressure came to bear upon actors to work together more effectively in this policy domain. Her study shows us that, whilst it appears there is much to gain from service integration, the on-the-ground experience illustrates just how challenging it is to implement this in practice.

In their chapter, Klaster *et al.* explore various experiments with cross-boundary working in education and employment in the Netherlands. Across these cases, we are shown how various forms and configurations are adopted to build bridges across boundaries. Their analysis points to several key tensions and broader lessons, including whether we seek to shift or cross boundaries and whether we pursue incremental or radical change. The Dutch central government, they show, is not simply crossing boundaries, but rather 'stumbling over boundaries; trying to climb some fences and tearing down others' (see page 242), thus revealing the complexity of boundary crossing within a specific policy domain.

The challenges of cross-boundary working in the health arena are faced by many nations. In their study, Korac and Saliterer explore attempts to overcome service gaps and fragmentation in the Austrian health system through the creation of multi-player health platforms. They consider whether changes to funding models and the adoption of collaborative decision-making structures can drive innovation, or not, in this complex arena.

The notion of partnerships as a mechanism for connecting across boundaries has been a popular one, especially in complex policy areas with many actors. In their chapter, Liddle and Diamond explore the area of community safety in England, where partnerships have taken centre stage. In doing so they confront a seemingly 'wicked' policy area and consider how factors such as leadership, 'place' and performance regimes come together in such arenas.

In the final chapter of this section, Donnet and Keast explore tensions in airport enclaves. The authors investigate a range of boundaries – physical, jurisdictional and sectoral – and explain how integrated planning methodologies may be used as a tool for crossing boundaries, including identifying conditions for collaborative planning approaches.

Together, these specific policy domain cases provide an opportunity to consider the fundamental questions in particular arenas of action, providing a basis for drawing broader lessons.

Conclusion

In the final chapter of this volume, the editors use the four fundamental questions to reflect upon the various themes presented by the contributions. They draw out important lessons from the exploration of solutions and cases and sketch future issues of interest to both scholars and practitioners.

References

Alford, J. and O'Flynn, J. (2012) *Rethinking Public Service Delivery: Managing With External Providers*, Palgrave: Basingstoke.

Frederickson, H.G. (1999) 'The repositioning of American public administration', *PS: Political Science and Politics*, 32(4): 701–711.

Kelman, S. (2007) 'The transformation of government in the decade ahead', in D.F. Kettl and S. Kelman, *Reflections on 21st Century Government Management*, Washington: IBM Center for the Business of Government.

O'Flynn, J. (2009) 'The cult of collaboration in public policy', *Australian Journal of Public Administration*, 68(1): 112–116.

2 Crossing boundaries

The fundamental questions in public management and policy

Janine O'Flynn

Introduction

The notion of working across boundaries receives considerable attention from scholars and practitioners of public management and policy. In recent times, much emphasis has been placed on notions of inter-organizational, inter-jurisdictional and inter-sectoral working, and a range of terms have emerged to capture this phenomenon: horizontal coordination, joined-up government, whole-of-government, holistic government, collaborative governance, to name just a few. Despite the flurry of terms, the core element that binds them is the sense that boundaries must be traversed in order to achieve goals.

Most of the post-New Public Management (NPM) models which have emerged over the last decade or so have put the notion of boundary crossing front and centre: the new public service model articulated by Denhardt and Denhardt (2000) focuses on collaborative structures and shared leadership; the new public governance model set out by Osborne (2006) includes a notion of inter-organizational management, inter-dependent agents and ongoing relationships; there is a strong relational, collaborative thread running through the public value management approach articulated by Stoker (2006); and Halligan's (2007) work on integrated governance demonstrates that new models of governing place horizontal collaborative, boundary-spanning ways of operating at their centre. Indeed, Kelman (2007) has argued that the topics of collaboration across government agencies ('connect the dots') and between government, private and non-government organizations (networks, or collaborative governance) are the 'most-discussed questions involving the performance of public institutions and achievement of public purposes' (p. 45).

In this chapter, I provide a review of the broad and varied literatures that connect to the notion of crossing boundaries in public management and policy. This is done by setting out four framing questions, which are explored throughout this chapter and which form the key threads drawing the contributions of this volume together. First, *what* do we mean by the notion of crossing boundaries? Second, *why* has this emerged, and what is the imperative for this phenomenon? Third, *what* does cross-boundary working involve – what are the forms and configurations? And, finally, what are the critical enablers and barriers which help us to understand *how* this works (or not)? In addressing these questions, I seek to bring some order to a diffuse and multi-disciplinary set of literatures which inform the theory and practice of crossing boundaries in public management and policy.

Working across boundaries: what?

Boundaries separate and demarcate, and they are complex, constructed entities which we use to understand behaviour and groupings (Aldrich and Herker 1977). Boundaries can be 'real', 'imagined' or 'objective' and, in the literature that explores this, various forms are set out. For some, the difference is between 'boundaries in the mind' and more solid, 'objective' ones (Heracleous 2004), or between symbolic and social boundaries (Lamont and Molnar 2002).

Symbolic boundaries are 'conceptual distinctions made by social actors to categorize objects, people, practices, and even time and space' (Lamont and Molnar 2002: 168). Such boundaries operate at the inter-subjective level and work to create distinct groupings. In contrast, social boundaries 'are objectified forms of social differences' that create patterns of association and structure social interactions, and manifest as groupings of individuals (Lamont and Molnar 2002: 168). Rather than boundaries of the mind, social boundaries are 'hard' formal demarcations. The intersection of symbolic and social boundaries matters; for example, symbolic boundaries often remain hardwired into social actors after formal, social boundaries have changed. This is often an important issue in work on culture and mergers, for example.

Others point to knowledge boundaries or interfaces for knowledge production (Lamont and Molnar 2002; see also Akkerman and Bakker 2011) and various approaches to this are explored in the literature: syntactic, semantic and pragmatic (see Carlile 2002 for a full discussion). Knowledge boundaries manifest in many ways, but are particularly important between professions, and they have the power to frustrate cross-boundary working. In a recent study of homelessness, for example, Cornes *et al.* (2011) argued that whilst the ideal was a seamless service which bought together a range of professionals to tackle the intersection of drug and alcohol abuse, health issues, mental health, sex work, begging and so on, the reality was that different professions worked in parallel, rather than together, to serve complex client groups.

Exploring boundaries points us towards relationality or, 'the fundamental relational processes at work across a wide range of social phenomena, institutions, and locations' (Lamont and Molnar 2002: 169). Developing an appreciation of relationality raises issues of separation, exclusion, communication, exchange, and inclusion (Lamont and Molnar 2002) and many pertinent questions. How rigid or permeable are boundaries? Are they fixed or malleable? Do they change over time? How are they created, bridged, traversed, or dissolved? (Lamont and Molnar 2002). These aspects are what make the concept of boundaries of interest to scholars and practitioners of public management and policy.

Thus, boundaries can be physical, social or mental. Regardless, however, they act as 'metaphors of containment' and as a means of determining who or what is in or out (Heracleous 2004: 100–101). Various types of boundaries are explored in the literature, with a heavy focus on the organizational ones which allow us to draw bounds of authority (Aldrich and Herker 1977). However, the issue of how to construct organizational boundaries is complex; that is, what principle should be used to create order? There are several means. It is common to design for *purpose* where all those from different functions, but focused on a common purpose, come together (e.g. development of specific regulations); by process or *function* where experts are separated into functional units (e.g. accountants, lawyers, marketing); by *clientele* where all those dealing with the same clientele are brought together (e.g. children's services or indigenous services); or by *place* where all those who deal with a specific geographical area are organized together (e.g. region, town) (Kelman 2007: 46, drawing on Gulick, 1937). Regardless of principle, when designing organizations we are in the boundary creation business, and each principle creates challenges of coordination. Indeed, Pollitt (2003) reminds us that coordination is an enduring issue in public management, and with all the focus on how to traverse boundaries we should not fall into the trap of considering boundaries 'a symptom of obsolescent thinking' (p. 39). This does not discount the coordination challenge, but recognizes that such boundaries will not disappear. Rather, boundaries are a central part of public management and policy which we must acknowledge; they can never be removed, despite our considerable attention to reshaping and moving them.

In addition to organizational boundaries, we are also concerned with policy boundaries as they delineate activity and create specific enclaves: health, education, employment, and urban development are all examples of discrete policy areas. We are interested in jurisdictional boundaries: those which reflect our institutional settings and political systems. And, finally, we are concerned with sectoral boundaries – public, private, non-profit – all of which are distinct, with various ways of operating, underpinning philosophies, and aims.

The notion of what we mean by boundaries has now been explored, and so now I consider the question of 'what do we mean by working across boundaries?' In a later section I will explore in more the detail various configurations, dimensions and forms.

In public management and policy boundaries abound – jurisdictional, organizational, policy, knowledge and so on. The existence of these boundaries requires us to develop means of crossing them. When addressing the question of 'what do we mean by crossing boundaries?' we enter into the world of various terms and notions from across different literatures. There is no clarity, and so here we point to a range of ways in which the crossing boundary issue manifests in different settings.

There are many variants, but all have in common a focus upon working across boundaries. As Williams (2002) noted, '[s]trategic alliances, joint working arrangements, networks, partnerships and many other forms of collaboration across sectoral and organizational boundaries currently proliferate across the policy landscape' (p. 103). In the United States, the answer to the question of what we mean by working across boundaries has been collaborative public management (Christensen and Lægreid 2007). In the United Kingdom, 'joined-up government' was a popular term which described a group of responses to the problem of the increasing fragmentation of the public sector and public services and a wish to increase integration, coordination and capacity (Ling 2002). Joined-up government, in the British context, sought to 'achieve horizontally and vertically co-ordinated thinking and action' (Pollitt 2003: 35) and represented a stark contrast to notions of departmentalism and vertical silos (Christensen and Lægreid 2007). In that sense, the answer to the 'what does it mean?' question was increased coordination. In Australia considerable attention was directed towards the notion of 'whole-of-government' models – formally, cross-portfolio approaches at the Commonwealth level, but, in practice, a range of experiments with working across various organizational, jurisdictional and sectoral boundaries. Christensen and Lægreid (2007) argued that joined-up government had, over time, developed into a whole-of-government approach. They also point to notions of collaborative public management and horizontal and holistic government as popular terms that have developed and provided potential answers to the question of what working across boundaries is.

The forms of cross-boundary working could conceivably be ordered in different ways, and this is discussed in more detail in the following section. However, there have been some attempts to categorize cross-boundary arrangements which may be helpful in making sense of the variety of labels that have emerged as the focus on cross-boundary working has increased. In his work on collaborative governance, Donahue (2004) points to eight dimensions which are readily applicable to broader forms of cross-boundary activity.

- *Formality* – does the arrangement operate formally (i.e. through contracts), or informally (i.e. through agreements, norms or understandings)?
- *Duration* – is the arrangement permanent, ad hoc, or somewhere in between?
- *Focus* – is the arrangement narrowly focused on a specific task or challenge, or more broadly focused, in order to encompass a range of issues and challenges?
- *Institutional diversity* – how diverse are the group of actors in the arrangement? Are they public, private, or non-profit organizations, or national, subnational or local governments?
- *Valence* – what is the number of distinct players involved in the arrangement? What is the minimum and maximum number of parties within which we can consider these to be something unique versus a norm of governing?
- *Stability versus volatility* – do the members share a normative view of successful governance, or do interests diverge?
- *Initiative* – which actors initiated the arrangement? Who is leveraging whom? Who defines goals, assesses results, and triggers adjustments?
- *Problem driven versus opportunity driven* – is the arrangement defensive

(i.e. constructed to solve a joint threat), or offensive (i.e. designed to pursue a shared opportunity)?

Working across boundaries: why?

In the previous section I gave a broad overview of *what* is meant by boundaries and working across them. Boundaries clearly demarcate and separate, and therefore the boundary construction process – symbolic, social, formal and informal – has, as its corollary, methods, models and attempts to traverse these boundaries. This is inevitable in any process of organizing, be it organizational, political or sectoral. In this section six major imperatives or 'stories' for crossing boundaries that have dominated in the practitioner and scholarly literature in recent times are explored. This addresses the 'why' question that I pose in this chapter – that is, 'why has this emerged?'[1] Each is relatively brief, but points us towards the various imperatives that have emerged, and many of these are explored in more detail by other contributors to this volume.

The twenty-first century modus operandi story

There is a view that crossing boundaries represents a *modus operandi* of governing for the twenty-first century. One of the most assertive cases has been presented by Cortada and colleagues (2008), who argued that, in order to cope with the looming challenges of the twenty-first century, governments must develop 'perpetual collaboration' capabilities that cut across boundaries: 'More connectedness and cooperation is needed than ever before: across agencies, across governments, and with more constituencies' (Cortada *et al.* 2008: 2). Others have argued that 'the future belongs to those who collaborate' (Economist Intelligence Unit 2007: 4), and that 'the fundamental performance improvement challenge facing government today is for leaders to achieve results by creating collaborative efforts that reach across agencies, across levels of government, and across the public, nonprofit, and private sectors' (Abramson *et al.* 2006: 22). McKinsey & Company, the global consulting firm (see Barber *et al.* 2007), has also focused on how cross-boundary working, and re-drawing boundaries, must be at the centre of how governments across the world operate in this century. These writers tend to idealise collaboration as the mode of coordination across boundaries and tend to be vague, normative and aspirational. Indeed, Glasby *et al.* (2011) argued that the focus on partnership approaches, for example, was 'faith-based' rather than evidence-based (p. 2). Many of these manifestos pick up on ideas from the other five imperatives, which I explore below, constructing, in a sense, a meta-narrative which might encompass the others.

Governments across the world have also promulgated this story. For example, the 2010 reform manifesto from the Australian Government (AGRAGA 2010) points to a range of whole-of-government challenges, responses, outcomes, and modes of operating which will define the twenty-first century for the Australian Public Service.

In their work on public service delivery, Alford and O'Flynn (2012) argue that government organizations engage in multiple relational types, working across various boundaries, with different external parties, to deliver on governmental outcomes. The management of this, they argue, becomes the twenty-first century challenge:

> As we move further into the twenty-first century, the challenges confronting societies will force governments to consider new means of organizing and of engaging with other parties; to rethink public service delivery. This is redrawing the traditional boundaries of public sector organizations, and reshaping their work.
>
> (p. 256)

The coordination story

Cross-boundary working is also seen as a response to the enduring issue of coordination in a fragmented domain, rather than something new. This reflects an institutional and organizational architecture that creates various boundaries that demand coordination efforts. This enduring coordination effort has been the focus of scholars and practitioners for years. As March and Olsen (1989) noted, 'Coordination across boundaries is more difficult than within them. Different sets of rules tend to evolve independently in different domains' (p. 26). Three decades ago Schermerhorn (1975) argued that inter-agency cooperation was developing as a panacea to coordination gaps in social services, and Perri 6 (1997) claimed that in the UK, inter-departmental working has been on the agenda to increase coordination across boundaries. In this sense, the coordination challenge is nothing new.

There are multiple drivers for the coordination challenge. Clearly, there are jurisdictional demarcations that create objective boundaries, and there are sectoral ones that distinguish public, private and non-profit sectors. Organizational design also matters, especially in the public sector where we tend to organize functionally. As discussed in the previous section, there are multiple ways to organize – purpose, process/function, place, or clientele are always on the agenda. A purpose-driven agency might focus on poverty reduction, a functional agency on defence, a client-focused agency on children, and a place-based agency on a specific region; but each creates its own boundaries because there are pieces of each organizing principle missing.

Kelman (2007) noted that the driver toward collaboration within government has been an attempt to coordinate across the 'inevitable tensions and trade-offs amongst different organization-design departmentalization decisions' (p. 46). And Ling (2002) argued that the UK focus on joined-up government was a coordination solution for the problems of functional separation, with the aim 'to coordinate activities across organizational boundaries without removing the boundaries themselves. These boundaries are inter-departmental, central-local, and sectoral (corporate, public, voluntary/community)' (p. 616). Functionalism has been at the core of failed attempts to coordinate in the UK for many years, and, according to Perri 6 (1997), this is what continues to stymie attempts at horizontal governance. This reflects the fundamental point that policy problems do not respect organizational boundaries:

> Most public challenges are larger than one organization.... Think of any major public policy challenge: housing, poverty, the economy, education, and pollution, to name a few. In order to address any one of these challenges effectively, a 'full-court press' is needed, with collaboration across boundaries.
>
> (O'Leary *et al.* 2012: s70)

Functionalism also breeds particular power and control structures that are built on 'virtues of rationality, professionalism and compartmentalism', and which, because of this, create barriers to more postmodern forms and renewed attempts at horizontal coordination capacity (Williams 2002: 105). On the one hand, the fixation of functionalism as an organizational design principle, combined with sectoral and jurisdictional boundaries, ensures that the coordination challenge will endure. On the other, if we choose alternate design principles, boundaries do not simply disappear. In this way, the cross-boundary imperative reflects the never-ending quest for coordination in a boundary-rich world.

The disaggregation and fragmentation story

Whilst the crossing boundaries focus reflects an enduring coordination story, others propose that there is something new in this. Whilst coordination issues themselves have always existed, this has intensified as the dysfunctions of New Public Management (NPM), namely disaggregation and fragmentation, have emerged. Fragmentation occurs for different reasons, and was not created by NPM, but rather was exacerbated via disaggregation in particular. For example, it has been argued (Statskontoret 2007) that countries in the continental tradition such as Germany and France are fragmented by a Weberian heritage, Anglo-Saxon countries more so by a belief in the rational control of single organizations, and that Nordic countries mix these fragmenting influences.

The crossing boundaries imperative became a device to swing the pendulum back towards more coordination, a rational counter to fragmentation – especially in Anglo-Saxon nations – in order to link together the increasing number and types of actors operating in an increasingly complex governing environment.

There has been ample debate about the nature, content, effects and aims of NPM and it is not the intention of this contribution to revisit them. The important point is that, in assessing these reforms and focusing on crossing boundaries, arguments have been made which state that NPM-inspired reforms produced incentives for an intra- rather than inter-organizational focus within government. As a report by Sweden's Statskontoret (2007) argued, 'Modern ("new") public management is much focused on the contributions of individual organizations, which makes it difficult to handle collaboration and complexity' (pp. 27–28).

That this trend toward an internal focus happened at the same time as major contracting out, agencification, and disaggregation is a source of these tensions. Frederickson (2012: 235 cited in O'Leary *et al.* 2012: s81) argued that 'public administration, prompted by the fragmentation of the state, is steadily moving ... towards theories of cooperation, networking and institution building and maintenance'. In the UK, the reforms of the 1980s incentivized an organizational focus over system-wide aims and undermined more inter-organizational or horizontal work (Ling 2002). Halligan *et al.* (2012) reinforced these points, arguing that the cross-boundary imperative was in response to disaggregation, specialization of agencies, and the increasing number of actors involved in governance. Practitioners have also recognized the effects; for example, in a major government report in Australia (Management Advisory Committee 2004) it was noted that 'devolution of authority to agency heads and a clear vertical accountability for agency outcomes may make collaboration across organizational boundaries more difficult' (p. 6). This trend has been international, with Christensen and Lægreid (2007) arguing that the performance management systems of the era directed attention away from horizontal issues.

The corrective imperative emerged in this context as a response to the effects of disaggregation and fragmentation. On the one hand, this is the old coordination story but, on the other, there is something particular about the drive toward disaggregation that came from NPM and the increasing complexity of governing in that environment that intensified this imperative to work across boundaries in order to get the business of governing done.

The complexity story

Another imperative relates to the notion that governments are increasingly faced by complexity and that the answer to dealing with this is cross-boundary working. In their work on 'anticipatory governance', Fuerth and Faber (2012) argued that the:

> challenges presenting themselves today are increasingly fast-moving and complex: they involve concurrent interactions among events across multiple dimensions of governance; they have no regard for our customary jurisdictional and bureaucratic boundaries; they cannot be broken apart and solved piece by piece; and rather than stabilizing into permanent solutions, they morph into new problems that have to be continually managed.
>
> (p. 1)

Complexity emerges in many forms. Frederickson (1999) argued that one of the most important features of the contemporary state was disarticulation:

> The capacity of the state to deal with complex social and economic issues has eroded significantly. Crime, for example, often has its origins in other jurisdictions. There is evidence that North Korea is in the drug trade. Miami

is infested with Russian crime gangs. Acid rain and water pollution start in one set of jurisdictions and profoundly affect others. The oceans, seas, and rivers are polluted by sewage and fertilizer run-off. Immigrants and a growing number of refugees move across porous borders. As the borders and the sovereignty of jurisdictions decline in importance, there is a corresponding decline in the capacity of jurisdictions to significantly contain some public policy issues and, therefore, in the jurisdictions' ability to 'manage' them.

(p. 703)

This complexity story has been strong in both the scholarly and practitioner literatures. Several writers have sketched the drivers reshaping the environment for governing, making it more complex, which requires increasing attention to cross-boundary working. Old ways of working, it is claimed, will not suffice:

> Public administration systems inherited from the past will be insufficient to prepare government for the challenges of the 21st century. Public servants serving today are facing an increasing number of complex public policy issues and must contend with an environment characterised by uncertainties, volatility and cascading global crises. There are reasons to believe that the number and magnitude of disturbances will continue to increase.
>
> (Bourgon 2011: 15)

Many drivers for complexity have been identified: demographic change, globalization, environmental challenges, threat to social stability, technology, shifting centres of economic activity, data-driven management, amongst others (see Barber *et al.* 2007 and Cortada *et al.* 2008). In a recent report by the global consultants McKinsey & Company it was argued that the 'biggest challenges [facing government] cross the boundaries of public, private, and non-profit sectors. As such, they locate government in a changing ecosystem comprising new forms of organizations and new forms of service delivery that are rooted in partnership' (McKinsey & Company 2012: 7).

A substantial group of writers have contributed to the complexity story. These complex challenges have been described as those that 'bridge and permeate jurisdictional, organizational, functional, professional and generational boundaries' and are 'capable of metamorphosis and of becoming entangled in a web of other problems creating a kind of dense and complicated policy swamp' (Williams 2002: 104). A veritable catalogue has been identified in the literature – pollution, drugs, terrorism, health care, preventable diseases, urban sprawl, avian flu, natural disasters, climate change adaptations, and gang violence, to name a few (Bond and Gebo 2012; Christensen and Lægreid 2007; Head 2008; Leck and Simon 2012; Linden 2002). For some, one of the main goals of government will be addressing these increasingly complex problems; Gill *et al.* (2010) argue that governments will continue to face more complexity and increasingly differentiated populations in an environment of resource constraints. Such complexity has re-opened the debate about governance and put cross-boundary working at the centre of the complexity solution:

> As we grapple today with more complex issues such as globalisation, climate change, and ageing demographics, we have to rethink our paradigms of governance. [...] Certainly the world we operate in is too complex and too fast changing for the people at the top to have the full expertise and all the answers to call all the shots. For us to operate in the complex environment of the world today, we must have horizontal reach in a networked government, readiness to discover and experiment, in order to gain insight, decision and action.
>
> (Ho 2008: 6–7)

In some cases these challenges moved beyond complexity and toward being 'wicked' problems, as defined by Rittel and Webber (1971; see also Head and Alford (2013) on this topic). The connection between complexity, wicked problems, and cross-boundary working as a solution has been strong, with cross-boundary activity seen as a solution for addressing those wicked issues that fall between traditional structures (see Bryson *et al.* 2006 on collaboration; also Emerson *et al.* 2011; Jackson and Stainsby 2000; Talbot and Johnson 2007). This recognizes that:

> The answers will not be found within any one unit, agency or discipline. When we fully recognize this reality and organize ourselves to work across boundaries, we will be able to provide integrated solutions to the complex problems facing us. The public deserves no less. And the stakes have never been higher.
>
> (Linden 2002: 6)

Such ideas have permeated official reports focused on cross-boundary working. For example, in the UK the *Our Healthier Nation* report noted that 'Connected problems require joined-up solutions' (cited in Parston and Timmins 1998: 4), in Australia the *Tackling Wicked Problems* (Australian Public Service Commission 2007) report advocated a cross-boundary approach to address complexity, and in Singapore the former head of the civil service matched more networked cross-boundary approaches with complexity (Ho 2008). Alford and O'Flynn (2012) have argued that governments which seek to address wicked problems are increasingly adopting partnership approaches, and throughout this volume the contributors provide many examples. Whilst the cross-boundary working solution emerges as the panacea for complexity, some have questioned the state's capacity to deliver on these complex issues (Sullivan and Skelcher 2002), an issue we return to later when we explore barriers and enablers.

The strategic management story

Another rationale for working across boundaries comes from the synergies that may be realized by working with other organizations, sectors or levels of government, and this reflects a strategic management perspective. In this case we are concerned with the competences of organizations – that is, the clusters of specific assets that allow them to do distinctive things (Prahalad and Hamel 1990) – and examples of this might include speed, consistency, innovation, marketing or leadership (Jacobides 2006). For private firms, core competences form the basis for competitive advantage. Capabilities have been described as bundles of assets developed within an organization (Barney 1991) and which can drive competitive advantage for private firms and performance improvement for public ones (Pablo *et al.* 2007); capabilities to learn or be entrepreneurial are good examples (Jacobides 2006). Dynamic capabilities are those routines, structures and processes that support the productive activity of organizations and/or enable them to adapt and change (see Teece *et al.* 1997; Eisenhardt and Martin 2000). The specific assets of the organization – the competences and capabilities – feed into the dynamic capabilities which are underpinned by management processes and systems (Teece *et al.* 1997).[2] Thus, when writers speak of leveraging off organizations in other sectors, or synergies, this is part of the strategic management story: the idea that we can tap into the competences and capabilities of others to reach broader governmental outcomes.

> Collaborative governance harnesses all of America's capability – public and private, for-profit and non-profit, employee and volunteer – for the pursuit of the common good. And it unleashes the unpredictable resourcefulness of an entrepreneurial people to improvise fresh, flexible solutions.
>
> (Donahue and Zeckhauser 2011: 285)

Scholars have also been part of developing this story, although few draw on the strategic management literature to do so. Pollitt (2003) argued that synergies may be created by bringing together key stakeholders in a specific area of policy or within a network, or by improving the exchange of information between them. Kelman (2007) argued that inter-organizational collaboration between *sectors* is premised on the idea that organizations outside of government hold resources, capacity or legitimacy that can help address policy problems, and using collaboration to leverage these enables synergies to emerge. Cortada *et al.* (2008) made similar points, noting that collaboration across boundaries 'is intended to leverage available capabilities across all facets of a society, not just within the governmental environment' (p. 7). In an extensive report looking at hunger, malnutrition and basic education, the World Economic Forum (2006) set out a range of ways in which cross-boundary partnerships could address these issues. They adopted an overtly strategic management approach, discussing the core competences and capabilities of private firms, and how they could be harnessed to address these global challenges. An excellent example is in how to leverage the core competences of private firms to halve hunger:

Eliminating hunger requires an integrated approach that addresses poverty, builds markets and infrastructure, boosts agricultural production and nutrition, focuses on health and enables women's empowerment. Collaborative private sector efforts to reduce hunger are rare, but have tremendous potential to bring both practical solutions and political action to hungry communities. Key opportunities for applying core business competencies to the fight against hunger [exist].

(World Economic Forum 2006: 6)

These public goals can be achieved, it is argued, if private expertise can be leveraged through actions such as increasing fortified foods, sourcing from small-scale producers, extending infrastructure, and, in many cases, partnering with non-government organizations and weak government agencies to increase their capacity.

The United Nations recently produced a report which discussed how the competences and capabilities of other sectors could be interwoven into partnerships, drawing on a strategic management approach:

Partnerships ... have the capacity to transform the ways in which the UN [United Nations], civil society, governments, and other stakeholders work with business to secure sustained and rapid realization of development goals. Problems are addressed holistically, often across multiple sectors. Additionally, transformational partnerships leverage core competencies of participants, and are designed for scale and sustained impact. As a result, these partnerships can deliver transformative impact across sectors and geographies, addressing both public and private objectives through changes in policy, market structure, and/or social norms.

(United Nations 2011: 6–7)

The 'better value' story

To complete the imperative section, the final story focuses on what I term 'better value'. This brings together various strands of literature which have argued that cross-boundary working would improve one or more of effectiveness, efficiency or quality, particularly in the area of service delivery areas. Some have argued that joined-up government is a means of making better use of scarce resources (efficiency), eliminating duplication, removing contradiction and tensions between policies across government (effectiveness), and bringing together a range of services for citizens (Pollitt 2003). Entwistle and Martin (2005) also point to the service issue, arguing that more collaborative approaches might transform service systems. Glasby *et al.* (2011) have noted, however, that whilst there is a 'working hypothesis' that partnership approaches will deliver increased value in services, few of the proposed linkages have been proven.

The more general collaboration literature points to a range of reasons to traverse boundaries which are relevant here, such as pooling resources, leveraging new ones, or reducing transaction costs (see O'Flynn 2008 for a discussion).

In their writing on how government organizations can work effectively with external parties to deliver public services, Alford and O'Flynn (2012) point to a range of service benefits and costs from crossing boundaries.[3] They note that service value can be increased when government organizations work with external parties, be they other government organizations, private firms, non-profits, clients, regulatees, or volunteers. Such benefits arise through reduced cost or increased value or various combinations of both, with value increases driven by factors such as economies of scale or scope, specialization, flexibility, complementarity, and innovation and learning. Such ideas have driven major outsourcing programs across the world, the development of one-stop-shops, and movements in several countries towards increasing co-production with clients, for example.

In many areas of social services there have been attempts to better integrate, for several reasons. This is important because 'people do not live their lives according to the categories we create in our welfare services' (Glasby *et al.* 2011: 1). A good example is how services and providers might be brought together to deliver seamless services to address the complex needs of those experiencing homelessness, but who may also have health needs, be involved in sex work, or newly released from prison, amongst other factors (Cornes *et al.* 2011). This not only has the potential to increase service quality for clients, but also to reduce costs through shared client assessments, for example. Such ideas have become part of the policy discourse in Britain, where there is an expectation that those with long-term conditions and social needs will have tailored support plans developed for them, particularly in cases where they have 'chaotic lives' (Cornes *et al.* 2011). Several of the authors in this volume connect to this imperative for change.

What does working across boundaries involve? Forms and configurations

When we look into forms and configurations a veritable catalogue emerges. There is considerable overlap and ambiguity, so in this section I set out several approaches – including typologies, continua, and individual form. The important point is that, in the end, these all represent mechanisms for cross-boundary working, be that through vertical boundary crossing (i.e. across levels of government) or through horizontal boundary crossing (i.e. across various parts of one level of government) or between sectors, or through different relationship forms such as collaboration, cooperation, or the exercise of the authority of the state (see Hardy *et al.* 2003).

Cross-boundary working: some general approaches

When we look at the broader literature we can identify typologies or continua of cross-boundary working. Alford and O'Flynn (2012: 19) articulate a continuum of 'modes of coordination' between parties that includes compulsion, supervision, classical contracting, negotiation, and collaboration. In their work, Mattessich and Monsey (1992) set out three modes of working together:

- *Cooperation* is an informal relationship without common mission where information is shared on an 'as needed' basis, authority remains with each organization, there is little (or zero) risk, and resources and rewards are kept separate.
- *Coordination* is more formal than cooperation, with compatible missions, common planning and more formal communication channels. Whilst each organization retains authority, risk enters the equation.
- *Collaboration* is a more 'durable and pervasive relationship' (p. 39) which involves creating new structures within which to embed authority, developing a common mission, and engaging in comprehensive and shared planning, and in which formal communication across multiple levels occurs. Collaboration also includes pooling and jointly acquiring resources, sharing reward, but also increased risk.

Himmelman's (2002) approach is similar and he identifies four common strategies for working together, each requiring different commitments of trust, time, and turf.[4]

- *Networking* is an informal relationship where information is exchanged for mutual benefit and where there is no need for trust and no sharing of turf.
- *Coordinating*[5] is more formal: information is exchanged and activities are altered in pursuit of mutual benefit and achievement of common purpose. This requires more time and higher trust, but little or no access to one another's turf.
- *Cooperating* involves the exchange of information, altering of activities and resource-sharing for mutual benefit in pursuit of common purpose. Organizational commitments are higher, formal agreements may be used, and this linkage requires higher levels of time and trust vis-à-vis networking and coordinating. Each party will provide access to its turf.
- *Collaborating* is distinctive as it involves a willingness of the parties to enhance each other's capacity – helping the other to 'be the best they can be' (p. 3) – for mutual benefit and common purpose. In collaboration the parties share risks, responsibilities and rewards, they invest substantial time, have high levels of trust, and they share common turf.

Leat and colleagues (1999) set out eight options for working across boundaries – or 'governing in the round' as they refer to it – each reflecting higher degrees of integration: dialogue; joint project; joint venture; satellite; strategic alliance; union; and merger.

Outside of these broader typologies or continua, many writers focus on specific types of cross-boundary mechanisms, and in the following discussion four popular forms are briefly discussed: collaboration; joined-up government;

networks; and whole-of-government. Other authors in this volume explore different forms in their contributions.

Working across boundaries as collaboration

Collaboration has been *the* mode of crossing boundaries in much of the practitioner and scholarly literature, prized as the 'holy grail' of working together (O'Flynn 2008). Indeed, Morse (2011) has argued that 'It is not [an] overstatement to say that collaborative governance ... is becoming a dominant, if not the dominant frame for public administration today' (p. 953). And Emerson *et al.* (2011) noted that for many scholars it was the new paradigm of public administration.[6]

Much has been made of the competing definitions, opaqueness, and ambiguity of collaboration but I will not repeat this here (see O'Leary and Vij 2012 for an excellent overview). Collaboration has been defined as 'a process in which organizations exchange information, alter activities, share resources, and enhance each other's capacity for mutual benefit and a common purpose by sharing risks, responsibilities, and rewards' (Himmelman 2002: 3). As is discussed above, this makes it quite different to other modes of operating across boundaries. The use of the term in public policy circles, however, has become somewhat of a buzzword, and indeed it has been argued that there is a 'cult' of collaboration (O'Flynn 2008). This has obscured the broader set of options, many of which may be more or less appropriate means of connecting.

Some of the discussions around collaborative governance or public management illustrate this. Collaborative government is defined as an 'amalgam of public, private, and civil society organizations engaged in some joint effort' (Donahue 2004: 2) and collaborative public management as a 'process of facilitating and operating in multiorganizational arrangements' (McGuire 2006: 3). In such broad definitions, collaboration seems to be just 'working together' and no different from others forms. In their work Batley and Rose (2011) adopt the term 'relationship' for exactly this reason, namely because many forms of non-government and government working were not collaborative as they were not based on mutuality, equality, or maintaining the identity of each party.

Others are more precise: Alford and O'Flynn (2012) argue that collaboration is a mode of coordination which is heavy on communication, acting consistently with the other parties' requirements and where 'the more the parties empower each other, the greater the degree of collaboration' (p. 114). For many writers collaboration is something more than an amalgam or joint effort – it involves sharing across a range of dimensions (e.g. goal setting, risk, reward, resource and culture), a more strategic nature, and autonomy (Axelrod 1984, 1997; Economist Intelligence Unit 2007; Head 2004, 2006). Several of the contributors in this collection focus on collaboration in their studies of crossing boundaries in public management and policy.

Working across boundaries as joined-up government

One of the most popular descriptors of working across boundaries in public management and policy, especially in recent times, has been 'joined-up government' (JUG). The term originated in the UK and has developed into an umbrella term which can describe a range of ways of 'aligning formally distinct organizations in pursuit of the objectives of the government of the day' (Ling 2002: 616). JUG captured a range of forms and dimensions:

- new ways of working across organizations (e.g. shared leadership, pooled budgets);
- new ways of delivering services (e.g. joint consultations, shared customer interface);
- new accountabilities and incentives (e.g. shared outcome targets; performance measures); and
- new types of organizations joined in various ways (e.g. training, culture, information, values) (Ling, 2002).

Pollitt (2003) extends this somewhat, noting that joined-up approaches can be horizontal – across national government – or vertical, between layers of government, while also distinguishing between joined-up government (inter-agency arrangements) and joined-up governance (cross-sectoral arrangements). In the contributions to this collection, several joined-up experiments are explored.

Working across boundaries as networks

There is an extensive literature on the notion of networks as a form of crossing boundaries. Networks are 'structures of interdependence. They exhibit both formal and informal linkages and include exchange or reciprocal relationships, common interests, and bonds of shared beliefs and professional perspective' (Frederickson 1999: 704–705). In his work, O'Toole (1997) set out a range of forms, including:

> Interagency cooperative ventures, intergovernmental program management structures; complex contracting arrays; and public-private partnerships ... [and] service-delivery systems reliant on clusters of providers that may include public agencies, business firms, not-for-profits, or even volunteer-staffed units, all linked by interdependence and some shared program interests.
>
> (p. 446)

Various forms of networks have emerged in practice, and a useful typology was set out by Abramson *et al.* (2006):

- service implementation networks, which are intergovernmental programs;
- information diffusion networks which are networks for sharing information across boundaries;

- problem solving networks which set agendas related to important policy areas; and
- community capacity-building networks built to develop social capital to enable communities to better address a range of problems.

Networks are not always collaborative, although there is a strong normative thread in much of the writing on this topic that supposes that they should be. Some have argued that they are especially useful forms for confronting wicked public policy problems, and have provided empirical evidence to suggest that this is permeating practice in areas such as HIV/AIDS and teen pregnancy (see Ferlie *et al.* 2011 for a discussion on this).

In their description of multi-party service delivery networks, Alford and O'Flynn (2012) describe how, in simple networks, government organizations might have separate relationships with each member, but in complex networks the many and varied parties have multiple relationships with each other. In some networks there will be specific parties that will act as intermediaries, others will have chains with multiple links, and others will have dense clusters of relationships, and so on. These complex networks of actors working across boundaries will have multiple motivational bases and various modes of coordination, adding to the complexity (Alford and O'Flynn 2012). Networks appear often in the contributions to this book as an important form of cross-boundary working.

Working across boundaries as whole-of-government

Finally, I will look at the emergence of whole-of-government as a form of cross-boundary working in management and policy. Christensen and Lægreid (2007) argued that whole-of-government was an extension of JUG; or, more correctly, that JUG had developed into a whole-of-government model over time. Christensen and Lægreid (2007) defined it quite broadly (as noted above), but it Australia, where the term originated, it was specifically related to cross-portfolio working and pursuit of objectives which cross boundaries within government (Management Advisory Committee 2004). However, over time this definition has stretched to include inter-organizational, inter-jurisdictional, and inter-sectoral working in the Australian context (Australian Public Service Commission 2007). This version makes it more akin to the notion of joined-up governance discussed above, rather than joined-up government, although even there the notion has become quite elastic. In their work on horizontal, joined-up and whole-of-government, Halligan *et al.* (2012) point to four forms of whole-of-government: integrative and rebalancing; coordination and collaboration; integrating service delivery; and culture change.

Working across boundaries: (some) enablers and barriers

Previous sections have provided an overview of three main questions: what do we mean by 'working across boundaries'?; why has this approach emerged?; and what does it involve? In this section I point to several important enablers and barriers of working across boundaries. This helps us to address the question of *how* this phenomenon works, or not. Throughout this collection, the contributors explore enablers and barriers in various forms. Many of these have been positioned as both potential enablers and potential barriers and so they are dealt with together in this discussion.[7] Before delving into specifics, some clusters of enablers that have been identified in the literature are set out.

Clusters of enablers

Several writers have identified clusters of enablers for effectively working across boundaries, usually focusing on a specific form. Joined-up working relies on aligning 'cultures, incentives, management systems and aims', according to Ling (2002: 616), or three 'must-haves' according to Pollitt (2003): *long-term* relationships to facilitate skill development, trust building and participation; a *selective* approach where benefits outweigh risks and costs, or where issues are significant and specific; and a *cooperative* but not imposed approach. In official guides, one study found that governments focus on five requirements: goal setting; accountability; networking and alliances; skills and learning; and time and money (Ling 2002). In a review of the international experience of joining-up, five factors for success were found to be common: clearly defined, mutually agreed shared goals; systems to measure and evaluate progress toward the goals; sufficient and appropriate resources; strong leadership to direct relevant parties towards goals; and a sense of shared responsibility (Victorian State Services Authority 2007: 5). Drawing on the expertise of practitioners, Parston and Timmins (1998: 29) pointed to nine factors that made joined-up management work:

1   Those responsible for implementation should also be involved in design.
2   The focus should be on outcomes, and they should be measurable.
3   Genuine feedback and communication is required for those working toward common outcomes.
4   Greater clarity on the role of government, what it can be expected to do, and what it expects from delivery agencies.
5   A consensus to operate, or 'break the rules' between public service organizations and government, with freedom to experiment and innovate to achieve agreed outcomes.
6   Explicit accountability and responsibility for delivery, ideally vested in an individual given power to deliver.
7   New incentive and reward structures, coupled with tolerance for failure and learning systems, in order to avoid major problems.
8   Ongoing community consultation based on engagement, education and capacity-building.
9   Mechanisms for highlighting success, sharing good practice and learning from mistakes – communities of practice.

When exploring the collaborative mode, Linden (2002: 5) highlighted the need for: a shared purpose or goal that cannot be achieved alone; a desire (not a direction) to pursue a collaboration; having the right people at the table; an open, credible process; and a champion for the initiative. Bardach (1998), on inter-agency collaboration, pointed to key tasks: developing a high-quality operating system; acquiring resources; creating a steering process; and developing a culture of trust and joint-problem-solving. In their study of the partnership literature Glasby *et al.* (2011) put forth four principles for strengthening collaborative approaches: shared vision; clarity of roles and responsibilities; appropriate incentives and rewards; and accountability for joint working. They also point to five major barriers – structural, procedural, financial, professional and perceived threats to status, authority and legitimacy (p. 6) – some of which map onto those individual factors explored below.

These clusters of enablers provide a 'recipe' for successful working across boundaries, according to various writers. There has also been attention on specific factors that may be enablers or barriers and I explore this through six categories: formal structures; commonality/complexity; people, culture and leadership; power and politics; performance, accountability and budgets; and boundary objects. In this volume, the authors explore a range of these factors throughout their various contributions.

Formal structures

There is no doubt that structures matter for crossing boundaries in public management and policy, and most current structural arrangements act as barriers. In a major Australian government report it was noted that 'existing public sector institutions and structures were, by and large, not designed with a primary goal of supporting collaborative inter-organisational work' (Australian Public Service Commission 2007: 17). The enduring commitment to functionalism of governments across the world is seen to be a major impediment to more constructive cross-boundary working, even within government. As Halligan *et al.* (2012) noted: 'The imperative of the functional principle and the rigidity of organizational boundaries still loom prominently in all countries' (p. 94).

Perri 6 (1997) argues that functionalism remains the major blockage to holistic government because any attempt to work against functionalism 'cuts against the grain' and 'few gain in career terms from questioning the interests of their department. Few are promoted for cutting their own budgets. Few are thanked by their ministers for negotiating away any of their power' (6 1997: 22). He goes on to argue that functionalism pushes people into 'departmental cages', and creates 'defensiveness about functional turf' (pp. 18–21). However, we also know that any other principle of organizational design will create new and different boundaries. Boundaries do not disappear: 'Simply removing barriers to cross-cutting working is not enough; more needs to be done if cross-cutting policy initiatives are to hold their own against purely departmental objectives' (Cabinet Office 2000: 5). Creating new structures can help in enabling more effective working across boundaries and Perri 6 (1997) discusses a range of organizational design principles that may enable governments to better deal with cross-cutting issues. In their work on co-location models in Indigenous Affairs, O'Flynn *et al.* (2011) suggest that matrix-style structures, which combine horizontal and vertical reporting lines, may provide a solution to the vertical–horizontal tensions that emerge in practice.

For the most part, formal structures are seen to act as barriers to cross-boundary working in public management policy; however, several authors have explored how these could be adapted to become more enabling.

Commonality and complexity

Another important factor is commonality, especially when collaboration is the form of cross-boundary connection. A sense of shared goals or outcomes can enable working across boundaries; a lack of commonality can undermine such attempts. Parston and Timmins (1998) argue that cross-boundary work needs agreement on what the problem or mischief is, and also an outcomes focus. Outcome agreement can then foster dialogue on what each party will do to contribute to their achievement and the design of outputs to feed into the outcomes. Much of the work on collaborative approaches highlights the importance of shared or common goals; other means of working together across boundaries rely on cooperation or negotiation of networking, where commonality is perhaps less important (Himmelman 2002).

Commonality can sometimes be engineered in times of crisis or when confronted with complexity (i.e. the wicked problems imperative discussed above). Lundin (2007) found that inter-organizational cooperation was both reasonable and beneficial in situations where there was significant task complexity and, conversely, it was both costly and unhelpful when applied to simple tasks. As Huxham (1996) has argued in relation to collaboration: 'Most of what organizations strive to achieve is, and should be, done alone' (p. 3). Head (2004) agrees: 'Selection of inappropriate structures and processes can be a recipe for frustration among participants, and ensures under-achievement of goals (p. 3). Put more succinctly: 'don't work collaboratively unless you have to' (Huxham and Vangen 2004: 200).

Working across boundaries can be facilitated by commonality and complexity, and in many cases a lack of commonality, in particular, can stymie attempts to bring together various parties across boundaries.

People, culture and leadership

There is an expansive literature which considers the people, culture and leadership aspects of crossing boundaries – key issues related to these are explored in various ways in the chapters in this volume. Whilst much literature focuses on how organizations might work together, this is inevitably done by people (O'Leary *et al.* 2012). The success, or otherwise, is therefore partially attributable to the individuals that are called on to operationalize these notions and their ability to work across hard and soft structures. This 'people issue', then, raises the question of which enablers and barriers are related. There is much written on this – from the skills and competencies required, to the performance management systems constructed to assess them. Here, I look at some issues which are also explored in detail in several contributions to this volume.

Many terms have emerged for the individuals that enact working across boundaries: networkers; brokers; collaborators; civic entrepreneurs; boundroids; sparkplugs; and collabronauts (Williams 2002: 107). In describing the skills, competencies and behaviours of competent boundary-spanners, Williams (2002) set out several critical aspects that are bundled together:

- *building and sustaining relationships*: communicating and listening, understanding, empathizing and resolving conflict, personality style, and trust;
- *managing through influencing and negotiation*: brokering solutions, diplomacy, persuasion, networking;
- *managing complexity and interdependencies*: making sense of structures and processes, appreciating connections and interrelationships, interorganizational experiences, trans-disciplinary knowledge, cognitive capability;
- *managing roles, accountabilities and motivations:* managing multiple accountabilities.

Such skills develop outside of technical or knowledge-based expertise, and boundary-spanners 'will build cultures of trust, improve levels of cognitive ability to understand complexity and be able to operate within non-hierarchical environments with dispersed configurations of power relationships' (Williams 2002: 106). Williams argues that even at the most basic level, public servants are required to develop boundary-spanning skills to facilitate inter-agency cooperation. Others talk more broadly about the creation of boundary roles – those positioned on the boundary between an organization and its environment which carry out functions related to information processing and external relations (Aldrich and Herker 1977). Such roles are more conservative than those set out by Williams (2002), yet they play a critical role in enabling or blocking cross-boundary working.

O'Leary *et al.* (2012) set out the skill set of effective collaborators as identified by members of Senior Executive Service in the United States, showing empirically that the most important factors are individual attributes and interpersonal skills, rather than broader strategic-thinking skills.

Moving outside collaboration skills, Alford and O'Flynn (2012) synthesized several typologies in order to set out the range of individual competencies that underpin effective relationship management – that is, not just for collaboration, but across the range of externalization options from co-production to collaboration and contracting (see pp. 242–243).

When public managers are encouraged, or required, to work across boundaries they must balance the risk of sharing the achievement, cost and risk of broader cross-boundary outcomes and being held to account for the narrower, more focused requirements of their own agency: 'This requires visionary and daring approaches' (Parston and Timmins 1998: 23). Further, it is argued that to counter this risk a complex mix of rewards, incentives and freedom to achieve outcomes is required – again, pointing to recalibration of Human Resource Management (HRM) systems.

As well as being prime enablers of cross-boundary work, individuals face considerable challenges and barriers in attempting and undertaking this work. Membership of a single organization creates identity and focus for individuals, whereas creating and sustaining commitment to cross-cutting and cross-boundary objectives may be more challenging (Centre for Management and Policy Studies 2001, cited in Pollitt 2003: 39). Managing multiple memberships, for example, can pose a serious challenge for individuals and organizations. This can be 'volatile, elusive or confusing', because

> navigating in more than one world is a non-trivial mapping exercise. People resolve problems of marginality in a variety of ways: by passing on one side or another, denying one side, oscillating between worlds, or by forming a new social world composed of others like themselves.
>
> (Star and Griesemer 1989: 412)

One way of addressing this is to rotate individuals who act in boundary roles so as to ensure ongoing commitment and integration (Aldrich and Herker 1977); however, this produces issues of continuity and stability in relationships across the boundary.

Despite the wide recognition that specific skills and competencies are needed to facilitate these boundary-spanners, there is a strong argument that these have not really been cultivated. In the UK there has been little investment in building up the expertise required to fully realize JUG, despite general recognition that it was needed (Parston and Timmins 1998), and a similar story was told in the Australian context in experiments with whole-of-government approaches in Indigenous affairs, although this reflected a broader underinvestment (O'Flynn *et al.* 2011). Further to this is the need to adapt organizational and HRM systems to select, train, appraise and reward for these skills (Pollitt 2003). HRM systems which fail to adapt to these needs create powerful barriers to cross-boundary working, and various authors have pointed to the importance of rewards, incentives, empowerment, or other supporting architecture which will catalyze new behaviours (Alford and O'Flynn 2012; O'Flynn *et al.* 2011; Parston and Timmins 1998). Getting these 'right' in order to enable cross-boundary working relies heavily on HRM systems, organizational cultures, and leadership.

The role of culture is also central to the discussion of cross-boundary working, and is an issue addressed by several of the contributors to this volume. It has been argued that major cultural change will be required if cross-boundary working is to be successful, partly to shift people away from narrow perspectives, silo issues and objectives (Christensen and Lægreid 2007; Management Advisory Committee 2004). In part, this is because the pressures from functionalism are embedded and intense. Formal structural adaptation is not enough and attention must be placed on cultural change over time. Indeed, Osborne and Brown (2005) argued that informal aspects of organizations are often the greatest barrier to successful change programs. Others argue that change programs can become 'stuck' if culture is not well understood; this means that there must be considerable effort invested in understanding the underlying assumptions held by people within the organization (Lawson and Ventriss 1992; Schein 1985). An understanding of public sector culture is important in working across boundaries, and the ability to identify points of instability (i.e. lack of alignment between culture, processes and structure) can give great insight into what enables and what blocks successful working across boundaries (see Hood 1996).

Leadership, as fluid as the notion is, also emerges as a critical enabler and barrier in the literature. A major report by the OECD (2001), which explored public sector leadership in the twenty-first century, argued that leaders need the ability to address interconnected problems, and Broussine (2003) argued that in order to solve complex problems, leaders had to be able to 'initiate concerted action not only within their own organizations but among a set of stakeholders with different and competing interests' (p. 175). Similar threads emerged from Luke's writing, where he claimed that leaders had to 'reach beyond their own boundaries and engage a much wider set of individuals, agencies and stakeholders' (1998: xiii), and others have noted that such approaches to working also increase risks for individuals (e.g. accountabilities, sharing achievements and costs) (Parston and Timmins 1998).

Leaders are seen as important in enabling cross-boundary work as they can provide the force for operating, and for leveraging resources across boundaries (see O'Flynn *et al.* 2011 for an example). Thus we can anticipate that poor leadership, or a lack of attention from leaders, will present a serious barrier to working across boundaries. Without the endorsement of those in powerful positions, cross-boundary work is undermined. In a recent empirical study into public sector chief executives and collaboration in Catalan, Esteve *et al.* (2012) found that specific attributes influence the decision on whether to engage in collaboration, finding compelling evidence that these attributes matter with regard to whether a public organization collaborates or not. The evidence showed that younger managers, more educated managers, and those with an orientation toward self-development tended to collaborate more often. Neither gender nor tenure had an effect upon chief executive tendency to collaborate.

The simple fact that government now works with multiple actors across boundaries means that public managers must be able to lead across these boundaries in order to deliver on outcomes. There are several streams of literature that consider forms of cross-boundary leadership and this is seen as a distinctive form, quite different from that which is focused within organizations.[8] This is because it is focused on leading action in complex multi-actor environments, using both formal and informal influence (see Blackman *et al.* 2012 for a summary). Various forms are discussed in the literature. In their study of public managers in Wales, Sullivan *et al.* (2012) identified various configurations of leadership for collaborating across boundaries: co-governing through inclusive relationships; negotiating dynamic complexity; judicious influence by elites; achievement of key outcomes; and co-governing through expert facilitation. Different sets of competencies underpin each and public managers are active in adopting different forms. Some writers focus on inter-organizational leadership, whereby individuals or organizations build 'alliances, links and networks with and between several organizations to achieve synergies, integration and joint outcomes' (Hartley and Allison 2000: 38). Another is focused on orchestration, a more collective approach to leadership which involves 'coordinated activity within set parameters expressed by a network of senior leaders at different administrative levels ... across part or all of a multi-organizational system' (Wallace and Schneller 2008: 765). Meta-leadership represents another approach; it emerges from the emergency preparedness literature, but is focused on how individual leaders can move beyond 'silo thinking to achieve ... cross-agency and cross-government coordination of strategy and effort' that 'connects the purposes and the work of different organizations or organizational units' (Marcus *et al.* 2006: 129). When such meta-leadership is achieved it is:

> akin to carefully crafting interlocking gears: when it is time to move, the cogs link in a way that ensures movement and not stasis. For this reason, designing cross-system linkages of action is a strategic and methodical building endeavour, by which both the process and the outcome of the effort attest to the value and benefits of working toward common purposes.
>
> (Marcus *et al.* 2009: 17)

There has also been considerable work on network leadership (see Silvia 2011 for an example), which explores the difference between hierarchical intra-organization and more collaborative leadership across boundaries, noting that leaders need to behave differently than when they lead within their organizations. Network leadership requires a focus on activation (i.e. who to include), framing (i.e. setting out the mission and vision), mobilizing (i.e. gaining and maintaining support), and synthesizing (i.e. influencing members to get common understanding and drive common action) (pp. 68–69). The leadership challenge is to 'guide a group of independent but related entities toward the accomplishment of a task that all of the entities seek to achieve, but none of them is able to solve alone' (Silvia 2011: 70).

Not all aspects of people, culture and leadership were set out here – the contributors to this volume explore these in greater depth – but from this discussion we can see that each provides us with an understanding of how cross-boundary working can be enabled, or not.

Power and politics

Power is a critical issue and one that does not get as much attention as it deserves in studies of cross-boundary working, but it has been recognized as a critical resource for joint action (Emerson *et al.* 2011). As has been argued, 'power can be used to advance the joint efforts of the collaborators, resulting in mutual gain, or to empower others to participate more effectively in the collaboration, resulting in altruistic gain' (Purdy 2012: 410). Three types of power emerge as important in inter-organizational activities (Purdy 2012; see also Hardy and Phillips 1998): authority – an acknowledged right to exercise judgement, act or make decisions; resource-based – those that hold important or valuable resources can wield power; and discursive legitimacy – the ability to speak on behalf of the issue in public and manage the meaning related to it.

Cross-boundary activity has the potential to reshape power relations and this may pose a significant barrier to the ability to operationalize this mode of working. As Parston and Timmins (1998) argue, '[w]hile the ideal may be that people should not care if their organization is under threat, providing the desired outcomes are achieved, such selflessness will not be easy to achieve' (p. 24). In part this is because working across boundaries has the potential to disrupt existing power bases and structures, both political and administrative.

Powerful actors will need to lend their support to working across boundaries to enable it to work, in effect creating a mandate for action. The counter-argument, especially in more collaborative and network forms, is that these approaches should be cooperative, not mandated or imposed from the top. Pollitt (2003) argues that where this power is used, it should be focused on steering and facilitating, negotiation and persuasion. Success in cross-boundary working – collaborative forms in particular – relies upon power sharing and participation (Hardy and Phillips 1998), which can be difficult to put into practice.

The issue of politics and power is linked. It is not hard to see how political endorsements and brokering can enable working across boundaries, or how the lack of it can create incredible barriers. Endorsement is a valuable currency but, as Pollitt (2003) has noted, in order to make cross-boundary working effective politicians will need to cede some of their traditional authority. It is politicians that often must break stalemates between competing objectives and feuding administrative groups (Pollitt 2003), because the administrative machinery was not designed to be collective or collaborative (Wilkins 2002). It is political actors that give important signals to public servants; they set the priorities for action that indicate to civil servants whether or not cross-cutting approaches are valuable (O'Flynn *et al.* 2011; Pollitt 2003). A recent example has been the focus on high-performing government and cross-cutting goals in the United States. This has been advocated by President Obama, and is focused on getting federal agencies to work together on clearly specified goals such as increasing energy efficiency, or improving the career-readiness of veterans.[9]

The challenge arises because there are political turf battles to be fought and political actors have their own power to protect (see Perri 6 1997), and also because the accountability issues that emerge from this approach may place them at risk of not gaining kudos for successful outcomes, or of being blamed for problems that emerge outside their control. Hence, power and politics can be

36   *J. O'Flynn*

considered either as powerful enablers of action, or as powerful barriers against crossing boundaries in public management and policy.

Performance, accountability and budgets

The question of how to assess and account for cross-boundary working points us to another important set of potential barriers or enablers. First, if we consider performance systems, there are tensions between encouraging cross-boundary activity and the developments of the few decades, which have focused agencies inward onto enhancing *their* achievement of targets and goals. To break the silo focus, cross-cutting targets need to be given equal weight as organization-based ones or they will not get the attention they need (Pollitt 2003). With reconfigurations of performance systems or regimes – individual, organizational, and cross-organizations – the overwhelming attention given to individual organizations will serve as a powerful barrier. The reality of how government operates, working across boundaries with many other parties, requires some rethinking of performance regime design to ensure that these are fit for purpose, rather than fit for the past:

> We need more carefully designed performance regimes that reflect the complexity of contemporary governance. We need to caution against the belief that performance measurement will make the messy business of government simple.
>
> (Moynihan *et al.* 2011: i142)

Resetting these systems and restructuring incentives within them could better enable cross-boundary work. The recent work on setting clear, cross-agency goals in the United States has focused on this, setting out specific goals and also identifying who within each agency is responsible for delivering on them.[10] In Australia there has been increasing attention on how to design performance and financial frameworks around shared outcomes. In a reform blueprint released in 2010 it was suggested that work be done within government to facilitate this, including formalizing agreements between agencies, requiring budget reporting against them, and potentially linking secretaries' performance agreements to achievement of such outcomes (AGRAGA 2010).

Accountability systems can also act as a major impediment to crossing boundaries in public management and policy, in part because the focus is on 'individual contributions not joint outcomes' (Statskontoret 2007: 37). Christensen and Lægreid (2007) point to accountability and risk management as central tensions: 'how we can have WG joint action, common standards, and shared systems, on the one hand, and vertical accountability for individual agency performance, on the other' (p. 1063). A similar point was made by Edwards (2001), who questioned whether the multiple accountabilities and ambiguities in partnering approaches could be tolerated in practice. A major Australian report on tackling wicked problems questioned whether there was a lack of compatibility between the existing accountability framework – structured around delivering on tightly specified program outputs and outcomes – and a model which seeks to encourage cross-boundary activity and deliver on broader shared outcomes (Australian Public Service Commission 2007). In recent work by Edwards (2011), notions of shared accountability are explored. She notes that in Canada accountability was 'rethought' more than a decade ago, but such ideas still largely remain part of the talk in Australia, rather than concrete action, despite several major government reports pointing to its importance.

Others argue that the innovation and flexibility required for effective cross-boundary solutions are hampered by traditional accountability approaches. This takes us back to the issue of functionalism and the inability to allocate risk and reward in order to encourage cross-boundary work: 'How can we hold managers responsible for achieving collective results when they have little or no control over the partner agencies and citizens involved in co-productive delivery?' (Parston and Timmins 1998: 14). In his work on boundary-spanners Williams (2002) found that anyone who 'slavishly or dogmatically ploughs a representative furrow in partnership arenas and, irritatingly, has to "report back" everything to the home organization' was considered a poor partner. He argued that more effective partners were those who could negotiate within parameters, i.e. those who had a good feel for what would be acceptable. Others have argued that accountability requirements need to be relaxed in order for cross-boundary working to be effective. What is needed is freedom to break the rules to deliver outcomes – a 'consensus to operate' – along with safeguards to identify problems (Williams 2002: 21; see also O'Flynn *et al.* 2011). However, such ideas don't gel with traditional accountability approaches. Adapting some systems may work; Pollitt (2003) argues that formal agreements can underpin joined-up approaches (although this is not sufficient). On top of this, cultures must adapt to a mixture of horizontal and vertical accountability, and external oversight bodies need to consider more complex accountability approaches (Pollitt 2003). It is at these very points of horizontal–vertical tension that attempts at cross-boundary work flounder (see O'Flynn *et al.* 2011).

A complementary area of importance is that of budgets. When we think about how to get cross-boundary models to work, we run into the fact that, for the most part, budgets are hardwired into departmental silos and, more commonly, to specific and highly specified functions and programs, not outcomes (Perri 6 1997). This traps departments in short-term ideas, annual spending rounds, and battles for maintaining resources, and undermines cross-boundary work (Perri 6 1997), rather than encouraging longer-term strategic thinking which might privilege more cross-boundary activity. To overcome this major barrier and enable cross-boundary work, some have suggested that budgets should be pooled in pursuit of broader outcomes (e.g. Wilkins 2002). Perri 6 (1997), for example, has floated the idea of holistic budgets which are tied to outcomes or geographical areas (i.e. place-based budgets), rather than functions or organizations. Sweden, along with many other nations, has been looking for means of transforming its budget system to set and monitor joint targets (Statskontoret 2007). In the United States, Fuerth and Faber (2012) have argued that budgets need to be more strategic; that is, they need to link money with operations so that we can move beyond vertical silos and toward the 'total engagement of government assets' (p. 30).

However, here the accountability issue immediately emerges: considerable readjustment of traditional approaches will be needed to accommodate such ideas. In part this is because pooling budgets and effort makes it difficult to own success or assign responsibility for failure.

Boundary objects

Finally, there is an interesting literature which explores the potential for boundary objects to act as enablers of cross-boundary activity. Effective boundary objects connect parties because they 'provide a means of resolving the consequences that arise when different kinds of knowledge are dependent on each other' (Carlile 2002: 443). They 'are shared and shareable across different problem solving contexts' (Carlile: 451), or 'organic arrangements that allow different groups to work together' (Akkerman and Bakker 2011: 141).

The 'boundary' nature of an object is captured by its simultaneous concreteness and abstractness, its specificity and generality, and its customization and conventionalism (Star and Griesemer 1989). These objects have different meanings in different worlds, but they act as a tool of translation; they are critical to developing and maintaining coherence in intersecting worlds and tend to fit into one of four types (Star and Griesemer 1989):

- *repositories* – objects indexed in a standard fashion or modularized to enable people from different worlds to adopt them for their use (i.e. a library);
- *ideal type* – an object which abstractly describes the details of something but which is adaptable (i.e. an atlas or diagram) and used for symbolic communication and cooperation;
- *coincident boundaries* – common objects with the same boundaries but different components cooperating across large geographic expanses which create a common referent robust enough to enable different perspectives and local autonomy;
- *standardized form* – objects devised as a means of common communication across dispersed work groups. These objects produce standardized indexes and remove local uncertainties.

Examining boundary objects provides another means of considering enablers and barriers. Attention to creating effective boundary objects offers another opportunity to enable cross-boundary working.

Conclusion

Working across boundaries is not a new proposition; however, the intensity with which it is now promoted is. In this chapter I have provided a synthesis around the four critical questions that are explored by the contributors to this collection.

- First, *what* do we mean conceptually by working across boundaries?
- Second, *why* has the working across boundaries imperative emerged?
- Third, *what* does this actually involve?
- Fourth, what are the critical enablers and barriers in understanding *how* working across boundaries can work (or not)?

Articulating these questions, which are based on a range of literatures that inform cross-boundary working, sets out the fundamental questions in the theory and practice of public management and policy. This also provides a framework for analysis for the series of contributions, which explore the theory, the practice, the complexities, the puzzles, and the potential solutions to making cross-boundary activity work.

Notes

1 In their review of the literature, Esteve *et al.* (2012) point to three categories of imperative for collaborative approaches (noting that they use a broad definition): (i) environmental factors – in low-density population settings actors know each other well and will be more likely to collaborate, the existence of complex problems, and the existence of multiple stakeholders with conflicting values and goals; (ii) organizational factors – quasi-autonomous versus departmental status, standardized collaboration procedures, past experience, and size; (iii) top manager characteristics – education level and political attributes.
2 For a more detailed summary of competences, capabilities and dynamic capabilities see Blackman *et al.* (2012): http://papers.ssrn.com/sol3/papers.cfm?abstract_id=2130232.
3 They also look more broadly into relationships and strategic costs, factors often overlooked in the service delivery literature.
4 The different strategies can also be considered as developmental stages. For instance, a relationship may begin as coordination, but develop over time into cooperation.
5 The placement of cooperation and coordination differs in the typologies offered by Himmelman and Mattessich and Monsey, with Mattessich and Monsey placing coordinating before cooperating.
6 Emerson *et al.* (2011) set out an integrative framework for collaborative governance regimes that focuses on internal collaborative dynamics and actions.
7 Note the contribution by Blackman in this volume, which challenges this perspective and explores enablers and barriers in a quite different way.
8 For an excellent review of leadership in inter-organizational networks see Müller-Seitz (2011).
9 See www.performance.gov for more on this.
10 See www.performance.gov for information and examples.

References

6, P. (1997) *Holistic Government*, London: DEMOS.
Abramson, M.A., Breul, J.D. and Kamensky, J.M. (2006) *Six Trends Transforming Government*, Washington: IBM Center for the Business of Government.
Akkerman, S.F. and Bakker, A. (2011) 'Boundary crossing and boundary objects', *Review of Educational Research*, 81(2): 132–169.

Aldrich, H. and Herker, D. (1977) 'Boundary spanning roles and organizational structure', *The Academy of Management Review*, 2(2): 217–230.

Alford, J. and O'Flynn, J. (2012) *Rethinking Public Service Delivery: Managing with External Providers*, Basingstoke: Palgrave.

Australian Government Reform of Australian Government Administration [AGRAGA] (2010) *Ahead of the Game: Blueprint for the Reform of Australian Government Administration*, Canberra: Department of the Prime Minister and Cabinet.

Australian Public Service Commission (2007) *Tackling Wicked Problems: A Public Policy Perspective*, Canberra: Australian Public Service Commission.

Axelrod, R. (1984) *The Evolution of Cooperation*, New York: Basic Books.

Axelrod, R. (1997) *The Complexity of Cooperation: Agent-Based Models of Competition and Collaboration*, Princeton, NJ: Princeton University Press.

Barber, M., Levy, A. and Mendonca, L. (2007) *Global Trends Affecting the Public Sector*, McKinsey & Company. Online. Available at: www.mckinsey.de/downloads/publikation/transforming_government/2007/0707_Transforming_globaltrends.pdf (accessed 12 December 2012).

Bardach, E. (1998) *Getting Agencies to Work Together: The Practice and Theory of Managerial Craftsmanship*, Washington DC: Brookings Institution Press.

Barney, J. (1991) 'Firm resources and sustained competitive advantage' *Journal of Management*, 17(1): 99–120.

Batley, R. and Rose, P. (2011) 'Analysing collaboration between non-governmental service providers and governments', *Public Administration and Development*, 31(4): 230–239.

Blackman, D., Buick, F., O'Donnell, M., O'Flynn, J. and West, D. (2012) *Developing High Performance: Performance Management in the Australian Public Service*, Crawford School Research Paper 12–09.

Bond, B.J. and Gebo, E. (2012) 'Comparing the implementation of a best practice crime policy across cities', *Administration & Society*, published online before print October 8 2012, doi:10.1177/0095399712459721.

Bourgon, J. (2011) 'The new synthesis: preparing government for the challenges of the 21st century', *ETHOS*, Issue 10: 14–20. Online. Available at: www.cscollege.gov.sg/Knowledge/Ethos/Lists/issues/Attachments/1/ETHOS10.pdf (accessed 3 January 2013).

Broussine, M. (2003) 'Public leadership', in T. Bovarid and E. Loffler (eds) *Public Management and Governance*, London: Routledge.

Bryson, J.M., Crosby, B.C. and Middleton Stone, M. (2006) 'The design and implementation of cross-sector collaborations: propositions from the literature', *Public Administration Review*, 66(s1): 44–55.

Cabinet Office (2000) *Wiring it up: Whitehall's Management of Cross-Cutting Policies and Services*. London: Performance and Innovation Unit.

Carlile, P.R. (2002) 'A pragmatic view of knowledge and boundaries: boundary objects in new product development', *Organization Science*, 13(4): 442–455.

Christensen, T. and Lægreid, P. (2007) 'The whole-of-government approach to public sector reform', *Public Administration Review*, 67(6): 1059–1066.

Cornes, M., Joly, L., Manthorpe, J., O'Halloran, S. and Smyth, R. (2011) 'Working together to address multiple exclusion homelessness', *Social Policy and Society*, 10(4): 513–522.

Cortada. J.W., Dijkstra, S., Mooney, G.M. and Ramsey, T. (2008) *Government 2020 and the Perpetual Collaboration Mandate: Six Worldwide Drivers Demand Customized Strategies*, Somers, NY: IBM Institute for Business Value.

Denhardt, R. and Denhardt, J. (2000) 'The new public service', *Public Administration Review*, 60(6): 549–559.

Donahue, J.D. (2004) *On Collaborative Governance*, Working Paper no. 2, Massachusetts: Corporate Social Responsibility Initiative, John F. Kennedy School of Government, Harvard University.

Donahue, J.D. and Zeckhauser, R.J. (2011) *Collaborative Governance: Private Roles for Public Goals in Turbulent Times*, Princeton, NJ: Princeton University Press.

Economist Intelligence Unit (2007) *Collaboration: Transforming the way Business Works*, London: The Economist. Online. Available at: www.eiu.com/site_info. asp?info_name=Collaboration_Transforming_the_way_business_works&rf=0 (accessed 7 April 2008).

Edwards, M. (2001) 'Participatory governance into the future: roles of the government and community sectors', *Australian Journal of Public Administration*, 60(3): 78–88.

Edwards, M. 'Shared accountability in service delivery: concepts, principles and the Australian experience', paper presented to the UN Committee of Experts on Public Administration, Vienna Meeting, July 2011.

Eisenhardt, K. and Martin, J. (2000) 'Dynamic capabilities: what are they?' *Strategic Management Journal* 21(10/11): 1105–1121.

Emerson, K., Nabstchi, T. and Balogh, S. (2011) 'An integrative framework for collaborative governance', *Journal of Public Administration Research and Theory*, 22(1): 1–29.

Entwistle, T. and Martin, S. (2005) 'From competition to collaboration in public service delivery: a new agenda for research', *Public Administration*, 83(1): 233–242.

Esteve, M., Boyne, G., Sierra, V. and Ysa, T. (2012) 'Organizational collaboration in the public sector: do chief executives make a difference?', *Journal of Public Administration Research and Theory*, published online before print, 18 September 2012 doi:10.1093/jopart/mus035.

Ferlie, E., Fitzgerald, L., McGivern, G., Dopson, S. and Bennett, C. (2011) 'Public policy networks and "wicked problems": a nascent solution?', *Public Administration*, 89(2): 307–324.

Frederickson, H.G. (1999) The repositioning of American public administration', *PS: Political Science and Politics*, 32(4): 701–711.

Fuerth, L.S. and Faber, E.M.H. (2012) *Anticipatory Governance Practical Upgrades: Equipping the Executive Branch to Cope with Increasing Speed and Complexity of Major Challenges*, Washington DC: Elliot School of International Affairs, The George Washington University.

Gill, D., Pride, S., Gilbert, H., Norman, R. and Mladenovic, A. (2010) 'The future state project: meeting the challenges of the 21st century', *Policy Quarterly*, 6(3): 31–99.

Glasby, J., Dickinson, H. and Miller, R. (2011) 'Partnership working in England – where are we now and where we've come from', *International Journal of Integrated Care*, 11(7): 1–8.

Gulick, L. (1937) 'Notes on the theory of organization', in L.H. Gulick and L. Urwick (eds) *Papers on the Science of Administration*, New York: Institute of Public Administration.

Halligan, J. (2007) 'Reintegrating government in third generation reforms in Australia and New Zealand', *Public Policy and Administration*, 22(2): 217–238.

Halligan, J., Buick, F. and O'Flynn, J. (2012) 'Experiments with joined-up, horizontal and whole-of-government in Anglophone countries', in A. Massey (ed.) *International Handbook on Civil Service Systems*, Cheltenham: Edward Elgar.

Hardy, C. and Phillips, N. (1998) 'Strategies for engagement: lessons from the critical examination of collaboration and conflict in an interorganizational domain, *Organization Science*, 9(2): 1159–1175.

Hardy, C., Phillips, N. and Lawrence, T.B. (2003) 'Resources, knowledge and influence: the organizational effects of interorganizational collaboration', *Journal of Management Studies*, 40 (2): 321–347.

Hartley, J. and Allison, M. (2000) 'The role of leadership in the modernization and improvement of public services', *Public Money & Management*, 20(2): 35–40.

Head, B. (2004) *Collaboration: What We Already Know, And How To Do It Better*, Canberra: Australian Research Alliance for Children and Youth. Online. Available at: www.aracy.org.au/ (accessed 7 April 2007).

Head, B. (2006) *Effective Collaboration*, Canberra: Australian Research Alliance for Children and Youth. Online. Available at: www.aracy.org.au/ (accessed 7 April 2007).

Head, B. (2008) 'Three lenses of evidence-based policy', *Australian Journal of Public Administration*, 67(1): 1–11.

Heracleous, L. (2004) 'Boundaries in the study of organization', *Human Relations*, 57(1): 95–103.

Himmelman, A.T. (2002) *Collaboration for a Change: Definitions, Decision-Making Models, Roles, and Collaboration Process Guide*. Minneapolis: Himmelman Consulting.

Ho, P. 'Governance at the leading edge: black swans, wild cards and wicked problems', paper presented at the 4th Strategic Perspectives Conference, Singapore, August 2008.

Hood, C. (1996) 'Control over bureaucracy: cultural theory and institutional variety', *Journal of Public Policy*, 15(3): 207–230.

Huxham, C. (1996) (ed.) *Creating Collaborative Advantage*, Sage: London.

Huxham, C. and Vangen, S. (2004) 'Doing things collaboratively: realizing the advantage or succumbing to inertia? *Organizational Dynamics*, 33(3): 190–201.

Jackson, P.M. and Stainsby, L. (2000) 'Managing public sector networked organizations', *Public Money & Management*, 20(1): 11–16.

Jacobides, M.G. (2006) 'The Architecture and design of organizational capabilities', *Industrial and Corporate Change*, 15(1): 151–171.

Kelman, S. (2007) 'The Transformation of Government in the Decade Ahead', in D.F. Kettl and S. Kelman, *Reflections on 21st Century Government Management*, Washington: IBM Center for the Business of Government.

Lamont. M. and Molnar, V. (2002) 'The study of boundaries in the social sciences', *Annual Review of Sociology*, 28: 167–195.

Lawson, R.B. and Ventriss, C.L. (1992) 'Organizational change: the role of organizational culture and organizational learning', *Psychological Record*, 42(2): 205–219.

Leat, D., Stoker, G., Seltzer, K. and 6, P. (1999) *Governing in the Round*, London: Demos.

Leck, H. and Simon, D. (2012) 'Fostering multiscalar collaboration and co-operation for effective governance of climate change adaptation', *Urban Studies*, published online before print 26 October 2012: doi: 10.1177/0042098012461675.

Linden, R. (2002) 'A framework for collaborating', *The Public Manager*, 31(2): 3–6.

Ling, T. (2002) 'Delivering joined-up government in the UK: dimensions, issues and problems', *Public Administration*, 80(4): 615–642.

Luke, J.S. (1998) *Catalytic Leadership: Strategies for an Interconnected World*, San Francisco: Jossey-Bass.

Lundin, M. (2007) 'When does cooperation improve public policy implementation?' *The Policy Studies Journal*, 35(4): 629–652.

McGuire, M. (2006) 'Collaborative public management: assessing what we know and how we know it', *Public Administration Review*, 66(s1): 33–43.

McKinsey & Company (2012) *Government Designed for New Times: a Global Conversation*, Washington DC: McKinsey Center for Government.

Management Advisory Committee (2004) *Connecting Government: Whole of Government Responses to Australia's Priority Challenges*, Canberra: Australian Government.

March, J.G. and Olsen, J.P. (1989) *Rediscovering Institutions: The Organizational Basis of Politics*, New York: Free Press.

Marcus, L.J., Dorn, B.C. and Henderson, J.H. (2006) 'Meta-leadership and national emergency preparedness: a model to build government connectivity, biosecurity and bioterrorism', *Biodefense Strategy, Practice, and Science*, 4(2): 128–134.

Marcus, L.J., Dorn, B., Ashkenazi, I., Henderson, J. and McNulty, E.J. (2009). *Meta-Leadership: A Primer*, Cambridge MA: National Preparedness Leadership Initiative, Harvard School of Public Health and Kennedy School of Government, Harvard University.

Mattessich, P.W. and Monsey, B.R. (1992) *Collaboration: What Makes it Work*, St Paul, Minnesota: Amherst H. Wilder Foundation.

Morse, R.S. (2011) 'The Practice of Collaborative Governance', *Public Administration Review*, 71(6): 953–957.

Moynihan, D.P., Fernandez, S., Kim, S., LeRoux, K.M., Piotrowski, S.J., Wright, B.E. and Yang, K. (2011) 'Performance regimes amidst governance complexity', *Journal of Public Administration Research and Theory*, 21(supp. 1): i141–i155.

Müller-Seitz, G. (2011) Leadership in inter-organizational networks: a literature review and suggestions for future research', *International Journal of Management Reviews*, 14(4): 428–433.

OECD (2001) *Public Sector Leadership for the 21st Century*, Paris: OECD.

O'Flynn, J. (2008) 'Elusive appeal or aspirational ideal? The rhetoric and reality of the "collaborative turn" in public policy', in J. O'Flynn and J. Wanna (eds) *Collaborative Governance: A New Era of Public Policy in Australia*, Canberra: Australia and New Zealand School of Government, ANU e Press.

O'Flynn, J., Buick, F., Blackman, D. and Halligan, J. (2011) 'You win some, you lose some: experiments with joined-up government', *International Journal of Public Administration*, 34(4): 244–254.

O'Leary, R., Choi, Y. and Gerard, C. (2012) 'The skills set of the successful collaborator', *Public Administration Review*, 72(s1): 70–83.

O'Leary, R. and Vij, N. (2012) 'Collaborative public management: where have we been and where are we going?' *The American Review of Public Administration*, 42(5): 507–522.

Osborne, S. (2006) 'The new public governance?', *Public Management Review*, 8(3): 377–387.

Osborne, S.P. and Brown, K (2005) *Managing Change and Innovation in Public Service Organizations*, London: Routledge.

O'Toole, L.J. (1997) 'The implications for democracy in a networked bureaucratic world', *Journal of Public Administration Research and Theory*, 7(3): 443–459.

Pablo, A.L., Reay, T., Dewald, J.R. and Casebeer, A.L. (2007) 'Identifying, enabling and managing dynamic capabilities in the public sector', *Journal of Management Studies*, 44(5): 687–708.

Parston, G. and Timmins, N. (1998) *Joined-up Management*, London: Public Management Foundation.

Pollitt, C. (2003) 'Joined-up government: a survey', *Political Studies Review*, 1: 34–49.

Prahalad, C.K. and Hamel, G. (1990) 'The core competence of the corporation'. *Harvard Business Review*, 68(3): 79–91.

Purdy, J.M. (2012) 'A framework for assessing power in collaborative governance processes', *Public Administration Review*, 72(3): 409–417.

Rittel, H.W.J. and Webber, M.M. (1971) 'Dilemmas in a general theory of planning', *Policy Sciences*, 4: 155–169.

Schein, E.H. (1985) *Organizational Culture and Leadership: A Dynamic View*, San Francisco: Jossey-Bass.

Schermerhorn, J.R. (1975) 'Determinants of interorganizational cooperation', *Academy of Management Journal*, 18(4): 846–856.

Silvia, C. (2011) 'Collaborative governance concepts for successful network leadership', *State and Local Government Review*, 43(1): 66–71.

Star, S.L. and Griesemer, J.R. (1989) 'Institutional ecology, "translations" and boundary objects: amateurs and professionals in Berkeley's Museum of Vertebrate Zoology, 1907–39', *Social Studies of Science*, 19: 387–420.

Statskontoret (2007) *Joining-up for Regional Development: How Governments Deal with a Wicked Problem, Overlapping Policies and Fragmented Responsibilities*, Stockholm: Statskontoret (Swedish Agency for Public Management).

Stoker, G. (2006) 'Public value management: a new narrative for networked governance?', *American Review of Public Administration*, 36(1): 41–57.

Sullivan, H. and Skelcher, C. (2002) *Working Across Boundaries: Collaboration in Public Services*, Houndsmills: Palgrave Macmillan.

Sullivan, H., Williams, P. and Jeffares, S. (2012) 'Leadership for collaboration', *Public Management Review*, 14(1): 41–66.

Talbot, C. and Johnson, C. (2007) 'Seasonal cycles in public management: disaggregation and re-aggregation', *Public Money & Management*, 27(1): 53–60.

Teece, D.J., Pisano, G. and Shuen, A. (1997) 'Dynamic capabilities and strategic management', *Strategic Management Journal*, 18(7): 509–533.

United Nations (2011) *Catalyzing Transformational Partnerships Between the United Nations and Business*, New York: UN Global Compact Office.

Victorian State Services Authority (2007) *Joined up Government: A Review of National and International Experiences*, Working paper no. 1, Melbourne: State Government of Victoria.

Wallace, M. and Schneller, E. (2008) 'Orchestrating emergent change: the "Hospitalist Movement" in US healthcare', *Public Administration*, 86(3): 761–778.

Wilkins, P. (2002) 'Accountability and joined up government', *Australian Journal of Public Administration*, 61(1): 114–19.

Williams, P. (2002) 'The competent boundary spanner', *Public Administration*, 80(1): 103–124.

World Economic Forum (2006) *Harnessing Private Sector Capabilities to Meet Public Needs: The Potential of Partnerships to Advance Progress on Hunger, Malaria and Basic Education*, Cologny/Geneva: World Economic Forum.

Part II

Solutions to cross-boundary dilemmas?

3 The cross-organizational collaboration solution?

Conditions, roles and dynamics in New Zealand

Elizabeth Eppel, Derek Gill, Miriam Lips and Bill Ryan

> Others have asked about what we did but no one has asked before about why or how.
> (interviewee)

Introduction

From the late 1980s, New Zealand acquired an international reputation for a model of public management which, amongst other things, focused attention on the outputs of individual public organizations. In 2001, government signed-off on a formal but only partially successful move towards managing for outcomes (SSC, 2002a) and the need for greater coordination between departments and agencies (SSC, 2002b). By 2004 (SSC, 2004a), there was a clear understanding that many of these outcomes were shared outcomes involving more than one department and that complex policy problems required information, resources and action from multiple agencies. Accordingly, cross-organizational coordination was re-emphasized (SSC, 2007; see also Chapter 2 in this volume).

During those years, initiatives such as the 'circuit-breaker' projects (SSC, 2004b), in which selected teams where tasked with developing solutions to cross-cutting issues such as truancy, came and went but achieved little, barely progressing beyond the pilot stage. Yet, by 2008, we were aware anecdotally of other subsequent initiatives which, by reputation, were more successful – that, in pockets throughout the New Zealand public sector, some ordinary officials were doing extraordinary things and learning to do something very difficult: to work with people from other agencies in achieving outcomes. We were interested to explore these initiatives, to learn 'who, what, how and why?' and so the *Better Connected Services for Kiwis* project was set up, upon which this chapter is based.[1] It brought together academic and practitioner perspectives on what was happening on the ground in New Zealand, but also drew on practical experiences in Australia, Canada, the Netherlands and the United Kingdom, and on the public policy literature (e.g. Australian Public Service Commission, 2007a; 2007b; Firecone Ventures, 2007; Hopkins *et al.*, 2001; Ling, 2002).

Our review of the existing literature (Eppel, 2008) suggested that much of it was top-down, government-centric and managerial. We had reasons to suspect that the view from the front line might be somewhat different, that the genesis and creation of successful joining up might look different if approached from a different angle. Accordingly, we designed our project as a qualitative, case-study based research project, looking at the experiences of joined-up front line officials across a range of public sector agencies and domains of government activity.

Our research questions were similar to the four framing questions asked in Chapter 2 of this volume. However, rather than a top-down view, we were more interested in what the key actors in these cases had done. We wanted to learn how those already doing cross-organizational work understood, rationalized, and enacted and then re-enacted that work (or not). We wanted to focus on their interactions with others and any roles, practices and norms they created in doing so, as well as the conditions under which they did so – in short, what Giddens (1984) refers to as their 'practical consciousness'.

In selecting the cases we sought to include 'hard' and 'soft' policy arenas, a focus on complex problems, a spread across different geographical regions, and more than one level of government. Pre-field work interviews and discussion with a reference group of practitioners led to the selection of seven case studies identified by common agreement to be demonstrably successful in some significant way. They were:

- Autism case study: cross-agency collaboration in providing services to mainstreamed special-needs students in schools;
- Government Urban and Economic Development Office (GUEDO): an office set up by a consortium of central government agencies working with local government and business to coordinate policy in New Zealand's largest and most economically significant city (Auckland);
- Mayor's Taskforce on Jobs: a national initiative headed by a group of mayors focused on cross-agency and cross-government collaboration in regional development and reducing unemployment;
- National Maritime Coordination Centre (NMCC): a multi-organizational entity set up to coordinate flows of information regarding maritime traffic moving to and from New Zealand;
- Integrated Case Management in South Auckland: integrated service delivery across several government agencies and community providers, focused particularly on families at risk (health, housing, education, unemployment and crime);
- Recognised Seasonal Employer (RSE) scheme in Hawke's Bay: the creation of a national programme designed to facilitate labour supply by drawing on seasonal workers from the Pacific islands;
- Strengthening Education in Mangere and Otara (SEMO): a Ministry of Education initiative to encourage collaboration across underperforming schools in a region of South Auckland, including extensive mobilisation of and engagement with Māori and Pacific parents.

In terms of research design, in brief, we adopted an interactionist perspective within a structurationist ontology (Giddens, 1984) and an interpretivist approach to the analysis of evidence (Blaikie, 1993; Denzin, 1989). Ideally, observational, immersive methods would have been employed, but because time and resources were finite we relied on intensive individual and collective interviews with subjects within and across all cases, wherein subjects were asked to speak about their motivated actions and the conditions pertaining to their enactment. In classifying and analysing this talk our categories were, in the first instance, derived from the language of our subjects. Our approach therefore shares certain methodological similarities with Huxham and Vangen (2000), Thomson and Perry (2006) and Weber and Khademian (2008).

Individual and collective (several participants from the same initiative) interviews were conducted in the case localities (Auckland, Napier, Wellington, Christchurch). Over 60 senior managers, middle managers and frontline staff participated, including some who brought experience of cross-organizational work outside of the nominated case studies, which we encouraged them to add to the discussion. On completion of the draft analysis we asked the subjects to review and, if necessary, improve or correct our findings and interpretations. Subject validation was positive and consistent ('That's our world!', 'You've got it', 'Someone from Wellington finally understands'). Unattributed statements in quotation marks used in this chapter are drawn from the interviews.[2]

Three sets of findings are worth highlighting. One relates to certain preconditions for collaboration, another to the cluster of necessary relationships and interactional roles, and the third to the phases and dynamics of the work that calls out these roles. We deal with each of these in turn.

Preconditions

Three matters reappeared constantly in our case studies, such that we suggest that they are necessary conditions for effective cross-organizational work. They are a client–outcome orientation, a decisive disruption and a capacity to learn-by-doing.

'We cannot do it on our own' was an oft-repeated phrase amongst our subjects, but the underlying 'it' is worth unpacking. Their first commitment was to client outcomes ('client' here can refer to particular individuals, or a more abstract conception applied to a group or community). 'It' meant achieving for the client the kinds of goals and objectives sought under a particular policy, and finding effective ways to achieve them. This is the 'common aim' (Huxham, 2003: 404–406) connecting the collaborators and the underlying driver, helping them overcome whatever other confusions and tensions may arise (O'Leary and Bingham, 2007). They are driven to do what has to be done to meet the legitimate needs of the client or to resolve the problem that had been identified. It was not just the fact of structural fragmentation or system failure or a top-down injunction to work with other agencies that impelled the cross-organizational work, but non-achievement of the mandated outcomes for individuals, groups or communities. Outcomes were the end and everything else was the means; not cross-organizational work for its own sake, but the over-arching and collective goal providing the rationale for action. It underpinned their commitment, drove them on and carried them through the tough and difficult dynamics of the process (a matter we revisit later).

Next, each of our case studies was triggered by a disruption of some form, articulated in a significant and decisive moment of realization – an 'A-ha!' moment. It might have been sudden or incremental, with the tipping-point occurring at the front line of delivery, at a meeting, in a minister's or official's office, or at a consultation; it might have been an externally-enforced crisis, a critical evaluation report, an angry remark from a client, or a stakeholder at a meeting who quietly spoke an unacknowledged truth. But this moment of insight irrevocably changed the lens through which the participants viewed the issue, providing the impulse for change. Striking examples included the moment when a client silenced a meeting with 'Everyone here is talking crap'; an evaluation report which concluded that 'These schools should be closed'; a labour-only contractor overheard muttering 'It's not a miracle at all, it's a disaster'; and a frustrated senior manager banging the table and declaring 'If we continue to act like this, the same thing will keep happening'.

In each case, the effect was decisive in creating a condition for effective cross-agency collaboration (Crosby and Bryson, 2010: 217–218 and Weber and Khademian, 2008: 433–434 argue similarly). One or another of the key actors (usually, although not necessarily, an official) stopped in their tracks and understood in a flash that business-as-usual – 'standard operating procedure' – was not enough. Something different was required and urgency was paramount. Practices needed to change across not just one but several organizations. This was the moment that galvanized the 'public entrepreneur', the first of the constituent roles we discuss below.

The third precondition apparent in each case study was a willingness and capacity to learn-by-doing (see also Thomson and Perry, 2006 for 'trial and error learning'). New ways and means needed to be developed, but the settings and issues were complex and few answers were immediately obvious. Participants realized that they had to 'learn' their way forward, and had to do so in spite of the unhelpful public management system in which they work, often without much support from their organizations, and in the general absence of a learning culture. Subjects talked about 'making it up as we go along', 'bending the rules', and 'working under the radar'. At the same time, our subjects noted their obligations as public officials and the need to innovate 'within baseline' and 'within our mandate'. This tension of accountability and autonomy is a constant balancing act (see also Huxham, 2000; Thomson and Perry, 2006), but the overriding sense was of purposive innovation within the public sphere – hence we have invoked the notion of '(public) entrepreneurialism' (Kobrack, 1996; see also Klein *et al.*, 2010).

But learning cannot be done alone. In a fragmented public sector, and needing holistic policy solutions to 'wicked problems' (Rittel and Webber, 1973), collaboration first demands acknowledging that 'We can't do this on our own', that 'We need to join up to get results'. New forms of organization are needed as well as new practices. Accordingly, the key actors construct horizontal, non-hierarchical networks that flow within and between organizations and sectors and may extend outside government to the economy or civil society. These networks are energetic, flexible, responsive and innovative, working across organizational boundaries – but they also rely on the human and other forms of capital attached to being part of larger, vertically aligned organizations. Further, since 'no system will connect you up', the 'right kinds of connections with the right kinds of people have to be created'. Personal relationships, trust, reliability and legitimacy are essential in creating collaborative arrangements (see also Bryson *et al.*, 2006; Crosby and Bryson, 2005; Huxham, 2000; Huxham and Vangen, 2000; McGuire, 2006; Thomson and Perry, 2006).

Interestingly, our interview subjects regarded collaboration as a distinctive form of cross-organizational interaction, different from, but related to, coordination and cooperation. One described the essence of collaboration as follows: 'It's when the people in the room stop saying "I" and start saying "we"'. One of Thomson's subjects said something similar: 'Collaboration is when everybody brings something to the table (expertise, money, the ability to grant permission) … take their hands off and then the team creates from there' (Thomson and Perry, 2006: 20; their paper includes other similar quotes). The difference between coordination or cooperation and collaboration is marked in part by the shift in balance towards collective interest and shared responsibility and away from self-interest and organizational autonomy[3] (see also Thomson and Perry, 2006: 23, 26)

Roles and relationships

On the basis of our case studies we argue that the creation and enactment of a trio of roles created and enacted within a horizontal network – the 'public entrepreneur', 'fellow travellers' and 'guardian angels' (plus, where appropriate, 'active client') – are essential in enabling new ways of doing things as part of effective cross-organizational working. Note that, at the outset, there are certain connections between our findings and those of Williams (2002, 2010) in relation to 'boundary spanning'. We argue, however, that our findings bring a more interactional understanding to this emerging phenomenon and pay more attention to its dynamics; therefore, we argue that it is important not to reify the notion of 'role'. Those we identify are constructed, reconstructed and deconstructed in the course of collective action according to context, timing, resources and purpose. Nor are they properties or attributes of individuals or behaviours, but forms of socially motivated enactment emerging in a context of interaction amongst multiple actors around particular purposes. We found, for example, that roles are not attached to particular individuals, but that particular individuals my enact several roles simultaneously or move in and out of particular roles at different times in the course of a particular project (e.g. starting out as a public entrepreneur but then enabling others to take that role and becoming a guardian angel).

The 'public entrepreneur'

In some ways the public entrepreneur is the most critical role, certainly in relation to initiating new ways of working. At least one person recognizes the
importance of the decisive moment and responds by initiating new ways of
working with others to achieve the desired outcome. People who adopt this role
can be employed in a variety of formal positions, although, based on our case
studies, they are usually an official in the 'middle' of a setting (e.g. a line
manager in an organization, or a more senior manager reporting to their chief
executive. Often the key motivation for action is the need to achieve the desired
outcomes, and they realize that the previously prescribed ways for getting there
are insufficient and inadequate. New ways must therefore be created by 'making
it up as we go along'. In other words, work is treated as action learning and not
rule-following.

Public entrepreneurs are marvellous networkers, and their initial activity is
focused on pulling together 'fellow travellers' – people who are similarly
capable and motivated public entrepreneurs in their own right whom they can
trust to collaborate. In just over half the cases, the solution often cannot be
created without the active participation of the client. In these cases the public
entrepreneur therefore also establishes a new relationship with the client, listening closely and working 'with' (rather than 'over' or 'for') them in co-producing
the way forward and, if necessary, empowering the client to do so.

Characteristically, these public entrepreneurs do not regard 'rules' as fixed or
as a barrier. If and when these general rules get in the road of achieving organizational outcomes, public entrepreneurs work by 'bending the rules'. This
enables development of the new ways required to make the system work in the
cases concerned. Knowing there is no textbook, they 'learn as they go'.
However, they regard themselves as 'acting normally', doing no more than 'what
needs to be done to achieve the outcome for the client', justifying their actions
by the specifics of the case or context and what they need to do, as a public official, to make it happen. If there is a possibility of challenge they will often 'act
first and seek approval later'.

The public entrepreneur and their fellow travellers – the core of the policy
network being formed to take the response forward – will sometimes, especially
in the early stages, keep their activities below the organizational radar, largely
because of the risk-averse organizational cultures permeating the New Zealand
public sector ('I keep my head down ... my colleagues handle everything the
same way').

In short, critical to the role of public entrepreneur – the individual who initi-
ates a transformational response to a moment of problem recognition – is a 'can
do' attitude. These individuals, however, are not – any more than their fellow
travellers – organizational mavericks or loose cannons. They are often savvy
about power, influence, organizations and individuals, and seek to manage in
particular cases for the overall organizational outcomes while maintaining a
deeply felt grasp of the public interest and the proper and legitimate role of the

official. In other words, their personal and emotional commitment to the role, purpose and efficacy of the public servant is central to their personal and professional being. However, they do more than simply say the right things, follow standard operating procedures and conduct due process.

'Fellow travellers'

Fellow travellers are exactly as the term implies. No public entrepreneur responding to a complex policy issue can be effective by themselves: they need like-minded people with whom they collaborate, each or any of whom might themselves play the public entrepreneur role in another setting. This applies even more where the policy problem and solution span agency boundaries and demand joining up in order to achieve shared outcomes. The process that develops is one of collective policy learning.

It is worth noting that this process is inherently unstable and under perpetual risk of 'falling back to the old ways', and so must constantly be pushed forward. In our case studies, the network was held together by the degree of trust and reciprocity shared by the participants. It is notable that these networks were often well-established and the members valued not just the personal relationships but also their stability and longevity ('restructurings mean that key people move on'). Equally, potential members, even if new to the context, are recruited on the basis of their willingness and capability to work within this kind of culture.

For fellow travellers, the key issue is the extent of the resources they can put on the collective table for others to share and use; they do not regard themselves as agency representatives, calculating their self-interest. In this respect their behaviour is almost the complete opposite of the turf protection that bedevils much inter-agency work.

A 'guardian angel'

While the public entrepreneur and their fellow travellers might often keep the first stages of innovation to themselves and work below the organizational radar, there will usually come a point where, for the survival of the collaborative enterprise, they need a 'guardian angel'. This is an individual – often a more senior manager in or close to the lead organization – who can mentor, protect, advise, advocate for and otherwise generally 'ride shotgun' for the network. Interestingly, the people interviewed suggested that there were enough public entrepreneurs and fellow travellers scattered around the New Zealand public sector, but far too few high-level officials or other individuals capable of understanding collaborative working and enacting the 'guardian angel' role.

'Guardian angels' themselves value innovation, flexibility and new thinking and are all too aware of how conventional thinking and standard operating practice can hamper and close down innovation. Accordingly, a guardian angel will be keenly attuned to the context, reading the ebbs and flows, managing the authorizing environment and managing risk, for and on behalf of the public entrepreneur and fellow travellers, sensing the moment when opportunities and dangers arise. Equally, they know how to stand back and let an innovation develop (or more actively facilitate its development) even though the risks in doing so may be quite high ('they must not try to own but get out of the way'). They too know the value of working under the radar, but also recognize when it is possible to go public and when it is necessary to do so for reasons of ministerial or public accountability (including 'no surprises').

The guardian angel does not simply serve organizational interests as the innovation proceeds, but does ensure that vertical matters are aligned and that certain hard limits are not exceeded. In short, they manage the authorizing environment in which the public entrepreneur and fellow travellers are getting on with their work.

This trio of roles – each of which is not necessarily one person, and not necessarily one person all of the time – acts in a way that combines the vertical and the horizontal by:

- balancing overall strategic goals and particular circumstances;
- balancing system demands and case conditions;
- focusing all on the common goal; and
- creating new ways of working that involves all of the parties.

The 'active client' ('co-producer')

In the majority of the cases examined, the client was an active participant in the process and fully engaged as co-producer (Boyle and Harris, 2009). They are positioned thus because the public entrepreneur and fellow travellers know that this is essential (often complex problems cannot be identified or solved anew without the participation of those affected) and because they ensure that the client is empowered to participate (whether by providing resources or by removing obstacles). From another angle, it can be said that these agents are sensitive to power imbalances (whether between clients and officials or between officials themselves), and so wherever possible, where progress is impeded, they seek to minimize them.

The active engagement of the client, which seems so important in most of the cases examined, points to another set of findings arising out of this study. The most effective cases of cross-organizational working required different relationships between front-line staff, national office officials, ministers and clients from those given by the classical constitutional models, and the necessary interaction between policy development and implementation. They also raise questions about when national policy can be implemented without the discretion allowed for regional variations to suit the specificities of the context.

The dynamics of horizontal, cross-organizational interactions

The points made so far relate to the relationships, practices and roles constructed by the participants in each of the cases examined. We have also noted that each of the cases entailed a long, involved process of establishing and maintaining new ways of working. In other words, building from a set of preconditions, a group dynamic emerged that seemed more or less common to all cases. Our organizing framework reflects that of our subjects and highlights its contextual, dynamic and emergent character. We should note that much of what follows resonates with research findings and analytical discussion conducted by other authors who have dealt with such processes (e.g. Bryson *et al.*, 2006; Crosby and Bryson, 2005; Huxham, 2000; Kickert *et al.*, 1997; O'Leary and Bingham, 2007; Thomson and Perry, 2006; Weber and Khademian, 2008; Williams, 2002, 2010). Nonetheless, we have remained faithful to the accounts given to us by our subjects, retaining their emphases and terminology. They described four phases, labelled simply 'before starting', 'getting together', 'working together' and 'sustaining'. Further, each phase involves learning from each other and learning-from-doing. It also requires support at each stage if the collaboration is to bring about shared outcomes (see Figure 3.1).

Before starting

In this phase – before the critical 'A-ha!' moment occurs – the staff are working on the delivery of services within their vertically aligned organizations. Standard operating procedures apply. Then the moment of realization occurs – the moment when a disconnect between the theory and the reality suddenly becomes apparent, when conflict between the realities presumed by the normal ways of doing things and the ways needed to deal effectively with the new situation can no longer be ignored. This imperative – perhaps a crisis or emergency – creates a window where one or more officials in the right place at the right time and with the courage and imagination to see the possibilities, decide to grab the moment. Equally, of course, this person or persons realizes that the solution must involve more than one organization.

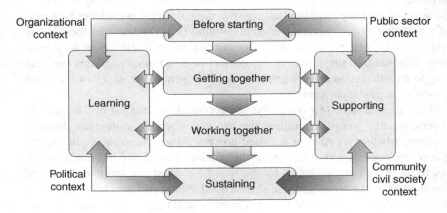

Figure 3.1 Cross-organizational collaborating.

Getting together

Bonding chemical elements in new ways takes energy and a catalyst. Similarly, in getting together, an initiating agent – the public entrepreneur – is required, one who has the passion, imagination, energy and credibility to break down the vertically aligned authority structures and organizational practices that prevent those caught up in them from recognizing the new realities and to start creating horizontal interactions. Organizations that encourage reflection and learning and that know how to manage risk create an environment and culture which makes this process easier.

The catalyst – the public entrepreneur – is someone able to activate the personal qualities, resources, 'nous', authority and trust within the system and who can galvanize and pull together a group of fellow travellers – like-minded people who are open to new possibilities, 'go to' people with an equally 'can do' attitude who are willing to engage with the unfamiliar. Not that those individuals will necessarily be available: many of our subjects mentioned the role of plain, simple good luck in ensuring that the various elements required to make it all work are present, when and where needed. Equally, as noted in the discussion of roles, this nascent network is sometimes (but not always) supported at this stage by one or more managers who know how to balance 'tight and loose' and allow the space for individuals to create new ways of working. In these respects, success also requires organizational cultures which empower (or, at least, do not prevent) bottom-up or middle-outwards problem solving, and which define their mission critical tasks broadly.

Working together

We were told that public entrepreneurs and their fellow travellers find it hard to create new ways of working together if the relationships and practices they are developing are not enabled in various ways. Effective joint working requires that staff from the various agencies have the permission and the authority to 'try out new ways of working', and the skills to span organizational boundaries by enacting a role that extend beyond the purely formal (e.g. the terms of their job or technical mandate). No matter how like-minded others might be, or how positively disposed to want to join in, the vertical organizational resources they can bring to the interaction are important in enabling them to act as fellow travellers alongside the public entrepreneur.

There seemed to be few fixed keys to successful governance of the group or process, as the group determines the process whereby individuals become members, whether an open or a closed process. Much the same applies to the style of governance and processes of monitoring (formal and informal), which tend to be shaped and reshaped by the specific context and the imperatives of the situation, particularly as these shift around. Similarly, we observed a wide range of leadership styles – although it must be said that commanding and controlling styles were rare. The commonalities were around matters such as the high value placed on 'heart' (the personal and often emotional commitment to making a difference) and 'smarts' (sufficient savvy, street sense and access to resources to know how to read the context and make the system work). With these conditions present, the participants slowly create a self-conscious network.

Supporting

Working together in achieving shared outcomes does not and cannot occur in isolation: horizontal networks need to be connected to the vertical organization(s) and supported as they work. Even in cases where the entrepreneur and fellow travellers initiated new ways of working and operated for some time without an official organizational mandate, the time would come when they needed support from the host organizations. This might be for assistance, scaling up, middle-outwards expansion, or simple risk-management. Here, the guardian angel is essential; if not already present, one must be found.

Our subjects spoke of 'working in the grey zone, not black and white'. Individuals in whichever role must be able to work collectively within a context of uncertainty and complexity, balancing the obligations of working in a public organization with the desire to work autonomously and to innovate. They must also be conscious of and work with the particular constraints or tensions operating upon any one of them and be willing to share organizational and reputational capital. They will be successful only if they maintain a high degree of legitimacy inside their organization and a sophisticated understanding of its formal and informal imperatives, structures, resources and limits. Conditions must be such that they – particularly the guardian angels – are able to engineer access to resources from host organizations that can be brought to the collective task, either as an earmarked budget within a silo or with flexible or horizontal expenditure rules. Without these forms of support, working together effectively over the medium to long term will not succeed.

Learning

Working differently in order to solve complex problems requires managing complexity, sometimes 'on the edge of chaos', where learning is crucial. As no one person has all the knowledge or resources, there is no received discourse or language, no cookbook or paint-by-numbers framework. It also requires an understanding that structure does not substitute for people or practice. What must be built up over time is a shared understanding and collective learning, a continual reframing of the problem, often from an outside-in view. Some described this as 'learning your way forward' (to probe > sense > act >, as Kurtz and Snowden (2003) might put it). However, doing so also requires the right reflexive, evaluative capability. In fact, some of the cases explicitly built an 'evaluator' role into the network, and several subjects spoke positively of having them in the process, walking alongside as 'critical friends'.

Sustaining

Support and learning are crucial in order for the group to sustain itself and develop. If reflection plus group learning and problem solving are expected of all participants and are part of the accepted organizational culture, the new structure of roles and the ways of working being developed by the trio of innovation will be sustained. Without this, without organizational support and a culture of learning, joining up will fail and the elements will return to their initial, ineffectual state.

The logic of bureaucracy in relation to processes is to identify repeatable tasks, create a rule and enforce its implementation. The cases examined in this project suggest that complex multi-agency work on shared outcomes often does not lend itself to being simplified and routinized in this way. In these cases everything depends on context, people, and responsiveness from the bottom-up and middle-outwards, as each continually changes. The process of collaboration cannot be set up and walked away from. Sustaining it is critical, achieved via enablement and definitely not control. The absence of active support at the organizational level was something keenly felt by our subjects and is a point to which we return in the conclusion.

Enablers and constraints

In considering the interplay between structure and agency in crossing organizational boundaries, several matters are frequently identified as barriers in the New Zealand context. Selected subject responses are worth noting, mainly because they reinforce the duality of structure – namely, that to agents, it can be both constraint and enabler.

What of budgetary silos and restrictions on spending within given output classes? New Zealand's strongly silo-ized budget system is often cited as a rationale for not collaborating, but, in most cases, the cross-organizational collaborators in these case studies did not regard it as an absolute constraint. What mattered more, they suggested, was the overall budget constraint, and how budgets and contracts were defined and monitored ('payments are tied to widgets not outcomes and ignore complexity'). Insofar as the budget system did constrain cross-organizational and cross-programme working, we were frequently told that 'these can be worked around', and 'when there is a will there is a way'. Here, as elsewhere, it seems that lesser mortals are stopped in their tracks by system limits, whereas public entrepreneurs are not deflected from their overall goals and can often find ways to make things happen.

Do other formal systems constrain? In an obvious sense the answer is 'yes', since that is what they are designed to do. Embedded organizational and sector-wide systems such as client/customer relationship management, management systems generally, information technology, and human resource and finance systems, are designed to operate hierarchically with vertical alignment and accountability in mind. As such, they do not support cross-agency processes, obliging those creating them, as they do with budget systems, to find legitimate and legal workarounds ('bending rules'). In fact, doing so emphasizes an essential aspect of learning how to work in new boundary-spanning ways. And working within public sector rules, conventions, and accountabilities means that they must learn to connect the vertical and the horizontal and make them work in achieving mandated client outcomes. An example is 'putting resources on the table but then spending them on behalf of the group'.

One formal system element that does appear to constrain is the Privacy Act, regarded in New Zealand as a powerful and important boundary by citizens and officials alike (although there are also important but unresolved questions in terms of delivery about whether some of the constraints are entirely a product of legislative requirements or risk-averse interpretation by officials). It is worth noting, however, that in these case studies, where cross-organizational working was created precisely to achieve the client outcomes sought by policy, the participants wanted to use methods and tools such as risk profiling and proactive case management, but felt unable to do so by the required privacy provisions.

Other unexpected matters did arise in discussion, however, which point to critical factors in creating and sustaining cross-boundary networks. One was how differences in regional and local government boundaries (and overlapping boundaries more broadly) can have significant consequences for relationships and the ability to work together. Another is the constant restructuring that has blighted organizations within the New Zealand state sector. This can seriously underpin the trust and continuity built up in networks which is important in maintaining them over time.

Perhaps the most significant finding regarding blockers, however, is that they do not sit around formal or hard systems. The main obstacles are the 'soft' issues: embedded organizational and sectoral cultures, values and routines, professional beliefs, values and preferences, and so on, which are also the hardest things to change. A positive, change-oriented dictum like 'no one ever got fired for doing the right thing' (the 'right thing' being defined in terms of client outcomes) has to compete with a culture of 'no one ever got fired for following standard operating practice'. Frustration and discouragement were traced back to risk-averse organizations and managers, senior managers who are busy managing upwards and not for outcomes, the dangers of 'putting your head above the parapet', the 'culture of busy-ness', and so on. A lack of leadership, a lack of permission and a lack of reward were also identified. Similar criticisms around the same issues were also made of the central agencies and other mechanisms of collective public sector leadership.

In that respect, an empowering rhetoric supporting cross-organizational working in place at the time of the research (but which subsequently lost currency following the change in government) – such as the 'shared outcomes' push identified at the beginning of this chapter, the community planning provisions of the Local Government Act (2003), and the State Services Development Goals (SSC 2008) – all contributed to supporting the work undertaken in the case studies but were not enough to make a major difference. Equally, the world-views of managers and staff in the regions were closely aligned and public entrepreneurs would frequently be supported by their local managers. Even within the same organization, managers in Wellington (i.e. central government policy shops) had a different world-view and would be significantly less supportive.

Conclusions

What are the major findings from the project? What conditions are required for officials and others to cross organizational, professional and other boundaries and start working horizontally?

- One is an outcome orientation, a determination in the face of system inadequacy or failure to create the outcomes for clients (whether individuals, groups or communities) sought by policy, to find ways to make them happen. This is particularly so when complex, dynamic situations defy easy description and are not amenable to detailed ex-ante planning or resolution through standard operating procedures. Outcomes and plans are best treated as emergent, being defined and refined along the way.
- Crossing boundaries, working together and working horizontally in networks are means to that end; no more, no less. Goal displacement needs to be avoided. Work practices, know-how and systems should be treated as conditional, subject to action learning and modified in line with experience and changing circumstances. Put simply, cross-organizational working should be treated as a perpetual pilot, an ongoing experiment, and be allowed to break the rules as it develops so that it can continue. Learning-by-doing is a pre-requisite orientation, as is an evaluative, reflective approach to action.
- Because crossing boundaries is a means to an end, not an end in itself, it will not succeed unless triggered by a decisive disruption – a crisis or emergency, an 'A-ha!' moment that demands a shift beyond conventional, vertical, single-organizational ways of working. It will not naturally evolve out of standard operating procedures, tweaking the existing system, or when commanded top-down as if an end in itself.
- Absolutely essential is a group of key actors who are able to enact the roles of public entrepreneur, fellow travellers and guardian angel as, how, and when required. If not fulfilled, the evolving dynamics of the interactions and the conditions for achieving shared outcomes to complex problems via cross-organizational working will not be present. Nothing else can follow.
- Co-production with individual and collective clients also seems to be important, certainly insofar as defining and realizing the particular form of the desired policy outcome is concerned. In many complex settings there must also be a process of empowerment in order for clients to overcome any power imbalances and to allow them to act proactively, as a contributing agent of change.

- Crossing-boundaries in order to achieve collective goals is an interactive, recursive process, constituted in and through its own dynamic through time. As such, it is hard work and requires purpose, energy and commitment from participants. It involves working on the edge and taking managed risks. It also requires managing the dynamics as the group goes through phases – initiating, working together and sustaining – and needs support from the authorizing environment.
- The most significant constraints to cross-organizational working are not so much those of existing structures, systems or rules – although these may not help. Moreover, access to authorized resources is essential for making the changes required; the horizontal must be made to work with the vertical. The major obstacle is embedded bureaucratic cultures and reified everyday practices – means of administration which have been transformed into ends. Those who can break through and learn to work horizontally understand that outcomes are the goal and construct ways and means of getting there over time. Again, the authorizing environment is critical in enabling them to do so and in sustaining their efforts.

Our overall finding, therefore, is that cross-organizational working is not an object that can be pre-defined and directed from the top-down. It is emergent work, something that must be enabled and allowed to spread outwards from the middle of organizations. If and when the conditions of possibility arise or are triggered, those who are capable of working these ways will rise to the task – but their efforts must also be protected, supported and sustained over time and in different ways, depending on the dynamics. Looked at from a managerial or leadership perspective, it demands a completely different approach to the command and control, risk-averse, top-down specification and compliance monitoring approach that typifies much public sector management from the top of organizations and from central agencies. Instead of directors and controllers, they need to become guardian angels of cross-organizational working. It also means clear and explicit signals to all and sundry that those already enacting the roles of public entrepreneurs, fellow travellers, and guardian angels should be allowed to come out from the bureaucratic shadows and be recognized for what they have done and continue to do. This injunction is definitely relevant to government and public service in New Zealand, but probably also to other similar jurisdictions as well.

Notes

1 This chapter is an abridged and sharpened version of a longer discussion document produced for practitioners: see Eppel *et al.*, 2008.
2 Unless otherwise indicated, all comments in quotation marks are non-attributable comments from state sector staff participating in the project workshops. Most are verbatim, although some are typified composites.
3 This entails not just 'communication' (talking together), 'coordination' (getting together) or 'cooperation' (working together), but something more: namely 'collaboration' (sharing work as one). This formulation differs slightly from the version given in Chapter 2 of this volume.

References

Australian Public Service Commission. (2007a) *Changing Behaviour. A Public Policy Perspective*. Online. Available at: www.apsc.gov.au (accessed 17 March, 2008).

Australian Public Service Commission. (2007b) *Tackling Wicked Problems. A Public Policy Perspective*. Online. Available at: www.apsc.gov.au (accessed 17 March, 2008).

Blaikie, N. (1993) *Approaches to Social Enquiry*, Oxford: Blackwell.

Boyle, D. and Harris, M. (2009) *The Challenge of Co-production: How Equal Partnerships between Professionals and the Public are Crucial to Improving Public Services*, London, NEF, the Lab and NESTA.

Bryson, J.M., Crosby, B.C. and Stone, M.M. (2006) 'The design and implementation of cross-sector collaborations: propositions from the literature', *Public Administration Review* (special issue): 44–55.

Crosby, B. and Bryson, J. (2005) 'A leadership framework for cross-sector collaboration', *Public Management Review*, 7(2): 177–201.

Crosby, B. and Bryson, J. (2010) 'Integrative leadership and the creation and maintenance of cross-sector collaborations'. *The Leadership Quarterly*, 21(2): 211–230.

Denzin, N. (1989) *Interpretive Interactionism*, Newbury Park: Sage.

Eppel, E. (2008) *Better Connected Services for Kiwis: Achieving Outcomes by Joining Up, A Literature Review*, Wellington: Victoria University of Wellington.

Eppel, E., Gill, D., Lips, M. and Ryan, B. (2008) *Better Connected Services for Kiwis: A Discussion Document for Managers and Front-Line Staff on Joining Up The Horizontal and the Vertical*, Wellington: Institute of Policy Studies, Victoria University of Wellington.

Firecone Ventures (2007) *Background Paper on Shared Services Models: Final Report*, Melbourne Victoria: State Services Authority.

Giddens, A. (1984) *The Social Constitution of Society*, Cambridge: Polity Press.

Hopkins, M., Couture, C. and Moore, E. (2001) *Moving from the Heroic to the Everyday: Lessons Learned from Leading Horizontal Projects*, Ottawa: Canadian Centre for Management Development.

Huxham, C. (2000) 'The challenge of collaborative governance', *Public Management Review*, 2(3): 337–357.

Huxham, C. (2003) 'Theorising collaborative practice', *Public Management Review*, 5(3): 401–423.

Huxham, C. and Vangen, S. (2000) 'Leadership in the shaping and implementation of collaborative agendas: how things happen in a (not quite) joined-up world', *The Academy of Management Journal*, 43(6): 1159–1175.

Kickert, W.J.M., Klijn, E.-H. and Koppenjan, J.F.M. (eds) (1997) *Managing Complex Networks: Strategies for the Public Sector*, London, New Delhi: Sage Publications.

Klein, P., Mahoney, J., McGahan, A. and Pitelis, C. (2010) 'Towards a theory of public entrepreneurship', *European Management Review*, 7(1): 1–15.

Kobrack, P. (1996) 'The social responsibilities of a public entrepreneur', *Administration and Society*, 28(2): 205–237.

Kurtz, C.F. and Snowden, D.J. (2003) 'The new dynamics of strategy: sense-making in a complex and complicated world', *IBM Systems Journal*, 42(3): 462–483.

Ling, T. (2002) 'Delivering joined-up government in the UK: dimensions, issues and problems', *Public Administration*. 80(4): 615–642.

McGuire, M. (2006) 'Collaborative public management: assessing what we know and how we know it', *Public Administration Review*, 66 (Special Issue): 33–43.

O'Leary, R. and Bingham, L.B. (2007) 'Conclusion: conflict and collaboration in networks', *International Public Management Journal*, 10(1): 103–109.

Rittel, H. and Webber, M. (1973) 'Dilemmas in a general theory of planning', *Policy Sciences* 4: 155–69.

State Services Commission (SSC) (2002a) *Managing for Outcomes: Guidance for Departments*, Wellington: Department of Prime Minister and Cabinet, Te Puni Kokiri, State Service Commission, The Treasury.

State Services Commission (SSC) (2002b) *The Review of the Centre – One Year On: Getting Better Results for Citizens, Ministers and Staff*, Wellington: State Services Commission.

State Services Commission (SSC) (2004a) *Getting Better at Managing for Shared Outcomes: A Resource for Agency Leaders*, Wellington: State Services Commission.

State Services Commission (SSC) (2004b) *Circuit Breaker Workbook*, State Services Commission: Wellington.

State Services Commission (SSC) (2007) *Factors for Successful Coordination: Helping State Agencies Coordinate Effectively*, Wellington: State Services Commission.

State Services Commission (SSC) (2008) *State Services Development Goals*, Wellington: State Services Commission.

Thomson, A. and Perry, J. (2006) 'Collaboration processes: inside the black box', *Public Administration Review*, 66 (Special Issue): 20–32.

Weber, E. and Khademian, A. (2008) 'Managing collaborative processes: common practices, uncommon circumstances', *Administration and Society*, 40(5): 431–464.

Williams, P. (2002) 'The competent boundary spanner', *Public Administration*, 80(1): 103–124.

Williams, P. (2010) 'Special agents: the nature and role of boundary spanners', paper presented at the ESRC Research Seminar Series – 'Collaborative Futures: New Insights from Intra and Inter-Sectoral Collaborations', University of Birmingham, February 2010.

4   The boundary-spanning solution?

Crossing boundaries in the United States

Kelly LeRoux

Over the past five decades, the practice of public management in the US, as well as many other parts of the world, has evolved in such a way that administrative action is rarely carried out through conventional notions of bureaucracy involving authoritative, hierarchically structured action. Rather, the structure of US government administration now resembles, and indeed requires, extensive horizontal webs of actors, none of whom have an exclusive claim to power. In recent years this transformation of government from vertical hierarchies to horizontal networks and public–private partnerships has been recognized with increasing frequency in the public management literature (Goldsmith and Eggers 2004; Salamon 2002; Kettl 2000; Frederickson 1999; Agranoff and McGuire 2004; O'Toole 1997).

The terminology used to describe this paradigm shift within the public administration field has varied, with references to the 'hollow state' (Milward and Provan 2000), collaborative public management (Agranoff and McGuire 2004; O'Leary and Bingham 2009), third-party government (Salamon 1987), government by proxy (Kettl 1988), the new governance (Salamon 2002), and, simply, governance (Frederickson 1999, 2005). Despite this diversity of terminology, each of these descriptions shares a common understanding of government as boundary spanner. Whereas governments are legally constructed institutions that are politically and spatially bounded, *boundary spanning* refers to the pursuit of public purposes through government-directed, but not necessarily government-produced, methods. Boundary spanning involves a strategic mix of service delivery arrangements, involving interdependencies between and among governments, citizens, and public and private (for-profit and non-profit) organizations. These interdependencies assume many forms, the most common of which are formal and informal networks, contracts for services, intergovernmental agreements, mixed-market approaches, and the use of public incentives to encourage desired behavior in the market place. By definition, boundary spanning is collaborative, requiring government to broker and manage partnerships with a wide variety of sub-national and non-governmental actors. This chapter examines the phenomenon of boundary-spanning activity within the US government, with particular attention to the question of 'what does it involve'?

Regardless of the terminology one uses, there is clear evidence that boundary-spanning activities by the US federal government are extensive. Salamon (2002) reports that roughly 72 percent of all US federal budget outlays are used to finance 'indirect government', such as contracts, grants, and vouchers, while only 28 percent of expenditures are for direct government services. This means that for every dollar spent by the federal government on direct services, nearly three more are spent on indirect services. These numbers illustrate the pervasive nature of administrative reliance upon third-party actors, and signal a permanent shift toward boundary spanning as the modus operandi of the US federal government.

This new era of governance, in which boundary spanning is the predominant mode of delivering public goods and services, is one that poses both challenges and opportunities for the US government and for the American public. The most obvious challenge is the potential loss of accountability, as government relinquishes some of its control over decision making and policy implementation to outside actors. However, for the federal government the trade-off in sharing power is that more effective and sustainable policy solutions may be crafted, and services might be delivered with greater efficiency and effectiveness and administered in ways that are more responsive to the needs and interests of the clients being served. The remainder of this chapter examines the factors contributing to the rise of boundary-spanning government in the US, and discusses some of the various policy instruments and methods through which government fulfills its obligations for public goods and services provision. The discussion concludes with an analysis and critique of how boundary spanning has worked in various US policy contexts, highlighting some specific examples from the health and human services arena and the implementation of federal initiatives aimed at enhancing public safety.

The emergence of boundary spanning in American public administration

Government reliance on third-party actors has a long history in the US, dating back to the Revolutionary War when colonial governments purchased arms through contractual arrangements with private suppliers (Salamon 2002). Yet boundary spanning activities did not become necessary or widespread in the US until the post-World War II era, when technological innovations began to give rise to new possibilities, and rapid population growth demanded new forms of public goods and services, requiring them to be delivered on a larger scale. While the reasons for the emergence of boundary spanning are many, they can be distilled into three key inter-related explanations, reflecting, in part, the key imperatives identified in Chapter 2 of this volume. The first is a deeply held American preference for limited government and the attendant political pressures to contain the size of the federal bureaucracy. The second reason is that the increasing complexity of public problems combined with a federalist system of government and a high degree of jurisdictional fragmentation has led to a growing recognition and acceptance by federal officials that effective policy responses cannot be crafted in isolation. The third explanation rests on technological innovation, globalization, and the rise of the information age. Each of these factors will now be examined in greater depth.

Preference for limited government

The first – and perhaps most distinctly American – force giving rise to the growth of government reliance on third parties is the long-standing and deep-rooted American preference for limited government. American exceptionalism, born out of the US revolution, has embedded the values of liberty, individualism, and *laissez-faire* government into the American culture, along with a general fear and distrust of 'big government' (Lipset 1996). As such, Americans have always preferred a limited national state system, and one with divided power amongst the states and federal government. Yet this has created an ongoing political challenge for federal lawmakers, as they have sought to strike a balance between limiting the growth of the federal bureaucracy while at the same time expanding public goods and programs to meet the diverse and growing needs and demands of American citizens. Contracting with private firms (both for-profit and non-profit) has provided a solution to this dilemma which has been politically attractive to both major US political parties.

Contracting with non-profits first began on a large scale in the 1960s, under Democratic president Lyndon B. Johnson, whose War on Poverty programs enabled unprecedented spending for domestic programs. The passage of the federal Medicare and Medicaid programs during this time created a new set of intergovernmental partnerships with states to implement these programs, but, even more importantly, fueled the growth of the health care sector, and served as the beginning of what is now an extensive program of government contracting for health-related services with private providers. This era also produced two new federal cabinet agencies with missions that require significant boundary spanning. The US Department of Housing and Urban Development (HUD) was formed in 1965, with a mission to combat urban poverty through extensive federal funding in the form of demonstration projects and grants made to cities and non-profit organizations across the country. Today, HUD is still a major federal grant-maker to local communities and non-profits, addressing problems of homelessness, shortages of low-income housing, and community development, among other things. The US Department of Transportation was also formed during this time, which created a vehicle for systematizing federal grants to local communities for transportation and gave rise to new forms of intergovernmental partnerships and new forms of non-profit and quasi-governmental institutions, such as councils of government and metropolitan planning organizations. Enabled largely by federal funding, today these institutions are located in every US metropolitan area, brokering inter-local cooperation and coordination among cities and counties in the region around issues such as regional land-use planning, economic development, environmental standards and safety, emergency management, disaster preparedness, and transportation.

The practice of contracting out for public services continued to grow throughout the 1970s and 1980s under Republican presidents Richard Nixon and Ronald Reagan, who campaigned on the promise of 'getting rid of big government'. Devolution also expanded during these administrations, pressing further responsibility for implementation of federal policies down onto state and local governments. Government contracting continued to flourish during the 1990s, bolstered by the managerial reform initiatives of that era, including the New Public Management and Reinventing Government, which prescribed increased contracting and a mandate that government should 'steer, not row' (Osborne and Gaebler 1992). Upon assuming office in 1993, Democratic President Bill Clinton embraced these reforms, as embodied in his own version of reform doctrine, the National Performance Review, which included a plan to reduce the size of the federal bureaucracy and expand the contracting of non-essential federal functions. Two landmark pieces of federal legislation which were passed during the 1990s also extended new funding to non-profits – the Americans with Disabilities Act, and the Personal Responsibility and Work Opportunity Act, more commonly known as 'welfare reform'. In the case of the latter, the federal welfare program was converted from an entitlement program comprising mainly income assistance to an intergovernmental partnership with the states, resulting in extensive contracting with non-profit and for-profit job training providers to help welfare recipients transition into the workforce.

Today, contracting remains a popular alternative to expanding the federal workforce, and one that has been widely embraced as 'good politics' by federal lawmakers in both parties. As Salamon (1995) has argued, particularly in the context of contracting for social services, government contracting creates a win–win situation for both federal agencies that contract out for services and for the recipient contractors. Private contractors benefit from increased legitimacy and from the funding which enables them to expand the scope and scale of their operations, and, in the case of non-profits, extend their missions to serve more people. Government benefits by expanding federal programs and services the public needs without increasing the size of the government workforce. By contracting with for-profit or non-profits that are experts in the manufacture of a particular good, or experts in the delivery of a particular service, government benefits by capturing innovative ideas and creative program that are often highly effective but not possible to implement in rule-bound bureaucracies. Sometimes efficiencies are gained, although this is not always the case, and it is rarely the motivation for contracting at the federal level where other public values such as effectiveness, equity, and responsiveness generally take precedence over cost-saving considerations.

Jurisdictional fragmentation and complexity of public problems

According to Agranoff and McGuire (2004, p. 4), 'collaborative management is a concept that describes the process of facilitating and operating in multi-organizational arrangements to solve problems that cannot be solved, or easily solved, by single organizations'. Without question, the nature and scope of public problems are becoming increasingly complex and can rarely be solved by a single organization. Pointing to milestone achievements in US history such as winning the space race and eradicating diseases, Frederickson (1999) has observed that every significant accomplishment of the twentieth century could be attributed to American bureaucracy. Yet today some of the most exciting innovations and discoveries are not being made by government, but in the private sector, often with the support and encouragement of government contracts or subsidies. In short, it is simply impractical, and not feasible from a technical or political standpoint, for government to employ all of the expertise needed to address today's complex problems. Yet a variety of forms of intergovernmental and public–private partnerships allow the federal government to still lay claim to these innovations, at least in part, and ensures that potential solutions to public problems evolve in ways that are consistent with the public interest.

Compounding the issue of problem-complexity is the fact that the American system of government is highly fragmented, which has presented an enduring challenge to the implementation of federal policies and programs. The US has one federal government, 50 state governments with distinct powers of their own, and roughly 89,527 local governments (US Census of Governments 2007), each with different values and preferences surrounding public services. Thus, the federal government must operate in a service-delivery environment that is not only sectorally fragmented, but is also jurisdictionally fragmented. The federal government engages in boundary spanning activities with state and local governments through intergovernmental grant programs and by regulating state and local implementation of federal policy mandates, both funded and unfunded. Not only does the federal government span intergovernmental boundaries in order to achieve national policy objectives, but significant boundary spanning occurs at the state and local levels as well. Nowhere is this more visible than in US metropolitan regions, which often contain hundreds of local government units that must work together on a purely voluntary basis in order to achieve regional goals.

Metropolitan fragmentation complicates the management of urban systems of commerce, communication, environmental issues and other realities of contemporary society that transcend political borders. This fragmentation is problematic for boundary spanning in the sense that each unit of government has its own set of rules, laws, and elected officials that often create barriers to cooperation. Despite these barriers, along with a strong preference for local control and a local tax system that creates economic incentives to compete rather than cooperate, in recent years local government officials have grown more receptive to cooperation with neighboring governments, as it has become increasingly apparent that local policy choices have implications beyond their own borders. As local problems have become increasingly trans-jurisdictional, and officials have accepted the fact that local problems add up to become global problems, they have increased their boundary spanning activities through interlocal service agreements, memoranda of understanding, coordinated environmental plans and standards, and greater participation in regional initiatives created by councils of government and metropolitan planning organizations.

Finally, the persistent threat of both man-made and natural disasters has resulted in a new set of mandates for intergovernmental collaboration in the areas of emergency management and disaster planning. Homeland Security and other federal mandates of the last ten years have redistributed federal funding to cities in ways that promote certain public objectives such as national security, while constraining cities' ability to deal with other pressing public problems.

Technology and the rise of the information age

The widespread availability of the internet, which began in the mid-1990s, has played a major role in enhancing the boundary spanning activities of government that existed before the onset of this technological innovation, and has also given rise to new forms. E-government has simplified and streamlined the process of doing business with government for private firms, and has expanded the opportunities for private organizations and local governments to become government partners. For example, state and local governments, as well as for-profit and non-profit firms, can now easily search a central federal government database for grants and apply for those grants electronically.

The internet has also allowed interest groups representing state and local offices and jurisdictions to more easily organize and present their agendas and policy priorities to federal agencies and lawmakers. Through organizations such as the National Governor's Association, National Association of Counties, National Conference of Mayors, and the National Conference of State Legislatures, state and local government administrators and elected officials can participate in webinars online, receive legislative updates by e-mail, and participate in online discussion forums relating to federal policies affecting their jurisdiction. Moreover, the internet has enabled more rapid diffusion of federal policy initiatives and ideas throughout the states, and created a vehicle for states and local governments to share stories and examples of best practices or problems in policy implementation.

Not only has the internet enhanced and expanded government's boundary spanning activities with private firms and sub-national governments, it has also created new avenues for government to span bureaucratic boundaries to connect with citizens. According to Smith (2010), 82 percent of US internet users had transacted with government in at least one way, such as looking up information on a public policy, obtaining information on services provided by a public agency, downloading government forms, applying for government benefits, paying a fine or bill, applying for or renewing a license, or applying for a government job, and 69 percent of internet users had engaged in more than one of these activities in the 12 months preceding the survey. Clearly, the internet and the quick, easy access to information it enables has been an influential force in the boundary spanning activities of the federal government and is likely to facilitate even more citizen contact, as well as inter-sectoral and intergovernmental cooperation in the future.

Boundary spanning in the United States: what does it involve?

The boundary-spanning activities of the federal government assume many forms, including the many 'tools of governance' described by Salamon (2002), as well as intergovernmental agreements, and networks, both formal and informal. A brief description of each is provided below, along with some examples of application in the US.

Policy tools of indirect government

Salamon (2002) identified a number of policy tools through which government provides public goods and services in partnership with the private for-profit and non-profit sectors. These policy tools include contracting, grants, vouchers, tax expenditures, loan guarantees, and government-sponsored enterprises. Contracts are the most common form of privatization (Savas 2005) and involve a legal agreement which specifies a *quid pro quo* relationship between a government agency and a private supplier. The government agency agrees to pay a specified sum or rate to the provider, at agreed upon timelines, whether it be for the manufacture of specialized military goods or for the ongoing provision of health care for senior citizens insured by Medicare. Contracts often also specify the expected quantity and quality of goods and services, along with other performance metrics. By contrast, grants are 'payments made from a donor government to a recipient organization (typically public or nonprofit); they are a gift that has the aim of either "stimulating" or "supporting" some sort of activity by the recipient, whether it be a new activity or an ongoing one' (Salamon 2002: 341). Common examples of federal grants are research awards made to universities and academic health centers through agencies such as the National Science Foundation, and demonstration grants made by the federal Office of Healthy Homes and Lead Hazard Control to local governments to help reduce exposure to lead-based paints.

Intergovernmental agreements

Intergovernmental agreements represent another important instrument that the federal government relies upon to provide goods and services, except in this case the cooperating partners are state and local governments as opposed to private providers. Interlocal agreements are used not only by the federal government to ensure local implementation of federal policies and services, but are also used to facilitate state–state cooperation, state–local cooperation, and, on the horizontal level, city–city or city–county cooperation. Indeed, a majority of cities and counties in the United States are party to at least one such agreement (ACIR 1985; Zimmerman 1973). Interlocal service agreements can assume a variety of forms. The Advisory Commission on Intergovernmental Relations (ACIR 1985) defined three types of interlocal agreements: (1) intergovernmental service contract, (2) joint service agreement, and (3) intergovernmental service transfer.

An intergovernmental service contract is a legally binding agreement between two or more general purpose government units in which one pays the other for the delivery of a particular service to the citizens residing in the jurisdiction of the paying government. Mutual aid agreements provide one of the most common types of intergovernmental service agreement. Mutual aid agreements are those in which local governments have an understanding to provide emergency 'back up' police and fire assistance to ensure public safety in the event of a disaster or other public safety threat.

Joint service agreements are those that exist between two or more units of government for the joint planning, financing, and delivery of a service to the citizens of all jurisdictions participating in the agreement. Thus, joint service agreements are different from intergovernmental contracts in that each participant in the agreement plays some role in the production of the service, whereas in contracting arrangements one unit produces the good or service and another (or others) purchase it. Finally, intergovernmental service transfers refer to scenarios in which total responsibility for the provision of a service is transferred from one governmental unit to another. Such transfers may be permanent or temporary. According to ACIR (1985), 18 of the 50 US states had legal provisions for intergovernmental transfers.

Formal networks

Extensive government contracting has led to a proliferation of formal networks, most often created for the purpose of public service delivery. Formal networks are multi-actor arrangements explicitly constituted by public managers to produce and deliver public services. McGuire defines such networks as 'public policy making and administrative structures involving multiple nodes (agencies or organizations) with multiple linkages ... structures through which public goods and services are planned, designed, produced, and delivered' (McGuire 2002: 600). Formal networks now serve as the preferred service delivery method for many forms of health and human services provision in the US, including public mental health (Provan and Milward 1995), child welfare (Romzek and Johnston 1999), and housing/homeless services (Hoch 2000). Local governments also rely on formal networks for managing economic development (Agranoff and McGuire 2004), public safety (Andrew 2009), environmental management (Lubell *et al.* 2002), and a host of other local services such as fire protection, parks and recreation, sewerage, and solid waste management.

Service delivery networks are typically made formal by contractual relationships between each network actor and a convening federal, state, or local government agency. Contracts serve to legally bind network actors together and specify the roles and responsibilities of participants. These networks of providers are generally convened and led by a public agency, acting as a 'network administrative organization (NAO)' (Provan and Milward 2001: 418), which specifies the nature of the formal relationships and interactions to occur between and among network actors, including the NAO itself. While many formal networks in public administration are bounded by contractual relationships, this is not universally the case. For example, mutual aid pacts and memoranda of understanding create formal networks in which actors share a set of collective goals, have clearly defined roles, and display sustained commitment to these roles over time, even in the absence of legal obligations to fulfill network responsibilities.

For the past 15 years, the study of formal networks has been a central focus of public management research. During this time, empirical network studies have produced important insights for the practice of managing complex, multi-organizational arrangements. Despite this knowledge, networks remain one of the most challenging forms of boundary spanning and pose the greatest difficulties for public managers, who must reconcile the diverse and often conflicting goals and agendas of various network actors and keep their activities aligned toward collective network goals.

Informal networks

In contrast to formal networks, which are typically designed, informal networks tend to emerge for the purposes of information sharing, capacity building, problem solving, and service delivery (Provan and Milward 2001). The diffusion of the drug court concept in the US provides an excellent illustration of how informal networks can emerge to fulfill all of these purposes. Hale (2011) has shown how a national information network comprised of non-profit organizations was instrumental in diffusing the drug court concept as a policy innovation among the states, demonstrating that networks can enhance the capacity of government to effectively confront the most difficult public problems. Hale (2011) has compellingly shown that states achieved a greater degree of success in policy implementation and policy outcomes when they were more extensively linked into the national information network. Perhaps even more importantly, this work demonstrates how participation in an information network led to improved policy outcomes: in her 50-state study, more extensive implementation of drug courts at the state and local levels resulted in lower crime rates, and higher arrest rates, even after controlling for rival explanations (Hale 2011).

Although it is only one of the many types of informal networks that help to bridge information gaps or build capacity for dealing with public problems, this example from the US drug policy arena helps to demonstrate the fact that government participation in informal networks can generate direct benefits for public organizations and the clientele they serve.

What makes boundary spanning work (or fail)?

The boundary spanning activities of public managers are unquestionably easier when the activity involves hierarchically structured interaction with a single party or a small number of parties, such as in contractual arrangements. Indeed, public administration scholarship over the last decade has yielded some important insights about how to hold accountable and measure the performance of government partners in hierarchically structured collaborative relationships (Moynihan *et al.* 2011). By contrast, the management of networks and other loosely coupled arrangements is more difficult: as the number of organizational participants increases, so does the probability of competing goals and interests. The need for network actors to be responsive to multiple principals often leads to role ambiguities and uncertainty on the part of actors about how to prioritize goals and activities. Even though network participants are united by a common policy objective, networks actors 'face the challenge of reconciling the needs of multiple stakeholders, diverse expectations, and varying organizational missions and roles, while delivering a complex public service' (Romzek 2008: 6).

Nevertheless, there are several factors that appear to facilitate the process of boundary spanning activities. Principal among these is trust among the actors engaged in an inter-organizational partnership. Indeed, the norm of trust has been recognized as being pivotal in cooperative service delivery relationships (Edelenbos and Klijn 2007; Isett and Provan 2005; Van Slyke 2007). Trust-building actions and behaviors not only foster productive working relationships, but also increase mutual accountability to collective goals. Trust reduces transaction costs for both network managers and network participants. Informal relationships among network actors often strengthen formal network ties and may give rise to other types of cooperation: for example, Thurmaier and Wood (2002) found that social networks among city managers and functional specialists were the underlying force creating and sustaining the use of interlocal contract networks among cities in the Kansas City metropolitan area. They credit the formation of these contractual service networks to the high levels of trust and norms of reciprocity, which in turn reinforced the contractual agreements.

The responsibility for fostering trust among multi-organizational actors in a collaborative partnership often rests with the public manager. Frequent and sustained contact (and particularly face-to-face contact) is a key factor in building trust and facilitating inter-organizational collaboration (Romzek *et al.* 2012). Axelrod's (1984) theory of cooperation evolution, a widely accepted starting point in understanding cooperation problems, posits that a pattern of cooperative interactions is most likely to take hold when there is an opportunity for repeated future interactions among the actors. According to Axelrod (1984: 21), 'the evolution of cooperation requires that individuals have a sufficiently large chance to meet again so that they have a stake in their future interaction'. In short, frequent and ongoing face-to-fact contact is essential to building trust and cooperation. With an indefinite number of interactions looming on the horizon, the opportunity exists for a pattern of reciprocity to develop, and thus cooperation can emerge.

There are other norms and behaviors that may help to enable cooperation when exhibited by participants in a multi-organizational collaborative arrangement. In a study of social service delivery networks in four Midwestern US states, Romzek *et al.* (2012) found that norms of trust, reciprocity, and respecting institutional turf led to a set of behaviors that facilitated cooperation, including information sharing, following through on commitments, frequent and sustained communication, extending favors, acknowledging mistakes, and taking action to fix mistakes. In turn, the display of these behaviors by network participants helped to reinforce the cooperative norms of trust, reciprocity, and respect of institutional territory. Romzek *et al.* (2012) also found that network actors developed an informal system for rewarding partners who abided by these norms and behaviors, as well as a system of informal sanctions to punish partners who failed to abide by them. Informal rewards included public recognition, enhanced reputation, extending favors such as loaning staff or cutting through red tape, and advance notice of opportunities for funding or future collaboration. Informal sanctions used by network participants to punish uncooperative behavior included diminished reputation, being cut out of the information network, and loss of opportunities for future funding or collaboration (Romzek *et al.* 2012).

Collaborative management skills can also play a significant role in enabling effective boundary-spanning relationships by government. Public managers in the US are increasingly engaged in activities of brokering, negotiating, managing, and overseeing multi-actor and multi-organizational arrangements. To do this effectively, public managers require skills in facilitation, negotiation, bargaining, consensus-building, and conflict resolution. Moreover, if they are to be successful in leading these partnerships to accomplish their mission they must bring not only this set of skills to the task of managing multi-organizational partnerships, but also a nuanced understanding of the institutional environment.

Of course, barriers sometimes emerge, posing challenges to inter-organizational collaboration. Chief among these barriers is politics. At times the preferences of political leaders conflict with those of managers or administrators who conceive plans for multi-organizational responses to public problems, and sometimes the political conflicts are among elected officials themselves, who cannot achieve consensus on the need for collaborative action. In the context of interlocal cooperation for public services in the US, Frederickson (1999, 2005) has argued that professional public administrators govern from a long-term perspective, and thus they often value opportunities for multi-jurisdictional, regional responses to public problems. On the other hand, locally elected officials govern from a short term perspective and thus prefer to avoid the risks associated with collaboration.

Management failures account for another reason why inter-organizational collaboration sometimes does not function as smoothly as anticipated. In delivering services through a network for the first time, many public network administrators underestimate the challenges of implementation, and fail to intervene quickly enough to remedy service delivery problems before they worsen (Romzek and Johnston 1999). This lack of preparation puts public officials in a poor position with regard to holding network participants accountable. The failure of network administrators to clearly specify expectations of network participants a priori can also lead to poor network performance. Although it is a challenge for government to establish performance expectations when contracting for complex services that are difficult to measure, establishing some level of performance outcomes can enhance the accountability of network actors and the performance of the network as a whole (Romzek and Johnston 2002).

Finally, along with intra-organizational changes, competition and turf battles can create barriers to effective inter-organizational collaboration. Romzek *et al.* (2012) found that competition among human service organizations for increasing shares of business within the local service market complicated their roles as collaborators. Moreover, they found that changes to legal rules and reimbursement structures also hampered cooperation by crowding out the time that staff were able to spend on building trust and relationships prior to these changes. Another barrier to inter-organizational collaboration is the loss of trust and social capital that occurs as a result of the exit of key agency staff. The stability of collaborative partnerships is predicated on the consistency of the participants. Trust evolves from repeated social exchanges over time, so staff turnover can create implementation delays and function as a major obstacle to the formation of the bonds that promote effective inter-organizational collaboration (Romzek *et al.* 2012).

Conclusion

The practice of spanning boundaries has become routine among public managers in the US as they seek to manage and lead an administrative state that is jurisdictionally, functionally, and sectorally fragmented, while public problems increasingly transcend these categorical boundaries. Public managers have embraced the daily use of policy tools connecting them to other sectors and governments in order to achieve their goals of serving the public interest. These policy tools take the shape of networks, service contracts, grants, intergovernmental agreements, the use of public incentives such as tax subsidies, and so on. These tools are employed by government managers to provide for a variety of public needs, spanning policy domains from housing and social services, to economic development and public safety.

This new era of management by spanning boundaries has created a new set of challenges and dilemmas for public managers as they seek to further the public interest. Foremost among these challenges is the quest to preserve accountability. Another challenge involves the need to balance diverse public goals and values in the context of a service delivery system that often places competing demands upon them. Managerial reform initiative, such as Reinventing Government and the New Public Management for example, demand improved government performance and better 'customer' service, while at the same time calling for a shift toward more market-based governance (Osborne and Gaebler 1992). As a result, government agencies now face the somewhat ironic mandate of providing citizens with high-performing programs and services, while at the same time outsourcing much of their work to private providers, networks, and other governments. Public managers equipped with skills of facilitation, negotiation, conflict resolution, and team building will ultimately fare better in their attempts to manage these competing demands and to foster and maintain effective boundary spanning collaboration on behalf of their organization.

References

Advisory Council on Intergovernmental Relations (ACIR) (1985) *Intergovernmental Service Arrangements for Delivering Local Public Services: Update 1983*, Washington, DC: Government Printing Office.

Agranoff, R. and McGuire, M. (2004) *Collaborative Public Management: New Strategies for Local Governments*, Washington, DC: Georgetown University Press.

Andrew, S.A. (2009) 'Regional integration through contracting networks: an empirical analysis of institutional collective action', *Urban Affairs Review*, 44(3): 378–402.

Axelrod, R. (1984) *The Evolution of Cooperation*, New York: Basic Books.

Edelenbos, J. and Klijn, E.H. (2007) 'Trust in complex decision-making networks: a theoretical and empirical exploration', *Administration & Society*, 39(1): 25–50.

Frederickson, H.G. (1999) 'The repositioning of American public administration', *PS: Political Science & Politics*, 32: 701–711.

Frederickson, H.G. (2005) 'Whatever happened to public administration? Governance, governance, everywhere', in E. Ferlie, L. Lynn Jr and C. Pollitt (eds) *The Oxford Handbook of Public Management*, Oxford: Oxford University Press.

Goldsmith, S. and Eggers, W.D. (2004) *Governing by Network: The New Shape of the Public Sector*, Washington, DC: Brookings Institution Press.

Hale, K. (2011) *How Information Matters: Networks and Public Policy Innovation*, Washington, DC: Georgetown University Press.

Hoch, C. (2000) 'Sheltering the homeless in the US: social improvement and the continuum of care', *Housing Studies*, 15(6): 865–876.

Isett, K.R. and Provan, K.G. (2005) 'The evolution of dyadic interorganizational relationships in a network of publicly funded nonprofit agencies', *Journal of Public Administration Research and Theory*, 15: 149–165.

Kettl, D. (1988) *Government by Proxy: (Mis?) Managing Federal Programs*. Washington, DC: CQ Press.

Kettl, D. (2000) *The Global Public Management Revolution: A Report on the Transformation of Governance*, Washington, DC: Brookings Institution.

Lipset, S.M. (1996) *American Exceptionalism: A Double-Edged Sword*, New York, NY: W.W. Norton & Company.

Lubell, M., Schneider, M., Scholz, J. and Mete, M. (2002) 'Watershed partnerships and the emergence of collective action institutions', *American Journal of Political Science*, 46(1): 48–63.

McGuire, M. (2002) 'Managing networks: propositions on what managers do and why they do it', *Public Administration Review*, 62(5): 599–609.

Milward, H.B. and Provan, K.G. (2000) 'Governing the hollow state', *Journal of Public Administration Research and Theory*, 10(2): 359–380.

Milward, H.B. and Provan, K.G. (1998) 'Principles for controlling agents: the political economy of network structure', *Journal of Public Administration Research and Theory*, 8(2): 203–222.

Moynihan, D.P., Fernandez, S., Kim, S., LeRoux, K.M., Piotrowski, S.J., Wright, B.E. and Yang, K. (2011) 'Performance regimes amidst governance complexity', *Journal of Public Administration Research and Theory*, 21(suppl 1): 141–155.

O'Leary, R. and Bingham, L.B. (2009). *The Collaborative Public Manager: New Ideas for the 21st Century*, Washington DC: Georgetown University Press.

Osborne, D. and Gaebler, T. (1992). *Reinventing Government: How the Entrepreneurial Spirit is Transforming the Public Sector*, New York: Plume.

O'Toole, L. (1997) 'Treating networks seriously: practical and research-based agendas in public administration', *Public Administration Review*, 57(1): 45–52.

Provan, K.G. and Milward, H.B. (1995) 'A preliminary theory of interorganizational network effectiveness: a comparative study of four community mental health systems', *Administrative Science Quarterly*, 40(1): 1–33.

Provan, K.G. and Milward, H.B. (2001) 'Do networks really work? A framework for evaluating public sector organizational networks'. *Public Administration Review*, 61(4): 414–423.

Romzek, B. (2008) 'The tangled web of accountability in contracting networks: the case of welfare reform', paper presented at the Kettering Foundation Symposium on Accountability, Dayton, Ohio, 2008.

Romzek, B.S. and Johnston, J.M. (1999) 'Reforming Medicaid through contracting: the nexus of implementation and organizational culture', *Journal of Public Administration Research and Theory*, 9(1): 107–139.

Romzek, B.S. and Johnston, J.M. (2002) 'Effective contract implementation and management: a preliminary model', *Journal of Public Administration Research and Theory*, 12(3): 423–453.

Romzek, B., LeRoux, K. and Blackmar, J. (2012). 'The dynamics of informal accountability in networks of service providers', *Public Administration Review*, 72(3): 442–453.

Salamon, L.M. (1987) 'Of market failure, voluntary failure, and third-party government: toward a theory of government-nonprofit relations in the modern welfare state', *Nonprofit and Voluntary Sector Quarterly*, 16(1): 29–49.

Salamon, L.M. (1995) *Partners in Public Service: Government-Nonprofit Relations in the Modern Welfare State*, Baltimore: Johns Hopkins University Press.

Salamon, L.M. (2002) *The Tools of Government: A Guide to the New Governance*, New York: Oxford University Press.

Savas, E.S. (2005) *Privatization in the City: Successes, Failures, Lessons*, Washington, DC: CQ Press.

Smith, A. (2010) *Government Online: The Internet Gives Citizens New Paths to Government Services and Information.* Washington, DC: Pew Research Center. Online. Available at: http://pewinternet.org/Reports/2010/Government-Online.aspx (accessed 18 October 2011).

Thurmaier, K. and Wood, C. (2002) 'Interlocal agreements as social networks: picket fence regionalism in metropolitan Kansas City', *Public Administration Review*, 62 (5): 585–598.

US Census Bureau (2007) Census of Governments 2007. Online. Available at: www.census.gov/govs/cog/ (accessed 19 October 2011).

Van Slyke, D.M. (2007) 'Agents or stewards: using theory to understand the government-nonprofit social service contracting relationship', *Journal of Public Administration Research and Theory* 17 (2): 157–187.

Zimmerman, J.F. (1973) 'Meeting service needs through intergovernmental agreements', in *Municipal Yearbook*, 79–88, Washington DC: International City Management Association.

5 The culture solution?

Culture and common purpose in Australia

Fiona Buick

Introduction

It has been argued that joined-up working is the solution to many contemporary problems faced by governments around the world. Recognition of the increasingly multidimensional and cross-cutting nature of such problems led to the trend towards joined-up working in many countries, but perhaps most fervently in Australia, Canada, New Zealand and the United Kingdom, during the late twentieth and early twenty-first centuries. This chapter discusses the joined-up experience and how organizational culture was argued to be a critical enabler for the success of these initiatives. In particular, it focuses on the Australian Public Service (APS) context, where culture was positioned as the panacea for joined-up working. This chapter addresses the question of 'how does working across boundaries work?', one of the key themes of this volume. It does this by exploring themes evident in two regional integrated service delivery sites, as well as the interplay between organizational culture and common purpose in this context.

Organizational culture as central to joined-up success

As discussed in Chapter 2, during the late twentieth century and early twenty-first century, the trend towards joined-up working was most evident in the Anglo-Saxon countries, such as Australia, Canada, New Zealand (NZ), and the United Kingdom (UK) (Christensen and Lægreid 2007; Pollitt 2003). In all contexts, organizational culture was argued to be the cornerstone of the joined-up movement. Governments placed significant emphasis on culture as a means for eliciting the desired attitudes and behaviors of public servants, with calls for a cultural transformation that would support, model and enable joined-up working (Briggs 2005; Cabinet Office 1999; Management Advisory Committee [MAC] 2004; Ministerial Advisory Group 2001; Performance and Innovation Unit [PIU] 2000; Privy Council Office 1996; Shergold 2003b, 2004a, 2004b).

Culture was the particular emphasis of public sector practitioners in Australia, with key senior figures in the Australian Public Service (APS) promoting cultural transformation as the panacea for joined-up success. The centrality of this view was reflected in arguments that it was the 'make or break' factor for joined-up success (MAC 2004: 45). A previous Secretary of the Department of the Prime Minister and Cabinet (PM&C), Dr. Peter Shergold, proclaimed that joined-up 'success lies not in their structure but in the culture that governs their behaviour' (Shergold 2004a: 13). Joined-up success was particularly centered on cultural change, with Shergold (2003a: 50) announcing: 'if we do not change the culture of the Public Service *we will not genuinely establish* a whole-of-government approach' (emphasis added). In essence, it was assumed that joined-up working would not happen without the desired 'horizontal' culture.

This chapter discusses how working across boundaries operated in two integrated service delivery sites – Indigenous Coordination Centres (ICCs) – in Australia. This case study is used to describe how cultural norms established in the ICCs enabled joined-up working to address the broader governmental goal of addressing Indigenous disadvantage, a wicked problem identified by the Australian Government.

Australian case study: Indigenous Coordination Centres

The ICCs were established in 2004 as part of the Australian Government's 'bold experiment' with joined-up working to address Indigenous disadvantage (Shergold 2004a). Indigenous Australians consistently score lower on measures such as life expectancy, infant mortality, educational attendance and attainment, literacy and numeracy skills, health, employment, and income than do non-Indigenous Australians. Moreover, they are at more risk of adverse living conditions and homelessness than non-Indigenous Australians (Australian Institute of Health and Welfare 2011; Steering Committee for the Review of Government Service Provision 2011). Because of its intractable nature, Indigenous disadvantage has been labelled a 'wicked problem' (Australian Public Service Commission 2007: 2) that is 'primed for a joined-up solution' (O'Flynn *et al.* 2011: 246). There was a clearly stated belief that working across boundaries was *the* solution to addressing this complex public policy problem.

As part of the new joined-up arrangements for Indigenous Affairs 30 ICCs were established in urban, regional and remote locations[1] to work with Indigenous communities in order to determine their local needs and priorities (KPMG 2007). The ICCs built on previous experiments, specifically the Council of Australian Governments (COAG) trials[2] which had aimed to enhance the participation and involvement of Indigenous communities (Office of Indigenous Policy Coordination 2004). The COAG trials formed the basis for the creation of the ICCs which became the 'permanent hubs' for policy coordination, service delivery and community engagement (O'Flynn *et al.* 2011: 247). The aim was to present a 'single face of government' or a 'one stop shop' for Indigenous communities, with the then Minister for Indigenous Affairs portraying the ICCs as akin to Australian embassies overseas: 'they represent the Australian Government, even though not every department is represented in the embassy' (Vanstone 2005: np). The ICCs comprised representatives from multiple government organizations operating in a co-location model, with the key organizations responsible for Indigenous programs, such as education, employment, community services, legal aid and health, to be represented on site (Shergold 2004a).

This chapter discusses two ICCs which were located in regional sites outside of the major capital cities in Australia (referred to as Redvale and Waytown ICCs).[3] Regional ICCs were established to deliver customized Indigenous-specific programs and coordinate mainstream programs for Indigenous communities; special provision was also made for coordinating an intensive place-based intervention strategy for those communities identified as being in crisis (ANAO 2007; Brough 2006). Because little empirical research had been undertaken in the ICCs, this study utilized a case study research design in order to understand and explore the phenomenon under examination *in situ* (Merriam 1988; Stake 2000; Yin 2003). Twenty-four semi-structured interviews and one focus group discussion were conducted between April 2009 and June 2010; non-participant observation of joined-up meetings was also used to explore the impact of organizational culture on joined-up working.

Common purpose and organizational culture as enabling for joined-up working in the regional Indigenous Coordination Centres

Organizational culture is socially constructed, acquired, learned and transmitted by members of a group (Cooke and Rousseau 1988; Geertz 1973; Lundberg 1988, 1990; Wilkins and Dyer 1988). Through working together over time, members develop expectations regarding what constitutes appropriate behavior. In order to fit in to this environment, individuals must learn and conform to these expectations (Cooke and Rousseau 1988; Deal and Kennedy 1983). According to Schein (2004), expectations regarding appropriateness stem from views regarding what it takes for a group to collectively succeed and survive in their environment, defining organizational culture as:

> A pattern of shared basic assumptions that was learned by a group as it solved its problems of external adaptation and internal integration, that has worked well enough to be considered valid and, therefore, to be taught to new members as the correct way to perceive, think, and feel in relation to those problems.
>
> (Schein 2004: 17)

According to Schein (2004), basic assumptions fall into two categories: those of external adaptation and those of internal integration. External adaptation incorporates assumptions about a group's reason for existence and how it will cope with the demands of its environment – essentially what to do and how to do it. Internal integration incorporates assumptions regarding the most appropriate way of building and maintaining a group through relationships amongst members. Over time, the assumptions associated with external adaptation and internal integration that repeatedly and reliably work are likely to operate uncon-sciously and are therefore less open to discussion and are no longer questioned (Schein 2004).

Basic assumptions are reflected in a system of values: the collective sense of what 'ought' to be and should be striven for or avoided, with assumptions shaping and determining what organizational members value (Denison 1990; Dyer 1985; Hatch 1993; Lundberg 1988, 1990; Schein 2004). Consequently, values direct the behavior of organizational members by providing guidelines regarding the thinking and behavior expected of them (Deal and Kennedy 1982; Lundberg 1988, 1990; Wiener 1988). These implicit expectations govern the day-to-day norms and behavior of individuals in the workplace, with Deal and Kennedy (1983: 501) describing these patterns as 'the way we do things around here'. This provides an explanation as to why organizational culture was argued to be so essential for joined-up success: such success would rely on officials assuming joined-up working was essential to their survival.

The reason both Redvale and Waytown ICCs existed was to serve Indigenous communities on behalf of the Australian Government. Their aspiration, articu-lated by ICC members, was to ensure that community members' basic needs were adequately met and that they had the same access to resources and oppor-tunities as the non-Indigenous population. In both sites, members had extensive experience of working with Indigenous communities. This had allowed them to develop a reservoir of local knowledge regarding regional issues and Indigenous communities. The knowledge and experience of ICC members was accumulated through their physical location in the regions where their communities resided, their identity as a local, and frequent contact with community members. More-over, due to their proximity to, and interaction with, Indigenous communities, they saw themselves as directly accountable to community members for the actions of the Australian Government.

Because the Redvale and Waytown ICCs were dominantly focused on deliv-ering services to communities on behalf of the Australian Government, ICC members perceived their role holistically and as one that went beyond that of an organizational representative. They saw the interconnectedness of issues faced by Indigenous communities and how their ability to deliver organizational pro-grams and satisfy organizational accountability demands relied upon the resolu-tion of issues in other areas. Therefore, the assumptions regarding what it took to succeed as both a community member and government employee were that success largely relied upon their ability to deliver and coordinate solutions for community members; joined-up working was considered to be essential to their success. Through the development of a horizontally-oriented core mission, the Redvale and Waytown ICCs established a highly internally derived common purpose. This purpose had emerged from cultural learning processes, thus becoming deeply entrenched within the day-to-day norms of the ICCs.

In the Redvale and Waytown ICCs, assumptions regarding their core mission were reflected in the values and norms of ICC members. Of particular interest to this chapter are three common themes across these two sites: community and outcomes orientation, cooperative mindsets, and communication and information sharing. This section discusses these common themes and leads to a discussion regarding how the prominence of these elements resulted in high cultural compatibility with joined-up working.

Community and outcomes orientation

A dominant theme across the Redvale and Waytown ICCs were the espoused values of adopting a community and outcomes orientation. The value of a community and outcomes orientation manifested itself in norms regarding community engagement, such as the importance of engaging community members in order to identify and understand community needs, gaps that needed addressing, and desired outcomes that guided action. This engagement was also necessary for the ICC members to understand community issues and to identify relevant stakeholders required to engage and identify appropriate solutions.

In the Redvale and Waytown ICCs, the adoption of a community and outcomes orientation was fundamental to the development of a holistic perspective. This orientation enabled ICC members to think outside silo boundaries and towards the desired outcomes. Rather than thinking within organizational boundaries, ICC members framed their focus towards what they were able to do and where they could make an impact. ICC members facilitated dialogue between various stakeholders and community members to ascertain community needs, connections across boundaries, the contribution of each stakeholder, and where existing services complemented one another.

The adoption of a community and outcomes orientation are factors that have been argued to be a component of the desired supportive culture for joined-up working (MAC 2004; Ministerial Advisory Group 2001; Privy Council Office 1996). In the Redvale and Waytown ICCs the focus on, and identification of, community needs and desired outcomes instilled a common purpose for those joining-up. This common purpose provided the impetus for cooperative and coordinated action across organizations and jurisdictions because the imperative to join up was clear. Reflective of Bardach's (1998) craftsmanship approach, the community and outcomes orientation provided a clear purpose and reasons to join up and established the platform for joint problem-solving and integration. This craftsmanship leadership style was important for shaping programs in order to fit with community needs, think broadly to marshal resources and reconfigure them to achieve outcomes (O'Flynn et al. 2011). This finding supports claims by Peters (1998) that joining-up at the bottom, where services to citizens is the dominant concern, leads to more cooperative behaviors.

Cooperative mindset: networks and relationships

Another cultural characteristic that was common across the Redvale and Waytown ICCs was the cooperative mindset and the value of developing and utilizing networks and relationships both inside and outside the ICCs. In these

ICCs, networks and relationships were essential for the ability of the ICCs to coordinate Indigenous-specific and mainstream services. In both sites, a cooperative mindset was an essential part of routine work, primarily because of the belief in the necessity for conducting business in this way in order to coordinate services for Indigenous people.

The development of long-term professional relationships amongst ICC members was essential to joining-up at the two ICCs. These relationships were formed prior to working in the ICCs examined in this study, with members having worked together in the Indigenous Affairs policy domain for long periods of time. This was particularly apparent in the Redvale ICC, where senior ICC members and their staff had worked together for over a decade.

Due to their history of working together, members in the regional ICCs had developed trusting relationships that evolved and strengthened over time. Trust has been defined as the confidence that people are 'disposed to act benignly' (Alford 2004: 3) towards one another and the belief that their incentives are oriented towards cooperation with and support of others (Hardin 1992). These relationships formed the foundation for ICC members to work as a team in a joined-up way, with collegiate and cooperative ways of operating evident in both the Redvale and Waytown sites. They were crucial for the ability of members to cope with the challenges they faced on a regular basis, including those in the political and administrative domains, demands from the Indigenous communities themselves, and tensions that emerged from operating in an environment that demanded joined-up working yet also required them to deliver on vertical targets.

In the Redvale and Waytown sites, members also utilized relationships and networks outside of the ICCs to find solutions, coordinate services and achieve outcomes for communities. In these ICCs, particular attention was paid to informal networks as a means of accessing the knowledge of others, maintaining awareness of current events, obtaining information to fully understand the issues members were dealing with and brokering solutions to address community issues. Through utilizing relationships and networks, ICC members could resolve issues quickly and draw on diverse perspectives to ensure their approaches were appropriate and value-adding.

This study found that a cooperative mindset, with values and norms around networks and relationships, was central to the survival and success of the Redvale and Waytown ICCs in three ways: first, long-term relationships provided a sense of stability and cohesive teamwork environments within the ICCs and the ability to cope with day-to-day challenges; second, it enabled ICC members to maintain awareness of current issues, projects and information, thereby enabling members to identify and capitalize on opportunities; and third, it provided ICC members with a mechanism to facilitate the access of Indigenous communities to the coordinated services they required.

These characteristics have been argued to be important for joined-up working, and all have featured prominently in government manifestos for joined-up working around the world (MAC 2004; Privy Council Office 1996; Ministerial

Advisory Group 2001). They have also been argued to be essential for eliciting the ongoing commitment of staff to the broader public policy agenda (O'Flynn *et al.* 2011). Moreover, trust has also been portrayed as the glue that holds a joined-up initiative together (Hopkins *et al.* 2001; Jackson and Stainsby 2000). In addition to adopting a united front and mutual support, a cooperative mindset underpinned by trust established the platform for frequent communication and information sharing in the regional ICCs.

Communication and information sharing

In the Redvale and Waytown ICCs, long-term relationships based on trust were critical for the willingness to openly communicate and share information. Open communication and information-sharing behaviors were role-modeled from the ICC managers down. Because of trust in their staff and faith in their ability to differentiate between confidential and non-confidential matters, both ICC managers emphasized their willingness to communicate openly and share information with their staff. By role-modeling information-sharing behaviors – one of Schein's (2004) primary mechanisms for transmitting and reinforcing culture – the ICC managers symbolized the importance of sharing information. In doing so, they encouraged their staff to share information and communicate frequently with one another (O'Flynn *et al.* 2011).

The importance of information sharing at the ICCs was reflected in the common practice of regular and daily communication, both formal and informal, with open discussions regarding all facets of work. ICC members espoused values concerning frequent and open two-way communication and beliefs that information sharing was critical for the internal working of the ICCs. Over time, ICC members learned that rich communication allowed them to deal with daily demands and challenges and work together as a team. Issues could be resolved in a prompt and effective manner and problems prevented through having open discussions, by working through issues, and by mitigating risks. This belief was reinforced over time as members encountered situations that could have had a different and negative outcome had they not worked together, communicated, and shared information.

Through encountering situations where a negative outcome was mitigated or avoided, the propensity to share information and communicate openly was reinforced. The recurrent experience of these situations also served as a trust circle, whereby trust in one another was also reinforced. Over time, this resulted in the establishment of deeply embedded values and norms around upholding a high level of timely communication, with members getting together on a regular basis to brainstorm ideas, troubleshoot issues, share best practices, and collectively engage in reflective learning. New approaches to working were shared, as were templates that served to minimize duplication and enhance efficiency through streamlining processes, thus enabling members to focus on more strategic matters. Members engaged in an active process of knowledge generation and transfer, building their collective knowledge base and enhancing each individual's ability to broker solutions for communities and enhancing member empowerment and ownership of issues.

Cultural compatibility and joined-up working

This study found that organizational culture was an enabler for joined-up working in the Redvale and Waytown ICCs. Whilst operating in different contexts, there were similarities across the two ICCs, including a community and outcomes orientation, cooperative mindset, networks and relationships, and communication and information sharing. Collectively, these values and norms were essential to the ability of ICC members to balance vertical and horizontal demands, engage in cooperative practices, and coordinate services for Indigenous communities.

The Redvale and Waytown ICCs were characterized by all of the desired cultural characteristics espoused by practitioners as being critical for joined-up working (see, for example, Cabinet Office 1999; Hopkins *et al.* 2001; MAC 2004; Ministerial Advisory Group 2001; PIU 2000; Privy Council Office 1996; Shergold 2003a). The mission – or high common purpose – of both the Redvale and Waytown ICCs derived from within the ICCs in response to environmental demands for joined-up working and accountability to community members. To achieve their core mission, ICC members adopted a community and outcomes orientation which enabled them to perceive community issues in a holistic manner, rather than being constrained by adopting a narrow orientation focused on their home organizations. Consequently, this orientation overcame a broader trend toward silo mentalities and enabled them to see where the interconnections with other organizations, jurisdictions and sectors existed, and where these could be utilized. By initiating and leading joined-up working, members also demonstrated their propensity to think and act outside organizational boundaries, their flexibility and adaptability of approach, and their persistence in striving towards outcomes. Finally, members of the Redvale and Waytown ICCs reflected collaborative modes of operating through valuing relationships, networks, and cooperative and collegiate modes of operating, as evidenced through their norms around relationship development. A solid foundation of trust and the ability to openly communicate and share information – all of which are requirements for joined-up working – facilitated these relationships. These factors all demonstrated the shared culture and values underpinning the day-to-day operation of the ICCs.

These findings can be partially explained by relating the cultural norms of the ICCs with the literature on cultural compatibility. Cultural compatibility, or alignment between new approaches and existing values and assumptions, has been argued to be a contributing factor to the successful implementation of new organizational approaches and public sector reform principles (Brunsson and Olsen 1993; Christensen, Lægreid *et al.* 2007; Frost and Gillespie 1998; March and Olsen 1989; Schein 1985; Schneider 1995; Schwartz and Davis 1981). The Redvale and Waytown ICCs were characterized by the cultural characteristics deemed by practitioners to be essential for joined-up working, and thus were assessed to have high cultural compatibility with joined-up working.

In this study both ICCs exhibited high cultural compatibility with joined-up working – a factor that was an important precondition for the success of joined-up working. However, our study found that a necessary precondition for high cultural compatibility was the generation of a high common purpose, and that this common purpose could be internally developed through cultural learning processes. These two factors, therefore, worked together in a complementary manner to create an environment conducive to joined-up working.

Common purpose and high cultural compatibility: creating an enabling environment for joined-up working

The presence of high cultural compatibility within the Redvale and Waytown ICCs meant that it could be assumed that this compatibility alone resulted in joined-up working. However, we found that it was the interaction between, and mutual reinforcement of, common purpose and organizational culture that resulted in joined-up success.

Through a continuous feedback loop, a virtuous circle emerged that involved the self-perpetuation of common purpose and organizational culture. With this virtuous circle, organizational culture may be perceived as the essential requirement, and the critical enabling variable, for joined-up working. However, rather than being the sole enabling variable, organizational culture is the manifestation of this interplay and the obvious explanation for joined-up working. Within this virtuous circle, each variable reinforced the other to the extent that they became so intertwined that they were virtually indistinguishable from one another.

These dynamics in the Redvale and Waytown ICCs reflect Schein's (2004) description of cultural perpetuation, with assumptions regarding their core mission influencing assumptions regarding the most appropriate means of achieving this mission. This means that norms concerning the adoption of a community and outcomes orientation, cooperative mindsets, networking, relationships, and frequent communication and information sharing were all perceived as critical for the achievement of this common purpose. These norms were encapsulated in rituals: the repetitive and habitual behaviors and routines that convey the values, goals and activities of organizations and depict expectations of employee behavior, as repeated on a daily basis through work practices and modes of operating (Deal and Kennedy 1982; Ott 1989; Pettigrew 1979; Trice and Beyer 1984, 1993). In the Redvale and Waytown ICCs, as these norms continued to contribute to successful outcomes, they were continually reinforced as the correct way of interpreting and responding to their environment. This reflects Schein's argument that assumptions that work repeatedly and reliably are likely to be taught to new members as the correct way to perceive, think, and feel in relation to commonly experienced problems (Schein 1990, 2004).

Conclusion

This chapter discussed how organizational culture *can* be a central element for joined-up working; however, it also showed that it is the coupling of cultural compatibility with common purpose that is critical for success. In many nations it has been assumed that culture would be important for eliciting the desired attitudes and behaviors considered as essential for joined-up success. Underpinning this rhetoric was the proposition that cultural compatibility between organizations was critical for the success of joined-up initiatives. This chapter addressed the question of 'how does working across boundaries work?' through utilizing two regional ICCs . In this case study, evidence of high cultural compatibility was found to be a key enabler of joined-up working. However, cultural compatibility in itself was not the sole explanatory variable: a high common purpose was also needed to create an environment conducive to joined-up working. The interplay between high cultural compatibility and a high common purpose meant that joined-up working was the modus operandi for the regional ICCs. In this chapter, this interplay was portrayed as a 'virtuous circle' whereby elements of the circle continually reinforced one another, thus leading to the self-perpetuation of high cultural compatibility and common purpose. Therefore, the key argument of this chapter is that, despite the emphasis placed upon it by practitioners, organizational culture is not the sole critical factor for joined-up success; it is the interplay between organizational culture and common purpose that provides the most valuable insight into joined-up success.

The findings of this study suggest that when joined-up working occurs in a more intensive, ongoing and longer-term manner, it creates the opportunity for a culture that is conducive to joined-up working to emerge. This opportunity is likely to emerge if the group frequently encounters similar problems, as it is required to respond to similar environmental demands and to establish ways of integrating to ensure that these demands are met (Schein 2004). As a consequence of these conditions, it can be argued that if the environment demands joined-up working – for example, if the environment consists of citizens, communities or joint stakeholders who demand a holistic and joined-up approach – then this creates the necessary precondition for the development of an internally derived common purpose. This study has found that, if these demands are compelling, they will shape collective assumptions regarding the core mission of the group, provide a common purpose, and lead to values and norms around joined-up working. Over time, if these values and norms lead to successful outcomes and enable the group to satisfy environmental demands, then it is likely that this common purpose will ultimately result in the evolution of a joined-up culture.

Notes

1 As at January 2012, there were 29 ICCs across Australia (Department of Families Housing Community Services and Indigenous Affairs [FaHCSIA] 2011).

2 In April 2002, COAG agreed to trial new ways of working with Indigenous communities. The COAG trials occurred across eight sites in each state and territory, with
   the aim of the 'shared responsibility' of government and Indigenous communities in
   addressing the intractable issue of Indigenous disadvantage. The trials were focused on
   community needs and greater inter-departmental and inter-governmental coordination
   (Morgan Disney and Associates Pty Ltd 2006).
3 Pseudonyms used for de-identification purposes.

References

Alford, J. (2004) 'Building trust in partnerships between community organisation and
   government', paper presented at Changing the Way Government Works, Institute of
   Public Administration Australia (IPAA) Seminar, Melbourne, October 2004.
Australian Institute of Health and Welfare (2011) *The Health and Welfare of Austral-
   ia's Aboriginal and Torres Strait Islander People: an overview 2011*. Cat. no. IHW
   42. Canberra: AIHW.
Australian National Audit Office (ANAO) (2007) *Whole of Government Indigenous
   Service Delivery Arrangements*, Audit Report 2007–2008 no. 10, Commonwealth of
   Australia, Canberra, Australia. Online. Available at: www.anao.gov.au/Publications/
   Audit-Reports/2007–2008/Whole-of-Government-Indigenous-Service-Delivery-
   Arrangements (accessed 16 October 2012).
Australian Public Service Commission (2007) *Tackling Wicked Problems: A Public
   Policy Perspective*, Commonwealth of Australia, Canberra, Australia. Online.
   Available at: www.apsc.gov.au/publications-and-media/archive/publications-archive/
   tackling-wicked-problems (accessed 16 October 2012).
Bardach, E. (1998) *Getting Agencies to Work Together: The Practice and Theory of
   Managerial Craftsmanship*, Washington, DC: Brookings Institution Press.
Briggs, L. (2005) 'Synergies: new approaches to working together in government',
   paper presented at Annual Government Business Conference: The Future of the Aus-
   tralian Public Service, Gold Coast, May 2005.
Brough, M. (2006) 'Blueprint for action in Indigenous affairs', speech delivered at the
   National Institute of Governance – Indigenous Affairs Governance Series, Univer-
   sity of Canberra, 5 December 2006.
Brunsson, N. and Olsen, J.P. (1993) *The Reforming Organization*, London: Routledge.
Cabinet Office (1999) *Modernising Government*, Cm 4310, London: Stationery Office.
Christensen, T. and Lægreid, P. (2007) 'The whole-of-government approach to public
   sector reform', *Public Administration Review*, 67(6): 1059–1066.
Christensen, T., Lægreid, P., Roness, P.G. and Røvik, K.A. (2007) *Organization
   Theory and the Public Sector: Instrument, Culture and Myth*, Abingdon, Oxon:
   Routledge.
Cooke, R.A. and Rousseau, D.M. (1988) 'Behavioral norms and expectations: a quant-
   itative approach to the assessment of organizational culture', *Group & Organization
   Studies*, 13(3): 245–273.
Deal, T.E. and Kennedy, A.A. (1982) *Corporate Cultures: The Rites and Rituals of
   Corporate Life*, Reading: Addison-Wesley.
Deal, T.E. and Kennedy, A.A. (1983) 'Culture: a new look through old lenses', *The
   Journal of Applied Behavioral Science*, 19(4): 498–505.
Denison, D.R. (1990) *Corporate Culture and Organizational Effectiveness*, New York:
   John Wiley & Sons.

Department of Families Housing Community Services and Indigenous Affairs (2011) *Indigenous Australians: Overview*. Online. Available at: www.fahcsia.gov.au/sa/indigenous/overview/Pages/default.aspx (accessed 5 December 2011).

Dyer, W.G. (1985) 'The cycle of cultural evolution in organizations', in R.H. Kilmann, M.J. Saxton and R. Serpa (eds) *Gaining Control of the Corporate Culture*, San Francisco: Jossey-Bass.

Frost, S.H. and Gillespie, T.W. (1998) 'Organizations, culture, and teams: links toward genuine change', *New Directions for Institutional Research*, 100: 5–15.

Geertz, C. (1973) *The Interpretation of Cultures*, New York: Basic Books.

Hardin, R. (1992). 'The street-level epistemology of trust', *Analyse & Kritik*, 14(2): 152–176.

Hatch, M.J. (1993) 'The dynamics of organizational culture', *Academy of Management Review*, 18(4): 657–693.

Hopkins, M., Couture, C. and Moore, E. (2001) *Moving from the Heroic to the Everyday: Lessons Learned from Leading Horizontal Projects (CCMD Roundtable on the Management of Horizontal Initiatives)*, Ottawa: Canadian Centre for Management Development.

Jackson, P.M. and Stainsby, L. (2000) 'The public manager in 2010: managing public sector networked organizations', *Public Money & Management*, 20(1): 11–16.

KPMG (2007) *Department of Families, Community Services and Indigenous Affairs Evaluation of Indigenous Coordination Centres Final Report*, Australia: KPMG. Online. Available at: www.fahcsia.gov.au/our-responsibilities/indigenous-australians/publications-articles/evaluation-research/evaluation-of-indigenous-coordination-centres (accessed 20 November 2008).

Lundberg, C.C. (1988) 'Working with culture', *Journal of Organizational Change Management*, 1(2): 38–47.

Lundberg, C.C. (1990) 'Surfacing organisational culture', *Journal of Managerial Psychology*, 5(4): 19–26.

Management Advisory Committee (MAC) (2004), *Connecting Government: Whole of Government Responses to Australia's Priority Challenges*. Canberra, ACT: MAC. Online. Available at: www.apsc.gov.au/publications-and-media/archive/publications-archive/connecting-government (accessed 15 November 2012).

March, J.G. and Olsen, J.P. (1989) *Rediscovering Institutions: The Organizational Basis of Politics*, New York: Free Press.

Merriam, S.B. (1988) *Case Study Research in Education: A Qualitative Approach*, San Francisco: Jossey-Bass Publishers.

Ministerial Advisory Group (2001) *Report of the Advisory Group on the Review of the Centre*, Wellington, New Zealand: State Services Commission. Online. Available at: www.ssc.govt.nz/roc (accessed 25 September 2011).

Morgan Disney and Associates Pty Ltd (2006) *A Red Tape Evaluation in Selected Indigenous Communities: Final Report for the Office of Indigenous Policy Coordination*, Canberra, ACT: Morgan Disney and Associates. Online. Available at: www.fahcsia.gov.au/sites/default/files/documents/05_2012/indigenous_redtapereport.pdf (accessed 19 January 2009).

Office of Indigenous Policy Coordination (2004) *Indigenous Coordination Centre Model for Rural and Remote Australia*, Canberra, ACT: Commonwealth of Australia.

O'Flynn, J., Buick, F., Blackman, B. and Halligan, J. (2011) 'You win some, you lose some: experiments with joined-up government', *International Journal of Public Administration*, 34(4): 244–254.

Ott, J.S. (1989) *The Organizational Culture Perspective*, Pacific Grove, CA: Brooks/Cole Publishing Company.

Performance and Innovation Unit (PIU) (2000) *Wiring It Up: Whitehall's Management of Cross-Cutting Policies and Services*, London: Cabinet Office. Online. Available at: http://webarchive.nationalarchives.gov.uk/+/www.cabinetoffice.gov.uk/media/cabinet-office/strategy/assets/coiwire.pdf (accessed 15 November 2008).

Peters, B.G. (1998) 'Managing horizontal government: the politics of co-ordination', *Public Administration*, 76(2): 295–311.

Pettigrew, A.M. (1979) 'On studying organizational cultures', *Administrative Science Quarterly*, 24(4): 570–581.

Pollitt, C. (2003) 'Joined up government: a survey', *Political Studies Review*, 1(1): 34–49.

Privy Council Office (1996) *Deputy Minister Task Forces: From Studies to Action*, Canada: Government of Canada.

Schein, E.H. (1985) *Organizational Culture and Leadership: A Dynamic View*, San Francisco, CA: Jossey-Bass.

Schein, E.H. (1990) 'Organizational culture', *American Psychologist*, 45(2): 109–119.

Schein, E.H. (2004) *Organizational Culture and Leadership*, 3rd edn, San Francisco CA: Jossey-Bass.

Schneider, W.E. (1995) 'Productivity improvement through cultural focus', *Consulting Psychology Journal: Practice and Research*. 47(1): 3–27.

Schwartz, H. and Davis, S.M. (1981) 'Matching corporate culture and business strategy', *Organizational Dynamics*. 10(1): 30–48.

Shergold, P. (2003a) 'On leadership, management and the Australian Public Service', *Canberra Bulletin of Public Administration*, 110: 48–51.

Shergold, P. (2003b) 'Been down so long it feels like up to me: working in Commonwealth–State relations', paper presented at the Institute of Public Administration Australia: Spotlight on Spring Street Series, September 2003.

Shergold, P. (2004a) 'Connecting government: whole-of-government responses to Australia's priority challenges', *Canberra Bulletin of Public Administration*, 112: 11–14.

Shergold, P. (2004b) 'Connecting government', paper presented at Institute of Public Administration Australia Queensland Policy Leadership Series, Brisbane, September 2004.

Stake, R.E. (2000) 'Case studies', in N.K. Denzin and Y.S. Lincoln (eds) *Handbook of Qualitative research (2nd edn)*, Thousand Oaks, CA: SAGE Publications.

Steering Committee for the Review of Government Service Provision (2011). *Overcoming Indigenous Disadvantage: Key Indicators 2011 Report*. Melbourne, Australia: Commonwealth of Australia. Available at: www.pc.gov.au/gsp/indigenous (accessed 30 November 2012).

Trice, H.M. and Beyer, J.M. (1984) 'Studying organizational cultures through rites and ceremonials', *Academy of Management Review*, 9(4): 653–669.

Trice, H.M. and Beyer, J.M. (1993) *The Cultures of Work Organizations*, Englewood Cliffs, NJ: Prentice Hall.

Vanstone, A. (2005) 'Minister discusses changes to the handling of indigenous affairs and the establishment of the National Indigenous Council', Paper presented to the National Press Club, Canberra, February 2005. Online. Available at: http://parlinfo.aph.gov.au/parlInfo/search/display/display.w3p;query=Id%3A%22media%2Ftvprog%2FSVA F6%22 (accessed 10 October 2012).

Wiener, Y. (1988) 'Forms of value systems: a focus on organizational effectiveness and cultural change and maintenance', *Academy of Management Review*, 13(4): 534–545.

Wilkins, A.L. and Dyer, W.G. (1988) 'Toward culturally sensitive theories of culture change', *Academy of Management Review*, 13(4): 522–533.

Yin, R.K. 2003, *Case Study Research: Design and Methods*, (3rd edn), Beverly Hills: SAGE Publications.

6   The structure solution?

Public sector mergers in the United Kingdom

Carole Talbot and Colin Talbot

This chapter turns its attention to mergers as the most intensive form of joint work within public sector settings. It addresses the four themes of this book by viewing mergers as a form of cross-boundary working and focusing on why, in the selected cases, mergers were chosen over less demanding forms of cross-boundary working. We draw on Mintzberg's (1979) conceptualization of task structures in order to explore organizational forms and identify the enablers and barriers to effective cross-boundary working created by task structures.

Given the problematic nature of many collaborative ventures between public organizations, mergers, which offer to eradicate troublesome boundaries, can reasonably be considered as a potential solution. However, such mergers can also be problematic. Three cases are reviewed in full within this chapter, with additional reference to the case of the Children's Trusts reviewed in Chapter 12 in this volume. In doing so we consider the role that task structures can play in facilitating or impeding the objectives of public sector mergers.

Whilst much research has focused on partnerships, joined-up government, whole-of-government and collaboration more generally, comparatively little attention has been paid to the impact of more intensive forms of joint work such as integration and mergers. These structural adaptations may, potentially, offer solutions to cross-boundary dilemmas, yet there has been little focus on them in public sector writing.

Mergers are not rare occurrences. Indeed, in the UK there is a long history of bringing public sector organizations together to address boundary issues. In the UK context, higher education institutions, health service organizations and inspection and regulatory bodies have all been prime targets for merger activity. In some cases these mergers have been mandated by central government, whilst in other cases public sector organizations have taken the strategic decision to merge, albeit in an environment where mergers were seen as a means to increase efficiency and/or effectiveness. In this chapter, we compare three merger cases: the successful merger which created Jobcentre Plus, and two less successful attempts which created Her Majesty's Revenue and Customs (HMRC) and the National Offender Management Service (NOMS).

Mergers can be vertical, where they involve dissimilar businesses – a TV company and newspaper business, for example – or horizontal, where they combine similar businesses – the main form in the UK public sector sense historically (Skodvin 1999; Fulop *et al.* 2002, 2005). King and colleagues (2004) argue that vertical mergers do not improve the performance of the acquiring organizations as they present higher levels of risk than horizontal mergers. Furthermore, other research demonstrates that the effects of mergers are similar, regardless of whether they take place between public or private organizations (Schraeder and Self 2003). This raises some interesting questions regarding the increasing use of vertical mergers in the public sector, in terms of whether the hoped-for efficiencies will be realized.

This chapter is organized as follows. First, we set out the policy context in which these mergers have taken place. This is followed by a discussion of Mintzberg's (1979) task structure concept and insights from the cultural perspective on mergers: together, these suggest that culture clashes between merger organizations can impact upon effectiveness. The analysis of the cases follows, highlighting how the variation in task structures creates situations where one organization in a merger setting tends to dominate the others. Furthermore, we can consider how an analysis of task structures might help to avoid problematic mergers.

Policy context

Recent mergers in the UK public sector have occurred against a backdrop of continual restructuring activities among public sector organizations, ranging from government departments through to frontline services (Talbot and Johnson 2007). The rationale given for mergers is generally a combination of service improvement and cost efficiency (Frumkin 2003). Mergers are often seen in terms of 'collaborations of missions', and sometimes merely as consolidations. Rarely are they viewed in the more aggressive acquisition mode redolent of the private sector. Public sector researchers have tended to relate mergers to other forms of joint work, such as cooperation and coordination (Algie 1973; Harman and Harman 2003), rather than the broader private sector merger literature. This failure to engage with the experience of the private sector has meant that many important insights have been neither explored nor built into public sector merger activity.

It may also be the case that UK Governments have been slow to generate and disseminate learning about mergers and reorganizations within government. More recently, the UK Cabinet Office (2010) has acknowledged that restructuring may be disruptive and lead to a decline in performance and increased costs, whilst the National Audit Office (2010) argues that it can create low morale. The Cabinet Office's good practice handbook was published in 2010 to support such change processes (too late, of course, for the mergers that we explore in this chapter). Prior to this date a Cabinet Office team existed to support restructuring, and which published material on restructuring, although this was considered rather too theoretical (NAO 2010). However, this seemingly weak knowledge at the centre did not deter public sector mergers, where the depth of 'cross-boundary' change can be greatest, so they went ahead with little a priori analysis or detailed implementation plans.

There has also been a lack of interest in evaluating post-merger outcomes, which may stem from a combination of continual restructuring, existing common ownership, and assumed shared goals and cultures. This situation has been identified historically where the UK Government tended to believe that the separate health and social care organizations, which clearly have overlapping roles, particularly with regard to the medical and social care of the elderly, would simply coordinate their activities vis-à-vis strategic direction and resourcing because they were both publicly funded bodies ostensibly working towards the same end (Bridgen 2004).

Whilst we have ample evidence of merger activity, Frumkin (2003) states that not all public sector mergers are likely to produce positive results. He argues that more attention should be given to the motives for mergers, that there needs to be analysis of individual organizations prior to merger, and that more attention needs to be paid to the approach taken to implementation. We argue that exploring mergers through Mintzberg's (1979) task structure concept, which we explain in the next section, will assist in this analysis.

Task structure analysis

Our initial analysis of the cases led us to consider Mintzberg's (1979) task structures as a concept for explaining why mergers in the public sector faced difficulties. We bring this together with concepts from the cultural perspective in merger studies in order to explore how particular configurations of organizational structures may lead to certain deleterious outcomes for some merged organizations. Broader issues such as the motives for forcing mergers and differential sizes of organizations are also identified as important explanatory factors. In his work, Mintzberg does not refer to culture, but to ideology to describe shared beliefs within an organization. Despite this, his analysis discusses similar issues to those explored in the work of Harrison (1972), whose typology of organizational cultures informed Cartwright and Cooper's (1993) original consideration of culture as the main cause of merger failure.

In his early work, Mintzberg (1979) argued that organizations comprise five different parts: strategic apex; operating core; technostructure; middle line and administrative. Each of these parts, he explained, displayed a natural bias towards a particular structural form of organization. Two structural forms of particular relevance are drawn on here, in order to analyse our cases of public sector mergers. The first is the machine bureaucracy, which emerges from the pull towards standardization from the technostructure. The characteristics of a machine bureaucracy include high specialization within large units, routine and formalized operating tasks, rule-based decisions, centralized decision making and generally low employee discretion.

The second is the professional bureaucracy, which emerges from the dominance of professionals and which, in contrast to a machine bureaucracy, has standardization of skills, training, and indoctrination which occurs outside of the organization or is supervised externally and which leads to professional autonomy and control over their own work. Professional autonomy may remain largely true, but the autonomy of professions with less legitimacy (social workers, for example) has been challenged. Administrative and management functions still exist within professional bureaucracies, but these do not dominate the culture of the organization. These two organizational forms share a bureaucratic basis but the source of their standardization and authority differs, with the first being based within the organization and the second being based in professional expertise and bodies outside the organization which often exert control through a registration process.

Mintzberg (1983) outlines how power is linked to the structural configurations within which the cultures are embedded. Table 6.1 provides a summary of the ways that the strategic apex, middle line and operating core may exert power and influence within machine and professional bureaucracies.

Task structures, because they are formed through occupation-based cultures, varying professional values and working practices, are important in mergers due to their ability to undermine stated policy objectives. This is particularly evident in cases where, post-merger, organizations are required to align working practices very closely, creating greater potential for tensions to emerge. For example, the merger of children's social workers with education administrators might be reasonable in policy terms in order to address coordination problems in the protection of children; however, one party is a specialist professional service for a

Table 6.1 Framework for assessing shifts of power within mergers

Part of the organization	Resources upon which power is based
Strategic Apex (Chief Executive)	Centralizing work processes Use of formal authority Display of expertise Use of rewards and sanctions Increasing size and staffing of the organization
The Middle Line (Middle Management)	Similar to the Chief Executive but dependent upon the manager's status in the hierarchy Increased autonomy and power may be sought by assuming a leadership position within a division
The Operating Core	The operating core's power emerges from size, strength of unions or professionalization Professionals have a weaker identification with the organization, which limits integration and engagement but potentially draw power from: • Professionalization – standardization of skills, registration and licensing • Adherence to professional ethics

Source: based on Mintzberg (1979; 1983).

minority of children, whilst the other deals, at a more or less universal level, with administering state education for 'most' children. The size and scope of the Education Service lays the basis for the domination of social work.

Over time, particular task structures emerge as practical ways in which to organize in order to meet certain objectives. Services requiring standardization, such as the administration of tax and benefits, naturally resort to the classic machine bureaucracy, whilst services requiring professional input or those that do not conform to standardization, such as Customs and Excise, require a professional bureaucracy. In the public sector in particular, task structures are not necessarily formed within each organization but, rather, they are commonly derived from a long history of bureaucratic structures built up and developed around the particular needs of that function. This makes them enduring and much less susceptible to the whims of individuals or fashion. Therefore, rather than viewing integration and mergers as collaborations of missions from dedicated public sector organizations (Frumkin 2003), it might be more realistic to view them as potential acquisitions in which one organization will likely feel vulnerable to cultural domination by another organization (Cartwright and Cooper 1993).

Cultural perspective on mergers

Traditional explanations for the issues arising from mergers, mainly in the private sector, have focused on aspects of poor strategic fit, managerial incompetence in achieving anticipated economies of scale, or over inflated purchase prices which, post-merger, negatively affected the balance sheet. Later writers emphasized organizational cultures as the primary explanation for the lack of merger success. Cartwright and Cooper (1993), for example, drew on Harrison's (1972) culture typology, in which he put forward four types of what he termed 'organization ideologies': power oriented; people oriented; task oriented; and role oriented. Each of these types exhibits particular organizational features, such as what goals are specified, appropriate relationships, forms of control, rewards and punishment, norms on how members should treat each other, and how the external environment is dealt with (see Table 6.2). The characteristics of these typologies are similar to the characteristics within Mintzberg's organizational structures, as set out in Table 6.1. This allows us to use them in complementary ways in our analysis of public sector mergers.

In their review of the cultural literature as it relates to mergers, Schraeder and Self (2003) identified several contextual features which merged organizations often have to contend with when different cultures come together. These include:

- a power imbalance between organizations;
- how organizations are placed geographically i.e. on a national, regional or local basis;
- differences in size, structure or workforce, such as the balance between professionals and support staff and the merging of varying task structures.

Table 6.2 Harrison's (1972) original organization ideologies

Power orientation	Person orientation	Task orientation	Role orientation
Competitive	Organization exists primarily to serve the needs of its members	Superordinate goals exist	Rational and ordered
Control over subordinates	Consensus-based	Organization's structure and functions are the basis for evaluation of achievement of goals	Legality, legitimacy and responsibility
May be exploitative or benevolent	Management control is rejected in favour of professional control		Rules and rights are honoured and may be more important than effectiveness

In our work, each of these features emerges as an important factor in the relative success of mergers.

Cartwright and Cooper (1993) argued that, from the 1980s onwards, mergers increasingly occurred between related organizations where integration of some or all of their human resources was required. In this context, they argued, success becomes 'heavily dependent upon human synergy' (p. 58). Given the nature of the joined-up government agenda in the UK, where the goal has been the reinforcement of interventions between different organizations to address deep-seated social and economic problems, this has considerable relevance (6 *et al.* 2002).

Cartwright and Cooper (1993) identified two key problems which have particular relevance for the current cases. The first is that the acquiring or lead organizations lack expertise in the business of the second organization. This can inhibit the recognition of changes to current practices and cultures necessary within the new, merged organization. The second is that the 'successful' culture and performance of the acquiring or lead organization will not necessarily transfer readily to the second organization. Cartwright and Cooper (1993) termed mergers where this transfer of successful culture and performance was expected '*redesign* mergers'.

Cartwright and Cooper (1993) were trying to discover what constituted good managerial practice in mergers; however, they found that the pre-combination cultures were the most important determinant of merger outcomes. Mergers were problematic where the weaker organization valued and considered their culture to be satisfactory and held a negative evaluation of the other 'dominant' organization's culture. These cultures were identifiable and the merger problems and outcomes from them were largely predictable.

Furthermore, they found that although mergers may have been intended to be collaborative, 'employees invariably failed to recognize an intended collaborative merger' (p. 64) and responded to the merger as being redolent of acquisition, in which one organization assumes a natural superiority. This suggests that mergers, particularly those that are vertical in nature and require a high level of integration, need to be managed carefully so as to limit this natural tendency. At the extreme end, where two organizations have quite different roles but the level of integration required is high, this may represent the limits to effective mergers: i.e. where the outcomes of the merger might be so dissatisfactory that there is little rational justification for it. In the public sector, the degree to which employees automatically assume it to be a redesign merger may rely upon their expectations emanating from the varying task structures of the merging organizations. Such expectations might be more likely in a professional bureaucracy, where autonomy is highly valued. They might readily see their autonomy under threat if they are mandated to merge with a machine bureaucracy. This will not necessarily be the intention of the lead organization, but it may occur because of the usual way that business is organized within that organization.

Three public sector merger cases

In this section we explore three cases of public sector merger to examine the extent to which structural change in the form of mergers represents a solution to cross-boundary dilemmas.

Jobcentre Plus

The 2002 merger of the Benefits Agency and the Employment Service (Jobcentre Plus 2003) was intended to provide a modern and more personalized service for jobseekers. Reflecting the government's desire to cut unproductive welfare spending, the new integrated service placed searching for alternative employment at the centre of benefit claims, making it difficult to stay on benefits (Driver and Martell 1998).

The two organizations were of unequal size with, 32,300 employees from Employment and approximately 60,000 from Benefits, and the merged organization became the largest single government agency in the UK. During the merger 14,000 employees were made voluntarily redundant, and over the course of six years the estate was reduced from 1,500 single offices to 811 combined offices. Employees from the two organizations were initially co-located, which provided an opportunity for integration but also produced some tensions. Operational changes beyond the establishment of personal advisors to facilitate active job searching included automation, which reduced the requirement for a high level of integration between the two groups. Automation took the form of a customer management system through which necessary data was collated and stored for retrieval, and later through the implementation of the Benefits Processing System. This facilitated the processing of benefit claims in specialist Benefit Delivery Centres from 2007 (NAO 2008).

The merger led to a significant degree of change in organizational structures and a significant impact on the workforce through the required retraining or redundancy. Despite this, Jobcentre Plus was praised by the NAO for its efficient and effective management of change (NAO 2008). Whilst this effective reform should not be dismissed, the case demonstrates that an accommodation took place between the two organizations whereby the hard silos of individual organization were replaced by internal or soft silos within the new organization.

National Offender Management Service (NOMS)

The creation of NOMS in 2004 was prompted by the Carter Review of correctional services (2003). It found that more severe sentencing had led to overcrowding in prisons, poor rehabilitation services which were often not continued on release, and ultimately poor targeting of resources. The merger sought to enable more effective use of resources through a mix of better offender management and contestability in service provision. The new system, it was hoped, would address high rates of reoffending and increase public confidence through delivery of a more joined-up and targeted service focused on the offenders' needs rather than on maintaining organizational boundaries (Faulkner 2005). The Ministry of Justice (2007a) argued that it would provide the 'end-to-end' treatment of offenders through a joined-up approach centred on Offender Managers who would act as key workers. It was suggested that this would help reduce reoffending.

The Prison Service was the much larger organization, with 54,000 officers and governors, whilst the National Probation Service had just 7,210 officers. The bulk of the reforms impacted upon the Probation Service.

The current NOMS emerged from a series of structural reforms. In 2001 the National Probation Service was created, replacing 54 local services, and in 2004 it became part of NOMS. The so-called 'new' NOMS was created in 2007 and subsumed the Prison Service; finally, alongside this, the Offender Management Act (2007) provided the legislative basis for the creation of Probation Trusts. These Trusts both 'commission' services and 'provide' them in collaboration with the Regional Commissioner (Ministry of Justice 2007b). The Act 'lifts' the statutory duty from Probation Boards (and therefore Trusts) to provide probation services, placing this with the Secretary of State who will contract these services from the Probation Service or other providers.

One major outcome of the merger has been the effective dismantling of the Probation Service. A recent Select Committee Report suggested that rather than a merger, the new NOMS represented a takeover of probation by the Prison Service (Justice Select Committee 2011). There is no head of the probation function, and there are few representatives of probation in NOMS and none in senior management. Efficiency savings have fallen disproportionately on the Probation Service, as the number of officers has been cut despite an increase in work. Alongside this there have been increases in funding and employment functions within NOMS (Robinson and Burnett 2007). Training was temporarily halted in 2007 and the Secretary of State was made responsible for national guidelines on standards and the qualifications, experience and training required from those dealing with offenders, thus removing responsibility from the probation professionals (Fletcher 2009). Formal performance has not suffered, according to evaluations, but neither has the merger itself produced improvements as most of these began prior to the joining of the organizations. Moreover, reviews suggest that there has been 'no appreciable improvement in the "joined-up" treatment of offenders', a key driver of the merger program (Justice Select Committee 2011: 3).

Her Majesty's Revenue and Customs (HMRC)

The two UK tax bodies, Inland Revenue (IR) and Customs and Excise (CE), were merged in 2005. The merger was the outcome of the O'Donnell Review (2003), which focused on improving the organizational arrangements for tax collection. At the time the UK was one of only two countries in the world with two tax collecting bodies. Reform was sought to reduce costs whilst increasing

The structure solution? 101

compliance, improve customer service, and coordinate services. Alongside the organizational merger, policy-making powers were transferred from both bodies to the Treasury (HMRC 2005).

Due to pressures to create a more efficient system, reorganizations were already underway prior to the merger. The number of London offices had been reduced, corporate functions had been merged, and call centres were being established across the country. Following the merger, the largest ever IT project was introduced to build inter-agency compatibility and work processes were reorganized using lean technology, which involved breaking down the steps in the tax and tax credit assessment systems. As a result, a higher proportion of lower-killed employees (including temporary workers) could be used, and the previous method of case-loading requiring more highly skilled staff was reserved for the more complex cases. The merger involved closing offices, the co-location of IR and CE staff, and a gradual reduction in employees. By 2007, 79 offices had been closed and the number of people working for the new agency had reduced by 18,940 to 90,950 (HMRC 2007). This trend has continued: the workforce in 2011 was 66,900, with further reductions in office space recorded (HMRC 2011).

Much change, both structural and operational, has been implemented in HMRC. Culturally, these changes have challenged both sets of employees, producing particularly toxic results. The larger service had been IR, with 82,180 employees, whilst CE had 23,380 (HMRC 2005). In many ways IR has dominated, with a shift to industrialization with an over-reliance on IT, lean technology and the increasing use of semi-skilled personnel reflecting their (the IR's) top-down culture. Changes have also been made which reflect the culture of CE and their more aggressive ways of operating. The outcomes have not been favourable, with measurable over-payments of benefits, under-collection of taxes, loss of child benefit data, issuing of incorrect tax codes, aggressive tax demands, and poor customer service. For example, letters and phone calls have been systematically ignored in favour of online interaction – the emphasis is always on the speed of individual transactions rather than on fully addressing customer concerns (Treasury Select Committee 2011b). Furthermore, since the merger, staff morale has been the lowest in the UK Government (HMRC 2009). The Treasury Select Committee has stated that the culture prevents employees from highlighting problems, which further prevents achievement of the merger outcomes. Complaints have also been voiced over the removal of policy-making powers, which has led to poor policy implementation (ICA 2007).

Identifying task structures in merged organizations

The characteristics of the operating cores for each of the eight merging organizations are summarized in Table 6.3, and are used to define the task structures of those organizations (children's services departments, discussed in Chapter 12, are also included here). A comparison of the task structures demonstrates that the merger between the Employment Service and Benefits Agency had the potential for success. This is because they shared a basic task structure comprised of strong internal management and a large group of semi-skilled administrators with weak unions. Certain structural reforms also reduced the disparity in the size of the individual workforces in the merged organizations, which may have also had a positive impact. Furthermore, this case is characterized by both organizations retaining policy legitimacy. This is something the other cases lack, including that of the Children's Services case discussed in Chapter 12. It has also been highlighted that the Jobcentre Plus merger was effectively managed, something we would not want to belittle. However, this in itself can be seen as a reflection of the shared task structures, which are likely to provide the conditions for shared definitions and agreed upon courses of action.

Such homogeneity was not shared by the other merging organizations, which combined machine and professional bureaucracies. Whilst we would not argue that it would be impossible for such mergers to ever be successful, nor that this is the only identifiable reason for merger issues in these cases, task structures do seem to be relevant for understanding merger outcomes. At the very least, they may point to the need for pro-active management in order to avoid predictable issues. Alternatively, it may suggest that a merger will be of little benefit if the perceived costs of managing the merger outweigh the hoped-for benefits. What these cases do demonstrate is that heterogeneous task structures do not support merger processes. This is important because the intention of government, albeit implicit in the merger plans, that 'successful' cultures would transfer from dominant organizations to the others, thereby producing positive outcomes, is misguided. The hoped-for transfer can be construed by the expressed policy legitimacy and performance of the education, prison and revenue services within central government and, by contrast, the concerns expressed at the centre concerning the weaker policy legitimacy and performance of social services, probation services and customs.

The NOMS case combined a uniformed semi-skilled Prison Service, with both strong management and unions, with a weakly managed and unionized professional bureaucracy (the National Probation Service). The two revenue agencies might be assumed to share the same task structure, but CE operated in ways more akin to professional groups. They were intelligence-led, held a key role in policy-making, and employees had a degree of autonomy not found in IR, which operated as a machine bureaucracy with strong top-down management. Harrison's (1972) distinction between role and task culture provides a valuable frame for analysis: CE focused on achieving the task, whilst IR focused on conformity to rules whereby 'the correct response tends to be more highly valued than the effective one' (Harrison 1972: 122). Examples of the impact of these task structures operating within the newly merged organizations are explored in the following paragraphs under the headings 'Organizational Size' and 'Policy Legitimacy'. These two aspects appear to be the most important factors in the cases for understanding how easily one organization can come to dominate within a merger. Differential sizes, we suggest, may not be necessary, but they can hasten the domination of organizations considered to have low policy legitimacy.

Table 6.3 Characteristics of the individual organizations' operating cores

Merged agencies	The operating cores	
Jobcentre Plus 2002	Benefits Agency Machine Bureaucracy Top down management. Semi-skilled administrators. Weak unions.	Employment Agency Machine Bureaucracy Top down management. Semi-skilled administrators. Weak unions.
National Offender Management Service (NOMS) 2004–2007	Prison Service Machine Bureaucracy Uniformed semi-skilled service. Strong internal management and unions.	Probation Service Professional Bureaucracy Professionals with weak professional bodies. Poor support from central government and poor standing within policy community.
Her Majesty's Revenue and Customs' (HMRC) 2005	Inland Revenue Machine Bureaucracy Traditionally operated through rule-based system with semi-skilled administrators dominating routine work and senior officials applying discretion. Weak unions.	Customs and Excise Professional Bureaucracy High level of autonomy associated with professionalism and a more flexible operating model. Key policy input. Weak unions.
Children's Services Departments 2004	Education Service Machine Bureaucracy A range of semi-skilled and skilled administrators. Low levels of autonomy, but divisionalization creates some power for the department.	Children's Social Service Professional Bureaucracy Professionals often poorly trained and lacking support from within organization and central government. Weak professional associations and poor standing within policy community.

Note
Children's Services Departments are included here for comparison.

Organizational size

Without exception, the mergers considered here were of differently sized organizations. This suggests that size alone may not be a key factor, but, more likely, related to task structure and policy legitimacy. Where the task structure was shared and both organizations were considered legitimate, as in Jobcentre Plus, the relative size of organizations was not an issue. In the remaining cases both size and legitimacy were important factors in the merger outcomes. The difference in size has augmented the dominance of the prison function in the merger, for example, in relation to the widespread exclusion of probation staff in NOMS headquarters and their total exclusion from the senior management ranks. In HMRC, although some influence from CE is identifiable, the thrust of the reforms have been driven through the machine bureaucratic structures, with the outcome being an over-reliance on IT, lean processing and low-grade staff (Treasury Select Committee 2011a, 2011b). The size differential has been detrimental to the power bases of the weaker merged organizations. Where a particular group are weak and also in a minority, they have less opportunity to take management roles and influence decision-making in relation to the operational changes involved as part of the merger process. In the longer term, this means that their power is likely to continue to dissipate.

Policy legitimacy

It would be easy to see the cultural clashes borne out of the task structure variation merely as an unintended consequence of the mergers. However, the evidence demonstrates that in each case, government, to a greater or lesser degree, desired some transfer of culture from those organizations who were evaluated as successful to those whose culture was seen as problematic. Again, Jobcentre Plus can be differentiated from the other cases: culture change within Jobcentre Plus was largely customer-oriented – a passive claimant culture would no longer be accepted. Some changes in orientation were introduced for the staff, but this operated equally with respect to the two groups of employees. This could also be identified positively as job enhancement.

The National Probation Service (now organized as Trusts under direction from NOMS) has long been negatively compared against the Prison Service. Its professional roots in social work have been viewed as an issue for government keen on creating a stronger management culture (Gregory 2007). The merger facilitated the spill-over of the Prison Service management style to the probation function within NOMS. The Prison Service argues that probation managers need to develop a 'crunchier' style. Probation managers argue that they operate on a model which relies on the consent and motivation of offenders to improve their own circumstances, which the Prison Service does not understand. The probation function also has no recourse to 'withdrawal of privileges', unlike the prison system (Fletcher 2009). HMRC was a merger which ostensibly affected both organizations, but the IR culture appears to dominate in the new task structure (although the more aggressive style of tax collection has transferred from CE). As the larger service, IR has bestowed a top-down management style which has clashed with the flatter hierarchies in CE. In the Children's Services case the Education Service was seen to have performed well, responding positively to reforms. Social Services, like probation, have been viewed as being problematic. This relates particularly to their long-standing rejection of management, and of performance management processes more particularly (Coulshed 1990). The merger of these organizations appears to have provided a vehicle for addressing the lack of legitimacy of certain groups within the policy community by removing much of their power. The degree to which this process creates a properly functioning public service is questionable. Redesign was part of the process as planned; however, whether those mandating the mergers understood what the impact would be upon key public sector employees and the services which they deliver remains an open question.

Conclusion – managing mergers

Given the potential complexity of public sector mergers that we have described, making effective decisions with regard to how to manage change becomes critical. Frumkin (2003) pointed to several areas of focus for public sector mergers: effective communications; swift implementation; creating a new culture; and being prepared to make adjustments. This is especially important if his first principle is taken seriously, namely that 'Public sector mergers are only successful if they satisfy or exceed the expectations of the constituents that are served by the agencies under consideration' (Frumkin 2003:4) – in other words, mergers have to add value. This value might be added by an accepted rationale for the merger, and also by effective management. It is clear from the two problematic cases detailed here that the 'constituencies' have not been satisfied and that, in both cases, issues of reduction in service quality can be identified even where more formal performance measures have improved. None of the cases other than Jobcentre Plus could be described as having been well-managed at the centre, even if much good work has occurred in local areas.

Identifying task structure variation provides a useful starting point in analysing organizations in order to highlight potential merger problems. Unlike in the private sector, there appears to be a poor understanding of the potential negative impact of mergers within UK Central Government. This is not to suggest that many of the aims and objectives were not reasonable, including that a degree of cultural change within organizations and professions might be beneficial for quality improvement in public services. However, there has been a failure to proactively manage mergers. In this study, the only merger reported to have been managed well was Jobcentre Plus. Interestingly, its Chief Executive transferred to HMRC to help address merger-related problems there; however, they have been unable to reproduce the same degree of effectiveness. The success of Jobcentre Plus has been widely attributed to effective management, which may have played a significant part, but this analysis raises the question of whether this merger was simply more straightforward to manage due to common task structures, just as those with varying task structures have been problematic? Our analysis suggests that organizations with varying task structures are not necessarily viable merger partners, and, when weighing up potential mergers, at the very least the benefits should outweigh the costs, in both financial and non-financial terms.

The variation in task structure between merging organizations is not the only factor that created merger-related issues in our cases – the complexity of the contexts in which mergers have taken place is also an important factor. Extensive operational and structural reform has been pursued alongside these mergers and was inextricably linked to the merger process. Greater complexity is added when vertical rather than horizontal mergers are attempted due to the potential for greater variation in task structures: differences which make it more difficult to reap gain. Furthermore, in addition to these new cases representing vertical mergers, there is another sharp contrast between the cases here and the earlier horizontal public sector merger studies in higher education and health. In these cases the merger was of a limited number of locally-based organizations, which presents a fairly limited management task as compared to recent mergers which affected whole sectors with hundreds of organizations across the whole of England, and sometimes the whole of the UK. These organizations are characterized by being geographically dispersed and centrally managed. This adds an additional layer of complexity to the already problematic nature of vertical mergers. The UK Government underestimated the potential difficulties mergers would encounter in these complex contexts. More analysis and pro-active management was required if they were considered essential reforms, to driving service delivery improvements.

The ensuing complexity also leads to the problem of attributing poor outcomes to specific elements of change – to the merger or to other individual factors of change such as the implementation of IT projects or market contestability. In this sense mergers suffer from the same methodological 'Achilles heel' that applies to other coordinative attempts within the public sector. In such contexts there is a problem in isolating variables, to the extent that it can become difficult to attribute success or otherwise to any single intervention. Whatever the outcome, the weaknesses in being able to isolate the 'causes' of success or failure tend to lead to more scepticism regarding the value of cross-boundary working. Without solid evidence that cross-boundary working improves efficiency and effectiveness, scepticism will continue. Finding new and better ways to analyse cross-boundary working remains essential.

This is particularly so as these cases demonstrate that both structural and operational reforms take place in the public sector in order to drive potential service improvements and efficiencies. In the HMRC case we can see the complex interplay between merger and related reforms. Tax credits predated the merger, but the bringing together of these organizations made it much more difficult to solve problems, and arguably harder to convince the Treasury that the system was actually unworkable. Whilst it might be difficult to attribute deficiencies to the merger alone, it is also difficult to claim that it had no effect. Furthermore, reforms continually take place within public sector organizations and rarely create persistent problems as their implementation takes place in a more stable organizational context.

Size differentials might be seen as an intervening factor which shifts more power to already strong organizations. The larger organization will more likely have greater capacity, both in terms of numbers of staff and also in terms of seniority and experience, which can facilitate their taking over administrative and planning roles. Even without legitimacy problems, size differentials could inadvertently empower one organization over another. However, legitimacy problems were identified, and although explicit statements did not always exist within the policies for merger, the choices made put one organization in the lead, thus allowing their task structure to dominate. Even where the choice was explicit, as in relation to education taking the lead in Children's Services, the understanding that their varying task structures would allow dominance was absent.

Frumkin (2003) argues that attention should be paid to merger motives as they are not always fully articulated, as shown in these cases. Given the effort required to make mergers work, questions have to be raised concerning the rationales and motives for UK public sector mergers. It appears that restructuring has been seen as a cure-all for outstanding policy issues as well as a means of reaping cost savings from economies of scale. The National Audit Office (2010) suggests that there is little evidence of cost savings in relation to reorganizations. Furthermore, systematic reviews of the overall benefits are rare at best. Given the lack of evidence of such added value, we raise of the question of whether the mergers we set out in these cases were really worthwhile. Whilst logically it is difficult to argue for the maintenance of two tax collecting agencies, the rationales for Children's Services departments and NOMS are more difficult to support. In these cases, mergers have not always facilitated the achievement of the objectives set out and, in some instances, have created new problems to be solved.

This chapter has outlined the issues which public sector integration and mergers face, and in doing so we have challenged the notion that mergers are an easy solution to addressing cross-boundary dilemmas. Mintzberg's (1979) notion of task structures was used to identify variation between merging organizations and explain the potential for power to be exerted by dominant organizations, which can produce unintended consequences for government.

The analytical framework provides an appropriate approach for understanding the potential problems of mergers in the public sector which are often put forward as cross-boundary solutions. Overall, it suggests that whilst the merger to create Jobcentre Plus was appropriate and delivered on outcomes, there are serious issues relating to the long-term viability of the other three cases as effective public sector organizations. Indeed, after the Coalition government took power in 2010 it set local areas free to organize Children's Services as they wish, thus diluting the role of the Director of Children's Services (Stewart 2011). The National Association of Probation Officers are campaigning in Parliament for the restructuring of NOMS (NAPO 2010), and HMRC is likely to come under increasing scrutiny as the government attempts to manage fiscal stress through welfare payment reform (HM Treasury 2010). Doubts about the effectiveness of HMRC in introducing a means-testing approach to the long-held universal child benefit system were aired in 2012 (Dalton 2012; Joyce 2012b).

There are two main lessons from this analysis that should inform governments that seek to use mergers to address cross-boundary dilemmas, especially where this involves vertical integration. First, it is necessary to set out more clearly articulated rationales for mergers, to identify whether there is variation in task structures between the organizations in proposed mergers, and to determine what level of complexity will be created from structural and operational reforms. Such pre-merger analysis would provide a more realistic preview of the costs and benefits of the potential merger and enable more strategic decisions to be made.

Second, if mergers are to remain an advantageous solution, then an active change management process needs to be implemented. Recognition must be given to the demands upon human synergy which mergers make in complex service environments. Ultimately, in public services activities have to be connected through employees committed to the organization. Too often in these mergers certain employees' roles have been undervalued: in HMRC, employees across the two organizations have felt undermined and have been left unable to carry out tasks effectively; in NOMS the profession of probation officer has been weakened in preference to the administrative management of offenders. Other providers produce the services and there is little influence from probation within NOMS; social workers have complained that education dominates Children's Services and they are not always able to exert autonomy. On the basis of these cases it seems unlikely that a merger would be truly successful where one organization experiences domination by another.

References

6, P., Leat, D., Seltzer, K. and Stoker, G. (2002) *Towards Holistic Government*, London: Palgrave.

Algie, J. (1973) 'Merging public services', *Management Decision*, 11(5): 280–293.

Bridgen, P. (2004) 'Joint planning across the health/social services boundary since 1946', in S. Snape and P. Taylor (eds) *Partnerships Between Health and Local Government*, London: Frank Cass.

Cabinet Office (2010) *Machinery of Government Changes: Information.* Online. Available at: www.gov.uk/government/publications/machinery-of-government-changes-information (accessed 30 December 2012).

Carter, P. (2003) *Managing Offenders, Reducing Crime*, London: Prime Minister's Strategy Unit.

Cartwright, S. and Cooper, C. (1993) 'The role of culture compatibility in successful organization', *The Academy of Management Executive*, 7(2): 57–69.

Coulshed, V. (1990) *Management in Social Work*, London: Macmillan.

Dalton, R. (2012) 'IFS says child benefit reforms are "bizarre and damaging"', *IFAOnline*,

1 February 2012. Online. Available at: www.ifaonline.co.uk/ifaonline/news/2143015/ ifs-child-benefit-reforms-bizarre-damaging (accessed 25 September 2012).

Driver, S. and Martell, L. (1998) *New Labour: Politics after Thatcherism*, Cambridge: Polity Press.

Faulkner, D. (2005) 'Relationships, accountability and responsibility in the National Offender Management Service', *Public Money & Management*, 25(4): 299–305.

Fletcher, H. (2009) *Probation Under Stress*, London: National Association for Probation Officers.

Frumkin, P. (2003) *Making Public Sector Mergers Work: Lessons Learned*, Washington: IBM Center for the Business of Government.

Fulop, N., Protopsaltis, G., Hutchings, A., King, A., Allen, P., Normand, C. and Walters, R. (2002) 'Process and impact of mergers of NHS trusts: a multicenter case study and management cost analysis', *British Medical Journal*, 325(7358): 246.

Fulop, N., Protopsaltis, G., Hutchings, A., King, A., Allen, P. and Normand, C. (2005) 'Changing organisations: a study of the context and processes of mergers of healthcare providers in England', *Social Science and Medicine*, 60(1): 119–130.

Gregory, M. (2007) 'Probation training: evidence from newly qualified officers', *Social Work Education*, 26(1): 53–68.

Harman, G. and Harman, K. (2003) 'Institutional mergers in higher education: lessons from international experience', *Tertiary Education and Management*, 9(1): 29–44.

Harrison, R. (1972) 'Understanding your organization's character', *Harvard Business Review*, 5(3): 119–128.

Her Majesty's Revenue and Customs (HMRC) (2005) *Annual Report 04–05 and Autumn Performance Report 2005 Her Majesty's Revenue and Customs*, Cm 6691, Norwich: Stationary Office.

Her Majesty's Revenue and Customs (HMRC) (2007) *Departmental Report 2007: integrating and growing stronger*, Cm7107, Norwich: Stationary Office.

Her Majesty's Revenue and Customs (HMRC) (2009) People Survey – Main data report 50233290 – HMRC Carried out by ORC International on behalf of HMRC. Online. Available at: www.hmrc.gov.uk/research/ss-spring2009.pdf (accessed 12 December 2012).

Her Majesty's Revenue and Customs (HMRC) (2011) *Annual Report and Accounts 2010–11*, HC 981, London; Stationery Office.

Her Majesty's Treasury (2010) *Spending Review 2010*, Cm7942, London Stationery Office.

Institute of Chartered Accountants (ICA) (2007) 'Memorandum submitted by the Institute of Chartered Accountants in England and Wales (ICAEW), in Treasury Committee', *The Efficiency Programme in the Chancellor's Departments: Eighth Report of Session 2006–07: Volume II Oral and Written Evidence*, HC 483-II, London: Stationery Office.

Jobcentre Plus (2003) *Annual Report and Accounts 2002–03*, HC 941, London: Stationery Office.

Joyce, R. (2012) *Tax and Benefit Reforms Due in 2012–12, and the Outlook for Household Incomes*, IFS Briefing Note BN126, London: Institute for Fiscal Studies and ESRC.

Justice Select Committee (2011) *The Role of the Probation Service*, HC 519, London: Stationery Office.

King, D.R., Dalton, D.R., Daily, C.M. and Covin, J.G. (2004) 'Meta-analyses of post-acquisition performance: indications of unidentified moderators', *Strategic Management Journal*, 25(2): 187–200.

Ministry of Justice (MoJ) (2007a) *National Offender Management Service Agency Framework Documents*, London: Ministry of Justice.

Ministry of Justice (MoJ) (2007b) *A Guide to the Offender Management Act 2007*, London: Ministry of Justice.

Mintzberg, H. (1979) *Structure in Fives*, New York: Prentice-Hall International.

Mintzberg, H. (1983) *Power In and Around Organizations*, New York: Prentice-Hall International.

National Association of Probation Officers (NAPO) (2010) *Performance of NOMS: the case for restructuring*, BRF21–10, London: NAPO.

National Audit Office (NAO) (2008) *The Roll Out of the Jobcentre Plus Office Network Report by the Comptroller and Auditor General*, London: National Audit Office.

National Audit Office (NAO) (2010) *Reorganising Central Government*, London: National Audit Office.

O'Donnell, G. (2003) *Financing Britain's Future: Review of the Revenue Departments*, London: Stationery Office.

Robinson, G. and Burnett, R. (2007) 'Experiencing modernisation: frontline probation perspectives on the transition to a National Offender Management Service', *Probation Journal*, 54(4): 318–337.

Schraeder, M. and Self, D.R. (2003) 'Enhancing the success of mergers and acquisitions: an organizational culture perspective', *Management Decision*, 41(5): 511–522.

Skodvin, O. (1999) 'Mergers in higher education: success or failure', *Tertiary Education and Management*, 5: 65–80.

Stewart, W. (2011) 'Councils move to unbundle "joined-up" children's services', Times Education Supplement 4th February 2011.

Talbot, C. and Johnson, C. (2007) 'Seasonal cycles in public management: disaggregation and re-aggregation', *Public Money & Management*, 27(1): 53–60.

Treasury Select Committee (2011a) *The Administration and Effectiveness of HM Revenue and Customs: Sixteenth Report of Session 2010–12: Volume I*, HC 731, London: Stationery Office.

Treasury Select Committee (2011b) *The Administration and Effectiveness of HM Revenue and Customs: Sixteenth Report of Session 2010–12: Volume II Additional Unpublished Evidence*, HC 731, London: Stationery Office.

7 The people and structure solution?

Collegial administration in Norway

Dag Arne Christensen, Tom Christensen,
Per Lægreid and Tor Midtbø

Introduction

The focus of this chapter is cross-boundary activity in the civil service in the form of participation in collegial bodies aiming at increasing coordination. Our aim is to use structural and demographic theories of civil service organizations to test general hypotheses about variation in cross-border activity on a set of survey data from the Norwegian central civil service in order to understand better how these organizational forms work, and whether they have the potential to provide a solution to cross-boundary challenges and dilemmas. Such instruments and tools might enhance the integration and cross-cutting capacity of the government apparatus.

Bureaucratic and networked organizations are usually portrayed as alternatives based upon hierarchical authority and cooperation (Olsen 2004). In this chapter we challenge this view and argue for the need to go beyond single principles when seeking to understand how public organizations operate (Olsen 2006). Cross-border collegial activities in civil service organizations are actually an old phenomenon supplementing hierarchy, but the concept of working across boundaries has become increasingly important in public administration and in management theory and practice over the last two to three decades (Sullivan and Skelcher 2002; O'Flynn *et al.* 2010). We may see this as a reflection of the complexity and fragmentation that New Public Management (NPM) reforms have brought, which have strained political and administrative leaders' capacity to solve societal problems, particularly those cutting across levels and sectors (Christensen and Lægreid 2007).

Different sets of rules tend to evolve independently in different domains, as do interests, norms and values (March and Olsen 1989: 26). As a result, there is currently a stronger focus on the notion of increased coordination. Such efforts are typically referred to as post-NPM or joined-up government, whole-of-government, holistic government, integrated governance, new public governance collaborative governance, networked government, connected government, cross-cutting policy, horizontal management, partnerships, and collaborative public management (Gregory 2003; Pollitt 2003; Christensen and Lægreid 2011). We expect an increase in such cross-border collegial working groups in recent years owing to post-NPM reforms and explore this through two sets of questions. First, how common is the use of internal ministerial working or project groups across ministries and between ministries and central agencies, and how has this changed over time? And, second, why are there differences in cross-boundary collegial activities? A structural perspective and a demographic perspective will be used to look at the importance of formal organizational features and personnel characteristics, respectively (Christensen and Lægreid 2007). Our empirical analysis examines the effects of both the individual features and the organizational conditions of the ministries, which represent civil servants' working environment.

We go beyond single level models and argue that a meaningful understanding of organizational behaviour requires an approach that cuts across levels and seeks to understand organizational phenomena from several perspectives (Klein and Kozlowski 2000).

Theoretical approaches

The context of cross-boundary activities

A basic assumption in organizational theory is that individuals are influenced by their organizational context as well as by individual socio-economic or career features. We look not only at 'individuals in organizations', but also at 'organizations of individuals'. The challenge is to examine the interplay between individual characteristics and organizational features in order to understand the behaviour of civil servants (Klein and Kozlowski 2000). The linkage between the individual and organizational levels is determined by the extent to which the characteristics of one level influence the characteristics of the other (Simon 1973). 'Individuals in organizations' act 'on behalf of' the collectivity. However, they also bring previous experiences, which may alter collective norms and values. The term 'organizations of individuals' alludes to the challenges of making actors work in the same direction to achieve the same goals.

The organizational factors we focus on are of two types: individual–structural, related to formal position and tasks; and relational or aggregate, related to size and tenure profile. Individuals go through learning processes both outside and inside the civil service (Eriksson 2007: 57). In turn, norms and attitudes are modified and shaped by individual structural and collective organizational variables.

Previous Norwegian research has dealt with civil servants' perceptions of coordination (Christensen and Lægreid 2008). This article, too, explores variations in actual participation in both vertical bodies across levels and horizontal collegial bodies across all ministries. So far research has focused on how individual resources affect the attitudes and behaviour of civil servants, rather than the organizational context. Still, the behaviour of civil servants is likely to be influenced not only by who they are and what they think, but also by the place where they work (Pfeffer 1983). Hypotheses about how civil servants perform should therefore be tested with *both* individual and aggregate, cross-ministerial data.

A structural perspective

According to the structural perspective, political–administrative leaders design the formal structure of public organizations so as to control the activities of participants in decision-making processes. Leaders influence such processes by utilizing, in a bounded rational way, the frames and leeway of the formal public structure, and by controlling change, reorganizations or reform processes, thus influencing the structural context (Christensen *et al.* 2007). Gulick (1937) identified specialization and coordination, and the dynamic relationship between them, as the important structural dimensions in public organizations. The more specialized a public organization is, the greater the pressure for increased coordination, as currently exemplified by the dynamic between NPM and post-NPM (Christensen and Lægreid 2007).

The main leadership coordinative instrument is hierarchical control. However, the challenges of coordination do not always lend themselves well to hierarchical direction (Wise 2002: 141). The tasks of the modern state are complex and fragmented, and they do not fit into the traditional sectoral structure. Therefore, leaders have to design coordinative, collegial structures, which arrive at decisions via argument, bargaining or voting, rather than through command (Egeberg 2003). As our empirical focus is on project and working groups in the central civil service, we seek to explain the participation of civil servants in such coordinative structures.

We have divided the independent variables into two groups: individual and organizational. The individual variables concern how authority, roles and tasks are allocated vertically and horizontally. This allocation may potentially be part of a conscious design of public organizations to further or to channel decision-making in certain directions in order to achieve public goals (Simon 1957). Organizational variables capture the structural characteristics of public organization that may have implications for coordinative collegial participation.

Empirical expectations

First, concerning variables on the individual level, we would expect leaders to be more in favour of coordination and also to see coordination differently than executive officers lower down in the hierarchy (Egeberg 2003). Leaders are expected to score highest on their participation in a broad range of coordination forms, especially along the external dimension. However, the fact that leaders often have problems of capacity and attention may modify this hypothesis.

This perspective also offers insights into how cross-border participation varies between different policy areas and among officials performing different tasks. Formal features determine how internally or externally directed their work is. Civil servants working with more general tasks, such as coordination, policy development, planning, regulation and preparatory legislative activities, will probably participate more in collegial cross-border groups than employees engaged in narrower, more inward-looking functions, such as single case-work.

Broad tasks involve more complex interdependence, which might lead to more insecurity, which in turn can be handled through collaboration and coordination (Thompson 1967).

Concerning structural organizational variables, we expect the size of the ministries to make a difference. Size may indicate capacity to initiate policies, develop alternatives or implement final decisions (Egeberg 2003). Our hypothesis is two-fold. On the one hand, civil servants in smaller ministries may be more involved in external cross-border activities because they have to 'defend' themselves vis-à-vis larger ministries with stronger decision-making premises or collaborate with external actors who are independent of the ministries (Thompson 1967). On the other hand, bigger ministries might have a greater need for internal cross-border activities because their policies and tasks are more complex and therefore require more interaction.

A demographic perspective

Demography may also explain cross-border collegial participation. Civil servants, through their socio-economic background or their individual careers, acquire certain norms and values that are relevant to their jobs (Meier 1973, Pfeffer 1983). Our focus is on where civil servants come from and what they bring into ministries and central agencies in the way of norms, values and competence – as well as what they experience during their careers there. This perspective deals with the development of professions and the interaction between educationally acquired norms and institutional norms in the civil service.

Individual demographic variables include gender and type of education. These represent early socialization; this is the 'baggage' of norms and values that public employees bring into the civil service. These features are important for the identities and mentalities of civil servants, and in turn they might affect decision-making behaviour – what Meier (1973) labels representative bureaucracy.

In a series of large surveys in the Norwegian central civil service, conducted every ten years since the 1970s, type of higher education is the demographic variable which stands out as most important for the opinions and contacts of civil servants, mainly because of pre-socialization (Christensen and Lægreid 2009a). Some professions, such as jurists, probably have a more distinctive professional identity, heightening the effects of this mechanism.

The effect of gender seems less clear. There are certainly gender differences, but their relevance to behaviour in the civil service is more debatable. What we do know is that women are under-represented in the civil service in general, and particularly so in leadership positions, something that might lead to gender differences in contact patterns (Christensen and Lægreid 2009b). Tenure differs from other individual demographic variables because it deals with the cumulative careers of civil servants (Christensen and Lægreid 2009a). Just like the institutions themselves, one would expect civil servants to develop more and more complex models of thought and action as a result of their diverse layers of experience and contacts.

On an organizational level, demographic variables may be important in terms of the thoughts and actions of civil servants (Pfeffer 1983). More general aggregate features may have an influence per se, and may also have a dynamic relationship with individual demographic features and structural factors, meaning that different individual backgrounds will play out differently in different aggregate contexts.

Empirical expectations

With regard to individual demographic variables, type of higher educational background may be important. For example, we expect political scientists and economists to be more involved in working and project groups, while jurists score lower on collegial cross-border activities due to their rule-oriented education and their focus on 'narrow' individual cases (Christensen and Lægreid 2009b). Another general expectation would be that women would be less involved in cross-border activities, based on the observation that women in organizational settings lack access to emergent interaction networks (O'Leary and Ickovics 1992). This may reflect both gender 'exclusiveness' (i.e. the fact that women are underrepresented in leadership positions) and the fact that they generally have shorter tenure. Further, civil servants with long tenure would be expected to participate more in cross-border activities as their experience and contacts would give them the wherewithal to do so (Christensen and Lægreid 2009b).

With regard to the aggregate demographic variables used, one would expect ministries with a large share of civil servants with long tenure to use cross-border activities more extensively than ministries with less experienced civil servants. The greater number of contacts associated with longer individual tenure should be reflected in a broader collective contact pattern.

The Norwegian context

Norway has a large public sector, and there is a relatively high level of mutual trust between central actors and public sector organizations. The central government in Norway is characterized by strong sectoral ministries and relatively weak super-ministries with coordination responsibilities across ministerial areas. The principle of ministerial responsibility is strong, meaning that the individual minister is responsible for all activities in his or her portfolio and in subordinate agencies and bodies.

The central government apparatus is generally characterized by strong hierarchy and strong specialization according to tasks, but these Weberian organizational forms have been supplemented by a variety of other features which have changed the internal organization of the central public administration, such as introducing internal team work, collegial network-based working, or project groups working across hierarchical levels and sectoral boundaries – the focus of our analysis.

Norway was a reluctant reformer and came late to NPM reforms (Olsen 1996), but over the past decade two development features in the Norwegian central government have affected the coordination pattern. First, the NPM reforms have increased vertical and horizontal specialization, while at the same time trying to balance this with a focus on vertical coordination, mainly within the government apparatus but also between central and local government. The problems of horizontal coordination have not been addressed to the same extent, but are reflected in reforms in policy, hospitals and welfare systems.

Data sources and method

This analysis draws on a comprehensive survey conducted among civil servants with at least one year of tenure in all 18 ministries. The survey was conducted in 2006, and included 1,846 respondents, ranging from nine in the Prime Minister's Office to 284 in the Ministry of Foreign Affairs (Christensen and Lægreid 2008, 2009b). The response rate was 67 percent. To obtain descriptive statistics over time, we used comparable surveys from 1976, 1986 and 1996. Our explanatory analysis is based on the 2006 survey and examines how ministry-level variables affect participation in coordination initiatives. The data from the civil servant survey are thus linked to data on ministerial characteristics, including ministry size and 'collective experience'.

The analysis distinguishes between three types of cross-border collegial activities. These three dependent variables were measured using a single survey question, which asked civil servants whether they had participated in various types of work-group/projects during the last 12 months. The first variable deals with participation in project groups *within* ministries. These groups have participants from different divisions and teams inside the ministries, and their purpose is to increase collaboration and coordination in establishing or implementing regulations and policies. The second variable deals with vertical coordination. Here the respondents were asked to identify participation in projects or groups with participants from the sub-ministry level, i.e., agencies. This variable deals with collaboration and coordination across borders, between organizations and levels. The last variable maps participation in work and project groups *between* ministries. This variable was intended as a rough indicator of horizontal coordination initiatives.

The scope and trajectories of cross-border activities

Table 7.1 shows, first, that cross-border activity, involving participating in inter-organizational working groups, is high in the Norwegian central government. The scope of such activity is non-trivial. The hierarchy is supplemented to a great extent by such collegial bodies.

Second, this is not a new phenomenon. Collegial working groups have existed for at least the entire period for which we have data. These activities were stepped up between 1976 and 1986, before NPM was introduced in Norway, and have remained stable and at a high level. Our expectation that these kinds of cross-border activity would have increased in recent years owing to post-NPM reform initiatives

Table 7.1 Ministerial civil servants participating in different working groups and project groups during the last year

	1976	1986	1996	2006
Within own ministry	58%	71%	75%	75%
Across ministries	40%	53%	58%	54%
With subordinate bodies and agencies	–	–	42%	40%
Number	759	1,171	1,393	1,768

is not supported by these data. Rather than radical pendulum shifts, we see gradual change: it appears to be an organizational form and a participation pattern that is rather resilient to reform initiatives, whether NPM or post-NPM. This is quite remarkable, since one would have thought that increasing the complexity of policy would lead to more collegial contact. On the other hand, there might also be increasing attention and capacity problems, having aggregate effects.

Third, internal groups working across the divisions and units within their own ministry are the most common and the least demanding. Two-thirds of the civil servants surveyed had participated in such collegial bodies over the last year, but there was also a high level of cross-border activity across ministries. More than half of the civil servants surveyed had participated in such activities, indicating that the strong siloization and departmentalization in the central government brought about by specialization by task or sector has been partly compensated for by high levels of activity in horizontal working groups and project groups crossing ministerial boundaries. There is also a rather high level of collegial bodies at the vertical level, bringing together ministerial civil servants and their colleagues in subordinate agencies and bodies. This shows ministerial capacity and structural preconditions for interaction (Egeberg 2003).

Explaining cross-border participation

We now turn from describing trends over time to explaining variation within and between two levels – the civil servants and the ministries – at one particular time. The 2006 survey data on the civil servants are embedded within the ministries, in the sense that the characteristics of the latter may influence the characteristics of the former. Among the many methods of analysing such data structures, there is a lot to be said for multilevel analysis (Steenbergen and Jones 2002; Hox 2002; Snijders and Bosker 2004).

The main findings of Table 7.2 are: first, that the main variation in cross-border activity is due to individual-level variables rather than organizational-level variables; second, there is a significant part of the variation that is related to organizational features which need to be included in the further analyses; and third, the importance of organizational-level variables is largest for participation in inter-organizational working groups and project groups that transcend ministerial boundaries both horizontally and vertically.

Table 7.2 Multi-level empty logistical regressions: participation in three types of ministry project groups

	Internal project group participation	*Project groups with subordinate bodies*	*Inter-ministry project group participation*
Fixed effects			
Coefficient	1.228*	−0.404*	0.315*
Odds ratio	3.42	0.67	1.37
Level-2 variance	0.168	0.213	0.243
Chi-square (*p*)	19.41*	53.03*	72.58*
Intra-class correlation	0.049	0.061	0.069
Plausible value range (95%)			
Lower	0.60	0.21	0.34
Mean	0.77	0.40	0.58
Upper	0.88	0.62	0.78
N-Level 1	1,561	1,539	1,542
N-Level 2	18	18	18

Notes
Random-effects with odds ratios, intra-class correlations, LR-test and plausible value ranges. Table entries are full maximum likelihood estimates with non-robust standard errors.
* Significant at the 0.00 level.

The subsequent step in the analysis is to include the explanatory variables in the model. Since there are only two such variables at the ministry level we present the effects for all of the explanatory variables simultaneously (Table 7.3).

Three results stand out: first, at the civil servant level two explanatory variables are especially important for participation in all three types of project group – being male and participating in policy development and planning. Both indicate a much higher probability than other civil servants of taking part in project groups. The odds of participating in internal project groups were 43 percent higher for male civil servants than for their female counterparts.

The odds that civil servants with policy development and planning as their main task will participate in project groups is 80 percent higher than for those with other tasks. This group stand out as important participants in all three types of project groups. Apart from these two variables, all others fail to reach significance for the first two types of project-group participation. It should come as no surprise that civil servants who are engaged in coordination activities participate more in inter-ministry project groups than other civil servants. Coordinators have an odds ratio of 1:68 for participation in inter-ministry project groups. There is a 68 percent increase in the odds of participating in these groups for coordinators, as compared to civil servants with other jobs.

Second, education does make a difference. From the second column of the table we see that educational background has a significant effect for internal project group participation and for cross-ministry project groups, although not

Table 7.3 Multi-level regressions: participation in three types of project group

	Internal project group		Project groups with subordinate bodies		Inter-ministerial project groups	
	Final model	Educational background effects	Final model	Educational background effects	Final model	Educational background effects
Fixed Effects						
Constant	0.89*	0.79**	−0.74*	−0.83*	−1.90	−2.03**
Civil-servant effects						
Structural features:						
Leadership position						
Coordination					0.52**	0.52***
Planning and development	0.60**	0.56**	0.66*	0.67*	0.71**	0.71**
Demographic features:						
Tenure						
Gender	0.36**	0.32***	0.24**	0.24***	0.26**	0.25
Jurists		−0.01		0.18		0.25
Economists		0.21		0.12		0.16
Social scientists		0.40		0.12		0.50
Ministry effects						
Ministry size					−0.002**	−0.002**
Ministry tenure					0.03***	0.03***
Variance Components						
Ministry level	0.138	0.161	0.187	0.197	0.014	0.016
Deviance compared to previous model	27.22*	7.43*	37.36*	1.55	66.50*	12.47***
N Civil-servant level	1,561	1,561	1,539	1,539	1,542	1,542
N Ministry level	18	18	18	18	18	18

Notes
Table entries are full maximum likelihood estimates.
* Significant at the 0.00 level.
** Significant at the 0.05 level.
*** Significant at the 0.10 level.

for participation in sub-unit project groups. In the two former groups, social scientists appear to be the most active participants.

Third, organizational-level variables make a difference. The two ministry–related explanatory variables in our model – ministry size and institutional/ministry tenure – are important for inter-ministry project group participation, but not for the other two types of participation. A high number of employees reduces the probability of individual civil servants participating in inter-ministry project groups, while institutional experience increases the odds of such participation.

Compared to the empty model, the ministry-level variance components show small reductions for internal and sub-unit project group participation. This is as expected given the small degree of freedom at Level 2. Hence, much of the variance at the ministerial level is still unaccounted for when it comes to these two types of project group participation. However, if we look at the ministry level variance components for inter-ministry project group participation we see that civil servant and ministry-level variables combined explain no less than 94 percent of the ministry level variance in inter-ministry project group participation.

Ministries do make a difference for participation in different types of work and project groups. Male civil servants working in the fields of planning and policy development are over-represented in all three forms of project group. At the ministerial level, size and institutional experience seem to be important for inter-ministry project group participation. However, when it comes to ministry-based coordination (internal and sub-unit project groups), the two ministry-level variables remain unimportant. The analysis also suggests that educational background plays a role for internal and cross-ministry project group participation, although not for participation in project groups with sub-units.

Discussion

Our analysis shows that structural and demographic features are important both at the individual and at the organizational level. First, starting with the effects of individual structural variables, it is rather surprising that our expectation that leaders would participate more is not fulfilled. One reason for this may be that there are many groups and they are of varying importance, so only some of them may attract leaders. One counter-argument to this would be that inter-ministerial groups would, relatively speaking, attract more leaders than other types, which is not the case. Another explanation is that administrative leaders increasingly have capacity problems, reflected in the finding of the surveys that the contact pattern of leaders has become more exclusive, meaning that executive officers are increasingly involved in such collegial participation (Christensen and Lægreid 2009b). A third explanation may be that leaders have other fora to interact in than project and working groups.

Further, we find, mostly as expected, that formal tasks matter, because having coordinative or planning/development tasks is connected with more participation. But why should having planning/development tasks have more impact overall than having coordinative tasks? One reason for this may be that planning/ development is in reality a broader task.

What about participation and structural organizational variables? Here, our expectations were rather divided, but the finding was that civil servants from larger ministries participate less in inter-ministerial working and project groups. As indicated, this may have something to do with smaller ministries having to engage a relatively higher share of civil servants in collegial coordinative efforts. Another factor may be that, as indicated, smaller ministries are at a disadvantage concerning the pattern of influence in the civil service and must use more resources and efforts to counter the influence of larger ministries

With regard to the individual variables, we did not find that long tenure results in more participation, reflecting that a career factor where civil servants build up a close network of contacts is of less importance than the type of tasks in which they are engaged. A long career may also further specialization, which would decrease the need for cross-border participation.

In accordance with our expectations, men score higher than women on collegial participation. Since leadership position is not connected to participation, this probably does not have to do with men being over-represented in leadership positions, and, overall, women are not under-represented in the ministries (Christensen and Lægreid 2009b). However, tasks and profession are linked to participation, and there are some differences between men and women in their tasks and professional profiles that might affect this result. Whether our results reflects a male-biased network and identity, indicating that men recruit men into these bodies, is not easy to discern from these data.

Education had an overall effect on participation, with social scientists scoring highest. This may reflect differences in tasks, with social scientists being seen as more competent at performing cross-border related tasks, but it may also reflect differences in the content of their education, with social scientists trained to take into account a broader set of decision-making premises in their consequence-oriented thinking (Christensen and Lægreid 2009b).

Ministerial tenure, an organizational variable, showed, as expected, that ministries with an 'older' tenure profile engage more in cross-border activities. Since, as an individual variable, tenure does not lead to more participation, the share of civil servants is obviously more crucial. Interestingly, this would seem to indicate that a career approach is of less value for explaining participation than a generational one (Christensen and Lægreid 2009b). We showed in Table 7.1 that cross-border collegial activities were less frequent in the civil service 20–30 years ago.

This chapter builds on the assumption that coordination is a core activity in these inter-organizational collegial bodies in central government. Other studies show that participation in project and working groups across the ministerial level tend to have a positive effect both vertically and horizontally upon perceived coordination among civil servants (Christensen *et al.* 2010). Such participation definitely seems to enhance coordination within central government both vertically and horizontally.

Conclusion

The main purpose of this chapter is to deepen our understanding of how collegial bodies in civil service are working to handle cross-boundary challenges – i.e., what is characterizing these forms primarily concerning variation in participation. This insight has an applied potential, because it could be used by the executive leadership in designing and redesigning these units to further collective goals. There seems to be a mismatch between the problem structures and the organizational structures in central government. Important tasks are cross-cutting organizational borders, and coordinating arrangements that transcend organizational borders are needed to handle such challenges.

We have shown, first, that the hierarchical organization of Norwegian ministries has, to a large extent, been supplemented by collegial cross-border project and working groups. This phenomenon is not recent, but goes back at least 30 years and, despite some growth from the 1970s to 2006, does not seem to have been significantly affected by the NPM or post-NPM reform movements, which appears to be something of a paradox: NPM seems to have fragmented the civil service in many countries (Pollitt and Bouckaert 2010), which would probably decrease the use of collegial bodies, and the efforts of post-NPM to increase coordination have been seen as a partial remedy to this situation (Christensen and Lægreid 2009b). Cross-border collegial activities as a fundamental feature of formal organizations go beyond contemporary administrative reforms. Such reforms are compounded as organizational changes and as layering processes, where new generations of reforms add complexity in structure (Streeck and Thelen 2005).

Different types of coordination problems have received a renewed focus in the form of 'whole-of-government' and 'joined-up government' programs (Christensen and Lægreid 2006, 2007), but different kinds of cross-border collegial bodies are definitely an old tool used to enhance coordination in central Norwegian government. Vertically, supplementing hierarchy with collegial working and project groups with subordinate bodies is a popular and long-term strategy for political executives to regain political control and pursue consistent policies across levels. On the horizontal dimension, measures like crosssectoral bodies, programs or projects have been used to a great extent and for a long time to modify the 'siloization' or 'pillarization' of the central public administration, with a strong specialization by sector (Gregory 2003; Pollitt 2003).

Second, our analysis reveals the combined effects of individual and organizational features on cross-border activities. The effects of organizational-level features are, however, more important for participation in inter-ministerial project groups than in internal or vertical sector-specific project groups. That said, overall, individual features are more important than organizational features. In particular, individual demographic features seem to be important.

The conclusion is that participation in cross-border collegial activities cannot only be traced back to either a structural or a demographic perspective. We need to use a mixed perspective approach to understand these activities and their effects.

What we are facing is not 'individuals in organizations' or 'organizations of individuals', but the mutual relationship between individuals and organizations.

Rather than looking at hierarchy and collegial bodies as alternative and competing organizational forms, we should understand them as supplementing and complementing other organizational modes (Olsen 2009). As a coordination mechanism, networks supplement the traditional hierarchy rather than replacing it (Verhoest *et al.* 2007; Bouckaert *et al.* 2010). It is more a question of how they co-exist in a complex and hybrid combination – and how they may be traded off and balanced against each other – than of replacing one form with another. Networks and hierarchy co-exist and represent compound systems of mixed political orders (Olsen 2007). Blending different forms of government and organizations in this way makes administrative systems robust and legitimate. By its focus upon structure and people, it represents a potential solution to handling the challenges of cross-boundary dilemmas.

References

Bouckaert, G., Peters, B.G. and Verhoest, K. (2010) *The Coordination of Public Sector Organizations: Shifting Pattern of Public Management.* London: Palgrave Macmillan.

Christensen, D.A., Christensen, T., Lægreid, P. and Midtbø, T (2010) *Working Across Boundaries: Collegial Administration in Central Government: Scope, Variation and Effects*, Working Paper 08/2010, Bergen: Uni Rokkan Centre.

Christensen, T. and Lægreid, P. (eds) (2006) *Autonomy and Regulation. Coping with Agencies in the Modern State*, Cheltenham: Edward Elgar.

Christensen, T. and Lægreid, P. (2007) 'The whole-of-government approach to public sector reform', *Public Administration Review*, 67(6): 1057–1064.

Christensen, T. and Lægreid, P. (2008) 'The challenge of coordination in central government organizations: the Norwegian case', *Public Organization Review: A Global Journal*, 8(2): 97–116.

Christensen, T. and Lægreid, P. (2009a) 'NPM and beyond: leadership, culture and demography'. *International Journal of Administrative Sciences*, 74(1): 5–21.

Christensen, T. and Lægreid, P. (2009b) 'Living in the past? Change and continuity in the Norwegian Civil Service', *Public Administration Review*, 69(5): 951–961.

Christensen, T. and Lægreid, P. (2011) 'Beyond NPM? Some development features', in T. Christensen and P. Lægreid (eds) *The Ashgate Research Companion to New Public Management*, Aldershot: Ashgate.

Christensen, T., Lægreid, P., Roness, P.G. and Røvik, K.A. (2007) *Organization Theory and the Public Sector: Instrument, Culture and Myth*, London: Routledge.

Egeberg, M. (2003) 'How bureaucratic structure matters: an organizational perspective', in B.G. Peters and J. Pierre (eds) *Handbook of Public Administration*, London: Sage.

Eriksson, K. (2007) *Spelar adressen någon roll? En studie av områdeseffekter på medborgares politiska deltagande (Does the Address play a role? A Study of the Effects of Geographical area in the Political Participation of Citizens)*, Umeå: Statsvetenskapliga Institutionen Umeå Universitet.

Gregory, R. (2003) 'All the king's horses and all the king's men: putting New Zealand's public sector together again', *International Public Management Review*, 4(2): 41–58.

Gulick, L.H. (1937) 'Notes on the theory of organizations: with special reference to government', in L.H. Gulick and L.F. Urwick (eds) *Papers on the Science of Administration*, New York: A.M. Kelley.

Hox, J. (2002) *Multilevel Analysis: Techniques and Applications*, London: Lawrence Erlbaum.

Klein, K.J. and Kozlowski, S.W.J. (2000) 'A multilevel approach to theory and research in organizations: contextual, temporal and emergent processes', in K.J. Klein and S.W.J. Kozlowski (eds) *Multilevel Theory, Research, and Methods in Organizations*, San Franscisco: Jossey-Bass.

March, J.G. and Olsen, J.P. (1989) *Rediscovering Institutions: The Organizational Basis of Politics*, New York: The Free Press.

Meier, K. (1973) 'Representative bureaucracy: an empirical analysis', *American Political Science Review*, 69: 526–542.

O'Flynn, J., Halligan, J. and Blackman, D. (2010) 'Working across boundaries: barriers, enablers, tensions and puzzles', paper presented at the IRSPM Conference, Bern 7–9 April 2010.

O'Leary, V.S. and Ickovics, J.R. (1992) 'Cracking the glass ceiling: overcoming isolation and alienation', in U. Sekaran and T.C. Fredericks (eds) *Womanpower: Managing in Crises of Demographic Turbulence*, Thousand Oaks: Sage.

Olsen, J.P. (1996) Norway: slow learner – or another triumph of the tortoise?', in J.P. Olsen and B.G. Peters (eds) *Lessons from Experience*, Oslo: Universitetsforlaget.

Olsen, J.P. (2004) 'Citizens, public administration and the search for theoretical foundation', *PS Political Science & Politics*, 37, January: 69–79.

Olsen, J.P. (2006) 'Maybe it is time to rediscover bureaucracy', *Journal of Public Administration Research and Theory*, 16(1): 1–24.

Olsen, J.P. (2007). *Europe in Search of Political Order*, Oxford: Oxford University Press.

Olsen, J.P. (2009) 'Change and continuity: an institutional approach to institutions of democratic government', *European Political Science Review* 1(1): 3–32.

Pfeffer, J. (1983) 'Organizational demography', in L.L. Cummings and B.M. Staw (eds) *Research in Organizational Behavior*, 5: 299–357. Greenwich, CT: JAI Press.

Pollitt, C. (2003) 'Joined-up government: a survey', *Political Studies Review*, 1: 34–49.

Pollitt, C. and Bouckaert, G. (2010). *Public Management Reforms*, 3rd edition, Oxford: Oxford University Press.

Simon, H.A. (1957) *Administrative Behavior*, New York: Free Press.

Simon, H.A. (1973) 'The organization of complex systems', in H.H. Pattee (ed.) *Hierarchical Theory*, New York: Braziller.

Snijders, T.A.B. and Bosker, R.J. (2004) *Multilevel Analysis. An Introduction to Basic and Advanced Multilevel Modelling*, Sage: London.

Steenbergen, M.R. and Jones, B. (2002) 'Modeling multilevel data structures', *American Journal of Political Science* 46(1): 218–237.

Streeck, W. and Thelen, K. (eds) (2005) *Beyond Continuity: Institutional Change in Advanced Political Economies*, Oxford: Oxford University Press.

Sullivan, H. and Skelcher, C. (2002) *Working Across Boundaries: Collaboration in Public Services*, Basingstoke: PalgraveMacmillan.

Thompson, J.D. (1967) *Organizations in Action*, New York: McGraw-Hill.

Verhoest, K., Bouckaert, G. and Peters, B.G. (2007) 'Janus-faced reorganization: specialization and coordination in four OECD countries in the period 1980–2005', *International Review of Administrative Sciences*, 73(3): 325–348.

Wise, C. (2002) 'Organizing for homeland security', *Public Administration Review*, 62(2): 131–144.

8 The performance target solution?
Cross-cutting public service agreements in the United Kingdom[1]

Akash Paun and Kate Blatchford

One more peculiarity in the Civil Service remains to be noted. It is what might be called its fragmentary character ... Each man's experience, interest, hopes and fears are limited to the special branch of service in which he is himself engaged. The effect naturally is, to cramp the energies of the whole body, to encourage the growth of narrow views and departmental prejudices.

(Northcote and Trevelyan 1854)

Anyone with experience of Whitehall will know that it was easier to get the USA and USSR to cooperate at the height of the cold war than to get two Whitehall departments to work together.

(Peter Lilley, former Cabinet Minister, 2008)

Introduction

The challenge of coordinating the work of different parts of government is a challenge as old as government itself. Overcoming the 'fragmentary character' of the UK central government in Whitehall has been an objective of many modernizing governments over the years,[2] but progress has often felt slow, patchy or too difficult to assess.

The complexity of the work of government means that division into specialized departments with a significant degree of managerial autonomy is inevitable. The structure of British government remains based in large part on the 'functionalist' recommendations of the 1918 Haldane Report, which advocated 'defining the field of activity in the case of each Department according to the particular service which it renders to the community as a whole' (Ministry of Reconstruction 1918: 8).

Functionally specialized departments have important advantages, such as the development of policy expertise and clear accountability chains. But many pressing challenges and contemporary policy objectives cannot easily be addressed by a single department acting alone. As a result, government must endeavour to 'join up' government, meaning to 'align incentives, cultures and structures of authority to fit critical tasks that cut across organisational boundaries' (Mulgan 2005: 176).

British governments have often reorganized the machinery of government or departmental structure in order to improve coordination in certain areas.

Examples include the 2008 creation of a single Department for Energy and Climate Change (DECC) to better manage the trade-offs between these two policy domains, and the 2007 merger of responsibility for higher education and adult vocational skills into a new Department for Innovation, Universities and Skills (DIUS).

But the machinery of government change does not erase the boundaries between departments – it merely shifts them. Thus, the creation of DECC created a new requirement to work across boundaries to ensure that climate change was taken into account in agriculture and land-use policy, which had been left behind in the Department for Environment, Food and Rural Affairs (Defra), the previous lead department for climate policy. The creation of DIUS similarly created a divide between post-18 and pre-18 education policy, with resultant coordination challenges at this new departmental interface.

Consequently, departmental boundaries will always exist, and so too will the challenge of cross-cutting working. As a previous analysis of this issue argued: 'Just as the functional separation of state agencies is a necessary part of managing complexity and is a characteristic feature of the modern state [...], so too is the development of strategies to deal with the problems this creates' (Ling 2002: 617).

This chapter is about the creation and later abolition of one particular strategy for dealing with the complexity of government – the framework of cross-cutting Public Service Agreement (PSA) performance targets, which was introduced in 2007 and abolished in 2010 following a change of administration.

Through our discussion of this particular story, we address a number of the broader questions that frame this book. We discuss *why* 'joining up' is regarded as an important objective – and why it became a particularly important objective under the previous administration (and why it has been deprioritized since 2010). Through our analysis of the cross-cutting PSA framework we provide one answer to the question of *what* working across boundaries in government involves, and, through a discussion of barriers to and enablers of success, we assess *how* effective this particular approach was.

About the Public Service Agreement framework

Public Service Agreements were first introduced in 1998 as part of the new Labour government's Comprehensive Spending Review (CSR) (HM Treasury 1998), which set out expenditure plans for the three-year period from 1999 to 2002. In their initial form, PSAs consisted of a set of specific performance targets that each government department was required to commit to by the Treasury, as a *quid pro quo* for the rising departmental budgets provided under the CSR.

The government revised the PSA regime as part of each subsequent spending review: in 2000, 2002, 2004 and, finally, in 2007. Over this period, the nature of the system changed in a number of ways.

First, there was a reduction in the number of targets (Gay 2005: 2). In 1998, there were no fewer than 600 targets set out across government. This fell with each iteration of the system – down to 126 targets in 2004, and then to 30 head-line policy targets in 2007, each measured by between 2 and 8 indicators.

Second, the nature of the targets changed. In 1998, many PSA targets were defined in terms of processes followed or outputs delivered: for instance, there were commitments to inspect 20 per cent of schools, to audit the performance of every new local housing authority, and to reduce the average duration of various types of legal process. Over time, and particularly in 2007, the emphasis shifted to more complex social and economic *outcome* measures, such as labour market productivity, employment rates among socially excluded groups, teenage pregnancy, child obesity and gender inequality.

Third, and most relevant to the theme of this book, the PSA structure became progressively more concerned with working across departmental boundaries – a development related to the growing focus on outcome measures. Almost all of the targets in the early PSA frameworks were the responsibility of individual departments or agencies. But in the 2007 framework – the focus of this chapter – all 30 PSAs were formally cross-cutting, meaning that two or more departments were required to collaborate in order to deliver performance improvement in the stated areas (see Gash *et al.* 2008).

Our research

We first set out in 2009 to examine the rationale and the effectiveness of the PSA framework, conducting semi-structured interviews with 18 of the 30 senior responsible owners (SROs) of cross-cutting PSA policy targets (or, in a few cases, their deputies). These were senior officials designated as responsible for coordinating cross-departmental collaboration around each PSA. We also con-ducted interviews with ten officials working in cross-departmental policy units – small teams of civil servants from two or more departments working together on a day-to-day basis to formulate policy in cross-cutting areas typically linked to one or more PSAs.

Our research indicated that the PSA framework and supporting governance arrangements had delivered some improvements in working across boundaries, but that its effectiveness was limited by several structural problems. Notably, we found that collaborating across departmental boundaries was limited by incen-tive structures – for both ministers and officials – that encouraged a focus on departmental rather than corporate concerns, by the absence of shared evidence bases, by the failure to align budgets to cross-cutting challenges and objectives, and by the limited extent to which the central departments at the heart of White-hall could drive joining up. As one official put it to us, Whitehall remains more akin to a 'consortium' than 'an integrated joint venture', to the detriment of its effectiveness in tackling the complex problems it faces.

Following the abolition of the PSA system in June 2010, we conducted five follow-up interviews (in July–August 2011) with officials we had previously spoken to while the system was still in operation. These interviews provide a 'flavour' of what changed in Whitehall under the new administration, but further research is needed to test more rigorously the impact on Whitehall of the abolition of the PSA framework.

Why join up government? The civil service view

Our interviews with senior civil servants revealed a widespread view in Whitehall that working across boundaries represented a weakness of the UK government. Over 40 per cent of those we interviewed stated that Whitehall was 'not very' or 'not at all' joined-up, and nearly 60 per cent believed that Whitehall was a long way from where it needed to be in this regard.[3] This recognition within the civil service that failure to work across boundaries is a genuine problem helps to explain why joined-up government (in one guise or another) has been such a recurrent feature of administrative reform programmes in Whitehall.

It has been argued that failure to join up the work of different government departments can create three general types of problem: *redundancy, inconsistency* and *lacunae* (Hood 2005: 27). Our interviewees further confirmed that the UK government suffers from each of these, and that the PSA system was intended to help overcome or minimize such problems.

Redundancy

One 'completely mad' case of redundancy, or duplication, we were told about was the lack of joint case management between agencies in the criminal justice system, which raises costs and slows down processes. The 2009 Operational Efficiency Programme review also identified several billion pounds of savings that government could realize by taking collaborative approaches to procurement, facilities management, and shared back office functions (HM Treasury 2009).

Interviewees in delivery departments spoke too of the multiple lines of accountability between themselves and the centre of government, with competing parts of the Treasury, Cabinet Office and Downing Street imposing their own requirements. One argued that:

> It's not very helpful that we are being monitored by the centre against a set of different frameworks. So we have the Comprehensive Spending Review, and we are answering to the Treasury on a range of targets on that. We have another set with the Cabinet Office for the Capability Review, we have a third set with the PMDU [Prime Minister's Delivery Unit] on the PSA and they are often measuring similar things against different frameworks, so I think that in terms of holding departments to account and getting data systems across government I think there is quite a lot of room for closer coordination.

Inconsistency

Numerous examples of policy inconsistency were cited in interviews. Some can be taken as a sign of healthy debate between departments representing different stakeholder groups and worldviews. However, these tensions are often not resolved, but are instead left to coexist, thereby undermining the efficacy and external credibility of government action. One senior official painted the following picture:

> Lots of different departments are trying to influence organizational behaviour, so GEO [the Government Equalities Office] are saying it's really important you treat your people well, diversity, etc., and now BIS [the Department for Business, Innovation and Skills] are saying it's all about skills. DH [the Department of Health] and DWP [the Department for Work and Pensions] are saying no, it's all about health and well-being, BIS used to say it's all about flexible working, DECC [the Department of Energy and Climate Change] says it's all about climate change, and I could go on and on. So you have got all these different departments which for perfectly understandable reasons are saying, 'no I'm the most important,' but what you end up with is messages just getting lost in the noise. I mean there is no real attempt to coordinate or prioritize messages.

Another notable case was the inconsistency between the Home Office and the Department for Children, Schools and Families (DCSF) over how to tackle youth crime. The Home Office, driven by a target agreed under the previous PSA system, sought to improve the delivery of justice by 'increasing the number of offences for which an offender is brought to justice' (Ministry of Justice 2008). By contrast, DCSF had a target to reduce the number of first-time entrants (aged 10–17) to the criminal justice system as part of their PSA to increase the number of children and young people 'on the path to success'. Consequently, their objective was to deal with low-level offences by children through non-legal means – in direct tension with the Home Office approach.

Lacunae

Lacunae, where issues 'fall into the gaps' between departments, were cited by interviewees as a principal reason for Labour's early focus on multi-faceted problems such as social exclusion. More recently, cross-cutting PSAs (along with their local equivalent, Local Area Agreements) were designed to remedy this issue, by creating a shared focus on outcomes running from the centre to localities. However, ministers and officials still appear to be driven in large part by their own department's particular objectives, leaving Whitehall a long way from the vision of policies shaped around problems rather than institutional boundaries.

For instance, while Labour developed a range of mechanisms for ensuring coherence of policy relating to children, the equivalent machinery for other citizen groups (such as the disabled or the elderly) is far less well-developed. This increases the possibility of poorly-designed services for lower profile (and often vulnerable) groups. The National Audit Office found that a lack of coordination within the tax and benefits system between local authorities, the

Department of Work and Pensions (DWP) and the tax collection agency HMRC led to 1.5 million older people overpaying £250 million in tax, while also increasing the administrative burden falling on those the system is designed to benefit (National Audit Office 2009: 5).

Collective goods also risk being under-produced. In one interview we were told of a minister having to circulate Whitehall 'with a collecting tin' to try to amass sufficient funding from individual departmental contributions for a joint R&D project, of which all were in favour and which would attract matching investment funds from the EU, to the benefit of the country. The problem, it was noted, was the 'classic free rider incentives' that emerge 'where it is very difficult to identify what is the precise value to each of the participants'. Here, policy priorities may 'fall into the gaps' between departments because there is no collective internalisation of a particular policy's costs.

Certain problems or groups may be overlooked where action taken by one department has 'spillover' effects for other parts of government. For example, spending on drug-abuse treatment programmes in the National Health Service (NHS) can generate large savings, but mostly in the form of reduced crime rates, which means that the Department of Health may not have a strong incentive to spend on this activity. This reflects the point made by Mulgan (2005: 177) that 'vertical organisation by its nature skews government efforts away from certain activities, such as prevention – since the benefits of preventive action often come to another department'.

Why did joining up (re-)emerge onto the agenda?

While there may be widespread agreement among civil servants that working across boundaries is necessary, the extent to which Whitehall prioritizes cross-cutting working has varied significantly according to the political composition of the government of the day. Notably, the Labour government formed in 1997 placed great emphasis on tackling cross-cutting challenges, and popularized the phrase 'joined-up government' as emblematic of the new administration's ambition to modernize public services.

The government's stated objective was to overcome Whitehall's traditional malaise of 'departmentalism' (Kavanagh and Richards 2001: 1), as well as the fragmentation associated with the agencification and privatization agenda of the previous Conservative administration. From Labour's perspective, the fragmented nature of the state they inherited combined to 'inhibit the tackling of problems and issues which cross departmental boundaries' (Performance and Innovation Unit 2000: 6). These issues included top priorities of the government, such as social exclusion and neighbourhood breakdown.

Joined-up government was subsequently said to have declined from the status of '*the* big thing' to merely 'a good thing' as the focus of the government's public service agenda shifted to an emphasis on 'delivery' within the large public service silos, as the government sought returns from its large investment in public services such as healthcare and schools (Page 2005: 139). However, towards the end of

Labour's period in office, often under the alternative labels of 'collaboration' or 'partnership-working', cross-cutting working was once again spoken of as 'the new currency' of public service reform, as one interviewee put it.

The perception was that public services had been significantly improved by the sizeable injection of funding after 2001, but that more limited progress had been made in tackling 'wicked' problems: those 'whose causes are so complex, and whose solutions are so multi-factorial, that they require a multi-agency response' (Ling 2002: 622). The return to joining up was reflected in particular by the 2007 set of PSA targets, which – as noted – were for the first time all jointly owned by more than one department, and covered complex issues such as climate change, social exclusion, and public health issues from obesity to substance abuse.

The joint Public Service Agreement framework: did it work?

The 2007 joint PSA system was perhaps the most ambitious attempt of recent years to re-engineer government along more collaborative lines.

As discussed above, most targets in the early iterations of PSAs (starting in 1998) were narrowly focused and confined to a single department, but as the regime developed it took on an ever-broader focus upon cross-departmental outcomes. By 2007 the entire PSA framework was structured around shared targets, defined in terms of broad outcome objectives and measured via a small number of quantitative indicators.

The 2007 framework set out 30 priority goals, each with a lead ministry and a cross-departmental delivery agreement setting out how other departments would contribute (HM Treasury 2006: 150). The new system implied, and to some extent created, a web of connectivity across Whitehall, with key 'hub' departments including DCSF, BIS, the Department for Communities and Local Government (CLG) and the Home Office (which controls the police), due to their participation in a wide range of joint PSAs.

Each PSA was led by a senior responsible owner (SRO) – usually at director general (DG) level, one rung below the head of department – supported by a secretariat and a cross-departmental delivery board which met several times per year.

Progress was assessed by the PMDU, which had been created in 2001 to improve performance in areas of political priority. Its creation was widely regarded as representing a significant strengthening of the institutional power of the Prime Minister (Richards and Smith 2006). PMDU was staffed by around 40 officials and was located at the heart of government (initially in the Cabinet Office, and then in the Treasury). It was empowered to monitor performance by other government departments in meeting PSA targets, and was involved in carrying out analyses about what were the most effective ways of driving progress. Officials from PMDU sat on the delivery board for each of the 30 cross-cutting PSAs in the 2007 set and carried out biannual progress checks for each one, rating performance on a red–amber–green (RAG) scale on the basis of various criteria.

Our interviewees painted a mixed picture of the efficacy of the 2007 PSA regime. The simple fact of setting collectively owned targets with joint boards sitting above them was seen as helpful by almost all of the senior civil servants we interviewed: some 70 per cent considered PSAs to be very or quite effective as a mechanism for improving joint working between departments.[4]

For instance, we were told by different interviewees that the cross-departmental delivery boards had created 'a focal point for what you need to cooperate to do', and 'a pretty strong mechanism for aligning different departments, making sure there is an escalation mechanism if there are problems or if I, as an SRO, am not getting what I need from another department.'

The boards also created social networks that facilitated joint working. As one SRO told us: 'What [the board] does do is give you the contacts so when there is a big issue you can phone up the other DGs'.

The evidence barrier

While there was a general sense that the PSA system had improved the way Whitehall worked across boundaries, a number of factors limited its impact. First, the complex and multi-causal nature of many of the problems addressed meant that departments needed a rigorous shared evidence base to inform collective discussions about priorities for action. As several of our interviews showed, this was often lacking: 'When you are setting up PSAs [you have to think] about data sources and continuity and the robustness of that data. Clearly in many PSAs that had not been done rigorously'.

Many SROs interpreted their role as persuading departments to collate and present evidence about the contribution they were making to the shared goal. Ideally, this would have enabled the SRO to influence other departments' activities and to facilitate debate across departmental boundaries about how to develop a more coherent approach to the problem at hand, but in some cases flaws in the design of indicators and data collection systems meant that no assessment of progress could be made two years after the new system went live. For instance, PSA 16, which addressed social exclusion, had sub-targets relating to homelessness and worklessness among adults with mental health problems but, in the event, progress could not be tracked due to the high proportion of missing or poor quality data, which made it impossible even to establish a baseline measure of exclusion for this group (NHS 2010).

The accountability barrier

SRO influence was also undermined by the lack of hard accountability mechanisms in the system. International evidence suggests that the UK imposes relatively weak sanctions on departments for failing to hit targets. Unlike in several other OECD nations, in the UK a failure to hit performance targets has no impact upon the pay or career prospects of the individuals responsible, or upon departmental budgets (Parker *et al.* 2009: 27).

In the UK, linking bonuses or pay to PSA performance was reportedly considered but ultimately rejected due to the severe difficulties in attributing success or failure to the actions of individual officials, or even to government as a whole, when complex outcomes such as carbon emissions or worklessness among ex-prisoners are the indicators being measured.

Nonetheless, some SROs reported feeling a strong degree of responsibility, but this was not universal. One told us that: 'I feel bits of accountability. It's not very good if you are going to continually get amber–red or red ratings [from PMDU], but actually nothing ever really happens'.

And below the top level, these accountability problems became more acute. In particular, officials in 'contributing' (i.e. non-lead) departments did not necessarily feel a strong stake in shared targets, which made it difficult for the SRO to influence behaviour. One SRO was matter-of-fact about this: 'There are a set of issues to do with day-to-day pressures on people. Their prime line of accountability is to their own ministers and that obviously defines their priorities'.

The finance barrier

The weak accountability framework for cross-cutting issues was closely related to the weak connection between budgets and cross-cutting objectives. As the National Audit Office (2005) noted: 'Shared targets have a limited impact on working arrangements unless supported by structural innovations that allow joint budgeting arrangements'.

In practice, there was no serious attempt to align budgets with cross-departmental PSA targets, which were claimed to represent the government's top policy priorities.

This problem was particularly visible in relation to PSA targets that departments contributed to but did not lead. Thus, for instance, the Department for Work and Pensions led on PSA 17, which sought to 'Tackle poverty and promote greater independence and wellbeing in later life'. In 2009 the department declared that £84 billion of its expenditure had been aligned with this objective in the previous financial year (Department for Work and Pensions 2009). However, the other key contributing departments to this PSA (Health, Communities and Local Government) had no budget lines directly aligned to this target. With few exceptions (such as a ring-fenced pooled budget for conflict prevention overseas, shared between the Ministry of Defence, the Foreign Office and the Department for International Development), this was the pattern across the PSA set.

The weak linkage between policy objectives and budget plans had been highlighted by the House of Commons Treasury Committee at the outset of the PSA regime (2007: 55). The committee argued that: 'Given that a number of departments have agreed Comprehensive Spending Review spending plans without apparently agreeing Public Service Agreement targets at the same time, it is unclear what part Public Service Agreement targets play in spending settlements'.

Without dedicated cross-departmental budgets, SROs and the PSA delivery boards found it difficult to look across the piece at all budgets linked to achievement of the target, and to think strategically about how best to allocate funds. Interviewees told us that:

> It's definitely an issue for us that the money being spent is all within departmental budgets, so the scope for a PSA to go, 'actually we are doing loads here but we could more sensibly spend some of the money over there' is very limited and it's very difficult to get the evidence to actually know whether it's a sensible question to ask.

And:

> I could not make [department X] pay more attention and spend more money on this, [other than] by trying to convince them. But in the end [this] PSA was at the margin of what they wanted to do.

An even stronger statement we heard was that: 'If you split money and governance like that you almost neuter the project before it starts, it proves very difficult to do and you are almost doing it on good will'.

Such factors acted to weaken incentives for cross-departmental collaboration not just of officials but also of ministers, which reinforced civil servants' own propensity to prioritize departmental matters. A regular refrain heard in interviews was that when ministers gave a clear indication that collaboration was a priority, then civil servants followed suit: 'If the ministerial steer is to come to an accommodation then you will make much more effort to do it. So to me that is what lies at the heart of all of this'.

However, the signal that officials frequently received from ministers was that PSAs did not truly represent the top priorities for government, and in particular that PSAs led by other departments were lower priorities. Civil servants often did not believe that they would get the backing they needed, or that their careers would be advanced, by too much of a focus on collaborative activity.

Clearing the blockages? The role of the centre

At the centre of government, reporting directly to the Prime Minister and the Chancellor (Finance Minister), the Prime Minister's Delivery Unit (PMDU) played a central role in helping to overcome the barriers described, though with mixed success.

As noted above, PMDU was dedicated to assessing the performance of all departments in meeting their PSA objectives. PMDU was viewed by several interviewees as playing a positive role in focusing the minds of different departments on shared challenges. It achieved this partly through the monitoring and challenge function it played, and partly through lending additional analytical expertise to inform discussions about prioritization of resources between the departments involved. Quotes from two interviews illustrate this:

PMDU has been pretty effective at highlighting common issues bearing on the delivery of the PSA and highlighting good practice.

And:

They are very good at working with us to spot the problem areas and they are very good at putting their resources in and doing the deep dives when that is what we want to do.

But more critical voices argued that PMDU did little to solve deeper underlying problems. As noted above, despite its regular reporting requirements and its twice yearly assessments of each PSA, PMDU was not as successful in changing the incentives of those involved. As one SRO put it: 'I don't think the process that the PMDU has devised means that I feel directly accountable to anybody'.

Some of our interviewees also suggested that PMDU had not done enough to tailor its processes to meet the very different types of challenge to be found across the PSA set. The centre's monitoring and reporting requirements were often said to suit output-focused targets where progress was easy to measure and the policy levers were clearly visible – such as exam results and waiting lists – more than complex and long-term outcome objectives where success depends upon changing the behaviour of individuals and companies. As two interviewees put it:

I sometimes wonder whether their [PMDU's] approach is sufficiently subtle for quite tricky policy areas.

And:

All the PSAs are assessed for VFM [value for money] and they have got a template of evidence that is required for VFM. It fits beautifully for a health model: outputs and costs. It does not work for an 'influencing' [PSA].

The influence of PMDU was also closely connected to the interest in the PSA system taken by the central political leadership of government – especially the Prime Minister and Chancellor. By the time we conducted our research (two years after the joint PSA system was launched), economic problems, a tighter fiscal context and shorter-term electoral concerns had made it much tougher to focus on long-term goals: 'If you went to the prime minister today and said "tell me the 30 most important things facing the UK in government today" they [the PSAs] would not be the 30 things on that list'.

While it is natural for the government to change course in response to events, one could argue that the PSAs were too easily knocked off the top of the agenda. This reflects a general difficulty in embedding long-term strategic priorities within the Whitehall system deeply enough that they are not forgotten about as shorter term political challenges emerge.

The overall conclusions we drew from our analysis of the cross-cutting PSA system are as follows.

- Relationships are vital to cross-cutting working. Formal mechanisms such as joint boards can help establish and maintain these relationships, but collaboration can occur without formal structures.
- Setting targets for cross-cutting priorities can help to hone the focus of departments, but without clear accountability for these priorities and a supporting financial management system, it is difficult to embed collaboration as a standard mode of operation.
- Having a strong centre to monitor and challenge functional departments can help to encourage collaboration, but different approaches to target-setting and performance monitoring may be needed for different types of cross-cutting challenge.
- Without ongoing political support from senior levels, departments are unlikely to maintain their focus on difficult cross-cutting issues over the long term.

A retreat to departmentalism since 2010?

The point that Whitehall only prioritizes joining up when this is an explicit priority of senior ministers has been underlined since the May 2010 election, which led to the formation of a new Conservative–Liberal Democrat Coalition government. In its first few months the new administration made a number of radical changes to the way Whitehall operates. The PSAs and the supporting infrastructure developed under the Labour government to support cross Whitehall collaboration were all scrapped. In place of PSAs, Departmental Business Plans were unveiled as the key performance management framework for government departments.

The Implementation Unit in Downing Street was established as the core body at the centre of government with responsibility for overseeing the new framework and tracking and publishing updates on a range of indicators set out in the departmental business plans (Rutter and Atkinson 2011: 16). The Business Plan framework did not replicate the focus on shared targets and cross-departmental accountability embodied in the 2007 round of PSAs. There is also far less focus on outcomes: instead the plans are filled with process targets and milestones specifying the dates by which actions – such as the publication of legislation or the completion of a policy review – should be completed, in line with policy commitments in the Coalition's Programme for Government (see Stephen *et al.* 2011: 8).

There are a number of reasons why the objective to join up government was seen as less pressing than under the previous Labour government. One is the financial climate. The top priority of the coalition government formed in 2010 is to eliminate the structural deficit, requiring at least £81 billion in spending cuts by 2015, the biggest retrenchment in the size of the state in a generation (HM

Treasury 2010: 16). Departments have consequentially turned to their 'core business' and are focusing on how to achieve fiscal consolidation, both by taking money out of the central civil service in Whitehall and by making wider cuts to government expenditure.[5] This focus on consolidation has meant that cross-cutting problems have received less government attention since 2010.

A further explanation is that even to the extent that the Coalition does focus on complex cross-cutting problems, it differs on the best way to tackle them. Whilst in opposition, the Conservative Party (now the larger and dominant coalition partner) emphasized the importance of 'broken society' issues such as drug addiction, family and neighbourhood breakdown.[6] But the Conservatives (and to a lesser extent their Liberal Democrat partners) have long held deep suspicions of centralized, bureaucratic mechanisms to join up government. The abolition of the PSA system and associated local targets, after taking power, is a reflection of this different normative perspective on how government should operate.

The Coalition government instead expressed an ambition to 'shift power' from Whitehall in favour of giving 'new powers to local communities, neighbourhoods and individuals' to join up services at the level where policies are actually implemented (Cabinet Office 2010: 11). In some cases power would reside at the individual level. Here, quasi-market methods would allow service users to 'buy' packages of services that join up around their needs, funded by government through 'individual budgets' that the user themselves decides how to allocate.

Local government would also be freed from central controls and empowered to determine its own priorities. It is debatable how far the government has lived up to its early localist rhetoric (and this is not a subject for this chapter), but it has at least swept away much of the complex web of targets, assessments and data-reporting requirements to which local government was previously subject.

As well as a presumption in favour of local rather than central, the new government was also initially sceptical about the need for centralization *within* Whitehall, preferring to increase the autonomy of departments to manage their own policy domains, though subject to strict central controls as far as spending totals are concerned. Consequently, the Coalition government slimmed down the size of the centre, cutting the number of political advisers and scrapping not only PMDU but also the Prime Minister's Strategy Unit.

The abolition of the formal joining up machinery in 2010 provided us with an opportunity to reflect on whether collaboration is possible without formal cross-cutting governance mechanisms and to test some of the conclusions we reached in 2009. Based on interviews conducted in summer 2011, it is possible to draw a few provisional conclusions.

First, despite less direct pressure from the centre to join up policies, a culture of cross-cutting working may have survived in some departments and around certain policy challenges. In the absence of more formal mechanisms to join up, in some cases informal 'working groups' were created, bringing together civil servants from across government. In the Department for Education, for instance, we were told that the 'deep dive' culture created by the PMDU (where departments try and identify the impact that a range of departments have upon a policy problem) still existed to some extent. However, our interviewees emphasized that there was no guarantee that collaboration would continue given its dependence upon informal relationships and networks, which high turnover in the civil service since 2010 is likely to have subsequently eroded.

Second, interviewees raised concerns that central government had lost some of its strategic capacity and its capacity to hold departments to account for performance. They suggested that the centre was not as equipped to add value in the policy-making process by spotting gaps, areas of common purpose and 'joining the dots' where necessary. Indeed, after coming to power, the government soon (partially) reversed its adherence to departmental autonomy. Following a series of early policy setbacks and political embarrassments (around plans to reform the health service, and to sell off national forests, for instance), the central machinery was beefed up once more, with a stronger Policy Unit tasked with monitoring departmental performance more closely (Rutter and Atkinson 2011). However, it is not apparent that this unit, or the centre of government more generally, is focused on building collaborative networks across Whitehall. Instead, the priority remains the implementation of spending reductions, albeit with a closer eye being kept by the centre on the policy implications of these cuts.

Third, despite the government's claims to the contrary, it is also clear that the urge to set targets, including on cross-cutting matters, has not entirely gone away. For instance, following the urban riots across England in August 2011, the Prime Minister announced a determination to 'turn around' the lives of 120,000 'troubled families' (Cameron 2011), though without specifying how this would be measured or whether any new processes might be needed to join up Whitehall in order to meet this complex objective.

Conclusions

In this chapter we have argued that the creation of formal cross-cutting structures with clear reporting requirements to the centre of government can create a degree of meaningful joint working, but that where incentive structures and budgets remain in departmental silos the effects will be weak. Competing departmental priorities and cultures also reduce the impact of whole-of-government approaches. These findings shed light on the central questions of what governments can do to improve their capacity to work across boundaries, and what barriers they are likely to face in so doing.

The longstanding nature of these barriers to collaboration serve to remind us that joining up government is not a one-off problem that clever structural reform can solve in a permanent sense. Rather, joining up is an ongoing task that must adapt to the changing nature of policy priorities and external challenges.

We have also discussed why governments attempt to improve collaboration. An organization of the size and complexity of the UK central government is likely always to retain aspects of the 'fragmentary character' that has characterized it for at least 150 years, and so reformers will always seek to mitigate the inefficiencies and frustrations caused by the division of government into functional departments (wherever the boundaries are drawn).

But, as we have discussed, the extent to which working across departmental boundaries is a central objective of government action can shift dramatically in line with the priorities and prejudices of the government of the day. Under the present government Whitehall appears to have retreated from cross-cutting approaches, but history suggests that joining up will return to political favour. When that moment arrives, ministers and officials (as well as international observers) may well wish to revisit the innovations described in this paper as a source of useful learning.

Notes

1 This paper draws heavily on a chapter written by Simon Parker, Akash Paun, Jonathan McClory and Kate Blatchford (2009), *Shaping Up: A Whitehall for the future* (London: Institute for Government). At: www.instituteforgovernment.org.uk/publications/shaping. We are grateful to our co-authors on this report, as well as to our other colleagues David Halpern, Michael Hallsworth and Jill Rutter, for their comments and input.
2 Past examples of attempts to join up Whitehall include the 'ministerial overlords' appointed in the 1950s, the 'super-departments' created in the 1960s and 1970s, and the creation of numerous central coordination units over the years, including the Joint Policy Review Staff (1971), the Efficiency Unit (1979), and the Social Exclusion Unit (1997). A timeline of joining up initiatives is provided in Parker *et al.* (2009: 75).
3 These findings are from a mini-survey conducted as part of our interviews with the senior responsible owners of joint PSA targets (N = 17).
4 These findings are from a mini-survey conducted as part of our interviews with the senior responsible owners of joint PSA targets (N = 17).
5 A similar point is made by Peters (1998: 39–40).
6 See, for instance, Centre for Social Justice (2006), 'Breakdown Britain: Interim report on the state of the nation'. At: www.centreforsocialjustice.org.uk/UserStorage/pdf/Pdf%20Exec%20summaries/Breakdown%20Britain.pdf.

References

Cabinet Office (2010) *The Coalition: Our Programme for Government*, London: Stationery Office.

Cameron, D. (2011) *PM's Speech on the Fightback after the Riots*. Online. Available at: www.number10.gov.uk/news/pms-speech-on-the-fightback-after-the-riots/ (accessed 20 September 2011).

Centre for Social Justice (2006) *Breakdown Britain: Interim Report on the State of the Nation*, London: Centre for Social Justice. Online. Available at: www.centreforsocialjustice.org.uk/client/downloads/CSJ%20FINAL%20(2).pdf (accessed 6 September 2011).

Department for Work and Pensions (2009) *Resource Accounts 2008–09* London: Stationery Office.

Gash, T., Hallsworth, M., Ismail, S. and Paun, A. (2008) *Performance Art: Enabling Better Management of Public Services*, London: Institute for Government.

Gay, O. (2005) *Public Service Agreements*, Standard Note: SN/PC/3826, London: House of Commons Library.

HM Treasury (1998) *Public Services for the Future: Modernisation, Reform, Accountability: Comprehensive Spending Review: Public Service Agreements 1999–2002*, Cm 4181, London: Her Majesty's Stationery Office. Online. Available at: http://archive.treasury.gov.uk/pub/html/psa/csrpsa.pdf (accessed 22 January 2013).

HM Treasury (2006) *Pre-Budget Report: Investing in Britain's Potential: Building our Long-Term Future*, CM 6984, London: HM Treasury. Online. Available at: http://webarchive.nationalarchives.gov.uk/+/www.hm-treasury.gov.uk/media/4/3/pbr06_completereport_1439.pdf (accessed 20 September 2011).

HM Treasury (2009) *Operational Efficiency Programme: Final Report*, London: HM Treasury. Online. Available at: www.bis.gov.uk/assets/biscore/shex/files/oep_final_report_210409_pu728.pdf (accessed 20 September 2011).

HM Treasury (2010) *Spending Review 2010*, Cm 7942, London: Stationery Office. Online. Available at: http://cdn.hm-treasury.gov.uk/sr2010_completereport.pdf (accessed 20 September 2011).

Hood, C. (2005) 'The idea of joined-up government: a historical perspective', in V. Bogdanor, (ed.) *Joined-Up Government*, Oxford: Oxford University Press for the British Academy.

House of Commons Treasury Committee (2007), *The 2007 Comprehensive Spending Review: Prospects and Processes*, HC 279, London: Stationary Office. Online. Available at: www.parliament.the-stationery-office.co.uk/pa/cm200607/cmselect/cmtreasy/279/279.pdf (accessed 6 September 2011).

Kavanagh, D. and Richards, D. (2001) 'Departmentalism and joined-up government: back to the future', *Parliamentary Affairs*, 54(1): 1–18.

Lilley, P. (2008) 'Paying for success: the international experience of contracting out', in P. Lilley and O. Hartwich (eds) *Paying for Success: How to Make Contracting out Work in Employment Services*, London: Policy Exchange.

Ling, T. (2002) 'Delivering joined-up government in the UK: dimensions, issues and problems', *Public Administration*, 80(4): 615–642.

Ministry of Justice (2008) *Ministry of Justice Departmental Report 2007/08: The Government's Expenditure Plans for 2005–08*, CM 7397, Norwich: Stationary Office, Online. Available at: www.justice.gov.uk/publications/docs/annual-report-2008.pdf (accessed 20 September 2011).

Ministry of Reconstruction (1918) *Report of the Machinery of Government Committee*, Cmd 9230, London: HMSO.

Mulgan, G. (2005) 'Joined-up government: past, present and future', in V. Bogdanor, (ed.) *Joined-Up Government*, Oxford: Oxford University Press for the British Academy.

National Audit Office (2005) *Joint Targets*, HC 453, London: Stationery Office.

National Audit Office (2009) *Dealing With the Tax Obligations of Older People*, HC961, London: Stationery Office.

NHS Information Centre for Health and Social Care (2010) *Mental Health Elements of PSA 16 CPA Reviews*. Online. Available at: www.ic.nhs.uk/services/omnibus-survey/using-the-service/data-collections/mental-health-elements-of-psa16-cpa-reviews-disabled (accessed 7 September 2011).

Northcote, S.H. and Trevelyan, C.E. (1854) *Report on the Organisation of the Permanent Civil Service*. London: House of Commons. Online. Avaliable at: www.civilservant.org.uk/northcotetrevelyan.pdf (accessed 7 September 2011).

Page, E. (2005) 'Joined-up government and the civil service', in V. Bogdanor, (ed.) *Joined-Up Government*, Oxford: Oxford University Press for the British Academy.

Parker, S., Paun, A., and McClory, J. (2009) *The State of the Service: A Review of White-hall's Performance and Prospects for Improvement*, London: Institute for Government.
Performance and Innovation Unit (2000) *Wiring it Up: Whitehall's Management of Cross-Cutting Policies and Services*, London: Cabinet Office.
Peters, B.G. (1998) *Managing Horizontal Government: The Politics of Coordination*, Ottawa: Canadian Centre for Management Development.
Richards, D. and Smith, M. (2006) 'Central control and policy implementation in the UK: a case study of the Prime Minister's Delivery Unit', *Journal of Comparative Policy Analysis: Research and Practice*, 8(4): 325–345.
Rutter, J. and Atkinson, D. (2011) 'Number 10 and the Centre', in *One Year On: The First Year of Coalition Government, a Collection of Views*, London: Institute for Government.
Stephen, J., Martin, R. and Atkinson, D. (2011) *See-Through Whitehall: Departmental Business Plans One Year On*, London: Institute for Government.

9   The collaboration solution?

Factors for collaborative success

Brian W. Head

Over the last generation there has been a shift in theory and practice towards recognizing that collaboration across boundaries is important for tackling complex problems of government policy making and service delivery (Mandell 2001; Edwards 2001; Goldsmith and Eggers 2004). The traditional top-down models of public administration have been modified by more flexible models of partnering, contracting and incentives, often with a greater focus on 'horizontal' models of decentralized coordination. Much of the literature on collaboration of the 1980s and 1990s was concerned with marshalling arguments stating why collaborative approaches could be desirable and useful for reducing tensions and solving problems (Gray 1985, 1989; Gray and Wood 1991; Kanter 1994). The assumption that collaborative methods could resolve a wide range of previously intractable problems led to a normative bias in favour of collaboration, without the support of an empirical scholarship examining the costs and benefits under a wide range of specific conditions. However, recent research has made a more careful examination of the balance of costs and opportunities arising from working across boundaries (Gray *et al.* 2003; Goldsmith and Eggers 2004; Kamensky and Burlin 2004; O'Flynn and Wanna 2008).

This chapter considers solutions to cross-boundary dilemmas by re-examining the process factors associated with outcome success. In other words, the chapter assesses the factors that influence collaborative success, taking into account the importance of both process factors (e.g. key actors, governance, resources, capacities) and outcome factors (e.g. measurable service improvements, political legitimacy). The wide interest in collaborative approaches arises from the common observation that the combined efforts of multiple organizations addressing an agreed problem can achieve better outcomes than would be possible if they worked in isolation or if they tackled the problem from conflicting positions. Moreover, collaboration might achieve more than other governance approaches, such as traditional bureaucratic regulations and directives. Specifically, it is often suggested (see, for example, Head 2006) that collaboration across boundaries can:

- help to define important complex problems that have eluded past attempts;
- focus energy on the top priorities and set agendas;

- create momentum by bringing together all stakeholders;
- draw on wide expertise and diverse sources of knowledge;
- value the practical experience of those working in the field;
- learn from and further refine effective practice models;
- mobilize potential champions, sponsors, donors and funders;
- help with information-sharing and mentoring.

As noted earlier in this volume, it is generally accepted that there are at least four modes or levels of working together – networking, cooperating, coordinating, and collaborating. None of these is intrinsically superior; the key point is that each may be better suited for specific tasks and challenges. According to Himmelman, a strategy can be 'appropriate for particular circumstances', depending on, first, the extent to which 'three limitations to working together – time, trust and turf – can be overcome', and, second, the extent to which agreement can be achieved about 'a common vision, commitments to share power, and responsible and accountable actions' (Himmelman 1996: 27).

However, the literature on public policy and service partnerships lacks a clear, coherent framework for designing appropriate collaborative arrangements or for assessing network effectiveness (Bingham and O'Leary 2006: 161). For this reason, conceptual arguments about the potential benefits of collaboration often lack supporting evidence. In an era when greater use is being made of collaborative approaches, it is important for the quality of public governance that a sound base is developed for the design and management of collaborative arrangements where they are warranted. Fundamental issues include determining what kinds of cross-boundary networks are effective, for what purpose, and under what conditions. This evidence-based understanding is required in order to demonstrate value in the eyes of decision makers, network participants and the general public (Head 2010). Collaborative approaches need to demonstrate their practical efficacy as well as their normative values and principles (Lasker *et al.* 2001). Within the community sector, and in some government agencies, there is an increasing preference for collaboration over hierarchy in tackling messy or 'wicked' problems. Indeed, in recent years it has become more common for government agencies, foundations and other funding bodies to specify a particular form of collaboration as a condition for providing program funds (Milbourne 2009), but often with minimal evidence that such mechanisms are the most effective for achieving outcomes (Bryson *et al.* 2006: 45). The potential confusion of means (collaboration) and ends (solving problems) has become the subject of a new wave of empirical scholarship examining the conditions under which working across boundaries is warranted and useful.

Scope of recent research

The study of effectiveness needs to build upon a wide range of prior research and professional experience, in a field where we cannot rely on being able to design and evaluate future field experiments. There has already been substantial research on three themes concerning successful working across organizational boundaries. The first is the practical guidance literature, centred on the organizational steps required to establish, maintain and develop partnerships and networked arrangements over time. This management and community development literature generally contains checklists of key elements for each stage in the development of the shared arrangements, drawing attention to essential factors such as clarity in goal setting, jointly agreed decision rules, regular communication, respect for participants, conflict resolution mechanisms, progress reporting, celebration of milestones, and so forth. Recent contributions also include advice on using electronic communications and web-based software to enhance interaction. This literature is based on organizational network experience and is often written by consultants and facilitators (e.g. Himmelman 1996, 2001; Austin 2000; Linden 2002; VicHealth 2003; Coleman 2009; Wolff 2010).

A second, more analytical, theme has focused on classifying and mapping the variety of collaborative types. This is important because every collaboration has typically been built to 'fit' a specific local configuration of relevant actors, challenges and institutional contexts. Each example thus has unique characteristics, as well as features it may share with other collaborations. Hence, the analytical challenge is to identify a coherent set of key dimensions for comparing differences and similarities (Provan and Milward 2001; Keast *et al.* 2004; Maguire 2006; Provan and Kenis 2008; Head 2008a). Patterns of interaction across organizations and stakeholder groups vary widely. Cooperative networked arrangements sometimes develop in a 'bottom up' manner, without direct government involvement, with participants gradually agreeing to work together on certain issues over time. Some collaborations may consist entirely of non-government organizations, seeking to achieve business or community outcomes (Ebers 1997; Huxham and Vangen 2005). The business sector, driven by the profit motive, is generally hardnosed about whether joint ventures and business partnerships are likely to be commercially profitable. By contrast, 'social innovation' ventures, anchored in the not-for-profit sector, focus on client outcomes and work across the boundaries of the community, philanthropy, research, and business sectors (Mawson 2008). However, the majority of policy-relevant collaborations are substantially shaped and resourced by *government*. In particular, public agencies frequently initiate networks and multi-stakeholder projects around important areas of policy or service delivery, usually centred on managing specific projects or tasks, but occasionally addressing longer-term intractable or 'wicked' issues (Head 2008b).

A third important body of research has focused on describing and explaining the circumstances in which collaborations have actually emerged in the social, economic and environmental spheres. Major themes arise concerning how actors have been drawn into – or, sometimes, pushed into – collaboration when other methods have been exhausted. When issues are conflictual and problem-solving capacity has collapsed, collaborative processes might be attempted as an alternative to protracted litigation or regulatory gridlock. In other cases, collaboration is not a choice of last resort, but a preferred approach for groups with overlapping interests who perceive advantages in working together in a complementary manner in order to achieve mutual benefits (e.g. Mandell 2001; Sabatier *et al.* 2005; Huxham and Vangen 2005; Maguire 2006; Agranoff 2007). Over time, proven results may result in further consolidation of arrangements, embedding the long-term value of working across boundaries. In the latter case, the structures and processes within a long-term collaboration need to remain open to adjustment and renegotiation in response to changing needs and challenges.

There is disagreement among analysts about which elements are decisive in explaining collaborative success or failure, as discussed in Chapter 2 of this volume. For some, the circumstances of network formation are crucial – and positively so when there is a perceived interdependence of interests and a shared perception that the issues are important (high stakes). For other analysts, the actual design of the structures and processes may be decisive for the future successful evolution of the collaboration (Sullivan and Skelcher 2002; Goldsmith and Eggers 2004; Maguire 2006). Hennart (2006) boldly suggests that structures explain most of the variation underpinning the success or failure of alliances. On the other hand, some analysts place great weight on the human dynamics of network communication and leadership within and across sectors. For example, regularity of contact and good communication channels strengthen partnerships and enhance capacity for problem-solving (Agranoff 2006; Bingham and O'Leary 2006; Thomson and Perry 2006). Many commentators emphasize the significance of *trust* as a feature of successful partnerships (e.g. Mandell 2001; Sabatier *et al.* 2005), but it is an emergent feature that is built through respect and good processes rather than a pre-existing condition of network formation. The literature on conflict resolution and mediation also has useful lessons about how collaboration affects the negotiation of relevant knowledge and interests (Bingham and O'Leary 2006).

Bryson and colleagues (2006) surveyed the research literature and identified a series of 22 empirical propositions which have emerged to date. These are grouped around four dimensions: initial conditions, process components, contingencies and constraints, and outcomes. First, in relation to the initial conditions that might give rise to cross-sector collaborative responses, it is argued that collaborations are more likely to form in 'turbulent' contexts in competitive and institutional environments. Public policy makers are more likely to encourage such responses when the 'separate efforts' of the various actors are believed to be unlikely to 'fix the problem'. Collaborations are better grounded if there are pre-existing networks, shared views about the problems, and strong sponsors of joint action.

Second, with regard to process components, the nature of the initial agreement and its strategic purpose is seen as critical for subsequent working across boundaries. This foundation affects the perceived legitimacy of the collaboration as a vehicle for joint efforts and the willingness of champions to provide various types of supportive leadership. Working to enhance cross-group understanding, include key stakeholders in negotiations, and utilize their documentation, builds collaborative strength. Collaborations incorporate conflicting viewpoints, so it is important to equalize influence and manage conflict effectively (Bryson *et al.* 2006).

Third, with regard to contingencies and constraints, the research literature suggests that system-level planning activities are likely to involve more negotiation than administrative-level partnerships and service-delivery partnerships. Different institutional logics among the partners may hinder agreement on key elements of process, structure, governance, and desired outcomes, and collaborations work better if they employ strategies for addressing 'power imbalances and shocks'.

Fourth, with regard to the achievement of outcomes, the research literature suggests that achieving results will always be difficult. It is important to promote resilience, engage in regular reviews, and aim to pursue a range of direct and indirect benefits for stakeholders and clients. They are more successful if they can utilize each sector's strengths while compensating for any weaknesses. They are more likely to produce outcomes if they are rigorous in establishing and using a results management system that monitors information, tracks inputs and processes, and builds accountability for outcomes in close association with key political and professional groups (Bryson *et al.* 2006).

Evaluating effectiveness

Having better understood the variety of participants, purposes, forms and vulnerabilities in different types of collaborations, it becomes more realistic to assess their strengths, weaknesses and overall effectiveness. Collaborative processes are certainly different from conventional organizational processes based on authority, power and precedent. The unresolved question is whether they produce different and better outcomes:

> Collaboration is not a panacea; it is a choice that policy makers and public managers should make based on evidence about expected outcomes. As we enter the era of the collaborative state, we must buttress the enthusiasm for collaboration with a better understanding of its [social, economic and] environmental impacts.
>
> (Koontz and Thomas 2006: 111)

Collaborations entail costs in time and resources, which fall unevenly on the participants. Given the investments of skills, time, funding, and relational capital that are required by networks and partnerships, there are clearly substantial transaction costs and opportunity costs in managing networks over a period of time. Even where there are good results, there are typically a host of complaints, e.g. relating to 'the level of resources that need to be invested' for collaborative endeavours, the 'slow progress towards goals', and, in some cases, the 'lack of inclusiveness' in membership and 'domination by some partners' (Sullivan and Skelcher 2002: 7). Government agencies are sometimes the dominant members of multi-party collaborations, seeking to shape priorities and directions. They supply legitimacy and resources for collective activities. When there is a dominant actor – whether from the private or public sector – there is a risk that the collaboration will be shaped by the institutional logic of the dominant member, and will therefore be less likely to achieve the mutual benefits that underpin long-term commitment to collective action. The opposite problem – a large number of stakeholders with no shared focus on how to achieve strategic outcomes – is also unsatisfactory because any decisions may be 'lowest-common-denominator' and subject to a multitude of vetoes.

Proponents claim that the costs and risks of collaboration are worthwhile because collaborative approaches to complex issues can achieve better and more enduring outcomes than could the more traditional regulatory approaches or the new market-based (contracts and incentives) approaches. It has been argued that complex or 'wicked' problems are best tackled through dialogue and collaboration rather than through regulation and markets (Innes and Booher 2003). Collaborative approaches often emerge as a response to difficult or contested issues that do not have clear technical solutions and may therefore require an approach involving inter-organizational and cross-sectoral collaboration. Wicked problems usually involve myriad uncertainties. Koppenjan and Klijn (2004) have grouped such uncertainties into three major categories. The first, substantive uncertainty, refers to the technical uncertainty surrounding the very nature of policy problems. Disagreements over the knowledge base, including both science and belief systems, can mean that the parties involved do not reach a consensus regarding the nature of the problem. The second, strategic uncertainty, arises from the reality of different parties involved in a policy network having different interests and incentives. Managing the resulting complexities of interaction is important to achieving successful outcomes. Finally, institutional uncertainty is characteristic of network membership because stakeholders come from institutional environments with different modes of interaction, levels of trust, and communication with one other (Koppenjan and Klijn 2004). Gray (2004) has argued that the key success factor is to build through dialogue a common frame of reference among the different parties in the collaboration; without this shared sense of purpose the enterprise is likely to fail.

Considering these multiple layers of interests and uncertainties, the task of assessing network effectiveness is also very complex, much more so than the task of evaluating the performance of a single organization. Measuring organizational effectiveness has usually focused on satisfying key stakeholders, primarily the organization's clients. Public sector organizations tend to have several groups of 'clients' to satisfy, both internal and external, including 'whole-of-government' considerations. The effectiveness of networks led by public organizations is likely to entail financial performance, stakeholder satisfaction, and organizational capacity issues. The involvement of multiple organizations, and hence multiple constituencies, adds to the complexities of establishing the key measures of effectiveness (Saxton 1997; Provan and Milward 2001). The difficulty increases where tough social problems are believed to require collaborative efforts spanning different sectors (for example, involving partnerships between government, business, non-profit organizations, and so on). In concluding their review of the literature on the design and implementation of cross-sectoral collaborations, Bryson and colleagues conclude that:

Cross-sector collaborations are difficult to create and even more difficult to sustain because so much must be in place and work well for them to succeed. The challenge of designing and implementing effective cross-sector collaboration is daunting ... the normal expectation ought to be that success will be very difficult to achieve in cross-sector collaborations.

(Bryson *et al.* 2006: 52)

The evidence base for assessing all of these claims and counter-claims is still rapidly evolving and is not systematized. Skelcher and Sullivan draw attention to the interplay of structure and agency that enables and limits the activities undertaken:

what people are able to do is sometimes channelled and other times obstructed by prevailing ideas about what can and cannot be said, what is 'good' and 'bad' practice, and the norms that determine the logics of appropriateness within which actions are judged. Understanding the possibilities and limitations of the structure–agency duality offers the basis for developing a more refined understanding of the performance of collaborative ventures, for instance by locating the possibilities for leadership in their structural context.

(Skelcher and Sullivan 2008: 768)

Foster-Fishman and colleagues (2001) place less emphasis on the governmental context and greater focus on local leadership and collaborative capacity building in human services coalitions. They claim that by enhancing community-member competencies, building new relationships, strengthening intra-coalition operations, and promoting the design and implementation of effective community-based programs, 'coalitions can develop the collaborative capacity needed to succeed'. Because the contexts are constantly changing, collaborative capacities need to be continually assessed and developed, 'empowering communities to respond to new challenges by developing new competencies, new relationships and new solutions' (Foster-Fishman *et al.* 2001: 257). These dynamic and interactive perspectives underline the difficulties of establishing a simple framework for evaluating the effectiveness of working across boundaries; however, the multi-dimensional nature of the challenge must be grasped.

Evaluation frameworks: effective for whom?

The selection of a framework for evaluation depends on whether the purpose of the assessment is to provide opportunities for improvement (a learning frame) or to provide judgements on efficiency (an audit-review frame) (Edelenbos and Van Buuren 2005; Head 2008a). A concern with identifying enabling factors, such as stakeholder values, organizational alignment and process quality, will be more significant in the first approach, whereas the cost/benefit focus of the second approach leads to a concern with metrics to measure 'value for money' in agreed activities to achieve agreed results.

Sullivan and Skelcher (2002) have identified three main approaches to evaluation that have been adopted in recent decades. First, the value for money approach emerged in the 1980s, emphasizing efficiency and cost control, with attention to the efficient application of resource inputs to produce service outputs. This tended to be top-down expert analysis, with limited concern for stakeholder perceptions about quality and appropriateness. Second, the outcome-focused approach in the 1990s concentrated on improved service outcomes for clients, allowed more flexibility in how outcomes were achieved, and allowed for longer time-frames. However, it was difficult to demonstrate tight links between interventions and outcomes. Third, evaluation scholars have recently turned more attention to understanding the effective processes underlying the achievement of desired benefits. This requires a better understanding of contexts and the recognition that processes such as collaboration and service integration always occur in a variety of different and changing local and institutional contexts. Interventions are seen to take place under specific conditions, which may be difficult to replicate (Sullivan and Skelcher 2002: 188–194)

Evaluation from the perspective of a funding agency (measurable results, value for money) and from the perspective of various non-government players (benefits for local interests, greater voice in planning, reshaping service options) may be rather different. Thus, the perceived merits and achievements of collaborations reflect stakeholder positions, including their relative power (Head 2008a). The second complication for evaluation is that interdependent and multi-faceted issues involve complex causal pathways that are very difficult to document with precision. That is why the quantitative experimental designs that may be suited to simple interventions (e.g. changing the tax rate) do not work with broad social programs (e.g. urban regeneration) with multiple objectives and diverse target groups. Third, taking a longer-term viewpoint, one consideration may be whether the collaborative processes are capable of being sustained, based on shared goals and achievement of useful results.

A contested local example

A collaborative project had been established in 2000 in response to a series of major issues in a disadvantaged community (Goodna, near Brisbane, the capital of the state of Queensland, Australia). Known as the Service Integration Project (SIP), the collaboration was centred on improving the capacity of local decision makers, program managers and service providers in that disadvantaged locality to work better together in the interests of the local population. The project received Queensland state government funding for three years, and 'in kind' support from other governmental and community organizations. The final report describes the project as a complex, whole-of-government project designed to test and demonstrate how the community can work with government and non-government agencies to improve sustainable community well-being, by aligning, and integrating as appropriate, the services provided by agencies with the needs and aspirations of the community and with the Queensland government priority outcomes (Woolcock and Boorman 2003). Given the nature of this task, the Project involved a diverse range of activities and engaged a wide range of stake-holders. A (somewhat unrealistic) state government requirement was that the Project learnings would be able to be transitioned into sustainable practices in Goodna and other regions of the state by the end of the three-year funding period (Woolcock and Boorman 2003: 2). The membership of the collaborative network comprised state government officials from several agencies, local authority officials, NGO service providers, and researchers. The agreed complex 'problem' was identified as overcoming fragmentation and dysfunctional behaviour by decision makers and service organizations, in order to better respond to the service needs of the locality. In order to pursue this broad direction, a range of activities and pilot projects were implemented, mainly focusing on better information, consultation with diverse stakeholders, coordination issues, and capacity building by the professionals themselves. This was seen as the platform for then tackling service provision in a more cohesive and productive way. An experiential learning frame was developed for the multi-organization network, involving relationship building through intensive face-to-face interactions. This was accelerated when the Project established a graduate certificate course in 'inter-professional leadership', attended by three cohorts of network members, from 2000 to 2003. Attention was also given to improving the database for understanding changing socio-economic trends and service patterns in the locality and its surrounding region (Woolcock and Boorman 2003).

Judgements about the success of the Project were extremely varied. The Project failed to attract a further period of funding because, from a central finance perspective, there were few 'tangible' products or outcomes emerging from the three-year Project, and no other funders emerged. On the other hand, some impressive 'intangibles' were identified by participants, including a stronger sense of interdependence and the capacity for joint action among the members. The latter reportedly saw these as enduring and transferable capacities and processes. While the key funder/stakeholder was the state government, over this period a broad group of leaders across various levels of government and NGO organizations developed a shared leadership style. The core Project group disappeared and the coordination mandate was transferred back to the state regional managers' forum (from where the concept had essentially originated, some years earlier). Project champions continued to adopt the optimistic perspective that the SIP collaboration had made a real difference, at least for a few years, and that the new skills and outlook of senior personnel had become embedded in management behaviour within that region. A tougher view would be that the experiment could not have made a substantial impact in only three years, given the severity of the underlying problems, and that the governance arrangements were vulnerable to veto or withdrawal by the dominant player. The lesson for other collaborative place–management approaches seems to be that complementary processes are necessary to ensure: (a) ongoing support for the local champions who provide network-based coordination, energy and capacity building; and (b) ongoing political support at a high level (reflected in resource allocation and prioritization).

Collaboration patterns in human services

Human services are concerned with helping individuals and families in specific communities to access effective services to meet their needs for social care, education and health care. Some services are generic and widely available, while others are targeted towards particular aspects of social disadvantage and risk. Provan and Milward (2001: 416) identify three levels of analysis for evaluating the network collaborations that underlie much of human services planning and delivery: the community, the network, and the organizational participants. At the broadest level (community), networks can be considered as service delivery vehicles and can be evaluated in terms of the contribution they make to that local area. This can include the assessment of aggregate outcomes for the network's clients and their perceptions of service provision, the overall cost of service provision, and the creation of social capital. At the network level, effectiveness must take into account the durability and long-term viability/sustainability of the network as an organization. This includes its ability to operate with efficient coordination and low transaction costs, its ability to attract and sustain membership, and its range of valued services. Finally, evaluation of effectiveness at the organization/participant level should consider how well the network serves the interests of its individual members (Provan and Milward 2001: 416–419).

Agranoff (2003) offers a useful distinction between the various types and levels of collaboration. *Informational* networks involve a range of stakeholders coming together to exchange information and explore solutions to a problem. *Developmental* networks involve both information exchange and education, which improves the organizations' ability to apply solutions. *Outreach* networks exchange information and improve the administrative capacity of members, but also develop 'programming strategies for clients (for example, funding packages, usable technologies) that are carried out elsewhere, usually by the partner organizations' (2003: 11). Finally, *action* networks formally engage in collective action at the network level, which can include delivering services (see also Maguire 2006).

Based upon the perceptions of health service professionals, a study by Darlington and Feeney (2008) identified three broad areas for the improvement of interagency relationships, collaborative processes, and service outcomes for families. These suggestions clustered around three main content areas: improving communication, enhancing the knowledge base of professionals, and providing adequate resources and appropriate service models. Within these three areas of communication, knowledge development and resources, relevant strategies included both formal organization-led initiatives as well as informal initiatives that could be implemented by individuals or small groups. Additionally, strategies were suggested which required a multi-level approach, ranging from the frontline workplace to state-wide policy changes. Thus, a complex picture emerges of inter-sectoral collaboration that comprises several key domains and needs to be implemented at all levels of organizational influence (Darlington and Feeney 2008: 195–197). On the other hand, solutions which seem to require a very high degree of inter-organizational integration for success may be relying on unnecessarily complex service models; high levels of integration may be too difficult, in many instances (Reitan 1998; Longoria 2005; Phillips *et al.* 2009).

Collaboration patterns in environmental management

Natural resources and environmental planning has undergone major changes in advanced societies in recent decades (Wondolleck and Yaffee 2000; Kettl 2002; Imperial 2005; Koontz and Thomas 2006). To take one example, in the United States the traditional approach to managing water and natural resources in river watersheds was based on regulation by single function agencies, but there has been a shift towards a more collaborative approach, including more horizontal contributions from multiple stakeholders as well as more provision for public input (Sabatier *et al.* 2005: 3–4). This arose because the previous approach could not adequately deal with a range of persistent problems that required the coordination of multiple agencies and in-depth local knowledge. These included problems of pollution, water quality planning, environmental protection of coastal areas, and protection of biodiversity. The move towards a more collaborative approach was attempted in order to tackle more complex sets of interconnected problems. However, solutions that are 'good politics' and solutions that actually make a big difference to environmental outcomes are not necessarily one and the same:

> Two questions are important: Are the decisions good ones from an environmental and socioeconomic perspective? And can they be implemented from a political and legal perspective? Many of the 'solutions' reached in collaborative stakeholder settings may be good political compromises, but they do not really solve the environmental or socioeconomic problems plaguing a watershed. Conversely, many negotiated solutions may be appropriate from a physical environmental standpoint, but they may leave out key stakeholders who will pursue other avenues of blocking implementation. Many collaborative efforts create policies that rely on voluntary cooperation without any formal legal enforcement mechanisms, which often creates considerable doubt about the likelihood of policy implementation.
>
> (Sabatier *et al.* 2005: 10)

Thus, collaborative approaches in US watershed management are sometimes criticized as being politically symbolic arrangements which distract attention from ongoing water management problems. However, it is also strongly argued that collaborative processes provide the opportunity for engagement with more complex problems than regulatory approaches would allow.

Sabatier *et al.* (2005) have reviewed the US environmental management literature in relation to factors increasing the likelihood of collaboratives being formed and factors increasing the likelihood that these partnerships across boundaries will produce results and endure over time. While recognizing that institutional and legal arrangements are different in other countries and that the voluntaristic and bargaining character of US experience is not typical else-where, they provide the following suggestions with regard to situations when multi-stakeholder agreements are more likely to be successful (Sabatier *et al.* 2005: 197):

- there is a 'stalemate', making the status quo unacceptable;
- all major stakeholders are included in negotiations;
- there is a consensus decision rule;
- there is a respected, knowledgeable and neutral person leading negotiations;
- key stakeholders stay personally involved, report regularly to constituents and commit to longer-term negotiations;
- some of the major conflicts concern empirical topics;
- there is a higher level of trust between stakeholders, who take each others' concerns seriously, and stick to agreements;
- when funding is provided by more than one interest coalition.

Skelcher and Sullivan (2008) make the case for a broad approach to the appraisal of cross-sectoral partnerships. They argue that collaborative performance should be assessed not only in terms of the 'policy domain' (achieving desired policy/ program outcomes), but also in terms of the 'democratic domain' (democratic performance, mainly about legitimacy), the 'transformative domain' (path-breaking behaviour, new benefits not otherwise possible without collaboration), the 'coordination domain' (mutually dependent exchange of resources), and the 'political domain' (generating high-level ideas that integrate the actions of divergent groups). In other words, getting improved environmental or social values is not the whole story. There are broader governance considerations concerning legitimacy and the quality of change management behaviour. An important enabler may be the increasing role of 'boundary-spanning' individuals and organizations, which can connect diverse groups, facilitate and broker agreements, and bridge the 'silos' of knowledge and interest that cause rigidities and path dependence (Williams 2002; Berkes 2009).

Concluding observations

Multi-sectoral collaborations are generally seen as useful because they may bring together a wide range of expertise, knowledge and resources that enables new thinking about complex issues – for understanding the problems as well as formulating possible solutions. Importantly, a collaboration may also be helpful in improving the quality and effectiveness of implementation. Collaborative networks are more likely to emerge in those policy contexts where simple technical solutions for issues are neither relevant nor feasible. Thus, for resolving some types of complex problems, negotiated accommodations among stakeholders are seen as more appropriate than a rational–technical solution. Public managers will be aware, however, that investing material resources and 'political' capital in either a collaborative network or an intensive participatory policy process has potential costs as well as potential benefits. Collaborative networks generally have high transaction costs (Metcalfe *et al.* 2006: 30) in terms of time, energy and commitment, and therefore the benefits need to be substantial so as to outweigh the effort involved. It has been suggested (Irvin and Stansbury 2004: 62) that a streamlined process would be preferable in most situations, unless a broader mandate is required to break a deadlock on a major issue and key stakeholders are willing to participate in seeking a broad-based solution.

An increasing proportion of the research literature is written from the viewpoint of how public managers must come to terms with a more consultative and networked environment (e.g. Agranoff 2006, 2007; Maguire 2006; Goldsmith and Eggers 2004). However, creating and shaping networks is just one of many tools which public managers might choose to deploy to handle various types of difficult problems. They must also give major consideration to finding the appropriate balance between strategic work drawn from internal discussion (i.e. intra-government review and coordination) and that drawn from external liaison (i.e. stakeholder consultation and network processes). Public managers would seldom begin with the explicit goal of creating an enduring multi-party network entity – this might emerge on the basis of initial operational experience with consultation and coordination. Various combinations of hierarchy, market, community, and network approaches might be implemented in a series of attempts to address different public policy challenges. In terms of organizational choices within the public sector, several coordination and strategy development options are available for public agencies seeking to address complex challenges (MAC 2004: 42). These options do not always envisage a major role for multi-sectoral network governance, and more analysis is required to establish the conditions in which collaborative options are likely to be both timely and effective.

References

Agranoff, R. (2003) *Leveraging Networks*, Washington DC: IBM Endowment for the Business of Government.
Agranoff, R. (2006) 'Inside collaborative networks: ten lessons for public managers', *Public Administration Review*, 66(S1): 56–65.
Agranoff, R. (2007) *Managing Within Networks: Adding Value to Public Organizations*, Washington DC: Georgetown University Press.
Austin, J.E. (2000) *The Collaborative Challenge: How Nonprofits and Businesses Succeed Through Strategic Alliances*, San Francisco: Jossey-Bass.
Berkes, F. (2009) 'Evolution of co-management: role of knowledge generation, bridging organisations and social learning', *Journal of Environmental Management*, 90(5): 1692–1702.
Bingham, L.B. and O'Leary, R. (2006) 'Conclusion: parallel play, not collaboration: missing questions, missing connections', *Public Administration Review*, 66(S1): 161–167.
Bryson, J.M., Crosby, B.C. and Stone, M.M. (2006) 'The design and implementation of cross-sector collaborations: propositions from the literature', *Public Administration Review*, 66(S1): 44–55.

Coleman, D. (2009) *42 Rules for Successful Collaboration*, Silicon Valley: Super Star Press.

Darlington, Y. and Feeney, J.A. (2008) 'Collaboration between mental health and child protection services: professionals' perceptions of best practice', *Children and Youth Services Review*, 30(2): 187–198.

Ebers, M. (ed.) (1997) *The Formation of Inter-Organizational Networks*, Oxford: Oxford University Press.

Edelenbos, J. and Van Buuren, A. (2005) 'The learning evaluation: a theoretical and empirical exploration', *Evaluation Review*, 29(6): 591–612.

Edwards, M. (2001) 'Participatory governance into the future', *Australian Journal of Public Administration*, 60(3): 78–88.

Foster-Fishman, P., Berkowitz, S.L., Lounsbury, D.W., Jacobson, S. and Allen, N.A. (2001) 'Building collaborative capacity in community coalitions: a review and integrative framework', *American Journal of Community Psychology*, 29(2): 241–261.

Goldsmith, S. and Eggers, W.D. (2004). *Governing by Network: The New Shape of the Public Sector*, Washington DC: Brookings Institution.

Gray, A., Jenkins, B., Leeuw, F. and Mayne, J. (eds) (2003) *Collaboration in Public Services: The Challenge for Evaluation*. New Brunswick NJ: Transaction Publishers.

Gray, B. (1985). 'Conditions facilitating interorganizational collaboration', *Human Relations*, 38(10): 911–936.

Gray, B. (1989) *Collaborating: Finding Common Ground for Multiparty Problems*. San Francisco: Jossey-Bass.

Gray, B. (2004). 'Strong opposition: frame-based resistance to collaboration', *Journal of Community and Applied Social Psychology*, 14(3): 166–176.

Gray, B. and Wood, D. (1991) 'Collaborative alliances: moving from practice to theory', *Journal of Applied Behavioral Science*, 27(1): 3–22.

Head, B.W. (2006) *Effective Collaboration*. Discussion Paper, Canberra: Australian Research Alliance for Children and Youth.

Head, B.W. (2008a) 'Assessing network-based collaborations: effectiveness for whom?', *Public Management Review*, 10(6): 733–749.

Head, B.W. (2008b) 'Wicked problems in public policy', *Public Policy*, 3(2): 101–118.

Head, B.W. (2010) 'Reconsidering evidence-based policy: key issues and challenges', *Policy and Society*, 29(2): 77–94.

Hennart, J.-F. (2006) 'Alliance research: less is more', *Journal of Management Studies*, 43(7): 1621–1628.

Himmelman, A.T. (1996) 'On the theory and practice of transformational collaboration', in C. Huxham (ed.) *Creating Collaborative Advantage*, London: Sage Publications.

Himmelman, A.T. (2001) 'On coalitions and the transformation of power relations: collaborative betterment and collaborative empowerment', *American Journal of Community Psychology*, 29(2): 277–284.

Huxham, C. and Vangen, S. (2005) *Managing to Collaborate: The Theory and Practice of Collaborative Advantage*, London: Routledge.

Imperial, M.T. (2005) 'Using collaboration as a governance strategy', *Administration & Society*, 37(3): 281–320.

Innes, J.E. and Booher, D. (2003) 'Collaborative policymaking: governance through dialogue', in M.A. Hajer and H. Wagenaar (eds) *Deliberative Policy Analysis: Understanding Governance in the Network Society*, Cambridge: Cambridge University Press.

Irvin, R.A. and Stansbury, J. (2004) 'Citizen participation in decision-making: is it worth the effort?', *Public Administration Review*, 64(1): 55–65.

Kamensky, J.M. and Burlin, T.J. (eds) (2004) *Collaboration: Using Networks and Partnerships*, Lanham MA: Rowman & Littlefield.

Kanter, R.M. (1994) 'Collaborative advantage: the art of alliances', *Harvard Business Review*, 72(4): 96–108.

Keast, R., Mandell, M., Brown, K. and Woolcock, G. (2004) 'Network structures: working differently and changing expectations', *Public Administration Review*, 64(3): 363–371.

Kettl, D.F. (ed.) (2002) *Environmental Governance*. Washington DC: Brookings Institution.

Koontz, T. and Thomas, C. (2006) 'What do we know and need to know about the environmental outcomes of collaborative management?', *Public Administration Review*, 66(S1): 111–121.

Koppenjan, J., and Klijn, E.H. (2004) *Managing Uncertainties in Networks*, London: Routledge.

Lasker, R.D., Weiss, E.S. and Miller, R. (2001) 'Partnership synergy: a practical framework for studying and strengthening the collaborative advantage', *Milbank Quarterly*, 79(2): 179–205.

Linden, R.M. (2002) *Working Across Boundaries: Making Collaboration Work in Government and Nonprofit Organizations*, San Francisco: Jossey-Bass.

Longoria, R. A. (2005). 'Is inter-organizational collaboration always a good thing?', *Journal of Sociology and Social Welfare*, 32(3): 123–138.

Maguire, M. (2006) 'Collaborative public management: assessing what we know and how we know it', *Public Administration Review*, 66(S1): 33–43.

Management Advisory Committee (MAC) (2004) *Connecting Government: Whole of Government Responses to Australia's Priority Challenges*, Canberra: Management Advisory Committee.

Mandell, M.P. (ed.) (2001) *Getting Results through Collaboration: Networks and Network Structures for Public Policy and Management*, Westport: Quorum Books.

Mawson, A. (2008) *The Social Entrepreneur: Making Communities Work*. London: Atlantic Books.

Metcalfe, J., Riedlinger, M., Pisarski, A. and Gardner, J. (2006) *Collaborating Across the Sectors*, Canberra: Council for the Humanities, Arts and Social Sciences.

Milbourne, L. (2009) 'Remodelling the third sector: advancing collaboration or competition in community-based initiatives?', *Journal of Social Policy* 38(2): 277–297.

O'Flynn, J. and Wanna, J. (eds) (2008) *Collaborative Governance: A New Era of Public Policy in Australia?* Canberra: ANU e-Press.

Phillips, R., Milligan, V. and Jones, A. (2009) *Integration and Social Housing in Australia: Theory and Practice*, AHURI Final Report no. 129. Australian Housing and Urban Research Institute, Melbourne.

Provan, K.G. and Kenis, P. (2008) 'Modes of network governance: structure, management, and effectiveness', *Journal of Public Administration Research and Theory*, 18(2): 229–252

Provan, K.G. and Milward, H.B. (2001) 'Do networks really work? A framework for evaluating public sector organisational networks', *Public Administration Review*, 61(4): 414–423..

Reitan, T.C. (1998) 'Theories of inter-organizational relations in the human services', *Social Service Review*, 72(3): 285–309.

Sabatier, P.A., Focht, W., Lubell, M., Trachtenberg, Z., Vedlitz, A. and Matlock, M. (eds) (2005) *Swimming Upstream: Collaborative Approaches to Watershed Management*. Cambridge, Mass: MIT Press.

Saxton, T. (1997) 'The effects of partner and relationship characteristics on alliance outcomes, *Academy of Management Journal*, 40(2): 443–461.

Skelcher, C. and Sullivan, H. (2008) 'Theory-driven approaches to analysing collaborative performance', *Public Management Review*, 10(6): 751–771.

Sullivan, H. and Skelcher, C. (2002) *Working across Boundaries: Collaboration in Public Services*, New York: Palgrave Macmillan.

Thomson, A.M. and Perry, J.L. (2006) 'Collaboration processes: inside the black box', *Public Administration Review*, 66(S1): 20–32.

VicHealth (2003) *The Partnerships Analysis Tool*. Melbourne: Victorian Health Promotion Foundation.

Williams, P. (2002) 'The Competent Boundary Spanner', *Public Administration* 80(1): 103–124.

Wolff, T. (2010) *The Power of Collaborative Solutions*, San Francisco: Jossey-Bass.

Wondolleck, J.M. and Yaffee, S.L. (2000) *Making Collaboration Work: Lessons from Innovation in Natural Resource Management*, Washington DC: Island Press.

Woolcock, G. and Boorman, C. (2003) *Goodna Service Integration Project: Final Report: Doing What We Know We Should*, Brisbane: University of Queensland. Online. Avaliable at: www.uq.edu.au/boilerhouse/goodna-sip/images/Final%20Report.pdf (accessed 8 December 2011).

10 The soft power solution?

Managing without authority

Owen E. Hughes

Introduction

Managing across boundaries can be argued to be a subset of a larger phenomenon that can be termed 'public management without authority'. Authority means the direct application of hard power; working across boundaries means using soft power, deal-making, negotiation and compromise. Results are still required, but the practical utility of force is attenuated. In terms of the question posed – what does managing across boundaries involve – one possible answer is that working across boundaries involves public managers having to gain results in ways other than the use of force. They need to be able to manage effectively, but to do so without authority.

It is almost a truism that the traditional model of public administration is based on authority – the authority of the state with its full panoply of majesty, prestige and power. The traditional bureaucracy has always been assumed to be able to not only make authoritative rulings, but to make ones that are enforceable. And, in the final analysis, the enforcement of bureaucratic decree involves the use (or potential use) of the innate force held by the police and even the military.

Early forms of managerialism were similarly reliant upon authority, in the sense of being able to enforce decisions arrived at centrally and then implemented through the force of law. Edicts would be made, which were then expected to be enforced. There was, then, no essential change in the 1980s and early 1990s version of managerialism in terms of its basis in authority and even authoritarianism. In this aspect, there was substantial continuity with the traditional bureaucratic model.

However, as public management has developed since the mid-1990s, the role and utility of authority has receded. It could even be argued that if there has been a single trend in public management in the last decade, it has been away from the use and utility of the exercise of authority. The more discussion and action there is around collaboration, co-production, managing across boundaries, leadership, and governance, to name but a few of the newer theoretical constructs, the more necessary it is to re-examine the real implications of this for traditional authority mechanisms.

Public managers may still have formal authority and the ability to call upon force to carry out their roles, but the circumstances for the actual exercise of this force are much reduced. The legal basis of what they may do is unchanged, but the actual exercise of authority is muted. Much of the day-to-day work of a public manager involves areas where the formal ability to act may be blurred or absent altogether. It follows that managing across boundaries involves, in large part, managing without any direct authority. Managing across boundaries can mean crossing jurisdictions into areas where the manager has no formal authority at all. Even if he or she is a formal representative of an authority, any deal involving agreement of some kind that is made with other parties may be seen as their own personal deal rather than binding the authority of the agency they represent.

If public managers are required to operate in circumstances where they do not have real authority, they are then in the difficult position of having to get results by virtue of their role, but from players for whom they are not personally responsible in the sense of being able to direct or to make authoritative rulings. In turn, this means finding new organizational cultures and, for many public servants, a need to acquire a completely different set of skills. The skills required of traditional public servants were quite different from those required now. Management skills have become those which involve personality, deal-making, operating through networks, and coalition-building, with the use of actual authority being much more rare. Some public managers will thrive under such circumstances; others will not have the requisite skills and will flounder.

Government and authority

Governments have force at their disposal by axiom; indeed, the possession of lawful authority defines government itself. Governments can require compliance through laws, and the coercion implied by those laws is assumed to be able to be carried out. Governments can compel the payment of taxes and conscript soldiers; they can (legally) seize property or resume land, although usually with compensation. The key point about government is that, ultimately, force is behind it; no lawful authority other than government can compel people to act in the ways that it prescribes.

The coercive power of government is the very source of its authority. Government is 'endowed with certain rights of compulsion that private institutions do not have', such as forcing the payment of taxes and the right to seize property provided it pays compensation (Stiglitz 1989: 13). Birch (2001: 54) notes that authority in this sense is defined by the *Oxford English Dictionary* as 'the right to command, or give an ultimate decision' and states that it is the 'type of authority wielded by presidents and prime ministers and parliaments, by generals in charge of armies, by judges and police officers, by managing directors of business firms, or (in a weaker form) by school principals and teachers'. As Birch argues:

For the ordinary citizen of a modern democratic society in times of peace, the nature of political authority is not problematical. It is embodied in a complex series of laws and administrative regulations that most citizens accept without question and that the questioning or recalcitrant minority are forced to comply with by tax inspectors, police officers and other public officials holding what are commonly called positions of authority.

(2001: 54)

The actual exercise of authority can, of course, be exaggerated. For most people in democratic societies the need for enforcement is quite rare. In societies with some pretence at democracy, the use of force may be muted – the army and the police are nowhere near large enough to maintain the regime through force alone – and the legitimacy of government is maintained by some kind of popular sovereignty. Not all government actions derive from force and, even if many do, most people in a given society accept that their membership of it carries some obligations. In practice, 'the exercise of authority ... depends upon the readiness of the people over whom it is exercised to accept the decisions and orders that are given' (Birch 2001: 57).

The mere threat of force is most often force enough. Indeed, the exercise of real force can be counter-productive. As Birch adds, 'the actual use of force, as distinct from the implied threat of force, usually indicates a partial loss of authority'; however, in the real world of politics it 'must be accepted that the threat of coercion is always present' (2001: 57). In all of this it is clear that authority and government go together. Each depends upon the other, and for either one to exist without the other is almost inconceivable.

Authority in public administration

The traditional model of public administration was quite obviously based on authority and authoritative rulings that could be made and enforced. It was always assumed that individual bureaucrats were able to make decisions rationally, based on information and precedent, and that these would then have force behind them. That force could also be used to compel compliance, either implicitly or explicitly.

As is well known, Weber argued that there were three types of authority – 'legitimations of dominance' – and these are: the traditional – such as the authority of a tribal chief; the charismatic – the appeal of an extraordinary leader; and rational/legal authority (Gerth and Mills 1970: 78–80). Rational/legal authority is modern and efficient, as contrasted with the other forms of authority, which are essentially irrational and extra-legal.

Weber emphasized order and rationality. He also argued that military discipline is 'the ideal model for the modern capitalist factory' and that 'organizational discipline in the factory is founded upon a completely rational basis' (Gerth and Mills 1970: 261). To Weber, '[u]nfailingly neutral, discipline places itself at the disposal of every power that claims its service and knows how to promote it'

(Gerth and Mills 1970: 254). By the end of the nineteenth century formal bureaucracy was regarded as the very pinnacle of organizational effectiveness, and
thus there was in place a system which seemed to be rational and ordered in the
sense of the application of authority.

In theory, and in practice in many places, the bureaucracy was able to operate
as if Weber's ideal-type model prevailed and the work of government is funda-
mentally based on the ability to compel those falling within its jurisdiction. The
traditional model of public administration, based on rational-legal authority, is
essentially about authority and its use, about force and its exercise. Rationality,
authority and discipline, even of the military kind, all go together in the strict
bureaucratic model set out by Weber.

Authority in early managerialism

From the mid-1980s, managerial reform in many countries brought in newer
ways of operating within government. However, what they did not do in the
early years was change the use and utility of the exercise of force. Managerialism supplanted traditional public administration, but with no essential change in
authority relationships, at least in the early stages. It could even be argued that,
in some circumstances, managerialism involved greater use of authority.

One example of this is the introduction of Compulsory Competitive Tendering
(CCT) in Britain when Margaret Thatcher was Prime Minister. This reform was
introduced into UK services such as refuse collection by local governments in
1988. The compulsory aspect of CCT was certainly an exercise of authority: even
if economic theory predicted that it would be more efficient to contract out such
services (Szymanski 1996: 4), local authorities were, without question, forced to
comply with the edict issued by Whitehall. The authority of government was all
too visible in terms of compulsion, enforced by the police, culminating in the poll
tax riot of 1990. Even if the latter did lead to Mrs Thatcher's later resignation,
early managerialism was linked with authority and enforcement.

Managerialism did not mean a fundamental transformation in the historic role
of the nation state. It did not mean, contrary to Lynn, 'a different basis of legitimacy: perhaps different forms of rationality, different jurisprudential principles,
a different allocation of property rights' (Lynn 1997: 109–110). Indeed, the
authority basis of managerialism was really the same as it had been in the traditional administrative model, and was equally based upon force and its exercise.

What we have, then, is the traditional model of public administration, which
is very clearly based on authority and its exercise. In the 1980s, managerial
models began to supplant traditional bureaucracy; however, these, too, were similarly based on force.

Moving away from authority

The past decade has seen something of a quiet change in public management. As
the field has developed – with leadership models, governance, collaboration,

co-production, to name but a few theoretical changes – so too has the exercise of authority been reduced. As Michalski *et al.* argue, this is a wider phenomenon:

> Looking at governance as the general exercise of authority, it seems that over the long run there has been a clear reduction in the absolute or unconstrained power of those in positions of power. This has been a marked trend both at the macro-political level, where the state attempts to effect society-wide governance, and at the micro-level, where firms and families have experienced important changes in the exercise of authority.
>
> (2001: 9)

The traditional public administration approach was for the government to deliver public services in ways largely determined by the bureaucracy itself, at times of its convenience and with the underlying assumption of a one-way flow of information from the bureaucracy to its clients. The recipients of public services played very little role and could not change the distribution of public services that occurred by virtue of authority. Early managerial approaches did aim to involve clients and citizens, but really only in terms of quite low-level consultation and participation. However, as the process of public management reform has continued it has become apparent that more active forms of outside engagement can provide for better outcomes. For public services to concede that their edicts could be improved by active engagement with the outside was a very big change indeed.

The change posed fairly major problems for public managers. How could government, or governance even, operate without recourse to the kind of authority that it had always had? As Kettl argues:

> How could its hierarchically structured, authority-managed agencies effectively manage increasingly non-hierarchical, non-authority-based administrative systems? Hierarchy and authority worked, more or less well, in an era in which the government produced most of its goods and services itself. As government employed more indirect tools, however, the management strains grew.
>
> (2002: 46)

Kettl argues that 'as authority has become a less effective tool with which to solve problems, managers have struggled to determine what can best replace it' (2002: 59). Various ways have been put forward. These are variations on the theme of greater involvement of the citizenry, reduced power of government, and public managers being central to the processes even if they do not have the untrammelled scope for action and edict that they had during the traditional model. Ideas of governance, collaboration and co-production, and leadership all involve a substantial movement away from authority models, most of all Weberian rational–legal authority, and towards something else.

Governance

Government is essentially about authority, as discussed earlier. The more recent revival in the use of 'governance' arose in part from the need to look at kinds of relationship other than those involving authority. Government and governance may have the same derivation (Hughes: 2010), but they now have different meanings with regard to the use of authority. Both government and governance 'refer to purposive behavior, to goal-oriented activities, to systems of rule', but:

> Government suggests activities that are backed by formal authority, by police powers to insure the implementation of duly constituted policies, whereas governance refers to activities backed by shared goals that may or may not derive from legal and formally prescribed responsibilities and that do not necessarily rely on police powers to overcome defiance and attain compliance.
>
> (Rosenau 1992: 4)

In particular, governance is most often claimed to be different from government as a model assumed to be able to obtain societal outcomes without governmental power. As Keohane and Nye argue:

> Rulemaking and rule interpretation in global governance have become pluralised. Rules are no longer a matter simply for states or intergovernmental organizations. Private firms, NGOs, subunits of governments, and the transnational and transgovernmental networks that result, all play a role, typically with central state authorities and intergovernmental organizations. As a result, any emerging pattern of governance will have to be networked rather than hierarchical and must have minimal rather than highly ambitious objectives.
>
> (2000: 37)

Rhodes (1996) argues that 'current use does not treat governance as a synonym for government'; indeed, governance can occur without government. Bevir and Rhodes argue that governance 'consists of self-organizing, inter-organizational networks ... [which] have a significant degree of autonomy from the state. Networks are not accountable to the state; they are self-organizing' (Bevir and Rhodes 2003: 53). Even if this is a large claim, it does seem evident that governance does involve less use of authority than does government.

A further distinction, made by Tarschys, is between tight governance and loose governance. As he argues:

> Tight governance stands for a variety of steering methods based on clearly determined objectives, rigorous instructions and meticulous follow-up. Military organisations, totalitarian political systems, and industries organised along the principles of Taylorism and scientific management represent

archetypes of tight governance. Many elements of this strategy recur in the wave of proposals and reforms entitled 'new public management', in which imitation of the private sector is an important trend.

(2001: 37)

As noted earlier, traditional public administration and 'new public management' can be considered as examples of traditional authority relationships, or 'tight governance' in the Tarschys terminology. As he continues:

In what has come to be called neo-Taylorism, there is strong emphasis on control through economic and financial information, cost evaluation of everything produced in the public sector, monitoring of individual performance and actively using rewards and incentives. In these approaches, a strong goal orientation is combined with a relatively pessimistic or sceptical assessment of human nature. Individuals, if left to themselves, will pursue their own ends and disregard those of the organisation – hence a need for firm frameworks, active efforts to strengthen motivation, and vigilant supervision.

(2001: 37–38)

The pessimistic views of human nature in tight governance are of interest, noting that these are present both in the traditional administrative model and the early managerial model. However, as Tarschys continues:

Loose governance, by contrast, is built on a less suspicious view of human behaviour and is linked with more agnostic or empiricist ideas about the choice of organisational means and goals. In management theory this line of thought is represented by the human relations school, with its trust in the creativity and growth potential of employees and in their voluntary participation in joint projects.... Loose governance relies on confidence, subtle signals and co-operative environments. It tends to resort to recommendations and 'soft law' rather than commands and strict regimes. Key concepts are innovation, adaptability, and learning capacity. Organisations should preferably be flat if not altogether replaced by networks of independent actors.

(2001: 38)

Loose governance would include concepts such as collaboration and co-production, both of which are based on trust. However, loose governance requires a lot more of public managers than they would have been used to doing under the old bureaucratic model. There are real questions about how a government can co-exist with networks and how public managers can operationalize the links with networked organizations. It is much easier to simply require compliance and to use authority and force to ensure that compliance occurs.

In general, the concept of governance does assist in illuminating a long-standing preoccupation in public management with drawing a boundary for the exercise of authority. This is a valuable, if perennial, area of thought. In the search for a clear line, it has become evident that government and governance are not the same. Government is about the exercise of authority, while governance is more about inclusion; governance can occur without government (Rosenau 1992; Rhodes 1996). This could be extended even further, in that governance can occur without the exercise of authority.

Loose governance does have its issues, even if that is where public management is heading. Working in a network may lead to special deals or collusion. Collaboration may exclude other interested parties. Corruption and inefficiency are indeed possible. Tight governance may lead to 'complaints about overregulation, red tape, government failure and intrusive bureaucracies', but with loose governance, too, there is 'always a risk that trust turns into gullibility and that flexible arrangements give room to laxity, waste and corruption' (Tarschys 2001: 38).

Collaboration and co-production

Collaboration is where various parties, normally public officials and outside participants, actively work together to solve a problem affecting all. Bardach defines it as 'any joint activity by two or more agencies that is intended to increase public value by their working together rather than separately' (1998: 8). Even if 'collaborations are inherently more unstable, fragile, and idiosyncratic than hierarchical settings' (Norris-Tyrell and Clay 2010: 10) there are benefits in working together from an early stage.

It is evident, however, that collaboration involves less use of authority, and evident, too, that this is quite contrary to the precepts of a bureaucratic model. As Bardach argues:

> Almost nothing about the bureaucratic ethos makes it hospitable to interagency collaboration. The collaborative ethos values equality, adaptability, discretion, and results; the bureaucratic ethos venerates hierarchy, stability, obedience, and procedures.
>
> (1998: 232)

Bardach also points to the contradiction between working together to create new value using interpersonal trust and the bureaucratic culture:

> The cutting edge of interagency collaboration is interpersonal collaboration. If interagency collaboration is supposed to create new value, that value will almost certainly be bigger and better if the people involved can work together easily and constructively. One barrier to doing so is the bureaucratic culture. It is at its core hostile to the required spirit of pragmatism.... Interpersonal collaboration is to a large extent a process of negotiation within a matrix of interpersonal trust.
>
> (1998: 268)

A further step is *co-production* – the realization that the delivery of certain governmental outcomes requires the citizenry to be quite active co-producers in contributing time, effort, information, and compliance to the achievement of organizational purposes (Alford 2009).

Some co-production is relatively trivial – for instance, citizens may fill out at least part of their taxation forms themselves, and this then saves the government agency from doing so. But in some instances, effective co-production is required for the agency to fulfil its very function. It follows that managers need to actively work with clients, client groups and the wider citizenry, and those managers 'who ignore their clients will miss potentially significant capabilities and resources' (Alford 2009: 3). Co-production could be the extension of collaboration to the outside, as well as the recognition that public managers need outside help to fulfil their very roles.

Collaboration and co-production certainly involve less use of authority and less benefit from its use. Indeed, an authoritative form of collaboration or co-production would defeat the very purpose of getting together to find a joint outcome of some kind.

Leadership

In essence, leadership involves the use of forms of authority other than the Weberian rational/legal authority which was always seen as the basis of the bureaucratic model of administration. Even if one kind of leadership involves charisma – regarded by Weber as irrational – the authority of a leader depends upon there being willing followers. Leadership cannot depend on force, or if it does, it is not likely to last.

Public administration is so imbued with authority and authority relationships that it is hardly surprising that leadership is little discussed. Heifetz does refer to the possibility of leadership without authority:

> The scarcity of leadership from people in authority ... makes it all the more critical to the adaptive successes of a polity that leadership be exercised by people without authority. These people – perceived as entrepreneurs and deviants, organizers and troublemakers – provide the capacity within the system to see through the blind spots of the dominant viewpoint.
>
> (1999: 183)

Heifetz mentions excluded groups, including women, and such leaders as Mahatma Gandhi and Martin Luther King as instances of management without authority, although there could also be instances of Weberian charismatic authority rather than absence of authority. Heifetz makes a distinction between leadership and authority:

> As we often experience it in real-time, leadership means taking responsibility for hard problems beyond anyone's expectations. Ironically, many

people wait until they gain authority, formal or informal, to begin leading. They see authority as a prerequisite. Yet those who do lead usually feel that they are taking action beyond what authority they have.

(1999: 205)

This comment squares with actual practice. Most good managers do not need to manage by invoking their authority; indeed, to do so would be likely to be counter-productive. Even when a public manager does have formal authority, he or she is likely to find that the actual exercise of authority in the absence of broader support causes more of an issue with subordinate staff. At an earlier time, the exercise of authority was simply part of the job of being higher up the hierarchy. More often now, even in public services, the exercise of authority involves consensus-building and discussion with all levels of staff involved. It is much more of a political job, and much less involving of the exercise of authority.

It is apparent that changes in management practice have democratized the workplace. The view of the leader-as-dictator, the leader who everyone else fears, seems rather old-fashioned. It is less acceptable now for strict authoritarianism to prevail and an authoritarian leader would often be unwelcome to the rest of the staff, and be ineffective as a result. The idea of the leader who has all the wisdom for a group and to whom everyone defers does seem somewhat obsolete, as an OECD paper argues:

> Under the old autocratic model, leaders could expect to solve the problem, announce the decision, and get compliance, based on their authority. But public sector leaders today must gain commitment, not just compliance, and therefore a collaborative style is needed. Leaders now succeed only if they can influence others, and quite often those whose support they need do not report to them.
>
> (2001: 43)

Leadership should be able to occur without formal authority; indeed, that kind of leadership is much more in tune with an organizational culture that is participative. This is difficult for formal bureaucracies, and it is unlikely to work in such settings. But change has taken place, such that formal authority is much less useful; even if, as Heifetz notes, as we are not used to distinguishing between leadership and authority, 'the idea of leadership without authority is new and perplexing' (1999: 184).

As a result of the decline in authority, the leadership and management skills required of public servants will be different. They are perhaps more akin to diplomacy than to the recourse to force or edict that might have been more common during a more bureaucratic era. Management skills, then, become those of personality, of deal-making, of operating through networks, and of coalition-building, but with the invoking of actual authority being rare. As Kettl argues:

> In the last third of the twentieth century ... government began relying on new tools.... Unlike direct delivery of services by government bureaucracies, these tools operated more through incentives and partnerships with nongovernmental players than through governmental management with hierarchical authority.
>
> (2002: 51)

The new mechanisms require new skills, ones that are different from those of traditional public servants, as Goldsmith and Eggers note:

> Managing in a networked government environment demands an entirely different set of competencies and capabilities. In addition to planning, budgeting, staffing, and other traditional government duties, it requires proficiency in a host of other tasks, such as activating, stabilizing, integrating, and managing a network. To do this, network managers must possess at least some degree of aptitude in negotiation, mediation, risk analysis, trust building, collaboration, and project management. They must have the ability and the inclination to work across sector boundaries and the resourcefulness to overcome all the prickly challenges to governing by network ... self-directing, multifaceted, and multiskilled managers are scarce in the public sector.
>
> (2004: 157–158)

Collaborative managers need to 'know how to bargain and how to negotiate' (O'Leary and Bingham 2009: 266). Norris-Tyrell and Clay mention that skills in leadership, group process, change management, and 'personal characteristics such as flexibility, patience, and a cooperative spirit are important to success' (2010: 11). Leadership across organizational boundaries is even more difficult (Hartley and Allison 2000). Public managers need to learn to make deals, to be entrepreneurs of a kind. The skills involved are essentially about personality, quite contrary to the impersonality argued by Weber.

Leaders may possess authority, but leadership utilizes different kinds of authority than rational–legal authority. Leadership is a further step away from traditional bureaucracy and its authority based upon rules and the enforcement of them.

Soft power rather than hard power

Another discipline may offer something of a possible solution to the issue of authority. Within international relations there is much discussion of soft power – essentially the power of culture – as a counter and a supplement to hard power, meaning military power. Nye argues that 'One can affect others' behaviour in three main ways: threats of coercion ("sticks"), inducements and payments ("carrots"), and attraction that makes others want what you want' (2008:94). Soft power is based around the third of these ways:

Soft power rests on the ability to shape the preferences of others. At the personal level, we all know the power of attraction and seduction. Political leaders have long understood the power that comes from setting the agenda and determining the framework of a debate. Soft power is a staple of daily democratic politics. The ability to establish preferences tends to be associated with intangible assets such as an attractive personality, culture, political values and institutions, and policies that are seen as legitimate or having moral authority. If I can get you to want to do what I want, then I do not have to force you to do what you do *not* want.

(Nye 2008: 95)

A world of soft power is one where influence is still extended, but without the need for force. It is a world of negotiation, of deals, of getting to a result without the direct use of force. By analogy, this can also apply to the new world of public management.

Governments still have authority; they still have power and can coerce citizens and exercise that power. However, most of the time, and on most issues, they do not need to do so. Moreover, the outcomes in policy and delivery when raw power is used are likely to be sub-optimal. It would now be almost inconceivable for government to pass legislation without extensive consultation with stakeholders. It would now be most unusual for an agency in the public sector to implement policy without consultation.

It could be argued that public management takes place within government and that government is essentially about authority. Perhaps there is a limit to how far management without authority can really go. Perhaps it is wishful thinking that government does not need authority and that new models of management can be more effective in its absence. Perhaps there is no necessary decline in the power of government at all – rather, an increased realization that the formal, rational bureaucratic model is no longer appropriate and that it actually suits governments to involve a wide range of actors in what they do. This involvement may be aimed at making government more efficient and effective rather than ceding any real power to the outside at all.

Take, for example, a police force or a tax office as governmental organizations that have substantial, real power to force citizens to comply with rulings. Once, during the apogee of the traditional bureaucratic model, such organizations operated with little regard for the outside. The bureaucratic model assumed that all information was held inside and that the traditional bureaucrat made a decision in an entirely rational way. But agencies that act in a high-handed manner can lose public support, even though they may act entirely within their legal powers. And an agency that loses support may lose its 'authorizing environment' (Moore 1995) and have its status and standing decline in the public mind.

Those in charge of the tax office now realize that the views of clients, accountants and other players are quite valid inputs and, without changing its powers one iota, they actively solicit opinions from outside players. Rather than the government conceding power, it may be exercising its unchanged power more judiciously. It is no concession of power to a network to involve it in decision-making. Other organizations are assisting government in doing what it wants done, and 'despite the view of some who persist in seeing networks as a weakening of the state, networked government can also be looked at as a different way of implementing the goals of the state' (Kamarck 2002: 246).

Soft power is still power and is still based on authority. Most of the time, and for most public managers, there is no real need to invoke authority. Much public management can be carried out without the exercise of authority, but it is still there if needed.

Conclusion

Government is about authority and public management does involve the exercise of authority backed by force. Even if government is now less able to direct, to use force and to exercise its formal authority, it does not mean that government can occur in its absence. Government without authority is not government at all, although it may be governance. The maintenance of authority is central to the whole process of government: government is authority, authority is government, and to think otherwise is wishful thinking.

However, public management and public managers can and should exist, and even prosper, in many situations where formal authority is not used and does not need to be used. Moreover, the crude exercise of power and authority is often counter-productive. This points to a need for public managers to be able to work smarter than before, to be able to make deals, and to get outcomes in circumstances where they do not have real authority. Soft power can be just as effective in gaining results, and public managers who know how to exercise soft power the most effectively are not only likely to be successful, but to be more successful than those who resort to hard power and authority.

References

Alford, J. (2009) *Engaging Public Sector Clients: From Service-delivery to Co-production*, Basingstoke: Palgrave Macmillan.
Bardach, E. (1998) *Getting Agencies to Work Together: The Theory and Practice Of Managerial Craftsmanship*, Washington, DC: Brookings Institution Press.
Bevir, M. and Rhodes, R.A.W. (2003) *Interpreting British Governance*, London: Routledge.
Birch, A.H. (2001) *The Concepts and Theories of Modern Democracy*, London: Routledge.
Gerth, H.H. and Wright Mills, C. (eds) (1970) *From Max Weber: Essays in Sociology*, London: Routledge & Kegan Paul.
Goldsmith, S. and Eggers, W.D. (2004) *Governing by Network: The New Shape of the Public Sector*, Washington DC: Brookings Institution Press.
Hartley, J. and Allison, M. (2000) 'The role of leadership in modernisation and improvement of public service', *Public Money & Management*, 20(2): 35–40.

Heifetz, R.A. (1999) *Leadership Without Easy Answers*, Cambridge MA: Belknap.

Hughes, O.E. (2010) 'Does governance exist?' in S.P. Osborne (ed.) *The New Public Governance? Critical Perspectives and Future Directions*, London: Routledge.

Kamarck, E.C. (2002) 'The end of government as we know it', in J.D. Donahue and J.S. Nye Jr (eds) *Market-Based Governance: Supply Side, Demand Side, Upside and Down-side*, Washington DC, Brookings Institution Press.

Keohane, R.O. and Nye, J.S. (2000) 'Introduction', in J.S. Nye and J.D. Donahue (eds), *Governance in a Globalization World*, Washington, DC: Brookings Institution Press.

Kettl, D.F. (2002) *The Transformation of Governance: Public Administration for Twenty-First Century America*, Baltimore and London: Johns Hopkins Press.

Lynn, L.E. (1997) 'The new public management as an international phenomenon: questions from an American skeptic' in L.R. Jones, K. Schedler and S.W. Wade (eds) *International Perspectives on the New Public Management*, Advances in International Comparative Management, Supplement 3, Greenwich CT: JAI Press.

Michalski, W., Miller, R. and Stevens, B. (2001) 'Governance in the 21st century: power in the global knowledge economy and society' in OECD, *Governance in the 21st Century*, Paris: OECD.

Moore, M. (1995) *Creating Public Value: Strategic Management in Government*, Cambridge MA: Harvard University Press.

Norris-Tyrell, D. and Clay, J.A. (2010) *Strategic Collaboration in Public and Nonprofit Administration*, Boca Raton: CRC Press.

Nye, J.S. Jr (2008) 'Public diplomacy and soft power', in *The Annals of the American Academy of Political and Social Science*, 616: 94–109.

O'Leary, R. and Bingham, L.B. (2009) 'Surprising findings, paradoxes, and thoughts on the future of collaborative research', in R. O'Leary and L.B. Bingham (eds) *The Collaborative Public Manager: New Ideas for the Twenty-First Century*, Washington DC: Georgetown University Press.

Organisation for Economic Co-operation and Development (OECD) (2001) *Public Sector Leadership for the 21st Century*, Paris: OECD.

Rhodes, R.A.W. (1996) 'The new governance: governing without government', *Political Studies*, 44: 652–67.

Rosenau, J.N. (1992) 'Governance, order and change in world politics', in J.N. Rosenau and E.-O. Czempiel (eds) *Governance Without Government: Order and Change in World Politics*, Cambridge: Cambridge University Press.

Stiglitz, J.E. (1989) *The Economic Role of the State*, Cambridge, MA: Blackwell.

Szymanski, S. (1996) 'The impact of compulsory competitive tendering on refuse collection services', *Fiscal Studies*, 17(3): 1–19.

Tarschys, D. (2001) 'Wealth, values, institution: trends in government and governance' in OECD, *Governance in the 21st Century*, Paris: OECD.

11 The diagnostic solution?

Gauging readiness for cross-boundary working

Deborah Blackman

Introduction

Increasingly, public managers are faced with complex problems which require thinking and working across boundaries; they span agencies, portfolios and jurisdictions, necessitating actors to work across them. However, working in this manner requires inter-agency collaboration and cooperation and is based on the premise that important goals of public policy cannot be delivered through the separate activities of existing organizations. Such approaches are pursued due to common assumptions that the coordination or integration of activities will achieve a better result than each party acting individually, and that working across boundaries will enable more efficient and effective policy development, implementation and service delivery. However, in practice, constraints and barriers lead to less than optimal – and sometimes paradoxical – outcomes.

This chapter outlines an approach which may help to address these cross-boundary dilemmas. Drawing on data collected from a large-scale study of joined-up working experiments in the Australian Public Service (APS), critical enablers and major barriers to the operationalization of this approach are identified and ongoing tensions and emerging paradoxes considered. Based on this analysis, the chapter considers the question of 'How does working across boundaries work (or not)?' by offering an alternative way of conceptualizing barriers and enablers which permits an organization to gauge its readiness for joined-up working. Some tentative advice for developing more effective ways of working across boundaries is proffered.

The Australian context

Horizontal approaches have developed in the last decade or so in public sector practice in order to promote inter-agency collaboration and cooperation in the pursuit of government policy goals (Bogdanor 2005). These approaches reflect both traditional coordination and new forms of organizing, structuring and collaborating which have sought to connect distinct parts of the public sector. In Australia and internationally, such approaches represent a significant break with conventional ideas of public sector organizing, and a concerted response to dealing with complex public policy problems and environments. A range of joining-up instruments and principles have been adopted in order to address wicked problems and other issues which cannot be handled within a functional department.

Australia came late to joining-up, but the federal government's 'connecting government' agenda set out in 2004 (MAC 2004) was encapsulated within a broader reform programme of integrated governance. The Australian agenda was given high-level attention by the head of the public service at the time, Dr Peter Shergold, and was well-articulated and strongly supported. The new 'whole of government' concept, as he called it, was ambitious, with high-level commitment to a multi-layered approach which had at its core a focus on cultural change, centred on collegiality (Shergold 2004a; 2005). Horizontal governance was depicted as being located alongside vertical relationships and hierarchies, rather than replacing them.

The shift was expressed in three ways. First, at the political level, the government committed to a series of whole-of-government priorities for policy-making, which included national security, defence and counter-terrorism and other generally defined priorities such as sustainable environment, rural and regional affairs, and work and family life (Shergold 2004a). Second, traditional political coordination through cabinet was streamlined, including changes to processes aimed at strengthening its strategic leadership role. The priorities were pursued through a range of coordinating or whole-of-government processes, including: cabinet and ministerial processes; the Council of Australian Governments (COAG)[1] and Commonwealth-State arrangements (e.g. sustainable water management); interdepartmental taskforces (e.g. work and family life); integrated service delivery (e.g. stronger regions); and lead agency approaches (e.g. Indigenous initiative). Australia also emphasized the building of coordinating units within current structures, particularly within the Department of the Prime Minister and Cabinet (e.g. for national security where the whole-of-government approach to national coordination covered strategic and operational levels). Third, attention was given to developing approaches for agencies in working across boundaries with policy development, program management and service delivery. The agenda was given impetus through a report – *Connecting Government* – by the Management Advisory Committee (the primary vehicle for developing reform comprising departmental secretaries: MAC 2004), which indicated how to address issues of whole-of-government processes and structures, cultures, managing information and budgetary frameworks.

Whole-of-government was defined as 'agencies working across portfolio boundaries to achieve a shared goal and an integrated government response to particular issues' (MAC 2004: 1). Despite this specific definition, the boundaries were not readily drawn and whole-of-government was also viewed in terms of coordinating departments (i.e. central agencies), integration (i.e. reducing the number of departments) and cooperative federalism (MAC 2004: 6–7). Approaches could operate both formally and informally, ranging from policy development through program management to service delivery.

What is evident is the wide range of expected outcomes which made very different demands upon people and processes. Two implications resulted from this: first, that the probability of agreement as to the function and focus of a whole-of-government initiative may not be shared across those working within it and, second, that the methods of adaptation and implementation become critical in the development of potential outcomes.

Despite official advice on processes and structures (MAC 2004) and the apparently high profile and priority of whole-of-government initiatives, there was limited evidence of actual success, including improvement across a range of outcomes (APSC 2007). There was some evaluation of specific government initiatives (ANAO 2007a, 2007b) but, to date, there has been little academic research or systematic study into either the successes or limitations of such initiatives or the appropriateness of the implementation advice being given. This chapter seeks to address this gap and, in doing so, develop a new way of recognizing the readiness of an organization to work across boundaries, which could have potential.

Methodology and methods

A multiple case-study methodology was adopted, enabling an in-depth investigation into how agencies and departments were working across boundaries to implement joined-up working (Yin 2003; Stake 2000). The case studies developed provide an understanding of the social processes, dynamics and contextual factors affecting initiative outcomes (Eisenhardt 1989; Stake 2000). Key federal APS departments identified initiatives that they considered to be 'whole-of-government' for study. They were: (1) the Department of Agriculture, Fisheries and Forestry (DAFF), which nominated the Australian Government Land and Coasts (AGLC)[2] programme, for which they had to work collaboratively with the Department of the Environment, Water, Heritage and the Arts (DEWHA) with joint, co-located teams; (2) the Department of Families, Housing, Community Services and Indigenous Affairs (FaHCSIA), which nominated the Indigenous Coordination Centres (ICC), which had to work with a range of agencies in order to improve Indigenous outcomes using a co-location model; (3) the Department of Health and Ageing (DoHA), which nominated pandemic preparedness, wherein they had to coordinate a range of agencies and services to prepare a plan for a pandemic crisis; and (4) the Australian Public Service Commission (APSC), which had been given the role of enabling and developing joined-up working for the APS.

Each partner organization was visited over a period of time, enabling documentation collection and analysis as well as the undertaking of a range of semi-structured interviews at three levels within each organization: senior management (Senior Executive Service – SES), middle management/supervisory (Executive Level – EL), and general employees (Australian Public Service – APS). Sixty-six semi-structured interviews were conducted with 82 participants in both individual and group interview settings. Participants discussed where whole-of-government had been seen to work and/or fail, identified inhibiting and enabling factors, and prioritized the issues they had identified as crucial for supporting new collaborative initiatives and cross-boundary working.

Enablers and barriers

A range of enablers or barriers to whole-of-government working emerged from the data. Which had the most impact upon a given situation was contextually, culturally and outcome specific, but there was commonality across the majority of cases and interviews. This chapter is focused upon the three enablers and four barriers which were the most commonly raised. Clearly, these are not the only issues, but our analysis showed that they were dominant in these cases.

Enablers

This section outlines the three enablers: clear mandate and central leadership, pattern breaking behaviour, and shared understanding of objectives and outcomes

Clear mandate and central leadership

One of the first themes to emerge was the need for a clear, identifiable political mandate. By this, the participants meant that there was clarity at the ministerial level which was translated into policy, spelling out the objectives of a particular whole-of-government initiative and how it was expected to work:

> You'd really want to make sure that you've got a very, very clear mandate from the ministers on what they wanted out of this joint team situation. And, also an acknowledgement that this is an integrated whole-of-government approach and it's not just going to be a combination of DAFF and DEWHA.
>
> (DAFF, EL)

Two of the cases emerged from COAG initiatives, which involved inter-jurisdictional working, and it became clear that once the focus upon the issue waned, it became much harder to get the commitment of other agencies and involved parties at a senior level: 'Nothing like having the Prime Minister's mandate, or the Premiers' mandate, for other agencies to listen' (FaHCSIA; SES). It was seen as a fundamental enabler without which many projects would fail, because a whole-of-government initiative was considered to be something where a set of outcomes could not be achieved without some form of actively managed and supported collaboration.

A related element was leadership – more specifically, the issue of who was supporting the initiative at the senior level, either in the bureaucracy or politically and in the locality of that leadership. A policy might be seen to be important, but without powerful champions initiatives would soon fail:

In the ICC nobody has authority; it tends to work best when there's somebody, and to be honest that somebody is usually a central agency, which
comes over the top and has their thumbs on the forehead of the individual
agency and the people involved, because with the best will in the world it's
just swimming upstream otherwise.

(FaHCSIA, EL)

It was recognized that such legitimate power (French and Raven 1959) supporting a project was always important, but the added importance of high-level
support for a cross-agency initiative was highlighted across all of the cases.

In the whole-of-government space it needs to be someone at a whole-of-
government pinnacle. It's pointless doing a whole-of-government project
having a line agency minister trying to run it.

(APSC, EL)

The argument that not all agencies (or ministers) were equal led to the assertion
that senior support provided more opportunity to gain entry to another agency:

If we ring up Health and we say 'hi we're from the ICC, we need help with
this or that' then ... we're on the same sort of power level as them. Rather
than if ... you ring up and say, 'hey we're from PM&C [Prime Minister &
Cabinet] or Treasury', then it's a whole different relationship.

(FaHCSIA, APS)

It was determined that for there to be regular collaboration there would need to
be a real change in the way that most agencies worked, driven from the top: 'it
can't be changed from below, can it? It's got to be changed from high, you
would think, one way or another but it doesn't happen greatly' (FaHCSIA, EL).

Pattern-breaking behaviour

Several participants observed that effective whole-of-government working was a
skill such that, for successful outcomes, there needed to be a greater ability to
recognize, support and seize opportunities where whole-of-government could
thrive and enable what was described as 'pattern-breaking behaviour'. There
needed to be spaces where novelty could occur and where the accepted practices
could be changed, such as where a crisis or unexpected finding led to a change
not only in policy, but also its implementation, in some crucial way. An example
given in several contexts was where changes in funding enabled a move away
from a tightly structured programmatic approach. The Northern Territory intervention[3] was cited as a time when the way that money was allocated changed
dramatically. Instead of the usual programme funding there was a shared fund
which was allocated against an outcome, leading to a very different set of priorities and behaviours:

the funding agreements that government [makes] just make it really, really difficult to do whole-of-government work because you're funded by program, by department and joining that up is really hard. In the Northern Territory it was the emergency response that was changed. I mean it wasn't perfect, but we actually had flexible funding and that made a huge difference.

(FaHCSIA, SES)

The argument was that in order for there to be a real collaborative development, the traditional patterns of behaviour needed to be amended, ignored or actively put aside so as to enable real change. Several participants talked about being given the space to do something different and how that needed to be supported: 'people will step up if you give them the room to do it and support them in doing it' (FaHCSIA, EL).

The role of many of the employees within the ICC was a 'solution broker',[4] which was seen as a facilitating role. Some argued that the role needed to be that of a 'dealmaker' as that was a more positive, innovative and challenging idea that would then be outcomes- focused; it would also change the evaluation pattern considerably:

It seems to me the whole-of-government approach is about being entrepreneurial inside the Public Service, like whether you can do a deal ... it's focused on the outcome and that's the way business operates. And we can deliver social outcomes in a business-like way.

(FaHCSIA, EL)

Shared understanding of objectives and outcomes

The need for clearly articulated, shared outcomes was identified by many participants as a crucial issue in whole-of-government working:

Where we have had any traction and have actually had any kind of credence, to the ICC managers' authority around whole-of-government, has been where there's been a particular issue or a particular place that there has been some legitimate want for whole-of-government and that is what our experience has been. I could talk whole-of-government and attempt to coordinate the other agencies until the cows come home, just for the purpose of having whole-of-government and we'll never get any outcome.

(FaHCSIA, SES)

In another agency it was agreed that outcomes were vital to overcome inherent differences in the systems:

Well I think what makes it work is clarity from government, from the elected government, so having a clear objective or set of objectives that government wants to achieve, a clear policy objective which allows you to work across the differences, if you like, to identify how they should be done.

(DAFF, EL)

Glasby *et al.* (2011) have also identified shared vision and clarity of roles as important principles for strengthening collaboration. What was of note in the APS research is that the data showed that when the focus was not upon outcomes it moved to either process or inputs, which led to a reversion to previous practice:

> There is a tendency to not focus on the issue ... there is more of a focus on process/inputs, which results in the document not getting out – when the intention of the document is to inform people. This doesn't happen because they're so focused on getting it right.

(DoHA, APS)

This point is seen to link to the barriers of evaluation and programmatic focus, in that many participants were of the opinion that short-term funding, regular measurement and a pressure to work to the agency goals led to a loss of focus upon the planned whole-of-government outcomes.

Barriers

A barrier was seen as something that either prevented or inhibited effective working. This section outlines the four barriers: programmatic focus, operational structure and 'core business', staff turnover, decision making and capabilities, and misalignment of evaluation and accountability

Programmatic focus, operational structure and 'core business'

In all of the cases, issues of structure were raised as causing difficulties for collaborative working. It was suggested that the way that programs were developed and delivered led to a culture of competition and that, because all individual and agency outcomes would be measured against agency strategies and plans, a lack of communal development was inevitable:

> If you take the perspective of an agency in the process they will have a view about how the outcome has panned out from their perspective. And that's normal because so many people are involved. The dilemma is that you've also got a whole range of other requirements that are a burden to people and people tend to fall back on them if they're a little bit lost in the relationship stuff, which are the line manager relationships around delivering programs efficiently, effectively.

(FaHCSIA, EL)

It is of note that even where there is a clear mandate, inappropriate structures and systems can prevent effective working. These findings are supported by the work of Glasby *et al.* (2011), who also found that changing structure rarely achieves the stated objectives and, in conjunction with poor funding and resource mechanisms, is often a barrier to effective partnerships. In the APS study, where a structural solution to collaboration had been chosen, there were serious problems as the team tried to work together but the differences in their agencies', employment practices and historical focus, as well as the interests of their ministers, led to tensions within the relationship:

> At the moment every department has different wages and pay scales and whatever and it's very hard, I think, to get a whole-of-government – get the team, yes rah, rah team – when people that you're sitting next to are earning three or four thousand more than you might be going home a couple of hours earlier every night.
>
> (DAFF, EL)

The need for strong relationships was identified in terms of physical location as well:

> They're either forgotten out of meetings or decision making sometimes or they have lost their opportunity to influence because they're not physically here enough ... I'm surprised at what an impact it has.
>
> (DAFF, APS)

Nevertheless, putting people together is not enough to overcome other barriers:

> Some people do feel like they're losing their identity of their department but also losing the opportunity of being seen by the core of the department and what they can do and that sort of stuff. As far as thinking about their career and where they go next, if they spend too much time here, will they be losing opportunities in the rest of the department?
>
> (DAFF, EL)

Several participants raised the issue of tensions between 'core business' and the demands of collaborative working, even when the initiative had high priority:

> Turf always inhibits whole-of-government working: 'this is our area' more so 'this is your area to do things with'. I think the pressure on Health has been enormous because there has been a constant need from all of the agencies at once to help the other agencies, at the same time as Health has been trying to prepare a health response.
>
> (DoHA, SES)

Another issue was the programmatic funding allocation; each agency had to release funds and would not do so unless the new initiative fitted with their current agenda:

> I guess, that we struggle ... because allocated funds aren't available for a particular issue at a fixed point in time unless it's been put into a budget about two or three years prior.
>
> (FaHCSIA, SES)

All of these are related to the wearing of multiple hats and trying to match the needs of sometimes competing projects:

> It is a challenge between saying I'm here as part of a whole-of-government representing DAFF trying to get some integrated projects, so we need to take into consideration whatever other agencies, in this case DEWHA's interests as well, and trying to develop projects which, as I say, can help to meet both portfolios' outcomes.
>
> (DAFF, EL)

These tensions were felt not only at outcome level, but also at the personal level. Examples were given, especially from those at the regional level, of the need both to fulfil outcomes and to keep more senior colleagues on side. In some instances this led to a perceived need for dual reporting whereby only activities related to the department were reported, unless there were successes when all of the whole-of-government activity was declared.

Staff turnover

It was argued that, for effective collaboration, strong relationships were needed, which would emerge over time. The problems created by staff turnover were frequently raised as participants opined that the delivery of longer-term plans necessitated collaborator continuity:

> The contact you had in a state or territory is now a different person and you're getting this hideous situation where you bring a new person to the ... table and they unravel three years of work ... they haven't come to the discussion with the understanding and knowledge of what's been done before. So you actually have to go all the way back and start all over again to bring them up to where everyone else is at. So it's the one step forward and two back.
>
> (DoHA, EL)

Interestingly, one senior manager argued that one of the reasons why his integrated service delivery centre worked more effectively than others was because 'I tend to sit in place for a while because I believe you don't make a difference unless you do' (FaHCSIA, SES). This manager had stayed in jobs much longer than average, despite being urged to move on.

Decision making and capabilities

A major barrier, identified in all of the cases, was the location and level of those involved in the initiative. It was stressed that there was a need to access the appropriate level of decision making if anything was to happen: 'But what I need is if you actually have a gap you've identified in the service matrix or in a developmental matrix I need a portal straight to someone who can help and connect and manage and input' (FaHCSIA, EL).

It was argued, for example that one possible structural solution – co-location – did not work as the people in the shared space were not appropriate for the task in hand: 'So what happened initially with ICCs you had lots of different levels of people at the places. So some had delegation, some didn't. Decisions were made elsewhere; it's just a matter of scales' (FaHCSIA, SES)

Because only limited decisions could be taken within the ICC, over time it was perceived as an expensive, ineffective shopfront and agencies began to pull their staff back, increasing the inability of decision making within the ICC. This problem was exacerbated by the ICC manager having very limited formal authority, and so any successes were linked to the personality, influencing skills and perseverance of the individual on the ground. The need for the right people to be present in order to achieve appropriate outcomes was raised in other cases as well:

> I think if the voice of service delivery is not at the table then the risks of implementing it are great and ... [if] high level policy is not with service delivery, the risks are there. So the key players need to have equal voice and be at the table.
>
> (APSC, APS)

Capability to actually undertake whole-of-government working was also raised: 'People aren't engaged particularly in thinking that way I think and you have people here who aren't recruited to think like that' (DAFF, EL). This has also been linked to the training and development of staff, which reflects a lack of understanding regarding what whole-of-government actually is and how it operates:

> I don't think that there was sufficient investment in the new model; just with the benefit of hindsight, looking back because it does require a different way of working.
>
> (FaHCSIA, SES)

Difficulties undertaking whole-of-government working due to insufficient capabilities have also been linked to staff turnover. There has been evidence elsewhere (Blackman and Kennedy 2008) that staff shortages in the period 2000–2008 led to the rapid over-promotion of talented individuals, many gaps in the staffing levels, and a high turnover of staff as they were poached from agency to agency. These issues were confirmed by the current research and were cited as contributing to serious capability gaps throughout the case studies.

The timeframes given for decisions was also raised as an issue, because effective joined-up working took longer as multiple stakeholders were needed to buy into the process, which was not possible when given only a day to achieve something. This short timeframe focus has been identified as a barrier because being in reactive and responsive mode perpetuates short-term thinking and stifles potential collaboration: 'they tend to respond to day to day pressures and what ministers want, which is responding to the political pressures, and often whole-of-government stuff is long term complex policy so inevitably it's going to fail' (APSC, EL).

Misalignment of evaluation and accountability

It was clear that all projects needed to be seen to be effective and that evaluation was a key part of this. However, it was argued that there was a tendency to over-evaluate projects before they could be seen to deliver outcomes. Moreover, where there was evaluation it was potentially likely that it would be encouraging the wrong behaviours or outcomes unless the matters being measured were appropriate (Blackman 2006):

> The dilemma for me is I don't think we understand what evaluation means really, that we measure things that we do, but we don't measure impacts that we do and we don't really know how to measure impacts.
>
> (FaHCSIA, EL)

This misalignment indicates one of the interesting issues that emerged in this research: that whilst there has been long-term commitment to the concept of joining-up by the Australian Government, evaluations have indicated that there has been little real change over time in the way that the agencies are working. There has been considerable evaluation, yet each time similar issues are raised – namely that the structures, systems and processes in place do not support whole-of-government working.

Implications for working across boundaries

The above discussion highlights that although the Australian Government has been emphasizing the need for joined-up approaches for a number of years, there has not been the appropriate institutional support to work in this way. The lack of human resource structures, systems and processes to encourage and facilitate working across boundaries were all raised as indicators of a mismatch between the espoused desire to have whole-of-government working and the reality, whereby business as usual prevailed.

From the identified themes it is clear that, despite a push towards whole-of-government working which has lasted several years, serious issues remain concerning the potential and possibilities of effective collaboration. When reviewing the enablers and barriers outlined above, they can be seen as ways of trying to encourage whole-of-government on the one hand, in terms of building the rhetoric and strategic vision, whilst at the same time preventing it by making such ways of working too hard to achieve. Where successes were apparent, those involved had worked around potential obstacles in their way. The question then becomes: what lessons can be taken from the analysis to identify the key issues to be addressed in order to develop and sustain effective cross-boundary working?

An important reflection upon the data is that whilst, in some cases, a barrier may be overcome so as to move towards enabling, for the most part barriers and enablers are not opposites of the same thing. For example, developing structures to support collaborative working may remove barriers, but this alone will not be enough to promote whole-of-government working. Consequently, the presence of the enablers on their own is not enough; there needs to be a lack of barriers as well. In terms of a model of the way that enablers and barriers create an impact, they need to be seen as different triggers leading to different outcomes which are independent of each other. Whilst they remain seen as opposites of one another, strategies for supporting whole-of-government are likely to prove ineffective. Figure 11.1 depicts two conceptualizations of barriers and enablers. In the first one, barriers and enablers are seen as being on the same continuum, and so concentrating on one should enable movement in terms of whole-of-government development. This is the conventional wisdom; however, our research shows that thinking of it this way may actually contribute to a lack of progress in operationalizing effective cross-boundary working.

The second conceptualization locates barriers and enablers on different continuums, which leads to them being considered separately. A precedent for this approach has been seen with Herzberg's factors of motivation and demotivation, whereby only when they are perceived as separate triggers can behavioural outcomes be better understood (Herzberg 1968; Herzberg *et al.* 1959). This change alone will not be enough, but acts as an underpinning for better understanding the tensions to be found in supporting whole-of-government working, because it allows an overall picture of the potential for change to be determined. The relative impacts of the enablers/barriers can be seen as independent sets of

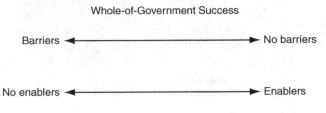

Figure 11.1 Conceptualizations of whole-of-government forces.

drivers and restraining forces, and if the barriers are stronger there is little point in pursuing a joined-up strategy until the enabler/barrier relationship has been changed. What emerges, unlike conventional readiness frameworks which tend to be sequential (see for example Glasby *et al.* 2011), is a framework which starts with a diagnosis of the actual state of readiness for a particular context. This forms the foundation for a diagnostic approach to addressing joined-up dilemmas.

Enabler/inhibitor analysis

In an adaptation of a Force Field Analysis (Lewin 1951), inhibitors are seen to be those things preventing a move away from the status quo, whilst enablers are the conditions which will support a desired change. The strength of the inhibitor or enabler is identified as a different-sized arrow leading to a picture of the forces at play (Figure 11.2).

Once it is accepted that the factors can be represented in this way, then it can be seen that a specific case of cross-boundary working, a potential project or a specific organization could be diagnosed in terms of its joined-up working readiness; a picture illustrating the likelihood of success can be developed.

Figure 11.3 is a generic picture of the types of barriers and enablers identified in the research and demonstrates their potential to influence outcomes. To be useful, an analysis needs to be undertaken which depicts the specific representation of the types of inhibitors and enablers present and the strength of their presence.[5] In the cases used for the research, the identification of the types and relative strength was determined from the qualitative analysis.

What can be seen in Figure 11.4 is that, at the time of the data collection in this particular case, inhibitors were stronger than enablers. In terms of the

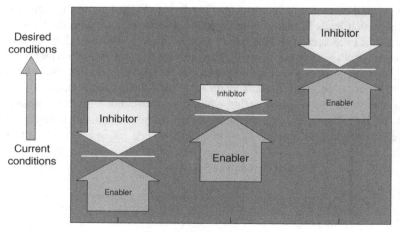

Factors affecting the development of
whole-of-government working

Figure 11.2 Factors conceptualized as a generic force field.

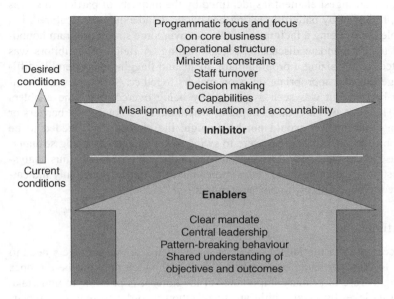

Figure 11.3 A generic model of enabler/inhibitor elements of whole-of-government working.

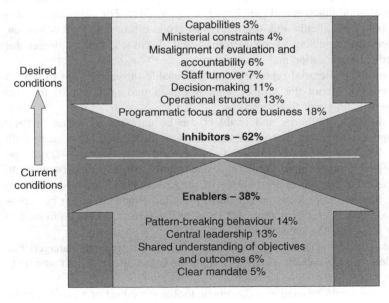

Figure 11.4 An example analysis.

enablers, the strongest element, as identified by the majority of participants, was mandate, followed by pattern-breaking behaviour. Leadership also featured, but the complexity of being a facilitator needing to overcome strong program boundaries led to the mandate discussion predominating. A range of inhibitors was highlighted, emphasizing a programmatic focus and flagging considerable difficulty in getting the appropriate decision makers together. Structure was identified as a barrier, but was seen as potentially being overcome by the enablers present. This case was a good example of where either removing the barriers or developing the enablers would not be enough: the elements all needed to be worked on together if the forces were to swing towards enablers being stronger. In this case, there were very different profiles in different locations, thus analysing each sub-case demonstrated some interesting differences, potentially indicating where there were likely to be better outcomes.

Implications

This process enables the identification of the elements senior managers need to focus on for any particular project being analysed, which may not be the ones they thought were of primary importance at the time. It is possible to undertake this analysis level by level within an organization in order to map differences and potential problems within the hierarchy.

Undertaking the analysis will have four managerial advantages:

1   The conversations that need to take place in order to develop the qualitative model will provide opportunities to explore potential problems, discover areas of good practice and gain buy-in for new ideas. The data can be gathered both individually and in groups. The group discussions will permit the barriers and enablers to be identified and discussed, and strategies for effective collaboration may then emerge;
2   The resultant pictorial representation will enable those involved to have a conversation about the project, with a shared understanding of the real issues affecting their likely success;
3   The different inhibitors and enablers can be assessed in terms of their strengths, with those that will make the most difference being dealt with first. In Figure 11.4 'Programmatic focus and core business' should be addressed as the primary inhibitor. Concurrently, efforts might be made to increase the 'Shared understanding of objectives and outcomes' and consider whether more focus on developing a 'Clear mandate' might be appropriate. What is crucial is that both sides of the force field are addressed in order to change the status quo;
4   By recognizing what is, and what is not, making a difference managers can develop strategies which specifically target the issues affecting their situation.

This technique could be used as a diagnostic tool at the outset of a project, or be utilized as an intervention if there are concerns during it. Comparisons between different data sets, such as levels of the organization, different sites within an agency or different agencies involved in the project, could be used to identify not only issues around the project but also, potentially, problems between the partners.

Conclusion

This chapter identifies enablers and barriers to cross-boundary working and reconceptualizes them to demonstrate that they are not opposites, but separate behavioural drivers. The implications for working across boundaries are that, in order to develop an environment which is conducive to, and supportive of, whole-of-government working, departments and agencies need to focus on both enhancing the enablers and minimizing the barriers. In this research context enablers have been identified in the form of a clear mandate and leadership, pattern-breaking behaviour, and a shared understanding of outcomes, whilst barriers are seen to be staff turnover, program focus, structure and 'core business', issues of decision making, and misalignments between evaluation and accountability. These were the strongest of the themes identified in this research, leading to the important conclusion that there needs to be a greater clarity as to the differences between enablers and barriers for a given context in order to improve potential collaborative strategies.

A diagnostic tool has been presented which offers insights into how to work across boundaries. It is argued that the use of that tool for a specific case or agency can provide managerial insights into the specific functioning of joined-up working in that context, enabling concentration upon strengthening the enablers and reducing the inhibitors in order to enhance the forces for effective working. The use of this diagnostic tool will increase the potential for effective joined-up work and can assist in providing solutions to cross-boundary dilemmas.

Notes

1 The role of the Council of Australian Governments (COAG) was to initiate, develop and monitor the implementation of policy reforms that are of national significance and which require cooperative action by Australian governments.
2 The Australian Government Land and Coasts (AGLC) is a joint venture between two Australian Government departments – Agriculture, Fisheries and Forestry, and Sustainability, Environment, Water, Population and Communities (previously DEWHA). It provides program delivery, liaison with state and territory agencies and regional bodies, and administration of funding for the Australian Government's Caring for our Country initiative, as well as a range of sustainable agriculture initiatives including landcare, environmental management systems, biodiversity and native vegetation, management of weeds and pest animals, and market-based alternatives to regulation.
3 The NT Intervention or, as it is more correctly known, Northern Territory National Emergency Response Act 2007, was a legislative response from the Federal Government to the Northern Territory Government's Inquiry into the Protection of Aboriginal Children from Sexual Abuse, or the 'Little Children are Sacred' report. It was a package of changes to welfare provision, law enforcement, land tenure and other

measures (for more information, see www.abc.net.au/indigenous/special_topics/
the_intervention/).

4 This role worked closely with Indigenous communities, individuals and stakeholders to
develop and implement partnership agreements which would support effective implementation of Indigenous specific programs and policies in a 'joined-up' way.

5 The method undertaken was based upon the qualitative analysis of semi-structured
face-to-face interviews with individuals at all levels of the organization. They were
analysed against the generic list of barriers/enablers identified from the cases. All the
responses relevant to the development of the figure were then added up and each
element was calculated as a percentage. It was decided a percentage was appropriate as
each case had differing numbers of interviews, and it is easier to compare like with like
in percentage terms. Other assumptions were that if an element was not mentioned in a
case study example then it was considered not to be contextually strong and, therefore,
was not seen as relevant, and where an element was mentioned it was of interest to the
case. The more times the element was mentioned, the more impact it would have upon
whole-of-government working. The format of the representation does not matter – it is
the presence of the element and its strength that matters.

References

Australian National Audit Office (ANAO) (2007a) *Whole of Government Indigenous
Service Delivery Arrangements*. Audit Report No. 10 2007–08, Commonwealth of
Australia: Canberra.

Australian National Audit Office (ANAO) (2007b) *Australia's Preparedness for a Human
Influenza Pandemic: Department of Health and Ageing, Department of Agriculture,
Fisheries and Forestry*. Audit Report No. 6 2007–08, Commonwealth of Australia:
Canberra.

Australian Public Service Commission (2007) *State of the Service Report 2006–07*. Canberra: Commonwealth of Australia.

Blackman, D. (2006) 'How measuring learning may limit new knowledge creation',
Journal of Knowledge Management Practice, 7(3). Online. Available at: www.tlainc.
com/articl117.htm (accessed 3 October 2012).

Blackman, D., Buick, F., Halligan, J., O'Flynn, J. and Marsh, I. (2010) 'Australian
experiences with whole of government: constraints and paradoxes in practice', paper
presented at International Research into Public Sector Management, Bern, April 2010.

Blackman, D. and Kennedy, M. (2008) 'Talent management: developing or preventing
knowledge and capability?', paper presented at International Research into Public
Sector Management, Brisbane, March 2008.

Bogdanor, V. (ed.) (2005) *Joined-up Government*, Oxford: Oxford University Press.

Eisenhardt, K.M. (1989) 'Building theories from case study research', *Academy of Management Review*, 14(4): 532–550.

French, J. and Raven, B.H. (1959) 'The bases of social power', in D. Cartwright (ed.)
Studies of Social Power, Ann Arbor, MI: Institute for Social Research.

Glasby, J., Dickinson, H. and Miller, R. (2011) 'Partnership working in England – where
are we now and where we've come from', *International Journal of Integrated Care*
11(7): 1–8.

Herzberg, F. (1968) 'One more time: how do you motivate employees?', *Harvard Business Review*, 46 (1): 53–62.

Herzberg, F., Mausner, B. and Snyderman, B.B. (1959) *The Motivation to Work*. New
York: John Wiley.

Lewin, K. (1951) *Field Theory in Social Science*. New York: Harper and Row.

Management Advisory Committee (MAC) (2004) *Connecting Government: Whole Of Government Responses to Australia's Priority Challenges*, Canberra: Commonwealth of Australia.

Shergold, P. (2004a) *Connecting Government: Whole of Government Responses to Australia's Priority Challenges*. Online. Available at: www.apsc.gov.au/_data/assets/pdf_file/0006/7575/connectinggovernment.pdf (accessed 5/10/2012).

Shergold, P. (2004b) 'Plan and deliver: avoiding bureaucratic hold-up', speech to the Australian Graduate School of Management/Harvard Club of Australia, National Press Club Canberra, November 2004.

Shergold, P. (2005) 'Foundations of governance in the Australian Public Service', speech delivered at launch of Foundations of Governance in the Australian Public Service, Canberra, June 2005.

Stake, R.E. (2000) 'Case studies', in N.K. Denzin and Y.S. Lincoln (eds) *Handbook of Qualitative Research*, 2nd edn, Thousand Oaks, CA: Sage Publications.

Yin, R.K. (2003) *Case Study Research: Design and Methods*, 3rd edn, Thousand Oaks, CA: Sage Publications.

12 The responsiveness solution?

Embedding horizontal governance in Canada

Evert A. Lindquist

Introduction[1]

Contemporary interest in and debate over horizontal policy and management emerged in Canada in the wake of the June 1993 restructuring of the federal government, the Program Review announced in the February 1994 Budget, and significant cuts in programs in the February 1995 Budget (Paquet and Shepherd 1996). The resulting staff reductions, program eliminations, and search for alternative ways to deliver services led to considerable interest in horizontal governance. In 2002, I wrote:

> The challenge of working across the traditional boundaries of government to deliver public services has seized the attention of political and administrative leaders across Canada. This encompasses designing and delivering a wide variety of programs across agencies, levels of government, and with partners in other sectors. Many different phrases are invoked to describe the challenge and purported solutions: horizontal government, collaborative government, 'joined-up' government, and public–private partnerships. The term 'horizontal' arguably now challenges 'strategic', 'performance', 'cost effective', and 'results' as the top adjective for describing the directions for public sector reform, and is often invoked as a noun – 'horizontality' – in effect, a condition, desired state, or mind-set for those working in the public sector.
>
> (Lindquist 2002: 153)

This observation was made not long after several task forces had published reports, the culmination of five years of internal discussion about managing horizontal initiatives in the Canadian Public Service. There had emerged views that decision making for the Program Review cuts were too 'siloed', that coordination ought to be achieved with non-structural approaches, and that the public service needed new ways of working with internal and external partners. The notion of 'horizontal initiatives' means very different things to different people: Box 12.1 provides examples of what officials and observers had in mind. Then, the interest in 'horizontality' showed no sign of peaking.

Box 12.1 Examples of horizontal issues in Canada, late 1990s

The Canadian Centre for Management Development (CCMD) Roundtable on Horizontal Issues (Hopkins *et al.* 2001) focused on the following examples:

- *Team Canada.* Prime Minister Chretien's initiative to launch and coordinate several visits of federal and provincial governments, along with business leaders from across the country, to foreign countries in order to expand markets for Canadian business.
- *Regional Councils.* Originally used to encourage information-sharing and coordination among federal entities in regions, the councils were increasingly used to implement system-wide reform initiatives, to assist with specific horizontal initiatives, and to serve as sounding boards.
- *Urban Aboriginal Strategy (Saskatchewan).* Sought to better coordinate federal departments, Aboriginal communities and organizations, and provincial ministries to deliver and tailor programs and services for urban Aboriginal people at risk.
- *Rural Team New Brunswick.* The New Brunswick Federal Regional Council coordinated 13 federal and seven provincial departments under the Canadian Rural Partnership program to increase leadership, capacity and access to government programs for rural communities and businesses.
- *St. Lawrence Action Plan.* A five-year collaborative initiative among eight federal and five Quebec departments and agencies, as well as NGOs, to improve water quality and coordinate policy in the St. Lawrence River.
- *Science and Technology (S&T) MOU for Sustainable Development.* Initiated in 1995, this initiative involved coordinating five departments to better support science to deal with sustainable development issues.
- *Implementing the Oceans Act (1997).* The Department of Fisheries and Oceans worked with 23 federal departments and agencies, provincial governments, and NGOs to develop an Oceans Management Strategy to improve ocean ecosystems, educate children and youth, and promote conservation, economic development, and sustainable communities.
- *Search and Rescue – Swissair 111 Disaster.* The Rescue Coordination Centre (RCC) of the Department of National Defense coordinated over one thousand people and seven departments, agencies and other organizations.
- *Voluntary Sector Task Force.* This involved 23 government departments and voluntary sector representatives in discussion tables, leading to the *Working Together* action plan (Voluntary Sector Initiative, 1999).
- *The Trends Project.* The Policy Research Secretariat and the Social Sciences and Humanities Research Council created multi-disciplinary networks of policy researchers from both inside and outside of government to identify and probe trends affecting policy making.
- *The Leadership Network.* This 1998 initiative, supported by several central agencies, sought to foster leadership and support the Assistant Deputy Minister (ADM) community as part of a broader public service renewal strategy driven by the Clerk.

Additional selected examples come from a study sponsored by CCMD, The Leadership Network, and the federal Quebec Regional Council (Bourgault and Lapierre 2000): a federal-provincial strategy to improve income security for First Nations in Quebec and Labrador; improving federal presence in Abitibi-Temiscamingue region; a federal strategy in support of Greater Montreal; the Lower St. Lawrence Model Forest with 40 partners, part of a larger national model forests program; the Saguenay–St. Lawrence Marine Park agreement between Canada and Quebec, involving many public partners; and initiatives by federal departments to improve locally shared support services in Shawinigan and Estrie. The Auditor General of Canada (2000) focused on the Family Violence Initiative, the Disability Agenda, and the Canadian Rural Partnership for an audit on horizontal management.

Over time, the pool of horizontal initiatives under the microscope has evolved, but is always an equally idiosyncratic, diverse mix. Bakvis and Juillet (2004) reviewed the Urban Aboriginal Strategy (1998), the Climate Change Secretariat (1998), the Vancouver Agreement (2000), and the Innovation Strategy (2002). A private firm hosted annual conferences on 'Horizontal Policy Management' with, for example, its 2006 event showcasing the Canadian Biotechnology Strategy, which manages science and technology at the community level, and implementing a cities and communities agenda for Infrastructure Canada (Federated Press 2006a, 2006b); its 2012 conference addressed topics such as Aboriginal issues, a Northern Strategy, policing and public safety, chemicals management, health emergency preparedness across the Canada–US border, and communities of practice for policy research across departments, etc. (Federated Press 2012). The Harper government's 2009 Economic Action Plan was a cross-government infrastructure and jobs initiative (Canada, Department of Finance 2009; Good and Lindquist, 2012). In short, the scale, locus, and range of partners of horizontal projects are incredibly diverse; developing typologies to make sense of them has not been successful.[2]

In Canada, discourse on horizontal management has proceeded from different vantage points. Traditionally it was seen as a 'coordination' or structural challenge, with the prime minister and top officials using more formal, top-down mechanisms such as: the mandate and scope of ministerial portfolios and committees; the structure and responsibilities of departments and agencies; monitoring and coordination by central bureaus on government priorities; internal task forces, committees and working groups with representation from across government to address specific horizontal initiatives; and cross-governmental committees and sector councils to deal with other governments and external stakeholders (Peters 1998). Conversely, Sproule-Jones (2000) proposed a bottom-up view of horizontal challenges, focusing on 'mutual adjustment' across departments. I have argued (Lindquist 2002) that, in initiatives and literature in the late 1990s and early 2000s, central agencies and top executives emphasized 'culture', seeking to inculcate values and repertoires disposed to collaboration across the public service, standing in contrast to a 'control' perspective emanating from the

Auditor General of Canada (1999, 2000), while common ground could be found on the need for sufficient 'capacity' to launch, co-design, and implement horizontal initiatives (i.e., resources, leadership, etc.).

Looking back, the early 2000s constituted the apex of Canadian interest and debate on horizontal governance. This chapter revisits Lindquist (2002) in light of more recent developments. It first reviews how horizontal management moved to the top of public sector reform agenda in the late 1990s, and delves into different perspectives on how to enable horizontal initiatives. The second section considers developments since the mid-2000s and beyond, arguing that while the government and public service leaders continue to rely on horizontal strategies, central-agency sponsored dialogue and research on practice has tapered off. The third section explores the reasons for this, arguing that, reinforced by a firm and directive government, there are fewer open discussions on initiatives, but that horizontality has been embedded as one of the core values of an executive group and way of doing business. The final section considers the prospects for horizontal initiatives and calls for a systematic review of the state of practice.

Horizontality moves up the agenda: late 1990s and early 2000s

Horizontal management moved to the top of the public sector reform agenda during the late 1990s as the government sought to handle cutbacks and avoid further structural change. First, this section reviews these developments and the efforts to build new skills and culture for this purpose; the second section is a response emphasizing control and accountability. The third part reviews a need that transcended these views: building sufficient capacity and enabling horizontal management at all levels for diverse issues in a system of distributed capacities.

Promoting horizontal management as culture and competency

In 1994 the Liberal Government announced a concerted government-wide Program Review process to reduce the federal deficit (Bourgon 2009). Each department had to meet strict expenditure reduction targets, ranging from 20 percent to as much as 50 percent, over three years. Ministers submitted plans for rethinking or eliminating programs (the phrase 'alternative service delivery' vaulted to the top of the lexicon) and decisions were announced in the February 1995 Budget. The Program Review has been hailed as a political and fiscal success (Bourgon 2009), but in the immediate aftermath public service leaders worried about the effects upon the Canadian Public Service. First, they wondered what 'new' public service would emerge over the longer term. Second, most decisions were not informed by analysis of their potential impact upon other programs (i.e., two departments cutting back or retaining similar programs for similar clients). Finally, executives wondered if the public service could have supplied the advice if asked – it was believed that the capacity to produce high-quality policy analysis and research had steadily declined following the managerialist reforms of the late 1980s and early 1990s.

In late 1995 the Clerk launched several task forces, led by deputy ministers, on different challenges for the federal public service. One was the Task Force on Managing Horizontal Policy Issues. Recognizing that there were several entities dedicated to working across departmental boundaries, such as the Council on Administrative Renewal, Personnel Renewal Council, and federal regional councils, this task force focused on how to better manage horizontal policy issues, not 'horizontality' more generally (Canada, Task Force on Managing Horizontal Policy Issues 1996).

The task force reviewed best practices and recognized that the extent of 'horizontality' for each policy issue would vary greatly, depending on the scope of the problem, the authorities assigned to departments and ministers, their respective capacities, the nature of stakeholders, and whether an issue was a government priority. The review pointed to the importance of properly defining issues, identifying lead institutions and providing proper mandates to lead officials, and securing the right level of support from central agencies (which could be assigned the lead, if necessary). The task force also recognized that there had to be realistic time frames and expectations, and sufficient resources to support initiatives. Finally, it called for accountabilities to be delineated in advance, followed by reviews upon completion of horizontal policy initiatives.

The task force did not propose structural changes – a reaction to the massive restructuring of the federal public service in June 1993, which was still working through the system. Rather, it sought to strengthen interdepartmental policy making by streamlining the cabinet and expenditure management systems, better utilizing the Continuing Committee of Deputy Ministers (CCDM) and the Assistant Deputy Minister Forum to manage cross-cutting issues, and striking standing committees or temporary task forces as required. This implied that the Privy Council Office (PCO) should be more collaborative as a strategic coordinator, better engage ministers on horizontal issues, and make more systematic use of the Committee of Senior Officials (COSO) and task forces.

Informed by the Task Force on Alternative Service Delivery, it was concluded that there was too much departmental turf protection and too little genuine cross-department collaboration. The proposed remedy was multi-faceted. Public servants were to take courses, adopt horizontal perspectives as part of their value system, take up new appointments across departments, and have their collaborative working appraised. The emerging functional policy community was to foster networking, hold more events to discuss issues, and support professional development. Executives were to model collaborative behavior, recognize horizontal achievements, and deploy sufficient resources to support horizontal initiatives. Pilots were to be identified by the Continuing Committee of Deputy Ministers' policy committee, and the Treasury Board Secretariat Advisory Committee was to develop more training opportunities. Central agencies were to have specific roles: PCO would anticipate and trouble-shoot on horizontal issues; TBS would facilitate mobility of executive recruits and incorporate horizontal issues into developing a broader learning policy; the Public Service Commission would include competencies relating to teamwork and managing horizontal issues for promotion to the executive ranks; and the Canadian Centre for Management Development would factor horizontal issues management into courses and seminars.

The Task Force recognized that much depended on deputy ministers who needed to 'walk the talk' with staff and other departments. It challenged them to inculcate a new culture in departments by encouraging executive teams to identify horizontal issues (i.e., designating an ADM to challenge the department on such issues), initiate reviews of programs and initiatives to determine their horizontal qualities, and take a government-wide view when proceeding with departmental business. Other suggestions included obtaining stakeholder and expert input from inside and outside government, encouraging ADMs to join interdepartmental committees, including horizontal activities in departmental appraisals and promotion decisions, and developing training programs and rotational assignments to facilitate horizontality. Finally, deputy ministers were to assess whether departments had sufficient capacity for short-term policy analysis, longer-term policy research, and longer-term anticipatory thinking.

In short, the Task Force report focused less on how to better manage specific projects, and more on building an enabling culture across the public service for handling horizontal issues and policy initiatives. As it completed its work, the Clerk created a Policy Research Committee, comprised of ADMs and other officials, to undertake a Canada 2005 scanning exercise – a precursor to the Policy Research Initiative (PRI) and the Policy Research Secretariat – which reached out across departments, and to think tanks and universities, with the Trends Project and other activities (Bakvis 2000). The themes of horizontal policy development and a 'borderless institution' soon appeared in the annual reports on the state of the public service from the Clerk to the Prime Minister (Bourgon 1998) and other communications.

Although the Task Force called for a two-year progress report (Canadian Centre for Management Development 1994; Canada 1996), in November 1999 the new President of CCMD (former Clerk Jocelyne Bourgon) announced a year-long Roundtable on the Management of Horizontal Issues.[3] It arrived at several conclusions. First, horizontal initiatives were unique, with their character and managerial challenges varying over time. Second, success required leadership, teamwork, and sufficient energy to work across boundaries, particularly the vertical incentives and accountability of public service systems. Finally, success often depended on building trust among partners, obtaining sufficient financial and human resources, and securing support from executive champions.

The Roundtable made practical recommendations for initiating and managing horizontal projects in several areas: (1) mobilizing teams and networks predicated on building trust and shared leadership, and crucial support of executive champions in home institutions at critical moments; (2) developing a shared framework and vocabulary on issues, balancing team responsibility with accountabilities to home organizations, and embracing creative ambiguity for unresolved issues; (3) matching support structures to needs, which could change as projects evolved, including possibly setting sunset dates; and (4) maintaining momentum in the face of inevitable setbacks, turnover in members, evolving needs, and unanticipated challenges. In contrast to the 1996 Task Force, the Roundtable offered a bottom-up view of how to further horizontal initiatives, essentially producing a guide on how to make horizontal projects work better and ensure other public servants could help further them.

The 1996 Task Force and 2000 CCMD Roundtable each endorsed horizontal, collaborative approaches for dealing with public-service-wide issues, relying on deputy ministerial leadership and ADM-level engagement. They focused more on creating an enabling culture of public service leaders than proposing new structural and coordination solutions. Cultural change would be achieved through better leadership, better training, a broader range of assignments, and appraisal and promotion which recognized horizontal experience. But there was no assessment of how the system might increase the ratio of successes to failures, how to reduce exposure to unnecessary risks without dampening innovation, or how to encourage innovation. Perhaps the most telling observation was that, too often, 'heroic individual effort' must 'overcome obstacles that the "system" could reduce or eliminate' (Hopkins *et al.* 2001: v).

Horizontal management and accountability: control and results

The Auditor General of Canada has closely observed public sector reform in Ottawa, often auditing progress using value-for-money precepts. Following the Program Review, the government entered into alternative service delivery arrangements across departments and with other governments and partners. He asked tough questions about how well the government managed horizontal arrangements, which was tied to an abiding interest in results reporting.[4] The Auditor emerged as a strong critic of how horizontal initiatives were managed, fearing that the government had insufficient controls and reporting.

The Auditor General's 1999 report noted the trend towards 'collaborative government' and alternative service delivery arrangements, observing that they could be 'an innovative, cost-effective and efficient way of delivering programs and services' (Auditor General 1999: 5–7). However, he worried about the increased risk to taxpayers and the public, particularly since the government was typically only one partner in such arrangements and this could potentially dilute accountability to parliament. The report sought to provide guidance on how to better participate and manage the risks in collaborative arrangements and questions to inform scrutiny by parliamentarians.

The audits did not review collaborative arrangements with other governments, conventional contractual arrangements, grants and contributions, or arm's-length organizations – the test was that decisions and oversight had to be jointly managed with other federal entities. The cases included Infrastructure Canada Works, the Model Forests program, the National Action Program on Climate

Change, the Labour Market Development Agreements, the Canadian Industry Program for Energy Conservation, and the North American Waterfowl Protection Plan. This set a low threshold: collaborative arrangements *should* be better managed *among* federal departments and agencies. The Auditor General concluded that collaborative arrangements are more challenging to manage than regular programs because: (1) a vision and effective leadership have to be developed among several partners; (2) they are more complex since each partner has distinct goals, interests, authorities, administrative styles, and accountabilities; (3) the coordination costs are relatively higher, with greater potential for conflict, requiring more capacity to manage; and (4) building trust and confidence are essential ingredients for collaboration, and this takes time.

Informed by previous audits of collaborative programs, the Auditor General built a framework around the general themes of serving the public interest, developing effective accountability arrangements, and greater transparency, leading to questions such as: Were objectives and the public interest best met by means of collaborative arrangements? Were the objectives, responsibilities, levels of performance, required capacities, and evaluation frameworks specified for each partner? Was sufficient information shared with partners, stakeholders, parliament and the public? The Auditor General believed that such questions should be answered *before* proceeding with collaborative arrangements, even though horizontal initiatives usually take considerable time and dialogue to establish.

Invoking such criteria raised the bar higher than it had been set for traditional programs because horizontal initiatives always have higher transaction costs for securing agreements and information. The Auditor General not only argued that departments should maintain reporting obligations to Parliament, but that they should also ensure that partners lived up to the reporting standards, even if partners had varying confidentiality needs. The Auditor presumed that parliamentarians, the public, and the media all clamor for this information, though evidence suggests that this is not so (Lindquist 1998; McDavid and Huse 2012). In short, the Auditor General placed paramount emphasis upon control, as opposed to the flexibility required for innovation and management.

The Auditor General's next audit was released in early 2001 after a federal election (Auditor General 2000). One of 18 chapters reviewed the government's progress on departmental results reporting and focused upon the challenges of reporting results on horizontal issues. The Auditor General had been closely involved in the pilots and roll-out of a new Estimates reporting system under the Improved Reporting to Parliament project (Lindquist 1998). The audit examined how results were used as a management tool in horizontal initiatives and the barriers to use with case studies of the Family Violence Initiative, the Disability Agenda, and the Canadian Rural Partnership – and other audit work, again involving only federal departments. They were assessed with respect to (1) coordination and management structures, (2) leadership from senior officials, (3) accountability frameworks, and (4) reporting frameworks.

While the departments had embraced results reporting, the Auditor raised concerns about the use of reports for accountability, monitoring, and planning.

The Auditor believed that the government and departments failed to clearly set out the expected results, and that evaluation was insufficiently used, calling on the government to move beyond a 'persistent state of planning' for results reporting (Auditor General of Canada 2000: 25). Treasury Board ministers and officials were singled out for insufficient leadership in moving results reporting to the next level by sharing information and practices across departments. The report went on to note recent government commitments required horizontal policy coordination and implementation, and the recommendations of the 1996 Task Force on Managing Horizontal Policy Issues. The Auditor reminded the government of its commitment to developing an accountability framework, consulting with stakeholders, setting realistic expectations for complex projects, providing sufficient resources, offering incentives and recognition for such activities, and the importance of evaluation and information sharing.

The Auditor recognized that informal coordination may be less burdensome and more productive, but favored a defined government strategy and structured coordination with shared frameworks, roles, responsibilities, and decision making protocols. This required a lead department and dedicated staff. The Auditor observed that coordination takes considerable time and energy to achieve, often longer than expected, posing a challenge for results reporting. Like the 1996 Task Force, the Auditor called for strong executive champions to secure resources and support managers, and suggested that formal accountability frameworks would be useful for more complex undertakings, particularly with regard to securing financial or other support for non-centrally funded initiatives. He argued that horizontal managers often do not have access to the incentives and tools required to ensure success, and central agencies needed to play a greater role.

The Auditor concluded that little results reporting occurred in the horizontal cases reviewed. Partner institutions had different reporting regimes, it took time to develop credible shared results regimes, and partners resisted developing detailed results frameworks and supplying information. The Auditor called for more systematic reporting on horizontal initiatives by lead departments because there was insufficient knowledge of program delivery costs. The Auditor worried that staff turnover might lead to insufficient institutional memory to inform subsequent initiatives. Finally, despite acknowledging TBS leadership in identifying and supporting horizontal initiatives, the Auditor worried that not all initiatives received appropriate scrutiny because many did not secure funds or approvals through the submission process, and that TBS approached horizontal initiatives in a piecemeal manner. The Auditor called on TBS to exercise strong central and strategic leadership so as to ensure sufficient resources for coordination and results reporting, and to facilitate sharing lessons and best practices. Like the report on *Collaborative Government*, Chapter 20 on results and horizontal issues set out clear markers for the government, executives, and managers.

Bridging culture and control: building capacity

That the Auditor General and sitting governments clashed over horizontal governance was not surprising given their institutional histories and interests, despite a common understanding of the challenges managers had to overcome when working across boundaries. However, Lindquist (2002) argued that the government, deputy ministers, the Auditor General, *and* working managers had a common cause in ensuring that sufficient capacities and resources were dedicated to horizontal initiatives. A common complaint of managers was that, unless leading a high-profile initiative, they typically managed 'off the corner of their desks' (this was before more onerous reporting requirements), often finding it difficult to secure resources and attention from executives and the centre.

Where and how should such capacities be created? The Auditor General felt that TBS should be more active, providing greater oversight and support. However, the sheer number and diversity of horizontal initiatives could easily overwhelm central agencies. Indeed, departments or other central agencies are often better positioned to lead many horizontal initiatives. Although the CCMD Roundtable was not asked to explore how central agencies could create a more supportive environment for horizontal initiatives, some follow-up did proceed with reports and courses (Rounce and Beaudry 2002; Bakvis and Juillet 2004).

Lindquist (2002) drew together suggestions about how to strengthen system support for horizontal initiatives given the volume and diversity of challenges:

1   *Support a training program on horizontal management* for leaders and staff, informed by case studies and accounts from previous initiatives.
2   *Support a mentoring network on horizontal management* with experienced officials contributing to training courses, providing advice and mentoring on horizontal projects, and increasing awareness of horizontal initiatives.
3   *Develop a central reserve/capacity in TBS to support and recognize horizontal initiatives* with limited-term assistance for staff support and performance pay as well as 'investment' support.
4   *Match machinery to address specific and unique horizontal management challenges* such as regional councils, department headquarters or regional operations, central agencies or deputy minister committees, etc.
5   *Raise awareness of executives and managers about horizontal challenges*, support, and expectations (also see recognition awards below).
6   *Encourage better reporting and accountability* by identifying ways to assist busy managers and partner organizations to more efficiently meet planning and reporting guidelines, with adaptable templates and other tools.
7   *Enhance existing recognition programs* by establishing a new category to recognize horizontal or collaborative initiatives.

These were presented as an integrated package, to be coordinated by a small Horizontal Management Secretariat in TBS, as a focal point for horizontal initiatives and to work with central and other entities to develop training programs, identify priorities for 'investment' support and mentoring contacts, and handle communications. However, these elements could be de-coupled and proceed independently; indeed, multiple lines of influence were identified since initiatives emerge and evolve in very different ways, requiring different kinds of engagement and support along the way. This effort to bridge the culture and control views from a capacity perspective provides one framework for evaluating progress from the early 2000s to the present.

Beyond the early 2000s: horizontal management – 'business as usual'?

Since the early 2000s, there has been a significant tapering in the number of reports and commentaries on horizontal initiatives, with a modest flurry in the mid-2000s. When I recently asked some public service executives about the state of horizontal initiatives in Ottawa, I received blank stares (i.e., it was not top-of-mind on the management agenda), and a couple mentioned that the Clerk had started to 'twitter'. This seems surprising given that no observer would argue that Ottawa has had fewer and less complex problems to grapple with.

Interest in horizontal issues seemed well-sustained into the 2000s, with reports from Canadian Policy Research Networks (CPRN), the Canada School of Public Service (CSPS) and the Auditor General. CPRN published a short study on housing as an example of horizontal social policy challenges (Hay 2005). CSPS published Smith and Torjman (2004) with two detailed case studies on the National Homelessness Initiative, and Bakvis and Juillet (2004) undertook four detailed case studies for the CSPS on the effectiveness of departments and central agencies in managing horizontal initiatives (the Innovation Strategy, the Urban Aboriginal Strategy, the Climate Change Secretariat, and the Vancouver Agreement). They noted the importance of executive champions, timely support, and appropriate skill-sets for enabling horizontal initiatives. However, they found that the costs of initiatives were usually underestimated, that staff had insufficient tools and support, and there was a lack of clarity about how accountability worked beyond reporting to home departments and agencies. They suggested that central agencies could clarify reporting via mandate letters and streamlined reporting, selectively increase the coordinating and policy capacity of central secretariats, and ensure that performance reviews squarely assessed the horizontal performance of executives. At the department level, Bakvis and Juillet (2004) suggested that executive teams could develop internal coordinating units and accountability regimes for horizontal initiatives, be more selective in choosing initiatives to pursue, and be more systematic in identifying staff with the skills and aptitude for collaborative work.

Lindquist (2004) built on this to suggest that central agency horizontal capabilities needed to be better managed for a range of specific upstream and downstream activities, as part of a distributed system. This first required assessing department capabilities and ensuring that central investments were complementary both for handling the design and implementation phases of horizontal initiatives, and for assembling data and analysis. Given the number of initiatives, too many horizontal units might grow at the centre, leading to too much interference, which would require intermittent culling. Second, while horizontal initiatives were 'soft change' attempts to work with existing authorities and structures (and avoid re-organizations or 'hard change'), the transaction costs of work-arounds as well as learning could, in some cases, auger for restructuring.

Revisiting earlier work in 2005, the Auditor General released an audit on how the federal government handled three high-profile initiatives: the Biotechnology Strategy, the Homeless Initiative, and the Vancouver Agreement, concluding that:

> Although there have been some recent improvements, much of the federal government's approach to horizontal initiatives is still on a case-by-case basis. Central agencies have not determined the kinds of circumstances that require a horizontal initiative and the kind of governance needed. They have not developed enough specialized tools for the governance, accountability, and co-ordination of federal efforts in such initiatives and have made little progress in developing means of funding horizontal programs.
>
> (Auditor General 2005: 1–2)

The Auditor General also pointed to insufficient planning for measuring and reporting on results in two of the cases. The report was sharply critical of the PCO and TBS. Since this report there has been no follow-up on horizontal initiatives as a cross-cutting theme, except on specific initiatives (see below).

TBS continued and furthered its capabilities on horizontal management. It issued a *Companion Guide* on program results and accountability (TBS 2002), but there were other pertinent corporate initiatives:

- A new results-oriented reporting architecture (Management, Resources and Results Structure, or MRRS) was developed to guide Estimates authorization and reporting for departments and agencies, providing a hierarchy of outcomes linked to programs and activities, which could be linked to cross-cutting or horizontal goals (Treasury Board of Canada Secretariat 2012).
- Renewed effort was made to create an Expenditure Management Information System (EMIS), to provide better data for budgeting, monitoring, and accountability because TBS could not easily pull comparable data from across programs on horizontal issues (i.e., on aboriginal issues, oceans, cities and communities, international issues, science and technology, etc.) and had to assemble finer-grained data from scratch with departments and agencies (Maloney 2005).
- The Treasury Board started to conduct horizontal strategic reviews of expenditures in broad policy and administrative areas, along with more systematic assessments of department capabilities under the Management Accountability Framework reporting process (Lindquist 2006b, 2009).
- The Treasury Board continued to publish the government's annual report on *Canada's Performance*, which started in 2001, and introduced a horizontal

and whole-of-government framework in the mid-2000s, focusing on a rolling handful of broad policy domains.[5]

• A TBS database of significant formal horizontal initiatives was created, with a small secretariat, since departments and agencies had to formally report on such initiatives in planning and performance documents (Fitzpatrick 2004).[6]

• TBS continued to house a small secretariat in support of regional councils across Canada to support the coordination of regional activities of departments and agencies (Juillet 2000).

Collectively, these initiatives gave expression to the vision of the Treasury Board as a 'management board' arising from the Modern Comptrollership (1996–1997) and *Results for Canadians* (Canada, Treasury Board Secretariat, 2000) initiatives. Both sought to improve the ability of the government and the public services to report and work better across boundaries. Whether the initiatives itemized above actually do so remains an open question.

There have been few reports and studies exploring horizontal themes since the mid-2000s. The strategic and operational reviews have not been released as public documents; only selected expenditure reductions and restructuring get announced in subsequent budgets. A task force report on horizontal tools for community investments was produced for Human Resources and Social Development Canada (Elson *et al.* 2007), and another examined how official languages programs were managed across the Canadian government (Savoie 2008), but the Canada School of Public Service's research program atrophied and no additional studies on horizontal management have emerged. The Canada School does not deliver courses focusing on horizontal management, but its offerings for current and aspiring executives rely on the precepts of systems thinking to encourage outward-looking and collaborative strategizing. The Auditor General has not revisited the matter of horizontal management.

Horizontal issues, however, remain salient. A consulting firm recently organized its eighth annual conference on horizontal policy and management, with federal and provincial government officials reporting on initiatives and experiences (Federated Press 2012). Organizations like the Public Policy Forum and the Institute on Governance have hosted events for departments and agencies to discuss horizontal challenges and prospects for collaborative, sustainable, and place-based governance models (e.g. Crossing Boundaries/Canada 2020 Working Group 2007; Public Policy Forum 2008; Motsi 2009; Bourgault 2010; Canada, Policy Research Initiative 2010). Recently, the Policy Research Initiative was revitalized into Policy Horizons Canada, governed with oversight from a committee of deputy ministers and with a mandate to build a cross-government foresight capability (Policy Horizons 2011). Reflecting broader trends, scholars have explored how collaboration and social innovation can address policy challenges and associated accountability and performance issues (e.g., Caledon Institute of Social Policy 2009; Rocan 2009; Fierlbeck 2010; Anderson and Findlay 2010). Recently, Howard and Phillips (2012) provide a conceptual analysis of whether horizontal and distributed models of public governance inherently carry accountability deficits.

With very few exceptions, though, little of this more recent work has produced new formulations or empirical information on the quality of the contemporary management of horizontal initiatives by the Canadian government. Indeed, this body of work tends to rely heavily on contributions and frameworks from the 1990s and early 2000s (e.g., Ferguson 2009).

Explaining the decline in corporate discourse on horizontal issues

What might account for this paradox, where governments and observers continue to respond to horizontal issues, but research and official, corporate discourse on horizontal governance has tailed off? This section reviews two sets of explanations: changes in the external governance environment, and the strategies used by the public service to adapt to this new environment.

Several changes in the external environment have been important. First, the Human Resources and Development Canada grants and contributions scandal of the early 2000s propelled and ensconced accountability as *the* management issue for government and the public service throughout the decade. It also made it increasingly difficult to use grants and contributions to fund horizontal and collaborative activities with partners because of new approval and reporting strictures (Good 2003; Phillips *et al.* 2010). Second, starting in February 2006, the Harper Government instituted a controlling, centralized, and disciplined style of governing, brooking little off-message commentary from Conservative caucus members and public servants alike, what Peter Aucoin terms the 'new political governance' (Aucoin 2008; Lindquist and Rasmussen 2012), and, not surprisingly, there are fewer task forces and roundtables with public reports. Third, the Harper Government has had to balance its interest in reducing and reallocating program spending, delegating responsibilities to provinces and territories, and securing marginal votes in elections to secure a majority government. This led to the identifying of specific initiatives closely aligned to the government's strategic policy and political agenda (e.g., the Economic Action Plan and the 2010 Olympics, etc.). Oversight and coordination of major projects and the public service has been closely handled by the Prime Minister's Office, which expects responsiveness and coordination of top-priority programs. And fourth, even when the Auditor General audited government programs such as the Economic Action Plan, horizontal management was not identified as a paramount theme to focus upon (Canada, Department of Finance 2009; Good and Lindquist 2012), even when collaboration across departments and central agencies was considered essential for success.

Relatedly, the public service has adapted to this new governance environment in several ways. First, since the mid-2000s the Treasury Board, TBS, and other central agencies have taken a low-profile approach to change and have eschewed announcing big reform initiatives (e.g., new expenditure systems), recognizing that, even if progress occurred, threshold improvements would take years of work and inevitably be superseded by overlapping initiatives (Lindquist 2009).

Second, resources devoted to supporting applied research and cultivating relationships with scholars have been pared back in TBS and the CSPS, leading to less open dialogue and research on internal developments and challenges, such as how horizontal initiatives are handled. Third, for over a decade the expectation of horizontal collaboration has been built into the culture of the executive group, no matter the agenda of sitting governments; careers are built through rotation, interaction at corporate events, and in the knowledge that the entire executive group is a corporate resource (Lindquist 2006a: 28–35).

In short, the combination of risk aversion due to a controlling government, lack of follow-up from the Auditor General, and a public service executive group which arguably has horizontal values embedded in its corporate culture, has led to insufficient incentive for TBS and other central agencies to support additional assessments of horizontal management.

Stepping back, it seems clear that considerations of 'coordination' and 'control' now dominate the landscape that leaders of horizontal initiatives must navigate, pushing aside the earlier interest in 'culture' and 'capacity'. And, presumably, in the context of the cutbacks and continued high scrutiny and transaction costs associated with grants and contributions so often used for horizontal initiatives (unless they are internal to government), the interest in promoting partnerships with outside groups and other governments may have waned, unless there is the prospect of genuine innovation in designing and delivering programs. However, if the executive cadre continues to embrace horizontality and collegiality as institutional 'cultural' values, and the external governance environment remains difficult in financial and political terms, there may be fertile ground for a quieter and more bottom-up 'mutual adjustment' approach for identifying and implementing horizontal initiatives within the federal government, with some potential to work across levels of government (Lindquist 1999).

Conclusion: assessing horizontal strategies in a tougher environment

This chapter reviewed studies and initiatives aimed at improving the quality of horizontal management in the Canadian government. It identified competing narratives about how to best handle diverse horizontal challenges – the coordination, mutual adjustment, culture, control, and capacity perspectives. The discourse of the late 1990s and early 2000s focused on building a new public-service culture in support of horizontal management, as response to the significant government restructuring and program cutbacks of the mid-1990s, while the Auditor General called for more systematic 'control' and reporting. Together, these studies, initiatives, and narratives identified myriad enablers for overcoming barriers to collaboration at all levels: leaders of projects, executive champions, department executive teams, and central-agency leadership.

Since the mid-2000s, horizontal issues seem to have tapered off as a top-of-mind reform challenge, at least with respect to central-agency exhortation and public administration scholarly research, even as complex policy challenges continue to multiply. Several explanations have been ventured to explain this state of affairs; of particular interest has been the ascendancy of the control perspective, along with the advent of top-down coordination from a controlling government in a tighter accountability environment, leading to less discretion and flexibility for public servants working with partners on a horizontal basis, but a great deal more political support for government priorities with horizontal qualities.

The drop-off in public discussion and research does not mean, of course, that ministers and public service executives are less interested in horizontal challenges – indeed, they may have found new, more efficient and effective ways to handle them (and this chapter suggests that 'mutual adjustment' might be a possible strategy). The Harper Government announced significant cutbacks to programs and the Canadian Public Service in the 2012 spring Budget, similar to those of the 1990s Program Review. Departments and agencies will be focused on controlling costs, increasing efficiency, and levering resources from other entities. The time is ripe for identifying what horizontal strategies are now favored by the government and the public service, their effectiveness, and the quality of central oversight and support. At the very least these announcements suggest a need for fresh research and dialogue (see Lindquist 2012).

Lindquist (2002) concluded on a speculative note, briefly considering future scenarios for how horizontal management by public servants might proceed. The trends identified remain salient: increasing complexity and interdependence of issues; increasing demands from citizens for better service; the accelerating pace of technological change; and increasing demands for accountability and results reporting. So, too, with the critical political uncertainties for public sector managers who grapple with horizontal issues: the extent to which governments will have more turf-oriented debates or engage in collaboration,[7] and whether citizens and other stakeholders will become more or less engaged in debating and shaping policy development and service delivery.[8] To these trends and uncertainties we can now add the significant pressures upon national budgets following the Global Financial Crisis and worries about the state of the US and European economies and public finances, and the Harper Government's tight control of the policy direction, communications, and the public service, and its determination to devolve responsibilities to provinces and territories.

Horizontal initiatives will continue moving forward in the midst of these challenges and uncertainties, and, as before, will be idiosyncratic and often frustrating experiences, handled by government in a distributed manner and in diverse ways. In the new governance and fiscal environment in Canada, it will be interesting to see whether decision making – and particularly longer term experimentation and solution-finding – becomes more collaborative and horizontal, whether governments and outsiders fully explore the possibilities of taking advantage of new technologies and the potential willingness of citizens and stakeholders to do things differently and change how government works, and whether the public service executives and managers leading the next wave of reform find themselves proceeding in supported environments or having to be 'heroic', navigating a vertically oriented government system. Providing credible assessments of how these trends and practices are handled by the Canadian government will require a new round of careful, systematic research.

Notes

1 This chapter was prepared in memory of Peter Aucoin (Dalhousie University), who passed away on 8 July 2011. Peter was initially invited to participate in the 'Connecting Across Boundaries: Making the Whole of Government Agenda Work' symposium on 18–19 November 2010 in Canberra. Not only was he Canada's foremost scholar in public administration, he was equally well-known and highly respected among scholars and public sector executives in Australia. He, along with other productive scholars of his generation in Australia and Canada, established footpaths and networks of collaboration from which subsequent generations of scholars and practitioners continue to benefit. Peter's research and presentations always combined taking up pressing issues and considering reform possibilities with an awareness of history, institutional constraints, and the core principles and ideals of Westminster government and public administration. This posture – along with his infectious enthusiasm, curiosity and collegiality – will be greatly missed. I would like to thank Deborah Blackman, John Halligan and Janine O'Flynn for their invitation to participate in the symposium, David Good and several officials in the Government of Canada for their perceptive comments on drafts of this paper, and Janine O'Flynn and Rosemary Lohmann for their editorial advice.
2 Attempts to produce typologies to categorize horizontal initiatives have proven unsatisfying: if one tries to richly capture their dimensions, the resulting typologies can be as complicated as the challenges; conversely, fewer dimensions cannot capture their distinctiveness and evolution. The first CCMD Roundtable explored whether cases under review could be grouped into the categories of service, research, policy, internal support, emergencies, and multi-faceted projects. A background report provided typologies based on: *function* (information, resources, work, authority); *goals* (support services, knowledge, policy development, program and service delivery); and *mechanisms* (a menu of formal structures and processes, and informal coordinating devices) (CCMD 2000). See also the Traverse Group (2006) typology.
3 The roundtable was one of four: the others were on the Learning Organization, Risk Management, and the Social Union Framework. The Roundtable on the Management of Horizontal Issues was led by an Associate Deputy Minister and consisted of ADMs, directors and two academics, supported by a small CCMD secretariat. The group was provided with a review of relevant literature and written summaries and presentations on case studies of different horizontal projects, had consultations in summer and fall 2000, and produced a practical guide for public servants. The author was a member of the Roundtable.
4 The Auditor collaborated with central agencies to institute a new estimates reporting regime following adoption of a new expenditure management system in 1995 (Lindquist 1998).
5 For the most recent *Canada's Performance* reports, see www.tbs-sct.gc.ca/reports-rapports/cp-rc/index-eng.asp; for the underpinning whole-of-government framework, see www.tbs-sct.gc.ca/ppg-cpr/frame-cadre-eng.aspx. The broad areas reviewed for the 2010–2011 report were demographic change, northern potential, economic prosperity, and domestic security.
6 The TBS Horizontal Initiatives Database for performance information defines a horizontal initiative as

> an initiative in which partners from two or more organizations have established a formal funding agreement (e.g., Memorandum to Cabinet, a Treasury Board

submission, federal-provincial agreement) to work towards the achievement of shared outcomes. Partners include other federal departments or agencies, other national governments, non-government and private sector organizations, etc. Major horizontal initiatives include initiatives that: have been allocated federal funds that exceed $100 million for the entire initiative; or are key to the achievement of government priorities; or have a high public profile.

See www.tbs-sct.gc.ca/hidb-bdih/home-accueil-eng.aspx.
7 The extent to which public sector managers can confidently proceed with horizontal initiatives has much do with how prime ministers organize and manage cabinets. In turn, how cabinets work can have significant implications for intergovernmental relations (Dupre 1987), and prospects for collaborative and horizontal government. If supportive and collegial cultures do not emerge at the political level, the leaders of central agencies and operating departments will have greater difficulty in collaborating, even if a prudent course of action is followed.
8 If buffered from the real work of our governments by technology and intermediaries, citizens will have decreasing knowledge of how public services are delivered; they might develop a better understanding as a result of better access to information and calls for greater coordination across institutions.

References

Anderson, L. and Findlay, T. (2010) 'Does public reporting measure up? Federalism, accountability and child-care policy in Canada', *Canadian Public Administration*, 53(3): 417–438.

Aucoin, P. (2008) 'New public management and new public governance: finding the balance', in D. Siegel and K. Rasmussen (eds) *Professionalism and Public Service: Essays in Honour of Kenneth Kernaghan*, Toronto: University of Toronto Press.

Auditor General of Canada (1999) 'Collaborative arrangements: issues for the Federal Government', Chapter 5 in *Report of the Auditor General of Canada to the House of Commons, Volume 1, April 1999*, Ottawa: Minister of Public Works and Government Services Canada.

Auditor General of Canada (2000) 'Managing departments for results and managing horizontal issues for results', Chapter 20 in *Report of the Auditor General of Canada to the House of Commons, Volume 3, December 2000*, Ottawa: Minister of Public Works and Government Services Canada.

Auditor General of Canada (2005) 'Managing horizontal initiatives', Chapter 4 in *Report of the Auditor General of Canada to the House of Commons, November 2005*, Ottawa: Minister of Public Works and Government Services Canada.

Bakvis, H. (2000) 'Rebuilding Policy Capacity in the Era of the Fiscal Dividend', *Governance*, 13(1): 71–103.

Bakvis, H. and Juillet, L. (2004) *The Horizontal Challenge: Line Departments, Central Agencies and Leadership*, Ottawa: Canada School of Public Service.

Bourgault, J. (2010) 'Utopia within reach: horizontal collaboration on place-based projects from a sustainable development perspective', *Horizons*, 10(4): 88–94.

Bourgault, J. and Lapierre, R. (2000) *Horizontality and Public Management*, Ottawa: Canadian Centre for Management Development.

Bourgon, J. (1998) *Fifth Annual Report to the Prime Minister on the Public Service of Canada*, Ottawa: Privy Council Office.

Bourgon, J. (2009) *Program Review: The Government Of Canada's Experience Eliminating the Deficit, 1994–99: A Canadian Case Study*, London: Institute for Government.

Caledon Institute of Social Policy (2009) *Collaboration on Policy: A Manual Developed by the Community–Government Collaboration on Policy*, Ottawa: Caledon Institute of Social Policy.

Canada, Department of Finance (2009) *Canada's Economic Action Plan: First Report to Canadians*, Ottawa: Department of Finance. Online. Available at: http://actionplan.gc.ca/grfx/docs/ecoplan_e.pdf (accessed 25 February 2012).

Canada, Policy Research Initiative (2010) 'Sustainable places', *Horizons* 10(4).

Canada, Task Force on Managing Horizontal Policy Issues (1996) *Managing Horizontal Policy Issues*, Ottawa: Privy Council Office and Canadian Centre for Management Development. Online. Available at: www.csps-efpc.gc.ca/pbp/pub/pdfs/actionc_e.pdf (accessed 25 February 2012).

Canada, Treasury Board Secretariat (2000) *Results for Canadians: A Management Framework for the Government of Canada*. Online. Available at: www.tbs-sct.gc.ca/report/res_can/rc-eng.pdf (accessed 25 February 2012).

Canadian Centre for Management Development (CCMD) (1994) *Continuous Learning: a CCMD report*, CCMD Report No. 1. Ottawa: Canadian Centre for Management Development. Online. Available at: www.csps-efpc.gc.ca/pbp/pub/pdfs/P34_e.pdf (accessed 25 February 2012).

Canadian Centre for Management Development (CCMD) (no date, *c*.2000) *Horizontal Management: Issues, Insights, and Illustrations: A Background Paper*, Ottawa: CCMD.

Crossing Boundaries/Canada 2020 Working Group (2007) *Progressive Governance for Canadians: What You Need To Know*, Ottawa: Crossing Boundaries/Canada 2020 Working Group.

Dupre, J.S. (1987) 'The workability of executive federalism in Canada', in H. Bakvis and W. Chandler (eds) *Federalism and the Role of the State*, Toronto: University of Toronto Press.

Elson, P., Struthers, M. and Carlson, J. (2007) *Horizontal Tools and Relationships: An International Survey of Government Practices Related to Communities: Report of the Task Force on Community Investments*, Ottawa: Human Resources and Social Development Canada.

Federated Press (2006a) *Presentations, Lecture Notes and Visual Aids Delivered at the Federated Press Horizontal Policy Management Course held in Ottawa on January 10 & 11, 2006*. Online Available at: www.federatedpress.com/FPWeb/Events/ConferenceReports/tabid/308/mid/380/ProjectId/42/wildRC/1/Default.aspx (accessed 22 December 2011).

Federated Press (2006b) *Horizontal Policy Management: Conference held in Ottawa on May 29–31, 2006*, Online. Available at: www.federatedpress.com/FPWeb/Events/ConferenceReports/tabid/308/mid/380/ProjectId/1252/wildRC/1/Default.aspx (accessed 22 December 2011).

Federated Press (2012) *8th Horizontal Policy Management Conference: Breaking Down the Silos: February 1, 2 & 3, 2012 Ottawa: Brochure*, Online. Available at: www.federatedpress.com/pdf/8HPM1202-E.pdf (accessed 22 December 2011).

Ferguson, D. (2009) *Research Brief on Understanding Horizontal Governance*. Montreal: The Centre for Literacy of Quebec.

Fierlbeck, K. (2010) 'Public health and collaborative governance', *Canadian Public Administration*, 53(1): 1–19.

Fitzpatrick, T. (2004) 'Reporting on Horizontal Initiatives: notes for a presentation on April 30, 2004', Ottawa: Treasury Board of Canada Secretariat.

Good, D. (2003) *The Politics of Public Management: The HRDC Audit of Grants and Contributions*, Toronto: University of Toronto Press.

Good, D. and Lindquist, E. (2012) 'Canada's reactive budget response to the Global

Financial Crisis: from resilience and brinksmanship to agility and innovation' in J. Wanna, E. Lindquist and J de Vries (eds) *The Global Financial Crisis and the Impact on Government Budgets and Debt: Responses, Reforms and Resilience in OECD Countries*, Cheltenham, UK: Edward Elgar.

Hay, D. (2005) *Housing, Horizontality and Social Policy*, Ottawa: Canadian Policy Research Networks. Online. Available at: http://cprn.org/documents/12_en.pdf (accessed 25 February 2010).

Hopkins, M., Couture, C. and Moore, E. (2001) *Moving From the Heroic to the Everyday: Lessons Learned from Leading Horizontal Projects*, Ottawa: Canadian Centre for Management Development Roundtable on the Management of Horizontal Initiatives. Online. Available at: www.csps-efpc.gc.ca/pbp/pub/pdfs/P99_e.pdf (accessed 25 February 2012).

Howard, C. and Phillips, S. (2012) 'Moving away from hierarchy: do horizontality, partnerships, and distributed governance really mean the end of accountability?', in H. Bakvis and M.D. Jarvis (eds) *From New Public Management to New Political Governance: Essays in Honour of Peter C. Aucoin*, Montreal and Kingston: McGill-Queen's University Press.

Juillet, L. (2000) *The Federal Regional Councils and Horizontal Governance: A Report Prepared for the Federal Regional Councils and the Treasury Board Secretariat*, Ottawa: Canadian Centre for Management Development.

Lindquist, E. (1998) 'Getting results right: reforming Ottawa's estimates', in L.A. Pal (ed.) *How Ottawa Spends 1998–99: Balancing Act: The Post-Deficit Mandate*, Toronto: Oxford University Press.

Lindquist, E. (1999) 'Efficiency, reliability, or innovation: managing overlap and complexity in Canada's federal system of governance', in R.A. Young (ed.) *Stretching the Federation: The Art of The State*, Kingston: Institute of Intergovernmental Relations, Queen's University.

Lindquist, E. (2002) 'Culture, control or capacity: meeting contemporary horizontal challenges in public sector management', in M. Edwards and J. Langford (eds) *New Players, Partners and Processes: A Public Sector Without Boundaries?*, Canberra and Victoria: National Institute on Governance and UVic Centre for Public Sector Studies.

Lindquist, E. (2004) 'Strategy, capacity and horizontal governance: perspectives from Australia and Canada', *Optimum Online: The Journal of Public Sector Management*, 34(4). Online. Available at: http://optimumonline.ca (accessed 22 December 2011).

Lindquist, E. (2006a) *A Critical Moment: Capturing and Conveying the Evolution of the Canadian Public Service*, Ottawa: Canada School of Public Service. Online. Available at: www.csps-efpc.gc.ca/pbp/pub/pdfs/P134_e.pdf. (accessed 25 February 2012).

Lindquist, E. (2006b) 'How Ottawa Reviews Spending: Moving Beyond Adhocracy?', in B. Doern (ed.) *How Ottawa Spends 2006–07*, Montreal and Kingston: McGill Queen's University Press.

Lindquist, E. (2009) 'How Ottawa assesses department/agency performance: Treasury Board's management accountability framework', in A.M. Maslove (ed.) *How Ottawa Spends 2009–2010: Economic Upheaval and Political Dysfunction*, Montreal, Kingston: McGill-Queen's University Press.

Lindquist, E. (2012) 'Horizontal Management in Canada Ten Years later', *Optimum Online: The Journal of Public Sector Management*, 42(3). Online. Available at: http://optimumonline.ca (accessed 16 December 2012).

Lindquist, E. and Rasmussen, K. (2012) 'Deputy Ministers and New Political Governance: from neutral competence to promiscuous partisans to a new balance?', in H. Bakvis and M.D. Jarvis (eds) *From 'New Public Management' to 'New Political*

Governance': Essays in Honour of Peter C. Aucoin, Montreal: Kingston: McGill-Queen's University Press.

Maloney, D. (2005) *Expenditure Management Current Challenges, Future Directions*, Notes for FMI Presentation (22 November 2005).

McDavid, J.C. and Huse, I. (2012) 'Legislator uses of performance reports: findings from a five-year study', *American Journal of Evaluation*, 33(1): 7–25.

Motsi, G. (2009) *Two Key Questions for Horizontal Policy Making and Implementation*, Policy Brief 34, Ottawa: Institute on Governance.

Paquet, G. and Shepherd, R. (1996) 'The Program Review Process: A Deconstruction' in G. Swimmer (ed.) *How Ottawa Spends 1996–97: Life Under the Knife*, Ottawa: Carleton University Press.

Peters, G. (1998) *Managing Horizontal Government: The Politics of Coordination*, Research Paper No. 21, Ottawa: Canadian Centre for Management Development.

Phillips, S.D., Laforest, R. and Graham, A. (2010) 'From shopping to social innovation: getting public financing right in Canada', *Policy and Society*, 29: 189–199.

Policy Horizons Canada (2011) *About Us*. Online. Available at: www.horizons.gc.ca/page.asp?pagenm=pri_index (accessed 18 October 2011).

Public Policy Forum (2008) *Collaborative Governance and Changing Federal Roles: a PPF and PRI Joint Roundtable outcomes report*, Ottawa: Public Policy Forum. Online. Available at www.horizons.gc.ca/doclib/RD_OTHER_roundtable_200802_e.pdf. (accessed 25 February 2012).

Rocan, C. (2009) 'Multi-level collaborative governance: the case of the Canadian Heart Health Initiative, *Optimum Online: The Journal of Public Sector Management*, 34(4). Online. Available at: http://optimumonline.ca (accessed 22 December 2011).

Rounce, A. and Beaudry, N. (2002) *Using Horizontal Tools to Work Across Boundaries: Lessons Learned and Signposts for Success*, Ottawa: Canadian Centre for Management Development.

Savoie, D.J. (2008) *Horizontal Management of Official Languages: Report Submitted to the Office of the Commissioner of Official Languages*, Ottawa: Office of the Commissioner of Official Languages.

Smith, R. and Torjman, S. (2004) *Policy Development and Implementation in Complex Files*. Ottawa: Canada School of Public Service. Online. Available at: www.csps-efpc.gc.ca/pbp/pub/pdfs/P125_e.pdf (accessed 25 February 2012).

Sproule-Jones, M. (2000) 'Horizontal management: implementing programs across interdependent organizations', *Canadian Public Administration*, 43(1): 93–109.

Traverse Group (2006) 'Cross-organizational Initiatives'. Online. Available at: www.traversegroup.ca/d5/cross-ndash-organizational-initiatives.php (accessed 22 December 2011).

Treasury Board of Canada Secretariat (TBS) (2002) *Companion Guide: The Development of Results-based Management and Accountability Frameworks for Horizontal Initiatives*, Ottawa: Treasury Board of Canada Secretariat. Online. Available at www.tbs-sct.gc.ca/cee/tools-outils/comp-acc-eng.pdf (accessed 22 December 2011).

Treasury Board of Canada Secretariat (TBS) (2012) *Policy on Management, Resources and Results Structures*. Online. Available at: www.tbs-sct.gc.ca/pol/doc-eng.aspx?id=18218&section=text (accessed 14 January 2013).

Voluntary Sector Initiative (1999) *Working Together: a Government of Canada/Voluntary Sector Joint Initiative: Report of the Joint Tables*, Ottawa: Government of Canada. Online. Available at: www.vsi-isbc.org/eng/knowledge/working_together/index.cfm (accessed 25 February 2012).

Part III

Cases of crossing boundaries in public management and policy

13 Children's services

The impact of service integration in England

Carole Talbot

This chapter explores developments in the integration of children's services in England. In doing so it feeds into the four central themes of this volume, namely:

- what constitutes working across boundaries;
- why we work across boundaries;
- theorizing organizational forms and configurations; and
- identifying enablers and barriers to effective cross-boundary working.

The Children's Trusts (CT) initiative was intended to address the long acknowledged weakness in the coordination in children's services through a broad range of integrative mechanisms. The 'Trust' concept was promoted as a particular organizational form providing a definitive solution to the coordination of various agencies around primarily child protection cases (DFES 2003). This occurred without the concept having been proven to be effective in social care settings. In this chapter I apply Provan and Milward's (1995) theory of network effectiveness to CT developments in order to explore how we can understand the limitations of this initiative by comparing the outcomes with those from alternative cases. This leads to a consideration of enablers and barriers to integration, and therefore how integration attempts may be better pursued. I argue that the initiative resulted in *expansive* networks – defined as expansive because they had many members of a heterogeneous nature pursuing multiple objectives. Although the initiative was laudable in principle, the outcomes have failed to impact positively upon children's services at the aggregate level. The reasons for this fall into four (often overlapping) areas, which constituted barriers to both the development of the Trust concept and to the development of effective cross-boundary working:

- a weak governance framework;
- a lack of resources, including capacity-building support;
- underdeveloped integrative systems; and
- the failure to address outstanding tensions prior to the advancement of integration.

This chapter is organized as follows: The next section discusses some evaluations of CT developments, demonstrating that the initiative has had some weaknesses. The chapter then discusses some of the 'theory' which has developed around the concept of network effectiveness and highlights the lack of coherent evidence on this issue. The CT initiative is then described more fully, prior to the application of Provan and Milward's (1995) theory of network effectiveness to analyse the CT case. The chapter concludes with a summary of the learning developed through the case with regard to expansive networks.

Continuing challenges for coordinating children's services

In England, children's services are continually in the spotlight as stories of the abuse of children are confounded by the apparent failure of public agencies to coordinate support for 'at risk' children. Policy analyses have repeatedly urged greater coordination in this area (DoH 2002). In England, following an inquiry into the death of Victoria Climbié in 2000, the Every Child Matters (ECM) Green Paper (DFES 2003) was published.[1] It has been described as representing 'one of the most far reaching programmes of reform for children and children's services anywhere in the world' (UEA and NCB 2007: 7). Among its recommendations was the aim to make the establishment of CTs a statutory requirement for each local authority with responsibility for children's services. This, it was hoped, would finally achieve children's services integration in England.

Joint work has developed in children's services, and some localities have moved some considerable distance towards the ECM objectives. The evaluation of the CT Pathfinders (UEA and NCB 2007) reported the emergence of some positive developments, among them that CTs had acted as catalysts for integrated working, had developed expertise in commissioning, had enabled joint approaches to workforce development, and had facilitated the establishment of new types of professionals able to work across organizational and professional boundaries through providing training. There were also indications that children and young people had experienced positive outcomes due to these pilot reforms. It is important to recognize that these organizations volunteered to develop some limited aspects of the CT initiative within the Pathfinder project (a pilot). These developments did not include the creation of new organizational entities (i.e. Trusts), neither did they represent a cross section of localities nor the piloting of the expansive approach which was implemented from 2004 onwards.

For the most part, and despite much effort, local areas have found the CT policy particularly problematic. Six years into the reform program a range of formal evaluations suggested that attempts to deliver integration through the creation of CTs had not met expectations (AC 2009). Despite the overwhelming improvement in local government performance in general since 2002, the performance of children's services had declined significantly. More authorities were delivering below minimum requirements in 2008 than in 2005, with eight judged as inadequate on the 'staying safe' outcome. Of a total of 150 councils, 139 were described as 'could improve' in 2006, and only 14 per cent showed improvement in the period 2005–2008. Children's services held back 47 per cent of councils from achieving four star status[2] (AC 2009). These trends suggest that the improvements which it was hoped would emerge from the CT initiative proved difficult to capture. In the context of the post 2010 coalition government's proposal to dismantle the CT initiative whilst still expecting extensive coordination to take place to safeguard children, this chapter provides important lessons based upon that experience.

Coordination: reflecting on the theories of effectiveness

Coordination has been described as 'the philosopher's stone of public administration' (Seidman 1998: 143). This is so not least because, whilst this single term is widely used within the public administration literature (Peters 1998; Pollitt 2003), in practice its meaning encompasses a wide variety of organizational forms and concepts. In general, 'coordination' is further classified into four main areas: (1) cooperative activities; (2) coordinative activities (Rogers and Whetten 1982); (3) collaborative or co-evolutionary activities (Pratt *et al.* 1999; Taylor 1998); and (4) integration, which is more closely associated with mergers (Perri 6 *et al.* 2002). This framework reflects the increasing depth of joint work required, as well as the potential impact upon an individual organization's autonomy. One criticism of the plethora of joint work initiatives has been the lack of accuracy in articulating the actual organizational concepts involved, which has left local actors struggling to translate policy ideas into concrete and purposeful action (Johnson 2005).

Coordination has been increasingly advocated as an approach for dealing with difficult social issues (DETR 1997a, 1997b, 2001; DoE 1977; Seebohm 1968). In the UK, particularly since 1997, the number of coordination initiatives has mushroomed. All manner of organizational forms have been used. CTs reflected two ideas in currency at the time which, on closer examination, appear contradictory. First, CTs represented strategic-level boards operating on local authority boundaries reflective of local strategic partnerships used for regeneration activities, i.e. cooperative strategies. These focused on creating consensus to support a strategy for development. Second, they were conceived as Trust organizations following a small number of similar developments in adult social care where departments from local authorities and healthcare were merged into single-focused bodies to address issues arising from the health–social care divide, i.e. integrative strategies.

It is the particular features of integration which are of core interest here, as the features emerging from the cooperative strategy could be seen to act as a barrier to achieving the desired outcomes. Perri 6 *et al.* (2002) have provided the most extensive analysis of UK holistic government strategies, and outline the key characteristics of integration as follows:

- the production of seamless services for the customer;
- integration to prevent conflict between mission-critical aspects of services;

- the possible involvement of mergers of existing organizations, or establishing new ones;
- the purpose of integration is to allow potential for services to reinforce each other.

Children's services, particularly child protection or the provision of complex sets of services to disabled or ill children, are clearly areas where providers may need to work in more integrated ways. It was intended that the CTs would promote seamless services to protect and prevent children falling through gaps between services. Integration into CTs was also intended to prevent the natural conflict arising from joint work, where organizations may lose control over their own resources. This idea was particularly applied to protection work, as well as to integration at a broader level, as it would allow children to receive all necessary services, which would collectively support their overall development. Such integration, it was argued, would break down professional and organizational barriers through joint strategy, funding and information sharing.

A problem for statutory or managed forms of joint work, which are crucial for integration, is the degree of external or internal control needed for effective implementation. Joint work suffers from an inherent tension between voluntary cooperation and persuasive strategies and the need, at times, to facilitate certain ways of working from member organizations. Thus, the need for control, hierarchy and top-down management of joint working are key areas for discussion in the public policy literature as joint work has become a key theoretical and practical issue (Kickert et al. 1997).

For policy makers, there is a need to know how to ensure effective joint work across different policy areas. Despite increasingly sophisticated approaches to managing networks by the UK Government – for example, in Local Strategic Partnerships (LSPs)[3] – failed networks remain. In some networks failure has little direct consequence for the quality of services citizens receive. In children's services, though, the ineffectiveness of joint work can have an impact upon the quality of services directly affecting children's circumstances. It is one clear area where joint work is a necessity, but there is little evidence on what constitutes an optimal level or how to best facilitate this.

Some conceptual progress in this direction was made by the UK Government's Cabinet Office, who published a report in 2000 outlining when and how to coordinate services. They provided a decision-making framework and proposed that cross-cutting approaches should be adopted only when they add value (PIU 2000). Furthermore, capturing all activity in a comprehensive set of cross-cutting objectives should be avoided as it can be counter-productive. However, it was also acknowledged that some areas may require 'coordination at the centre' (PIU 2000: 19). This approach suggests that a more selective approach, focusing on a few clear objectives and involving fewer agencies, was likely to be more effective for CTs. The option of centralization does not exist within the current governance framework of local authority accountability, and it is doubtful that such services could be better organized at the central level. Nevertheless, coordination at the centre was vital if children's services were to be prioritized. The wider strategy development could have been taken forward by the LSPs. As we shall see, neither of these arguments pervaded CT development.

In other areas of policy making, questions have been raised in relation to a consideration of what the limits to coordination are – what is actually worth doing? (Davis and Ritters 2009). There is scant empirical evidence concerning the effectiveness of attempts to integrate services judged on either financial or outcome criteria. Perri 6 *et al.* (2006) reviewed the literature in relation to the effectiveness of networks in healthcare and found little to support the idea that network forms brought about effectiveness in service delivery. This was especially true of research on joint work for specific client groups such as the elderly (Polivka and Robinson-Anderson 1999). This research may contain biases due to the inclusion of large-scale US-based quantitative studies focusing on Health Maintenance Organizations (HMOs), to the exclusion of UK based and other qualitative studies. However, evidence of effectiveness was reported in a few types of clinical network which offer both inter- and intra-professional support and exchange of best practice with the offer of comprehensive approaches for the treatment for chronic and life threatening disease (Foucaud *et al.* 2002). Yet even in these networks there has been no attempt to define what control mechanisms and formal financial and administrative infrastructure are necessary to facilitate effective clinical networks. Overall, the research suggests that effectiveness is limited, but it may occur where the focus is important to the involved actors as well as government (Perri 6 *et al.* 2006).

Provan and Milward's study (1995) focused on identifying the features of effective integration. This research found that coordinated networks are more effective than self-regulating ones in key areas of social welfare services delivery. This research, alongside previous citations, appears to have some applicability for understanding the weaknesses in the CT initiative. The focus of the research was mental healthcare networks in the US, and four of these networks were assessed using robust quantitative and qualitative methodologies within a case study design. Two basic sets of criteria were assessed: (1) the degree and type of interaction between agencies; and (2) a client perspective sought from clients, their families and key workers. The latter assessments included subjective statements on clients' quality of life and results from standardized mental health functioning tests.

Testing whether effectiveness was linked to the density of interaction, Provan and Milward (1995) found that the density of the network (i.e. the degree to which all parts were connected) was unrelated to how effective the network was judged to be. Families and patients judged the least dense (i.e. the least integrated network) as being the most effective. The success of the low-density cases related to centralized functions, such as hierarchical ordering within the network (i.e. one network actor/organization monitors and organizes work flow). A high concentration of influence led to high outcomes, whilst a low concentration of influence led to poor outcomes. However, centralized integration, and the direct non-fragmented control which it allows, are not the only key features of successful networks. Successful networks were also influenced by the context. If the system was stable and well resourced, the likelihood of effectiveness was increased. Indeed, it was stability and resourcing which allowed the central organization to retain control over the other network actors. The model of network effectiveness concludes that *Network Context* (system stability and high resource munificence) together with *Network Structure* (centralized integration and direct non-fragmented control) were the key characteristics of effectiveness in networks.

These findings suggest that a high degree of centralized and hierarchical coordination is necessary to support effective service delivery integration. However, much of the literature on UK experiences of partnerships promotes more pragmatic responses, highlighting the weaknesses in top-down instrumentalist management in effecting joint work where local actors are resistant or where professionals feel their knowledge-base is being undermined by central dictate (Perri 6 *et al.* 2006; Newman 2001). This views suggests that joint working can only be encouraged, not forced – a view that was eventually adopted in the case of CTs. This is because the Children's Act 2004 s10(1) merely states that 'Each children's services authority ... must make arrangements to promote co-operation between ... each of the authority's relevant partners'. Forcing the creation of new 'Trust' organizations was dropped, whilst the need to integrate operationally through the network's board structure and the information sharing mechanisms remained. The discussion above suggests that attempts to over-integrate may be fruitless in terms of effectiveness, suggesting that the UK Government were right not to force organizational integration. However, the theory of network effectiveness also implicitly undermines the utility of using large multi-sectoral networks for strategy development. In the most successful cases cited, a central organization was responsible for strategy, overseeing operational developments, and distributing resources. This suggests that the CT policy was subject to a number of contradictions between its roles and the organizational structure.

Despite the difficulties in promoting joint work, governments attempt to encourage local actors to take joint work seriously, in part by re-designing those institutions which shape regulatory, incentive, and sanction systems. In the case of CTs, the UK Government found it particularly hard to create the hoped for integration and soon reverted to allowing a looser cooperative type of partnership structure. However, this has produced rather more variation in outcomes than is desirable.

Integrating children's services – the CT initiative

The ECM Green Paper both introduced and embedded a number of reforms. The focus here is the formation of CTs as the administrative solution – how they have been operating and how they have interacted with other statutory structures such as the new Local Safeguarding Children's Boards (LSCBs). The Children Act 2004 set out the expectation that all areas would be under a statutory requirement to establish broad-ranging trusts which would provide strategic direction for most (if not all) services for children (UEA and NCB 2007). There was an assumption that funding would be pooled and that service provision agreed by the CT board in the Children and Young People's Plan (CYPP) would become subject to a commissioning process from the board.[4] This would ensure local coherence in public services spending and provision. Funding would be allocated effectively and duplication of services eliminated. Both universal and specialist services would be facilitated through the CT with the appointment of a Director of Children's Services (DCS) overseeing the newly merged education and children's social services departments within local authorities, while also providing effective leadership for CT developments.

The ECM policy was extensive, going further than the issue of protection from which it was conceived. It created five rather vague objectives: Be healthy; Stay safe; Enjoy and achieve; Make a positive contribution; and Achieve economic well-being (DFES 2003). Underneath these, a plethora of services could exist to improve outcomes for children. Furthermore, the policy was used as the basis for taking a 'determined effort' to address inequalities, with CTs becoming the vehicle through which child poverty could be further tackled. Local areas were given some flexibility in how they developed services to suit local circumstances, but there were key features of the ECM that were expected to be implemented across all areas (DCSF 2008).

Network effectiveness and the CT initiative

The initiative contained the potential to provide an effective structure for service planning and delivery. The Trust concept could have provided increased centralized integration and direct non-fragmented control, which have both been identified as key to effectiveness; however, the initiative failed to gain widespread support, although it was encouraged on a voluntary level. As the implementation phase wore on, it was described as moving from a policy for integration to a policy for locally networked relationships (UEA and NCB 2007); that is, it moved from an integration aim to a cooperation approach. Despite the organizational downgrading, CTs remained expansive in terms of the number of members, the heterogeneity of those members, and their policy objectives. In doing so, an unwieldy process has been created which exacerbates the problems of weak governance and resourcing structures typically found in joint work.

Arguably, the strategy that the CT and wider ECM policy represents is more about capturing all activity in a comprehensive set of cross-cutting objectives; a strategy that the Cabinet Office argued should be avoided. It lacks a clear rationale for how value is added, and the ECM cross-cutting objectives have a built-in 'collaborative inertia', which may impact negatively upon the development of key objectives (Huxham 1996).

This does not mean that added value has not been produced; rather, that the formation of strategic bodies to bring together joint work across the five objectives has overshadowed the key areas where reform was essential in getting professionals to work together and in providing effective support and resourcing for children's social care in particular. The positive vision of inter-professional relationships suggested by Harlow and Shardlow (2006: 71), in which the distribution of responsibility 'may mean that social workers enjoy a greater level of practical and emotional support', seems not to have materialized.

Centralized integration

The creation of Trusts as a new organizational form was an idea which increasingly gained popularity after 2000. However, these have developed slowly in adult social care, suggesting that it is a difficult area within which to integrate in this way. As CTs were more diverse as partnership boards, they would potentially face additional barriers. CTs are led by the local authority and since 2009 all agencies involved with children are under a statutory duty to cooperate. In the early development of CTs, they had many members, but there were important omissions too. In particular, the 2004 Children Act was criticized for not specifically including schools under the duty to cooperate, thereby leaving substantial gaps in the membership.

The roll out of CTs was expected to have been completed by 2008, yet the Laming Report on child protection (2009) and the Audit Commission's report (2008) suggested that we were some way from achieving the full aims of the integration policy even where services had been reorganized into Trusts. Ninety-six per cent of areas had created some sort of partnership board, but few had drawn on the provisions for an 'incorporated' partnership, i.e. a Trust. The Audit Commission (2008:4) report stated that 'Thirty-one per cent of directors of children's services said there was confusion about the purpose of children's trusts in early 2008'. Given that 2008 was the target for establishing CTs across the nation, this suggests a lack of clear workable guidance from the Department for Children, Schools and Families (DCSF). However, the Audit Commission report stated that belated and confused guidance from central government did not excuse a lack of development across the sector (AC 2008).

The Audit Commission (2008: 4) concluded that 'there is little evidence that children's trusts, as required by the government, have improved outcomes for children and young people'. Lord Laming, expressing some irritation, argued that, as the policy, legislation and guidance are in place, 'now, for goodness' sake, lets get on and do it' (Children, Schools and Family Committee 2009a).

In terms of network structure, CT developments have largely followed a looser structural approach than may have been optimal. CTs have been characterized by density of interactions over strategy and operations within an extensive policy context. These have dominated over purposeful interaction around a limited set of core activities, an approach which theoretically could have been more successful. In short, they have lacked the centralized integration found in the US cases. Of course, in the English governance context such integration would have needed higher levels of collaboration than the US cases where the network is based on simpler contractual relations, albeit that they tend to operate in a more collaborative form.

Direct non-fragmented external control

A key strength in the US cases was that centralized integration could create non-fragmented external control. A single organizational entity could act as a network manager, pulling in organizational contributions and allocating them in an efficient manner. Indeed, this is how the original model envisaged that CTs would work, and formed an important reason why it was rejected, particularly as a result of widespread concern regarding the loss of autonomy over individual organization's budgets. In the CT case, clear authority did not develop, leaving local actors to form a consensus as best they could on how to advance the integration aim. Where consensus has been absent, boards have had little opportunity for impact. Agreement among key organizational actors would have been required to support boards, and this ultimately relies upon the design of the institutional structure to facilitate integration. The CT initiative failed to get the institutional structure right; for example, there was widespread concern from professionals over aspects such as client confidentiality and information-sharing, which were not satisfactorily resolved (Blake and Beckwith 2009; Harlow and Shardlow 2006; Lord Laming 2009; UEA and NCB 2007).

A further issue identified was the expansive model promoted by DCSF, whereby the CT would influence the work of the LSP, tackling areas such as child poverty and infrastructure planning in providing housing, regeneration and transport (DCFS 2008). Thus, boards grew to provide representation for a broad range of service providers and became too unwieldy (UEA and NCB 2007). This often led to a waste of effort, as was discussed by a Trust Board Deputy Chair: 'We are supposed to be a strategic board – but we never get time to look at the big picture. The agenda is always filled with detail that should really be dealt with somewhere else' (AC 2008: 21). This suggests that boards neither effectively supported the key services envisaged by the ECM policy, nor provided a broader strategic planning function.

Alternatively, one area where external control was introduced was the merging of education and children's social services departments within local authorities. In theory, the use of local authorities as lead agencies should have aided effective integration. However, this merger, under the management of a single director, is less logical than it first seems. For education services there is little advantage besides becoming more centrally important within the authority, which may improve the status of and rewards for some employees. For children's social services – for which the change could have been important – it actually brought some potentially negative impacts, such as decreased morale and reduced professional autonomy. What it has not achieved is turnaround within a service which is struggling.

There is some evidence that the decision to place the education service in the lead role together with the expansive nature of the CT remit and membership has led to a further diminution of status for children's social services. This has contributed to the situation whereby social services have found it hard to achieve the 'stay safe' objective. The lead agency was always perceived to be the education department. This appeared to make sense in terms of the ECM's broad policy remit, as schools interact with the majority of children. This makes them key places for service development in terms of protection, prevention, and the broader well-being agenda. When ECM was published concerns were raised that children's social services would be lost in integration attempts, usurped by education and health (Community Care 2005). Although CT developments have not stampeded towards integrated trusts, the reforms have had a discernable impact upon social services.

Some notion of the influence of the education service and DCSF in relation to the CTs is demonstrated by the vision statement for CTs: 'Our vision is of 21st Century Schools, delivering excellent personalised education, contributing to all aspects of well-being; operating at the centre of the Children's Trust' (DCSF 2008: 6).

There is a clear emphasis on schools and education, and although preventative work is mentioned there is no explicit mention of protection work or joint work between social workers, health professionals and the police, which has figured strongly in child protection failures.

Furthermore, the evaluation of the Pathfinders reported that of the 31 CTs reviewed, the Local Authority (LA) chaired 30. In only six of those cases was the chair a social services director, with the remainder being education directors or, more commonly, other senior LA officers or members. In two-thirds of cases the new Directors of Children's Services posts were held by people with an education background, with a further quarter having a social services background. Whilst these Director's posts have been attributed to facilitating a more integrated approach, Laming (2009) concluded that many did not have first-hand experience of child protection work, and hence their role needed to be supplemented by another senior manager who did. To address this, education professionals have begun to be trained in child protection (Laming 2009); training for teachers was made mandatory in 2010 as part of the initial teacher training. The absence of a leadership with a good knowledge of child protection issues has not aided a small and struggling social care workforce to assert its value in protecting children.

It is not hard to understand why the CT initiative has not supported social care in its child protection work. CTs were managed from within a newly created DCSF, which was effectively the old Department for Education and Schools (DFES) with a wider joined-up remit. Unsurprisingly, the implemented policy was education-oriented and school-based, and the key DCS posts were mainly held by those from education.

The reason for this dominance lies partly in the fact that children's social care is a small service compared to education. Furthermore, for some time the status of social work has been recognized as problematic; training issues have been highlighted in relation to the quality of students, the quality of the curriculum and placements (Children Schools and Families Committee 2009b). A recent survey (Lombard 2009) stated that recruitment and retention of staff has been difficult, with 57 per cent of Social Services Departments experiencing difficulties in recruitment and 38 per cent in retention.

Despite good intentions, overall the CT initiative appears to have done little to address the status of social care, the support needed by social workers, or children at risk. The education services – which have always been larger, stronger and higher performing – have continued to do well, but their leadership has failed to assist social care in managing a turnaround. It is also interesting to note that the trajectory of improving performance in education services began to plateau alongside this reform (AC 2009).

System stability

The network context in which CTs were created could not be considered stable. First, they were one part of a broader reform of children's services, which included the mergers and establishment of DCSs and of LSCBs, and, second, children's services themselves were just part of a raft of reforms which sought to revolutionize public services at the local level, such as policies for Local Strategic Partnerships (LSPs) and Local Area Agreements (LAAs). These have further complicated the contextual environment within which CTs have operated. CTs themselves have been slow to develop stability through establishing Trust board arrangements.

A key relationship for protection work is that between CTs and the statutory LSCBs. The role of boards is in 'coordinating and ensuring the effectiveness of the work of partner bodies to safeguard and promote the welfare of children' (France *et al.* 2009: 1). They have a particularly important role in overseeing training, conducting serious case reviews (SCRs), and making sure that any learning gained is implemented. In relation to the protection of children, the operation of this board and the way it works alongside the broader CT arrangement is crucial on issues such as policies, strategies and resourcing.

Lord Laming (2009) argued that LSCBs have built stronger partnerships and, in many ways, represent an administrative improvement. However, their resources are insufficient in relation to their expected role. They struggle to fulfill all their roles with SCRs dominating work. Many are over-ambitious, and the wider agenda of preventative work has drawn away much of the additional resources for children's social care instead of focusing on narrower protection concerns. Communication channels remained weak and appropriate accountability arrangements have been difficult for local authorities to establish (France *et al.* 2009, 2010).

High resource munificence

Resources from central government could not be described as lavish. Whilst core funding for education, health and social services has been relatively generous over the period, the pressures to do more and make efficiency savings despite increasing costs has often left organizations in a poor position to continue with joint work initiatives. There has been a lack of recognition of the need to resource reorganizations and no specific funding has been granted for organizational development, despite this having been identified as useful for CT Pathfinders (UEA and NCB 2007). Local organizations have been unable to divert resources to CTs in the quantities required, and the boards do not have the authority to force organizations to either commit resources or to distribute resources differently. Rather than CTs being strong local organizations shaping the improvement of children's services, they have become weak steering bodies reliant upon consensus and the alignment of budgets to gain greater effectiveness.

Whilst creating integrated organizations, joint posts and pooled or aligned budgets for children's services appears to be appropriate, in practice it can leave less powerful services vulnerable to the loss of voice, status and funding. Laming (2009) stated that whilst 82 per cent of education funding is ring-fenced, the funding for safeguarding is not. Social services have contributed more funding into pooled and aligned budgets than any other service, while many health partners avoided making any contribution. On top of this, pressures to make efficiency savings have further thwarted social services. In relation to the LSCB, the funding problem is particularly acute: as no funding formula exists for this, boards rely on voluntary contributions. Boards have to agree with local agencies how much the board will receive in any given year, and securing an adequate budget can be difficult (France *et al.* 2010).

Overall, there was a lack of attention paid to resourcing such a significant change in the way children's services were organized. Such resourcing also goes beyond the needs of administering a partnership board, but also to the needs of essential – albeit weak – professions.

Learning from the CT experiment

The focus has been on the role of CTs as an integrative mechanism in supporting the improvement in the coordination of children's services. A number of learning points have emerged from this particular experiment in cross-boundary working. CTs ostensibly provided a solution to the problem of coordinating services around the needs of children, but as an administrative mechanism they appear to have had minimal impact. The preceding analysis identified several barriers to effectiveness:

- Governance structure – the policy objectives and structural organizational change was not matched by the governance framework. Guidance about how Trusts should operate and what exactly would be a statutory requirement was slow to emerge from the inexperienced DCSF. The legislation finally embedded a more cooperative style of organization with the expectation that it could still deliver high levels of integration. Legislation was particularly vague on membership until 2009. It could be argued that DCSF themselves were lukewarm collaborators on the CT project. The local governance aspect operating through the expansive board led to more opacity. The proposal for Trusts was ambitious and unrealistic within the English governance context.

- Resourcing – a major barrier to success has been inadequate resourcing: not just the lack of funding for CT development and the rather opaque funding mechanism for the LSCBs, but also the support which could have come from the centre in terms of training and professional development, specifically for social workers. We know from the pilots that the funding was important to support change and build capacity, yet it was not forthcoming. Local variation in capacity was not acknowledged in the policy at all.
- Underdeveloped integrative mechanisms – the ways in which the CT was to integrate the work of local service providers was poorly designed. Much was left to local development and due to the weak governance framework there was a tendency to move forward slowly. Because Trust formation was voluntary, the levels of resource contribution expected from each actor could not be mandated. No clear guidance was given for how the establishment of DCSs was to be implemented, or for how the smaller service might be integrated with education in a more collaborative way.
- Outstanding tensions – although all professionals coming into contact with children have a duty to report abuse, within the social work profession many weaknesses remain. Trying to address problems through administrative solutions will not necessarily work. The service is under-resourced and no amount of cross boundary working is likely to resolve the sorts of myriad and complex issues that social workers face. An unintended consequence of the CT and wider ECM policy has been to undermine the social care workforce, rather than strengthen it.

Applying Provan and Milward's (1995) framework to the case of CTs has provided important lessons for designing integration approaches in critical work environments. Theories of effectiveness may not translate well into situations which are not based on simpler contractual arrangements, although Provan and Milward's cases exhibited excellence in delivery. There is also no suggestion that children's services could or should be run on a contract basis as it simply would not work in the governance context of the UK. Nevertheless, it does highlight some of the basic elements which can provide effectiveness within joint work. If we compare CT developments against the US cases, we can see that in the US cases there was centrality of strategic decision making along with a stable context and resource munificence; this provides important lessons for the CT case, where these were absent.

Overall, this analysis highlights the importance of the focus of this book. The four themes are inherently intertwined – why we need joint work, what constitutes joint work, and what organizational forms and institutional configurations are needed to address the joint work problem in order to achieve the desired objectives. Unless this is done carefully, taking account of the governance framework in any given country whilst learning from evidence, these features will not necessarily achieve their objectives. In the UK, it might be fair to argue that cross-boundary working has been subject to political whim and fashion rather than looking for evidence and looking at the value chain within the production of services. CTs looked a lot like other forms of cross-boundary working which focused on much less critical areas of work and so were appropriate. More learning could have taken place from the Pathfinders regarding operational features, and potentially also from international examples of joint work, one of which was discussed here.

Notes

1 Victoria Climbié died in 2000 at the age of eight years following horrific abuse and torture by her guardians, who were later jailed for life. Her death exposed major problems in children's protection as she was known to numerous government organizations – four social services departments in different London boroughs, three housing departments, two hospitals, and a specialist centre focused on prevention of cruelty to children (Batty 2003).
2 The star ratings relate to the comprehensive performance assessment process used for English Local Government. Four stars was the highest rating, and was heavily reliant upon performance in the areas of resources and social care. In this environment, children's services became a critical measure of performance.
3 Local Strategic Partnerships were introduced in 2001. They are permanent board structures through which strategic decisions about localities can be influenced by broad representation from the community, business and service providers.
4 Funding is pooled from individual organizations to be spent according to the decisions of the partnership board. Increasingly, the term 'commissioning' has been used to put organizations under a contractual system.

References

6, P., Goodwin, N. and Freeman, T. (2006) *Network Organisations for the 21st Century*, London: Palgrave.
6, P., Leat, D., Seltzer, K. and Stoker, G. (2002) *Towards Holistic Government*, London: Palgrave.
Audit Commission (AC) (2008) *Are We There Yet? Improving Governance and Resource Management in Children's Trusts*, London: Audit Commission.
Audit Commission (AC) (2009) *Final Score: The Impact of the Comprehensive Performance Assessment of Local Government 2002–08*, London: Audit Commission.
Batty, D. (2003) 'Q&A: Victoria Climbié inquiry', *Guardian*, 30 January. Available at: www.guardian.co.uk/society/2003/jan/30/1 (accessed 28 November 2012).
Blake, H. and Beckwith, M. (2009) *Controversial ContactPoint Database Delayed Again Amid New Security Fears.* Telegraph. Online. Available at: www.telegraph.co.uk/news/uknews/5038572/Controversial-ContactPoint-database-delayed-again-amid-new-security-fears.html (accessed 23 March 2009).
Children, Schools and Families Committee (2009a) 'The Protection of Children: oral evidence taken before the Children, Schools and Families Committee on Wednesday 25 March 2009'. Online. Available at: www.publications.parliament.uk/pa/cm200809/cmselect/cmchilsch/379/9032501.htm (accessed 20 December 2009).
Children, Schools and Families Committee (2009b) *Training of Children and Families Social Workers*, HC 527–1, London: House of Commons.
Community Care (2005) *Knock it Down and Start Again. Community Care.* Online.

Available at: http://www.communitycare.co.uk/articles/20/10/2005/51331/knock-it-down-and-start-again.htm (accessed 13 January 2010).

Davis, H. and Ritters, K. (2009) *Linkage Plus National Evaluation: End of Project Report*, London: Department of Work and Pensions.

Department for Children, Schools and Families (DSCF) (2008) *Statutory Guidance Children's Trusts*, London: DCSF.

Department for Education and Skills (DFES) (2003) *Every Child Matters*, London: DFES.

Department of Environment (DoE) (1977) *Policy for the Inner Cities*, London: DoE.

Department of Environment Transport and the Regions (DETR) (1997a) *Building Partnerships for Prosperity: Sustainable Growth, Competitiveness and Employment in English Regions*, London: DETR.

Department of Environment Transport and the Regions (DETR) (1997b) *Regeneration Programmes – The Way Forward*, London: DETR.

Department of Environment Transport and the Regions (DETR) (2001) *Local Strategic Partnerships: Government Guidance*, London: DETR.

Department of Health (DoH) (2002) *Safeguarding Children: A Joint Chief Inspectors' Report on Arrangements to Safeguard Children*, London: DoH.

Foucaud, P., Rault, G., Sautegeau, A. and Navarro, J. (2002) 'Clinical networks and cystic fibrosis', *Archives of Pediatrics and Adolescent Medicine*, 3(1): 312–314.

France, A., Munro, E., Meredith, J., Manful, E. and Beckhelling, J. (2009) *Effectiveness of the New Local Safeguarding Boards in England*, London: Department for Children, Schools and Families.

France, A., Munro, E. and Waring, A. (2010) *The Evaluation of Arrangements for Effective Operation of the New Local Safeguarding Children Boards in England*, Research Brief, London: Department for Children, Schools and Families.

Great Britain (2004) *Children Act 2004: Elizabeth II. Chapter 31*, London: The Stationery Office.

Harlow, E. and Shardlow, S. (2006) 'Safeguarding children: Challenges to the effective operation of core groups', *Child and Family Social Work*, 11(1): 65–72.

Huxham, C. (ed.) (1996) *Creating Collaborative Advantage*, London: Sage.

Johnson, C. (2005) 'Strategic superboards: improved network management processes for regeneration?' *International Journal of Public Sector Management Special Edition New Localism and Regeneration Management*, 18(2): 139–150.

Kickert, W.J.M., Klijn, E-H. and Koppenjan, J. (eds) (1997) *Managing Complex Networks*, London: Sage.

Lombard, D. (2009) 'LGA: Baby P media treatment harms social worker recruitment', *Community Care*. Online. Available at: www.communitycare.co.uk/SearchServices/Search/aspx?SearchType=site&content=site&Keywords=Recruitment%20%20and20%20retention%20social%20work%LGA (accessed 02/10/2009).

Lord Laming of Tewin (2009) *The Protection of Children in England: A Progress Report*, HC 330, London: House of Commons Online. Available at: www.publications.parliament.uk/pa/cm200809/cmselect/cmchilsch/379/9032502.htm

Newman, J. (2001) *Modernising Governance: New Labour, Policy and Society*, London: Sage.

Performance and Innovation Unit (PIU) (2000) *Wiring It Up – Whitehall's Management of Cross-cutting Policies and Services*, London: PIU, Cabinet Office.

Peters, G. (1998) *Managing Horizontal Government: The Politics of Coordination*, Ottawa: Canadian Centre for Management Development.

Polivka, L. and Robinson-Anderson, R. (1999) *Managed Care for the Elderly and the Role of the Aging Network: Prepared for the Commission on Long-Term Care in Florida*, Long-Term Care Policy Series Volume IV revised edition, Tampa, Florida: The Florida Policy Exchange Center on Aging, University of South Florida.

Pollitt, C. (2003) 'Joined-up government', *Political Studies Review*, 1(1): 34–49.

Pratt, J., Gordon, P. and Plamping, D. (1999) *Working Whole Systems: Putting Theory into Practice in Organisations*, London: King's Fund Publishing.

Provan, K.G. and Milward, H.B. (1995) 'A preliminary theory of network effectiveness: a comparative study of four community mental health systems', *Administrative Science Quarterly*, 40 (1): 1–33.

Rogers, D. and Whetten, D. (1982) *Interorganizational Coordination: Theory, Research and Implementation*, Ames, IA: Iowa State University Press.

Seebohm, F. (1968) Report of the Committee on Local Authority and Allied Personal Social Services, Command papers Cmnd. 3703, London: HMSO.

Seidman, H. (1998) *Politics, Position and Power: The Dynamics of Federal Organization*, 5th edition, New York: Oxford University Press.

Taylor, M. (1998) *Top-down Meets Bottom-up: Neighbourhood Management*, Bristol: Joseph Rowntree Foundation and the Policy Press.

University of East Anglia (UEA) and National Children's Bureau (NCB) (2007) *Children's Trust Pathfinders: Innovative Partnerships for Improving Children and Young People's Well Being*, Norwich: UEA and NCB.

14 Education and employment

Stumbling across boundaries in the Netherlands

Esther Klaster, Celeste P. M. Wilderom and Dennis R. Muntslag

Introduction

The Dutch central government, like many other western governments, has been experimenting with new organizational approaches to deal with complex public-policy problems. In this chapter we describe four recent attempts by the Dutch central government to cross functional boundaries in the public policy fields of education and employment. All four cases reflect a specific approach to crossing boundaries: by changing a ministry's organizational structure; by synchronizing several ministries' policy instruments; by using policy content as a driver to cross boundaries; and by harmonizing educational legislation. Although the four cases are different in nature and scope, they show that there are certain common enablers and barriers for working across boundaries. We conclude this chapter with lessons learned.

Coordination is inherently an essential effect of specialization and the division of labor; every task that has been split up by a hierarchy eventually needs to be reintegrated (Thompson 1967; Crowston 1997; Heath and Staudenmayer 2000). When the task at hand involves a complex process, such as public policy making, the process of dividing and reintegrating may become even more complex compared to, for example, industrial settings. Dividing up public sector tasks thus creates boundaries. And those boundaries need to be crossed, as contemporary societies pressure governments to deliver seamless public services, one-stop-shop solutions, and efficient processes.

We start this chapter by sketching how the Dutch central government has evolved over the past 40 years, with regard to intra- and inter-departmental cooperation. These developments provide the context within which our four cases occurred. We then discuss key characteristics of the policy fields of education and employment, and describe our methods of data collection. Next, we present our four case studies. We conclude this chapter with a synthesis and lessons learned, as well as suggestions for future research.

Coordinative challenges faced by the Dutch central government: an overview of forty years of grand reforms

> Bureaucracy defends the status quo long past the time when the quo has lost its status.
>
> (Peter 1977)

After the Second World War, the Dutch central government grew rapidly; between 1942 and 1964, the number of civil servants doubled (Van Twist *et al.* 2009; Hovestadt 2007). This growth led to an increase of specializations. Up until the 1970s, this did not cause severe problems, but, prompted by developments such as emancipation of citizens, globalization, and growing welfare, specialization and fragmentation started to collide with increasingly complex public problems. The Dutch government realized that changes needed to be made.

What followed (between 1969 and 2011) was a long tradition of Dutch governmental reforms. Although the Dutch public sector reforms vary in nature and scope, they address three recurring themes: (1) the government's inability to be responsive to societal changes; (2) its inability to coordinate effectively across departments; and (3) a government that had become ever more over-weight. These three problems are interrelated: the larger a government grows and the more policies and regulations it makes, the greater the need to divide tasks into small bits and pieces, which increases the need for coordination across boundaries. Throughout the years, there has been increasing need for inter-departmental coordination. As we will explain in this section, the reforms largely resemble those of other western societies, but also have some distinctive characteristics.

The reforms of the early 1970s reflect the struggle with traditional bureaucracy. The core problem at that time was that policy areas were not divided efficiently across departments (Committee Van Veen 1971); this was the result of public problems that had grown in complexity and that subsequently started to cross the boundaries of traditional departments. The early reforms sought solutions via drastic departmental reorganizations (MITACO 1977). Although this temporarily addressed the problem, departmental reorganizations did not provide a solution in the long run because society and its problems kept changing. Moreover, many reform plans required large investments, thus they were often not executed at all (Van der Steen and Van Twist 2010).

Throughout the 1980s and early 1990s, several committees (e.g., Committee Vonhoff 1980; Committee Verbaan 1983) found that the level of fragmentation was still too high and the government was still unresponsive to society. The solutions these committees suggested included a smaller cabinet, outsourcing, decentralization, a higher mobility among civil servants across departments, and managing for results. These reforms that followed comprised a range of new public management (NPM) practices, including outsourcing, decentralization, privatization, separating policy making from execution, and an increased focus on results and efficiency (Kickert 2000). These changes were attempts to reduce the size of the central government and to cut back costs, as well as an attempt to improve the quality of policy making and implementation (Kickert 2000). The result of these efforts was that vertical accountabilities were strengthened and that incentives were aligned with the outputs of distinct departments and units within those departments, which is counterproductive in terms of inter-unit cooperation (Perri 6 2004; State Services Authority 2007). Outputs that were the result of cooperation across departments were much more difficult to define and measure, and were therefore given a lower priority. So, although NPM increased the public administration's efficiency, it reinforced the issues of fragmentation, duplication of services and a lack of cohesion (Williams 2000; Moore 1995).

Between 1990 and 2000, the central government still faced the old familiar problems: a too large and too fragmented central government, as a result of having too many civil servants, tasks, divisions and functions; a lack of responsiveness to society; and inefficient use of means. In short, departments had become unmanageable for ministers. Again, solutions were sought in terms of a smaller government, separating policy and execution, and having few core departments (Committee Wiegel 1993), but also in terms of having fewer policies and rules, ending policies and being reserved to start new ones, less overlap between departments and better coordination, and a results-driven organization (Program 'Andere Overheid' 2004–2006; Program 'Vernieuwing Rijksdienst' 2007–2010).

Recent Dutch developments in an international perspective

The 'post-NPM' paradigm has, under various labels,[1] made crossing boundaries its core concern. In the Netherlands, recent reforms also show characteristics of a post-NPM approach. A concept called 'fluid governance' (translated from the Dutch term '*Vloeibaar Bestuur*') comes closest to what can be seen as a Dutch equivalent to the post-NPM approach (Van der Steen and Van Twist 2010). Instead of having directorates with clear borders, the basic idea of fluid governance is an extremely decoupled government, in which civil servants work together in groups that may constantly vary in size and composition, depending on the political, administrative and societal needs of the moment (Van der Steen and Van Twist 2010). Although fluid governance is said to be based on actual reforms – and is thus partially descriptive – the concept remains rather abstract and academic, and has not been used as a guide or blueprint for governmental reforms.

When we compare the recent Dutch reforms to post-NPM approaches elsewhere in western countries, we notice two main differences. First, while joined-up government in the UK was primarily politically driven (initiated by the Blair government), the latest reform in the Netherlands was initiated and led by top civil servants rather than politicians (Vernieuwing Rijksdienst 2007). This reform concerned the coordination of support units, and not of policy units. Top civil servants leading the change program sought solutions in terms of shared services for information and communications technology (ICT) and human resource management, reasoning that fragmentation of operational systems leads to fragmentation in policy (Vernieuwing Rijksdienst 2007). Three of the four case studies described in this chapter are also departmentally driven, although they concern policy units.

Second, the Dutch approach has tended to focus on organizational structural solutions. During the 1990s, solutions to deal with complex public policy problems were sought in making use of additional structures instead of inter-departmental rearrangements. Examples of such additional structures are program ministries, thematic directorates, and task forces, which existed next to the traditional bureaucratic structures. The underlying argument is that the difficulty is not so much how to stimulate specialists and professionals to cooperate, but how to make sure that these people and their organizations are flexible enough to respond to political and societal changes (Van der Steen and Van Twist 2010). Our first case study is an example of a structural approach to overcome such organizational barriers.

This historical overview clearly reflects the persistence of the problems at hand. Large reforms at the level of central government often did not have the outcome one hoped for – and may not be the best way to address stubborn issues such as fragmentation. But, next to these large reforms, there have been efforts to cross boundaries within and between departments as well. We take a closer look at four of these, all situated in the area of education and employment, involving the Ministry of Education, Culture and Science and the Ministry of Social Affairs and Employment. First, we explore the need to cross boundaries in the policy areas of education and employment.

Crossing boundaries in education and employment

Working across boundaries in the policy fields of education and employment has received a lot of attention from the Dutch central government, for several reasons. First, the policy fields of education and employment are interrelated fields, because the education offered should meet the requirements of employers, and also because education and employment are intertwined with regard to the 'lifelong learning' principle. The latter states that adults should engage in life-long learning activities in order to increase the overall educational level of the working population. The interaction between the two policy areas requires them to be mutually adjustable, and thus requires inter-departmental collaboration.

Second, crossing boundaries within the policy field of education is important to address problems that occur in various educational sectors simultaneously, or that emerge at the intersection of educational sectors.[2] School drop outs are an example of such a policy problem: not only do school drop outs occur in various educational sectors, there are also frequent drop-outs when moving from one sector to the next, for example from secondary to vocational education. This leaves the problem of whose responsibility this is – the secondary schools, or the vocational schools? Tackling such a problem requires close cooperation and shared responsibility from both school types – and, subsequently, from both governmental directorates.

Our third and final argument involves the organization of the fields of employment and education in which decentralized networks have become a common practice for central government to translate national level ambitions into regional- and local-level action. These networks consist of, amongst others, representatives of local governments, schools, social security providers, and firms. In an earlier study, we learned that the same individuals tend to be involved in projects that were developed in distinct parts of the central government (Klaster *et al.* 2010). As a consequence, these actors notice fairly quickly when the policies and objectives of those separate projects do not gel together well. Distinct projects may reinforce one another, but may also conflict. To illustrate, a project for school drop outs (developed by the Ministry of Education, Culture and Science) and a project for youth unemployment (developed by the Ministry of Social Affairs and Employment) reinforce one another in the sense that certain instruments – such as coaches – can be used for both target groups. However, the two projects may also conflict at some level: the project for youth unemployment encourages schools to enroll unemployed youth, but because these youths have a heightened chance to drop out again, this complicates the policy objective of decreasing school drop out rates. Hence, in order to simplify the execution of policies and increase their effectiveness, well-harmonized objectives are essential at the central governmental level.

Introduction to the cases and methods of data collection

There are many ways of joining up. One may focus on horizontal or vertical linkages (e.g., between governmental layers), or involve groups from outside the government; also, it may concern policy development or policy implementation (Christensen and Lægreid 2007). Without wanting to be comprehensive, joining up may be fostered via pooled budgets, organizational mergers, joint teams, or informal agreements (Ling 2002; Hunt 2005); via new accountabilities and incentives, such as shared outcome targets and regulations; or via shared service deliveries (Ling 2002).

The types of joined-up government that we describe in this chapter concern policy development within the Dutch central government. They reflect four different attempts to cut across boundaries (both within and between ministerial departments) within the policy areas of education and employment.

Case I describes a *structural* approach to crossing boundaries: specialized directorates were installed to deal with complex and high-priority policy problems, both within the Ministry of Education, Culture and Science (intra-departmental) and between this ministry and others, including the Ministry of Social Affairs and Employment (inter-departmental). Case II describes an attempt to overcome policy barriers by harmonizing and integrating *policy instruments*, such as pooling budgets and establishing a shared client focus. It describes the efforts of an inter-departmental committee concerned with regional employment and education policies. Case III entails an attempt to cross organizational boundaries based on the *content* of policies: for a limited number of key policy topics that could not be effectively addressed within a single directorate, specialized working groups were to be set up. Finally, Case IV describes a *legal* approach to crossing boundaries, by trying to establish a single educational law out of five distinct sector-based laws.

The study was carried out between January 2007 and August 2011, when the main author was situated within the Ministry of Education, Culture and Science. During that period, several forms of data related to the cases were collected from interviews, archival documentation (e.g. research reports, minutes from meetings, audit reports), and participant observation.

The case studies

Case I. Thematic directorates – a structural solution

In 2005, the Secretary-General of the Ministry of Education, Culture and Science initiated a change program in order to address two core challenges: (1) responding to the changing demands of the external environment, and (2) tackling problems that required a collaborative effort between various directorates. One of the change program's components was the introduction of seven intra- and interdepartmental thematic directorates. These thematic directorates were to focus on a single, high-priority public policy problem that occurred in various school types simultaneously. An example of an intra-departmental thematic directorate was the directorate for School Drop-outs; an example of an inter-departmental directorate was Lifelong Learning. With the thematic directorates focusing on new, changing, or high-priority policy issues, the traditional functional directorates remained focused on their core tasks: to manage standing, ongoing policies. This separation was expected to reduce the workload of civil servants. Note that the structural solution implied that a topic was lifted out of the standing organization into a specialized unit, meaning that boundaries were shifted, rather than crossed.

Descriptive findings

Thematic directorates succeeded with regard to the first, externally oriented, objective. They were able to address a high priority issue and responded effectively to the external environment. They were praised, both by internal and external actors, for putting issues on the agenda and for turning plans into action. In addition, they appeared to have symbolic value; the mere fact that a specialized directorate was called into existence was a sign to external parties that a specific problem was being given high priority. However, an interesting paradox emerged. External actors saw inter-departmental directorates as an illustration that departments were collaborating intensively. At the same time, the thematic directorates were criticized for developing policies and funding that were too narrowly defined; they were seen to show little synchronization with those of other thematic directorates.

The second objective reflected an internal matter. Were thematic directorates better than functional directorates at addressing complex policy problems that required working across boundaries? Around the topics for which thematic directorates had been installed, less cooperation was needed across functional directorates, but now cooperation between thematic and functional directorates became crucial for effective policies. Some thematic directorates functioned as a catalyst for collaboration between directorates, but others had the opposite effect. In these instances, the thematic and functional directorates were felt to grow further apart, because the thematic directorates built a wall around themselves, while the functional directorates left the subjects at hand entirely to the thematic directorates. Moreover, cooperation between thematic directorates was almost non-existent, despite the fact that thematic subjects often affect each other. In other words, thematic directorates seemed to create new boundaries of their own: thematic ones. What seemed to be missing was a natural reflex to look beyond the borders of one's own directorate – whether functional or thematic – to see how the policies of other directorates affected their own.

In addition, the perceived workload went up instead of down, due to the extra coordination that was needed between thematic and functional directorates – since functional directorates still needed to cooperate with each other, but now also had thematic directorates to cooperate with – and because of struggles over who was responsible for what (Ministry of Education, Culture and Science 2009). And, finally, closing the – temporary – directorates down caused stress and insecurity for civil servants, as this took place in a time of personnel cut-backs. Based mainly upon these side-effects, the Secretary-General decided not to start up any new thematic directorates and to close three extant ones. Instead, he claimed, thematic policy problems should be addressed via lighter organizational forms than formal directorates, such as projects within existing functional directorates. In conclusion, thematic directorates were quite successful from the external actors' point of view, but less so from an internal organization perspective.

Case II. An inter-departmental committee – an instrumental solution

In 2009, the department heads of several ministries (including Social Affairs and Employment; Education, Culture and Science; Nature and Agriculture; and Economic Affairs) had come to realize that people who work at the regional level of the education and employment field were experiencing an overload of separate governmental projects, overlapping or conflicting objectives, and managerial stress. Together, the ministries installed an inter-departmental committee whose task was to make recommendations about how to remove and avoid fragmentation and duplication in regional employment policies.

Descriptive findings

The inter-departmental committee chose five key organizing issues that, together, were to provide better harmonized or even integrated regional employment and education policies. The first issue was the extant amalgam of specific and often temporary funding regulations (the accompanying recommendation being suggestions on which funding to integrate and which to end). The second issue concerned the fact that 'a region' was not a formal entity and every departmental directorate used its own delimitation. The third issue concerned account management: every directorate had its own account managers (i.e., civil servants who acted as linking pins between a region and the central government), which meant that regional actors had to deal with multiple account managers around often partially overlapping themes. The committee's recommendation included a three-fold solution: (1) account managers were to *inform* each other; or (2) *cooperate* with each other; or (3) account management should be *integrated*, so that every region would have a single account manager responsible for various related topics. The fourth issue concerned communication from departments and politicians toward the regions, which was at times conflicting, and information that was collected by distinct sections of the central government, instead of shared internally. Finally, the fifth involved avoiding duplicated or conflicting policy objectives.

When the committee began, it faced an amalgam of governmental projects, funding and national-level ambitions. The reason for this amalgam was that there had been enough money and political approval to develop all kinds of specific projects, but during the committee's existence, the tide changed drastically. The former cabinet fell and, after seven months of political silence, a new liberal and right-wing cabinet was installed. Faced with great economic challenges, this new cabinet announced major savings in almost all policy areas. Many projects were to be terminated and temporary funding regulations were either slashed or had to be integrated within the standard bulk budgets of departments. Despite the fact that reducing the number of distinct governmental projects had been one of the committee's ambitions, the new cabinet's drastic approach undercut the relevance of the committee. The committee reasoned that since many projects were to end, trying to coordinate and integrate policy instruments was not relevant anymore. Instead, the committee evolved into a platform whose members came together every two months to exchange information about what each department was working on, so as to detect possible conflicting policies.

Despite the committee not having the effect that had been hoped for, some gains were obtained. First, although the intensive interventions such as collaborating or integrating policy instruments were not executed, information exchange was given a permanent place on the agenda. Second, two 'no-regrets'[3] were implemented: a single regional delimitation used by both the Ministry of Social Affairs and Employment and the Ministry of Education, Culture and Science, and the sharing of information about schools between several executive agencies and the Ministry of Education, Culture and Science.

Case III. Common threads – a policy content approach

During the political silence of 2010, civil servants from the Ministry of Education, Culture and Science wrote their policy agendas in preparation for the yet-
to-be-formed cabinet.[4] Instead of writing separate ones for each of the
educational sectors – which would have been common practice – the departmental executives insisted that the agendas showed congruity and that so-called
'common threads' across sectors should be identified. When, months later, the
political agenda of the new coalition cabinet was published, civil servants
incorporated these new political priorities and objectives into the extant policy
agendas. Based on this renewed document, eight common threads were identified, such as simplifying and integrating funding, and increasing the number of
qualified teachers. The plan was that a working group, led by a director and consisting of policy makers from various directorates, would become responsible for
each of the common threads.

Descriptive findings

In practice, only one common thread was translated into a working group: the
one regarding the integration of funding regulations. For the other seven
common threads, there were no working groups at the implementation level.
Instead, these common threads were discussed once a month, at a strategic level,
in a steering committee, which comprised two Directors-General and directors.
As a result, the common threads evolved into quite abstract guidelines, rather
than becoming a concrete policy tool.

One reason for the limited follow-up of the initial plans was the lack of political attention that was given to the common threads. When the new minister and
vice-minister were appointed, their primary concern lay with realizing the budget
cuts and realizing quick wins, because the elections for the Senate were
approaching rapidly. In addition, presenting well-harmonized policy or legislation means that there is one publication moment, whereas several smaller pieces
provide multiple opportunities to gain political attention. The result was that directors and policy makers felt trapped between the priorities of their political
leaders and their departmental leaders. The minister also looked at the common
threads with suspicion: were civil servants doing things that actually belonged to
politicians? Via these common threads, Directors-General gained more influence
over policy content, which may have added to the initial resistance of politicians.
After the Senate elections, their resistance declined and their political priorities
became more congruent with the common threads' policy objectives.

What this had in common with Case I was the basic idea of lifting topics out
of the standard organization and creating specialized units; in Case I these were
formal directorates, whereas in Case III these were less formal working groups.
A director, who was opposed to the idea of lifting a topic out of the standing
organization, argued that crossing boundaries is more valuable than shifting
them. Others, who favored the idea of specialized units, indicated that the

common threads were too soft to be an effective intervention. Although the 'intensive variant' of working groups was never implemented for many of the common threads, the program did lead to an increase in information sharing and ad hoc cooperation between directorates.

Case IV. An integral educational law – a legal approach

In 2005, the then Minister of Education announced the desire to 'harmonize the extant legislation'.[5] At that time, five educational laws existed (for primary, secondary, vocational, special education for pupils with disabilities, and higher education), which overlapped substantially. Some of these laws required modernization – the oldest one dated back to 1963. Instead of modernizing each of the sector laws separately, the minister wished to harmonize the similar or overlapping parts into a single integrated education law. Only sector-specific subjects would have distinct legislation (such as regulations for doctorate studies, which is a matter exclusive to higher education). The minister wished to integrate these laws for two reasons. The first reason was an ideological one: it fitted with the good governance philosophy, because the new law was to be less detailed. The second reason concerned educational content: harmonized legislation could support a smoother flow of pupils throughout the educational system.

Descriptive findings

In 2007, the Good Governance program, including harmonization of legislation, started to lose political support, due to several incidents at schools. The political atmosphere became one of steering and control, and the new law ended up in a ministerial drawer. Later that year, the new Coalition Agreement largely neglected the harmonization of legislation and, also, the new vice-ministers of education did not seem to be particularly interested in an integrated law. One of the reasons for this was that 'education' had been split up amongst them: the minister was responsible for higher education, one vice-minister was concerned with primary education, and another vice-minister with secondary and vocational education. With each of them having their own concerns and objectives, the topic of the harmonization of educational legislation was given little attention.

Confronted with the economic crisis, the cabinet that was installed in 2010 announced major cutbacks, both in terms of reducing expenses and the slimming-down of the ministerial departments and executive agencies. These cutbacks gave a new boost to the harmonization of legislation discussion. The more detailed a law is, the more adjustments it requires, which means more work for civil servants – in other words, less detailed legislation is more sustainable. Simplifying the execution of legislation was also necessary for the executive agencies that operate at arm's length from the ministry. The cutbacks made it possible to discuss things that were not previously open for discussion, such as changes regarding the diffusion of tasks and responsibilities between the core department and the executive agencies. Thus far, the attempts to implement a single educational law have not succeeded, and it may likely not come that far. The program did, however, foster incremental changes to the several sector-specific laws, in that they became better synchronized and conflicting policies were removed.

Synthesis

We have described four different approaches towards establishing working across boundaries. Each of these four cases had a specific angle, focusing on structures, policy instruments, policy content, or legislation. In this section, we reflect on the cases with the purpose of identifying patterns throughout them in terms of enablers and barriers for working across boundaries and defining the lessons learned.

Throughout the cases we noticed that the motivation of key actors – or lack thereof – had a major influence upon whether the programs were implemented and succeeded. In literature on joined-up government, whole-of-government and other post-NPM approaches, a lot of attention is focused on the factors that determine success, including resources (e.g., time and means), incentives, leadership, skills and behaviors, communication, and ICT. Such incentives, resources, and skills may be different for different key actors. We therefore start this section with an analysis of the key actors – ministers, Directors-General, directors, and policy makers – asking ourselves the following question: what drivers do they experience for working across boundaries, and what inhibits them?

An actor perspective on motives and barriers for working across boundaries

Despite the four cases being initiated by departmental actors, political actors had a large influence upon whether the initiatives went through. In principle, a minster is responsible for all of the policies from his or her department, which means that he or she benefits from a well-harmonized set of policies – but the everyday reality is more complex. Cases III and IV illustrated that having multiple vice-ministers for one policy field hampered the emergence of harmonized or integrated policies. Also, political pressure to score 'quick wins' attracted attention toward sub-areas. Inter-departmental collaboration may be even more complex, because politicians usually prefer well-defined agendas for which they are solely responsible and recognizable. In contrast, crossing boundaries is inherent to a Director-Generals' function. As one Director-General put it: 'My directors are the experts in their fields. My added value is to make sure their fields are well harmonized.' According to other civil servants, Directors-General stimulate politicians to think and act across sectors, rather than the other way around.

The result is that directors and policy makers have to deal with two different priorities: those of their political leaders and those of their departmental leaders. Generally speaking, directors and policy makers seemed to lack clear incentives to work beyond borders. Directors' prime responsibilities are their own sector, and the internal incentive structure encourages directors to focus on what happens within their own directorate. Policy makers often lack the time to seek cooperation across the boundaries of their own directorate and department. What motivates them to work across boundaries is: (1) the knowledge that trying to harmonize policies that are nearly finished is more troublesome than adjusting those in earlier stages of policy development; (2) making use of scarce resources (e.g., cut backs in personnel); and (3) a genuine wish to do what is best for the public field. However, when the time pressure is high, the reflex of most directors and policy makers will be to focus on their own field.

Analytical findings and lessons learned

Shifting boundaries versus crossing them

One should keep in mind that no matter how boundaries are designed – whether functionally, thematically, or otherwise – policy problems hardly ever fit boundaries, and, inevitably, they will always need to be crossed. This finding is nothing new. As an illustration, a Dutch central government advisory committee acknowledged in 1977 that 'No matter how you change the departmental structure, inter-departmental coordination is and will always be of utmost importance.' (MITACO 1977: 13; translated from Dutch). Case I illustrated that structural solutions may benefit the content of the policy at hand, but may also create new isolations. Such structural solutions are likely to fall short if they are not accompanied by a cultural awareness of the necessity to cross the boundaries of one's own unit, as well as having the right incentives and skills (e.g., being able to collaborate, trust, and mobilize teams) to do so (Ling 2002). In comparison, whole-of-government initiatives elsewhere are often more concerned with working together pragmatically than with formalized collaboration (Christensen and Lægreid 2007). We conclude that organizational structures may work as a precondition, but they are not sufficient: '[S]tructure is not enough to fulfill the goals of whole of government initiatives. Cultural change is also necessary, and processes and attitudes need to be addressed' (Christensen and Lægreid 2007: 1062). The Lessons Learned (LL) that we can draw from these cases are:

> **LL1.** Lifting a topic out of the standard organization and into a specialized unit may benefit the policy content, but does not necessarily improve cross-boundary collaboration; and

> **LL2.** Structural solutions that are not accompanied by a cultural awareness that working across boundaries is needed are likely to fall short.

Ideological versus economic drivers of change

Pollitt (2003) described four rationales for joined-up governance which can also be applied to the Dutch situation. Three of those could be regarded as ideological or content-driven: (1) situations whereby different policies that undermine each other can be eliminated; (2) situations whereby it becomes possible to offer citizens seamless rather than fragmented access to a set of related services; and (3) situations whereby synergies may be created by bringing together different key stakeholders in a particular policy field or network. The final rationale is an economically driven one: (4) making better use of scarce resources. Throughout the above cases we saw that an economic drive was stronger than an ideological one. Initiatives that had stagnated in earlier years found their way back into current events under the pressure of the cutbacks in expenses and personnel. Rather than addressing wicked policy problems or fostering seamless services, increasing efficiency had become the main driver of collaboration across boundaries in the Dutch case. We therefore postulate that:

> **LL3.** Economic motives are stronger incentives for change than ideological and content-based motives.

When the economy recovers and the central government has opportunities to invest in new projects again, it should be interesting to see whether the initiated changes (as presented in Cases II, III and IV) prove to be the result of a paradigm shift or merely the result of budget cuts. A paradigm shift would imply that the government will continue its reduced role and continue to strive for harmonized policies, funding regulations, and legislation. If the changes turn out to be primarily based upon economic motives, the chance is that the government will return to initiating silo-based policies and funding, without considering what is going on across unit and departmental borders. In between these two scenarios, there is a third alternative: budget cuts may actually be a driver of gradually making a paradigm shift.

Incremental versus radical changes

Incremental changes are usually associated with continuous and evolutionary change, whereas radical changes are associated with discontinuous and episodic change (Mintzberg and Westley 1992; Beer and Walton 1987; Weick and Quinn 1999). However, in our view and experience, incremental changes may be the result of planned, radical changes. In all four of our cases something was set in motion, but none of them succeeded in their exact aim. Throughout the cases we noticed that the aim often entailed an intensive collaboration or integration, while the actual outcome was information exchange or cooperation.[6] In other words, radical change initiatives resulted in incremental changes. One might conclude that grand reforms and radical changes in the public sector do not work and should be omitted entirely, but we believe that without these radical change programs the incremental changes would not have been accepted and implemented. In psychology this is referred to as the 'door in the face' technique: a large request is made in order to realize a smaller one. We therefore postulate that:

LL4. Grand reforms may be a necessary means to achieve incremental changes.

Is an integral approach needed to foster integral policies?

The four cases were independent from one another – they were not part of any overarching program – yet they reflect the spirit of the time. As a result, these distinct cases showed elements of overlap. For example, the program for harmonizing legislation (Case IV) had the same objective as the common thread for simplifying funding regulations and execution (Case III), and, at the same time, simplifying funding regulations was also one of the topics of the interdepartmental committee (Case II).

The question arises as to whether integrated solutions can be effectively realized by change programs aimed at a single organizational aspect. One might argue that in order to realize integrated policies, an integrated approach is in order. According to Senge and colleagues (1999), many reforms fail because the actors involved lack understanding of the interconnections of the various changes that are simultaneously implemented. Having a holistic or integrated perspective on change programs would foster participation and understanding (Boonstra 2000). However, we believe that – in accordance with our previous Lesson Learned – a broad, integrated program might be a bridge too far. Rather, incremental changes in specific areas are likely have a more enduring effect, as long as the drivers of change (whether ideological or economic) push the various initiatives in the same direction.

Concluding remarks

The Dutch central government is stumbling over boundaries, trying to climb some fences and tearing down others. Overall, we believe that the Dutch central government is making slow, yet continuous, progress regarding crossing boundaries in education and employment so as to facilitate harmonized and more effective policies and less duplication for both the government and the field. The primary gain may be that crossing boundaries and fighting fragmentation was given a permanent place on departmental and political agendas. Although it may seem paradoxical at first sight, the economic crisis provides a 'window of opportunity' (Kingdon 1984), which both departmental and political actors may use in order to gradually pursue a paradigm shift.

Notes

1 Such as Joined-up Government in the UK (Newman 2001); Horizontal Management in Canada (Bakvis and Juillet 2004); Whole of Government in Australia and New Zealand (Christensen and Lægreid 2007); Collaborative Governance in the USA (Agranoff and McGuire 2003); New Public Governance (Osborne 2010); and Public Value Framework (Moore 1995).
2 The Netherlands' education system consists of primary education (for children from 4

to 12 years old) and secondary education (from 12 to 16–18 years old), followed by either vocational education (non-academic, basic level of professional education), higher professional education (sometimes referred to as 'universities of applied science'), or academic education (research-oriented universities).

3 'No regrets' are those propositions that are likely to be accepted by any coalition, regardless of its political color.

4 The former cabinet had resigned; new elections took place, and a new cabinet had to be formed, which took seven months (the longest period for this process in the history of the Netherlands). During this period, there was no actual political steering, which is usually a period in which civil servants reflect upon the central government's roles and steering philosophy.

5 Harmonization of legislation was part of a broader program called 'Good Governance.' This program entailed the central government withdrawing, focusing on outcomes rather than process (the 'what' instead of the 'how'), giving more autonomy to schools, and reinforcing horizontal control (by separating supervision from administration, for example).

6 We use a continuum for the intensity of cooperation, ranging from least to most intensive: informing, cooperating, coordinating, collaborating, and integrating.

References

6, P. (2004) 'Joined up government in the western world in comparative perspective: a preliminary literature review and exploration', *Journal of Public Administration Research and Theory*, 14(1): 103–138.

Agranoff, R. and McGuire, M. (2003) *Collaborative Public Management: New Strategies for Local Governments*, Washington, DC: Georgetown University Press.

Bakvis, H. and Juillet, L. (2004) *The Horizontal Challenge: Line Departments, Central Agencies and Leadership*, Ottawa: Canada School of Public Service.

Beer, M. and Walton, A. (1987) 'Organization change and development', *Annual Review of Psychology*, 38: 339–367.

Boonstra, J.J. (2000) *Lopen over water. Over de Dynamiek van Organiseren, Veranderen en Leren*, Amsterdam: Vosiuspers.

Christensen, T. and Lægreid, P. (2007) 'The whole-of-government approach to public sector reform', *Public Administration Review*, 67(6): 1059–1066.

Commissie Van Veen (1971) *Bestuursorganisatie bij de Kabinetsformatie*, The Hague: Staatsuitgeverij.

Crowston, K. (1997) 'A coordination theory approach to organizational process design', *Organization Science*, 8(2): 157–175.

Heath, C. and Staudenmayer, N. (2000) 'Coordination neglect: how lay theories of organizing complicate coordination in organizations', *Research in Organizational Behaviour*, 22: 155–193.

Hovestadt, D. (2007) *Concern over het Rijk of het Concern Rijk? Onderzoek naar de Governance, Inrichtingsmogelijkheden en Kansen van Rijksvrede Bedrijfsvoering*, The Hague: SDU uitgevers.

Hunt, S. (2005) *Whole-of-government: Does Working Together Help?*, Canberra: The Australian National University.

Kickert, W.J.M. (2000) *Public Management Reforms in the Netherlands. Social Reconstruction of Reform Ideas and Underlying Frames of Reference*, Delft: Eburon.

Kingdon, J.W. (1984). *Agendas, Alternatives, and Public Policies*. Boston: Little, Brown.

Klaster, E., Wilderom, C.P.M. and Muntslag, D.R. (2010) 'Regional meta-networks in

Dutch public policy implementation: an initial exploration in the field of education and employment', paper presented at the International Research Society for Public Management Conference, Bern, April 2010.

Ling, T. (2002) 'Delivering joined-up government in the UK: dimensions, issues and problems', *Public Administration*, 80: 615–642.

Minister of the Interior and Kingdom Relations (2007) *Policy Document on Central Government Reform in the Netherlands.* Online. Available at: www.vernieuwingrijksdienst. nl/actueel/nota's-vrd/nota-vernieuwing (accessed 15 September 2011).

Ministeriële Commissie Interdepartementale Taakverdeling en Coördinatie (MITACO) (1977) *Rapport van de Ministeriële Commissie Interdepartementale Taakverdeling en Coördinatie,* Letter to the House of Representatives (14 649 nr. 1–2), The Hague: MITACO.

Ministry of Education, Science and Culture (2009) *Internal Audit Report: Experiences with Thematic Directorates,* The Hague: Ministry of Education, Science and Culture.

Mintzberg, H. and Westley, F. (1992) 'Cycles of organizational change', *Strategic Management Journal,* 13: 39–59.

Moore, M.H. (1995) *Creating Public Value: Strategic Management in Government,* Cambridge: Harvard University Press.

Newman, J. (2001) *Modernising Governance,* London: Sage.

Osborne, S.P. (2010) *The New Public Governance?: Emerging Perspectives on the Theory and Practice of Public Governance,* London: Routledge.

Peter, L.J. (1977) *Peter's Quotations: Ideas For Our Time.* Online. Available at: http:// en.wikiquote.org/wiki/Laurence_J._Peter (accessed 13 September 2011).

Pollitt, C. (2003) 'Joined-up government: a survey', *Political Studies Review,* 1: 34–39.

Senge, P., Kleiner, A., Ross, R., Roth, G. and Smith, B. (1999) *The Dance of Change: The Challenges to Sustaining Momentum in Learning Organisations,* New York: Currency Doubleday.

State Services Authority (2007) *Joined Up Government: A Review of National and International Experiences,* Melbourne: State Services Authority.

Steen, M. van der and Twist, M. van (2010) *Veranderende Vernieuwing: Op weg naar Vloeibaar Bestuur: Een Beschouwing over 60 jaar Vernieuwing van de Rijksdienst,* The Hague: Nederlandse School voor Openbaar Bestuur.

Thompson, J.D. (1967) *Organizations in Action,* New York: McGraw-Hill.

Twist, M. van, Steen, M. van der, Karré, P., Peeters, R. and Ostaijen, M. van (2009) *Vernieuwende Verandering: Continuïteit en Discontinuïteit van Vernieuwing van de Rijksdienst,* The Hague: Nederlandse School voor Openbaar Bestuur.

Weick, K.E. and Quinn, R.E. (1999) 'Organizational change and development', *Annual Review of Psychology,* 50: 361–386.

Williams, D. (2000) 'Reinventing the proverbs of government', *Public Administration Review,* 60(6): 522–534.

15 Health

Overcoming service delivery gaps in Austria

Sanja Korac and Iris Saliterer

International developments in working across boundaries have been observed with interest in Austria's public sector, and, together with the challenge of complex public needs, have paved the way for new modes of public governance. Starting with an overview of the organization and structures of the Austrian health system, we clarify why cross-boundary strategic management and service delivery has emerged in one of the most complex policy fields, and then we explain how it has been implemented. This contribution explores the various levels of innovation that have been enabled by new governance structures, as well as their role in overcoming the historic service delivery gaps that have existed in health care in Austria. This allows us to provide an answer to the enduring question of whether working across boundaries leads to more efficient and effective service delivery. This is provided by an analysis of the impact of collaborative reform pool projects on different health system target fields, reflecting the system's performance, and ultimately, comprising efficient and effective health care delivery. Drawing on this research, we develop an innovation level/impact type framework for the assessment of the projects, before discussing the role of radical innovations in working across boundaries. The chapter concludes with critical views on the findings and implications for future research.

The fragmented challenge in Austria's health care system

The historical background of Austria's health care system offers an understanding of the key issue in health policy and management research – the fragmentation of health care delivery. Regulations for the federal republic's health care system can be found in national laws, which provide framework legislation and 'Länder' (federal state) laws which provide execution legislation (Mayer 2007: 85–87), under which the 'Länder' have significant autonomy in designing the preconditions for the inpatient health care sector. Successive enhancements of the Bismarck model oriented system led to substantial power being held by the 19 compulsory self-administered social health insurance institutions. Their overall amount of health care expenditures, accounting for 59 per cent or €12.98 out of €21.80 billion of total public health expenditures in 2008 (Statistics

Austria 2011; Hauptverband 2011a), the population's total insurance coverage of 99.3 per cent (Hauptverband 2011b: 13), and the lack of competition due to compulsory competencies all combine to strengthen the role of the social health insurance institutions as main p(l)ayers in the Austrian health care system. Serious financing problems in social health insurance since mid-1990s (Statistik Austria 2010: 387), however, have accelerated the successive outsourcing of financing responsibilities in service delivery, and more cost-shifting to private out-of-pocket payments and to national level grants in the late 2000s (Hofmarcher 2009). The resultant increasing power of the federal states explains the shift of Austria's health care system to a mixed financing and organizational form (Hofmarcher and Rack 2006: 95; Statistics Austria 2011) and in sum leads to greater organizational and financial fragmentation of the system (Figure 15.1).

Like many other industrialized countries, Austria has undergone several health care reforms since the 1970s (Berman 1995; Chernichovsky 1995; Busse and Schlette 2003; Casebeer and Hannah 1996; Dixon and Mossialos 2002; Docteur and Oxley 2003; Evans *et al.* 2001; Glassman and Buse 2008; Hussey

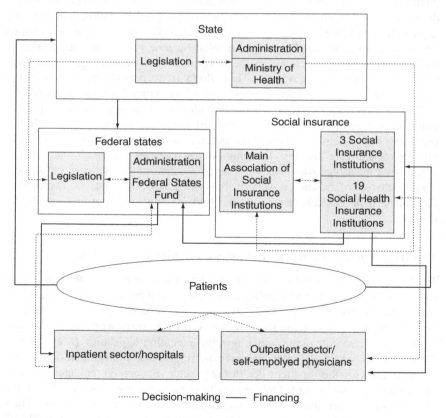

Figure 15.1 Traditional decision making structures (source: authors' design, based on Hofmarcher and Rack 2001).

and Anderson 2003; Maynard and Bloor 1995; Sturmberg *et al.* 2010; Figueras and Saltman 1996; Segal 1998; Toth 2010; Wendt and Thompson 2004). The aims of the reforms were mainly focused on accessibility, equity, effectiveness and efficiency or sustainable financing (Arah *et al.* 2003; Frenk 1994; Kelley and Hurst 2006: 12; Knowles *et al.* 1997: 13–41). Service improvements highlighting the patient focus have dealt with special topics (e.g. HIV/AIDS education, broadening of the obligatory social health insurance's services) with regard to either the inpatient or the outpatient sector, and were therefore constrained within the organizational boundaries of acute hospitals or medical practices. However, the latest health care reform (in 2005) included interface management between the sectors for the first time (BMG 2011; BGBl I Nr. 73/2005; Herber 2007: 38ff.; Laimböck 2009: 30; Spiel and Petscharnig 2009: 334; Unger 2007: 122–128.). It consisted of measures in three main areas: (a) overcoming the strict separation of health care sectors and better coordination in planning, regulation and funding; (b) ensuring sustainable financing of the health care system; and (c) the promotion of preventive health services and comprehensive quality improvement within the system (BMG 2008). From the structural view, however, the most drastic change in the organization of Austrian health care decision making and financing was an innovation in governance at a meta or macro level – the implementation of multi-player health platforms in the federal states (Figure 15.2), which distribute distinct funds, directly aiming at promoting innovations in health care, the 'reform pools'. The new funding structure allows the shift from an insular organizational mindset to collaboration across sectors.

The new health platforms consist of representatives from federal states, social health insurance institutions, the medical association, patient advocacy, churches (as providers of clerical hospitals), one representative from the national health ministry, and one from the Main Association of Austrian Social Insurance Institutions. These platforms make collaborative decisions about the inpatient sector, the outpatient sector, and the (virtual) so-called cooperation sector, mainly referring to service shifts between the previously mentioned sectors (Land Wien 2007: 12–13; BMG 2008), and realize innovation processes in governance at a macro-level (McNulty and Ferlie 2004: 51–55.). The establishment of the reform pool fund in the cooperation sector implies the long-targeted financing of the fragmented health system from one source, enabling projects of innovative, inter-organizational health care delivery (innovations at the meso-level). It was intended to dispose of a percentage of total funds for the inpatient and the outpatient health care sectors, but one restriction to the project implementation was set by the legislation regarding the reform pool funds: an amount of up to 1 per cent (2005–2006), and 2 per cent (2007–2008) of total funds for both the inpatient and outpatient health care sector had to be reserved from usual health care spending. This meant a lack of additional financial resources and an incentive for the federal states and social health insurance institutions to minimize reform pool initiatives in order to leave the usual funds for health care delivery relatively unaffected.

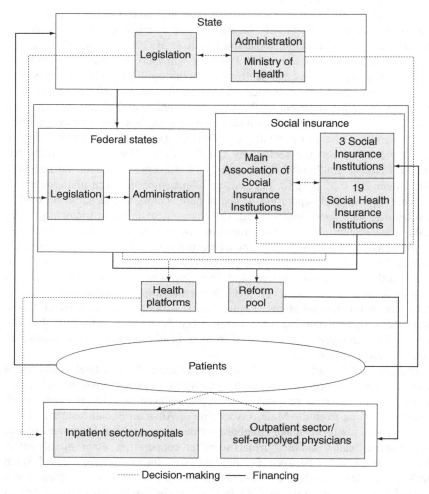

Figure 15.2 Decision making and financing structures since 2005 (source: authors' design, based on Hofmarcher and Rack 2006).

Building bridges by innovation

The strict separation of the two health care sectors has constrained continuous health care service delivery, inhibiting the adequate response to chronic diseases like asthma, cancer, cardiovascular diseases, etc., which account for a large part of the total burden of disease in Austria (e.g. Habl and Bachner 2010: 55–59, 63–64; Statistik Austria 2010: 38, 43; WHO 2009). In order to work across traditional health sector boundaries, innovative approaches ensuring high standards in system performance are needed. 'Innovation' is being used more frequently in the vocabulary and discourses of public service improvement as a result of the 'positive resonances' associated with this concept and the improvements that can be achieved (Albury 2005; Hartley 2005; Mulgan 2006; Osborne 1998; Potts 2009; Walker 2003). In the health care context, innovations often focus on medical goods (e.g. pharmaceutical industry, new medical devices) (Evans 2010; Gassmann *et al.* 2008; Kola 2008; May 2009: 144–146), or on single organizations (Duncan and Breslin 2009; do Carmo Caccia-Bava *et al.* 2009). With regard to health care services, these innovations are being explored from an objective view and classified into convenience-driving, higher effectiveness, and lower costs innovations (Herzlinger 2006: 3; Schultz *et al.* 2011). In recent decades, scholars have increasingly tried to categorize innovations (Garcia and Calantone 2002; Rowley *et al.* 2011; Zaltman *et al.* 1973), as the public sector innovates in a variety of ways. Research in this area – which is under-represented within 'classical' innovation literature – mainly concentrates on improving organizational performance (Walker *et al.* 2002: 201) through different types of product, process, and, to a lesser extent, ancillary innovations (Damanpour 1987; Damanpour *et al.* 2009; Kruger and Johnson 2011; Walker 2006).

Considering the given context, intra-organizational innovations are not intended to be fostered by the reform pool using the macro-level governance innovation as enhancements should be made between the sectors, and are thus inter-organizational. In the following, therefore, we use a threefold categorization of incremental, substantial, or radical innovations (Abernathy and Utterback 1978; Davila *et al.* 2006: 38–54; Bourque 2005: 72–73; Govindarajan and Trimble 2005; Pekkarinen *et al.* 2011; Perl 2003: 37–38). Incremental innovations are the most frequent form in single organizations, due to their greater feasibility, safety and predictability compared to other forms (Davila *et al.* 2006: 42). Incremental innovations can be seen as any type of improvement to existing services without significant changes to the production process (Bourque 2005: 72). Substantial, or semi-radical, innovations involve crucial changes to the organizational environment. They focus either on changes to the business model itself (Chesbrough and Rosenbloom 2002: 530) or on changes to the technology (production process) (Davila *et al.* 2006: 47–49). Radical innovations, however, provide significant changes to the business model, as well as to the technology or production process, which means fundamental changes to an organization's environment (Bourque 2005: 72; Godoe 2000: 1034; Pavitt 2004: 104–105; Sandberg 2008: 52–53).

Given the fact that health care 'remains among the most fragmented of industries' (Duncan and Breslin 2009: 13), and considering the boundaries between Austria's health care sectors and the strong negotiating power of actors, we identify a need to improve the business model as well as the production process, so that radical innovations are considered as the intervention of choice to bridge the health sector gaps. The derived hypothesis within our research, therefore, is that radical innovations have the highest impact upon health system performance fields. Following the definitions above, we draw an analogy of the levels of innovation in health care services as follows.

- Incremental innovations are improvements in existing services (e.g. better education of medical staff), with neither changes in the production process or technology nor changes in the business model.
- Substantial innovations provide changes within the health care system by bringing about changes in the business model, as the principle of how the health care system gains value for its stakeholders (e.g. utilization of profoundly new health care systems, new methods of treatment), or by building new structures for health care service delivery. These must be completely new to the system as a whole and exclude implementation of known structures (e.g. mobile home care in regions where the service was not available before). On the other hand, substantial innovations can be achieved by new technologies or by improvements in process quality (e.g. the application of new IT using electronic health records).
- Radical innovations, representing the highest level of innovation, realize both new health care systems or new structures for health care service delivery, and new technologies or process quality improvements. However, radical innovations might require high levels of investment, and so, given the fact of the lack of additional financial resources mentioned before, the main p(l)ayers in Austria's health care system have few incentives to implement radical innovations using high investment reform pool projects. We therefore assume that radical innovations are not prevalent within the Austrian health care system context as they require high financial resources.

We set up a framework consisting of the innovation level and the impact types, in order to allow a general assessment of the projects. We used document analyses and case studies to assess the two dimensions and to qualitatively test the impact of innovations. To further explore our hypotheses, we searched evaluations of the reform pool projects and evaluated the best-practice model of the reform pool projects using a multi-method qualitative and quantitative research design (interviews, questionnaires, statistical and document analyses) to validate the innovations' benefits in terms of the financial consequences and trans-sectoral collaboration – the overcoming of service delivery gaps. The prevalence of radical innovations was tested by comparing the innovation levels with budget figures for health platforms in general and reform pool projects in particular, considering financial resources approved and actual funds invested and/or spent.

Creating innovation-fostering governance structures

Traditional health care funding structures were innovation inhibiting due to the separate funding and strict regulations in decision making with regard to inpatient and outpatient health care. Fixed-rate hospital funding by social health insurance also formed an incentive not to invest in innovations, but to keep the structures and strive for an 'insourcing' of health care services into hospitals. Consequently, the costs for inpatient care to the social health insurees remained the same, whilst outpatient health care services (and thus costs for the social health insurance) were cut (Ivansits 2009: 73; Granig *et al.* 2011: 142–143). The new innovation-fostering financial and decision making structures of the cooperation sector enabled trans-sectoral funding and provided new structures in negotiation processes. These changes were designed to facilitate continuous and coordinated health care, which will be essential in dealing with future epidemiological and demographic challenges for industrialized health systems.

The performance of health systems consists of various dimensions, objectives or targets. The target fields – accessibility, effectiveness (health improvement), efficiency, equity, and patient focus, which were identified in a comprehensive study as the most prevalent in national or multinational health quality concepts (Kelley and Hurst 2006: 11–13) – can be linked to the aims of the reform pool: the conjunction of the health care sectors. The higher the impact upon health system performance fields, the higher the effect upon bridging the gaps between the inpatient and outpatient health sectors. The target field effectiveness corresponds to reform pool aim (a) enhancement of the effectiveness of the health care system by population's health status improvement (health improvement). Efficiency is equal to reform pool aim (b) efficiency improvement; and accessibility and equity strongly relate to (c) health service shifts with the realization of benefits for the federal states and the social insurance institutions. The link between accessibility and equity and health service shifts can be justified by looking at the definition more narrowly. Accessibility means the level of ease with which health services can be reached and requires health services to be available a priori. Equity is a dimension closely related to access and defines the extent to which a system deals fairly with the target groups or the distribution of healthcare and its benefits among the population (Kelley and Hurst 2006: 13). The patient focus was not mentioned in the aims of reform pool projects, but is indeed pursued by the integrated care approaches which were decreed as particularly eligible as a type of project (BGBl I 2008).

Bridging boundaries by radical innovations

Looking at the target fields accessibility/equity, efficiency, effectiveness and patient focus, for each one we can observe an achievement with a different impact. We cluster this using three impact types for each target field, as shown in Table 15.1.

Reform pool projects in transition vary in quantity and subject across federal states, but show some similarities in the subject (e.g. palliative care) or the overall project (e.g. Disease Management Program Diabetes Type 2 – being equal in the federal states implementing the project) (BMG 2009, 2011). In order to assess the different reform pool projects, we identified the innovation level by applying the previously mentioned definition of incremental, substantial and radical innovations, and carried out a qualitative document assessment of project objectives and measures based upon the impact type framework described above in order to explore the holistic approach in pursuing the reform pool principles. The assessment results are shown in Figure 15.3.

Table 15.1 Type of impact for target field

Target field	Expressed by*	Expressed by**	Expressed by***
Accessibility/equity	Accessibility is not affected at all, but equity is gained by standardization.	Barriers are built for one or few and minimized for other population groups, and equity predominates within the segmented groups.	Barriers are minimized for the whole population and/or equity is gained by changed care funding.
Efficiency	Increase in output, when overall real costs may be higher, but are relatively lower.	Increase in productivity, when overall costs are stable.	Increase in output or productivity, while overall costs decrease.
Effectiveness	Broadening the output to gain (higher or better) outcome.	Optimization of production to gain outcome.	Implementation of new evidence-based input.
Patient Focus	Patient focus is mentioned in project goals.	Services are adjusted to patients.	Direct patient involvement.

Applying the innovation level/impact type framework, we observe 16 incremental, 29 substantial, and six radical innovations in 2009, and 11 incremental, 14 substantial, and three radical innovations in 2011. With regard to the interrelations between the two dimensions, the innovation level and the impact type, we observe the following: incremental innovations tend towards a lesser impact upon the target fields. Substantial innovations, which arise by either the principle of the health system's value gain or the implementation of completely new technologies, show a varying picture, partly with similarities to the impact types of incremental innovations, and partly with higher, more 'radical' impacts. Radical innovations, implemented through the analysed reform pool projects, whilst applying both new health care systems or new structures for health care service delivery, and new technologies or process quality improvements (Discharge Management, Case and Care Management Tennengau, Best Practice Model TeleUlcus, and Patient Oriented Integrated Care), by trend show more impact within this assessment. Subsequently, the hypothesis that radical innovations have the highest impact upon health system performance fields can be qualitatively confirmed.

Radical innovations facing lack of evidence

Sustainability in terms of long-term funding was achieved for two incremental and four substantial innovations, but for none of the radical projects, leading to the assumption that incremental rather than substantial or radical innovations are pursued in the system. Of the six radical innovation projects in total, three are still in the implementation phase, and three are finished (however, one was finished without any evaluation). The radical innovation reform pool project with the greatest qualitative types of impact, Patient Oriented Integrated Care, accounts for over 6 per cent of total reform pool funds per year (Czypionka and Röhrling 2009: 3–4). It is a population and patient-centred care approach to bridging the boundaries of Vienna's health care by cooperation using five measures: hospital discharge management for patients with complex post-inpatient care; standardized electronic information transfer between care providers; promotion of contact to self-help groups during hospital stay; development of a web-based information platform for all health care and social services; and standards for prescription of medical devices and equipment. The combination of the first two measures generates a consistent interdisciplinary cross-boundary pathway, including an interdisciplinary discharge report and an electronic admission/discharge letter. The expected benefits of the cross-boundary pathway are: (a) reduced unplanned re-admission rates; (b) reduced length of stay; (c) increased patient and professional safety; (d) increased data security; (e) higher information quality and/or enriched data transfer; and (f) time savings for professionals. As a consequence, it should lead to a conjunction of the inpatient and the outpatient health care sector, which in the following should be validated using an evaluation of the benefits of the innovations with regard to financial consequences and trans-sectoral collaboration.

Federal State	Reform Pool Project	Status 2009	Status 2011	Innovation level	Impact Type Accessibility /Equity	Efficiency	Effectiveness	Patient focus
Burgenland	Disease Management Program Diabetes Type 2	I	I	s	*	**	**	*
	Colon Cancer Prevention	I	I	i	*	*	**	*
	Children and Adolescents Psychiatric Care	I	I	i	**	*	*	*
	Discharge Management	I	A	r	**	**	**	***
	Palliative Care	C	A	s	***	*	**	**
Carinthia	Speech Therapist Service Improvement	E	LTF	i	***	*	**	*
	Diabetes Type 2 Patient Training	F	LTF	i	*	*	*	**
	Palliative Care Concept	F	LTF	s	**	*	**	**
	Oncological Care	I	F, E missing	s	**	*	**	**
Lower Austria	Disease Management Program Diabetes Type 2	I	I	s	*	**	**	*
	Integrated Palliative Care	I	I	s	**	*	**	**
	Cardiological Care	F	F	s	**	*	**	*
	Interdisciplinary Admission Ward	F	LTF	s	**	**	**	**
	Discharge Management	F	F	r	**	**	**	***
Upper Austria	Integrated Stroke Care	E	LTF	s	**	**	***	***
	Structured Support Diabetes Type 2	I	E	i	*	*	*	*
	Health Network Perg	C	C	i	**	*	*	**
	Health Centre Kreuzschwestern Wels	C	I	i	*	*	*	*
	Integrated Care Dementia Concept	C	C	s	**	**	**	**
	Enhancement of Medical Care in Elderly Care Homes	C	C	s	**	**	**	**
	Fit 4 Life – Integrated Care for Children with Behavioural Disorders	C	I	i	*	*	*	**
Salzburg	Congestive Heart Failure Local Care	C	C	i	*	*	*	*
	Preoperative Diagnostics	I	E	s	**	**	**	*
	Case and Care Management Tennengau	I	F	r	**	*	**	***
	Disease Management Program Diabetes Type 2	I	I	s	*	*	**	*
Styria	„Herz.Leben" - Cardiological Care	I	I	i	*	*	*	**
	Palliative Care	E	LTF	s	**	**	**	**

Figure 15.3 Innovation level/impact type framework.

Region	Program	Phase	Impact	Level
	Disease Management Program Diabetes Type 2	I	s	**
	Integrated Care Coronary Heart Disease	E	i	**
	Integrated Stroke Care	F	s	***
	Interface Management Graz	F	s	**
	Nephrological Care	F, missing		*
	Pilot Project Trans-Sectoral Funding of the Outpatient Sector: MRI	E, missing	s	***
	Best Practice Model TeleUlcus	F,	r	***
Tyrol	Interdisciplinary Care Concept Back pain	F, missing		**
	High-cost Pharmaceuticals at the Interface	A	s	***
	Disease Management Program Diabetes Type 2	F	s	**
	Integrated Stroke Care	I	s	***
	Oncology in Practice	I	s	**
	Palliative Care	I	s	***
Vorarlberg	Mobile Child Care	I	i	***
	Mobile Palliative Team	I	i	***
	Discharge Management	I	r	**
	Disease Management Program Diabetes Type 2	I	s	***
Vienna	General Practitioner in the Hospital	A	s	**
	Patient Oriented Integrated Care	I	r	***
	Disease Management Program Diabetes Type 2	E	s	***
	Pediatrician Emergency Practice in Hospital	F,	i	*
	Integrated Stroke Care	E, missing		***

Legend:

C	Conceptual Phase	I	Implementation Phase
E	Evaluation Phase	F	Finished
A	Aborted	LTF	Long Term Funding
i	incremental	s	substantial
r	radical	*, **, ***	impact type

A multi-method evaluation of the Patient Oriented Integrated Care cross-boundary pathway – being the best-practice model of reform pool projects due to the high proportion of reform pool funds, the highest innovation level and impact upon health system and reform pool target fields – carried out in 2009 shows that expected benefits were achieved in varying degrees:

- The decrease in care-related re-admission rates could not be confirmed quantitatively, but is observed by health professionals qualitatively; partial improvements in the continuity of care are the result of timely and high quality information.
- There is no quantitative, but qualitative, evidence for the decrease in length of stay, too.
- Most of the hospitals involved show good results concerning the structural quality of the discharge expert standard, but barely 30 per cent reach the minimal achievement level within the process and result quality.
- There is a high degree of utilization of the discharge report (in more than half of total hospital discharges) compared to traditional data transfer (telephone, fax, hardcopy form), which means that a high increase in data security and transmission reliability is achieved.
- All professionals involved in admissions (nursing directors, discharge managers, nurse unit managers) know about the discharge expert standard, but the depth of knowledge of its content differs significantly between them; no difference was discovered in usage or non-usage of the standard between nurses and social workers in their function as discharge managers, but the expert standard is used implicitly by applying its guidelines in everyday work in a formless manner. All respondents confirmed the usefulness of the electronic admission/discharge report; it is used by different health professional groups, who show high satisfaction levels with the instrument, with the group of senders showing slightly better results than the group of receivers. Improvements in quality (fewer errors, comprehensive and complete information) in comparison to traditional transfer forms were confirmed.
- The satisfaction experienced by health professionals differs, but an increase in administrative efficiency was observed.

Hence, the results show that the cross-boundary pathway can act as a virtual bridge between the fragmented sectors. Future challenges for the project's success are the financial structures, which lead to competition instead of cooperation since the implementation of professional discharge management means a fixed sum of reform pool funds, but the long-term costs of the discharge management have to be borne by the hospitals themselves. Furthermore, voluntary participation in the cross-boundary pathway seems to enhance the motivation of staff, but the voluntary action also makes it difficult to achieve high participation rates, and thus to achieve standardization of information for Vienna as a whole.

Evaluations of other reform pool projects face restrictions in information value regarding the conjunction of the sectors. The evaluation focus is not on the degree of collaboration between the sectors on a meta level, but on the effects upon target groups, financial consequences for the reform pool payers and patients, as well as care provider satisfaction at the meso and micro levels (Bundesgesundheitsagentur 2008; Knopp 2009). Furthermore, because of the implementation phase of most projects (BMG 2011), the lack of any evaluations in three federal states, weaknesses in the operationalization of evaluations in many cases (Czypionka and Röhrling 2010), and evaluation reports not being publicly accessible, no absolute conclusions can be drawn regarding the contribution of other projects aimed at bridging the gaps of the two sectors. Rather, it would be better to guess which health system performance impact types have the greatest effect upon bridging the gaps between the inpatient and outpatient health sectors, although a trend is indicated within the largest project. The financial resources of reform pools could have enabled extensive changes and improvements in Austria's health system, but the funds are virtual and illustrate upper limits with no utilization obligations. Actual invested funds in reform pool projects are small shares of the intended resources, varying from 1.5 per cent to 33.7 per cent of overall reform pool funds (Czypionka and Röhrling 2009: 3–4), so we assume that there are few incentives to implement high investment reform pool projects. Budget figures, however, show no connection between the amount of resources and the level of innovation, so radical innovations seem to be feasible with lower funds, too. Hence, the assumption that radical innovations require high financial resources within the Austrian health care system context cannot be confirmed.

Missing links – conclusion

The assessment of implemented reform pool projects using the innovation level/ impact type framework reveals different levels of innovation in Austria's health system. Comparing the innovation levels and the impact types of the projects, radical innovations – which use new business models and process quality improvements or new technologies – have the highest impact upon the four target fields of accessibility/equity, efficiency, effectiveness and patient focus, which health care systems pursue in general. Furthermore, reform pool projects also aim at these in order to bridge the gaps between the inpatient and outpatient health care sectors in Austria, which represent one of the biggest challenges for Austrian health care policy in the near future. The evaluation carried out for one of the biggest reform pool projects, an example of radical innovation, shows a certain validation of the results from the framework.

Innovations in health care through cooperation were almost impossible before 2005 due to the decision making and financial structures of the health system. Nevertheless, there are shortcomings in the argumentation for reform pool projects as instruments of collaborative funding and decision making to overcome traditional health sector gaps, observable by the numbers of finished or aborted projects of substantial innovations (six finished and five aborted). On the one hand, there is a lack of sound cost-benefit analyses for the system as a whole, due to missing data and delayed records. On the other hand, the evaluation of priority setting for issues other than the conjunction of the inpatient and the outpatient sectors cannot prove benefits for the system. This also leads to the prolongation of the project statuses rather than the negotiation of long-run funding contracts between the federal states and the social insurance institutions as the payers for health care services. Given the experiences of the Patient Oriented Integrated Care, the financial structure of the project partly leads to competition instead of cooperative behaviour, whereas the voluntary participation of hospitals in the cross-boundary pathway, resulting from the general status of a project, seems to enhance the motivation of staff, but also counteracts the reasonable standardization of information transfer for Vienna as a whole. Health platforms signalize plans for the long-term funding of the innovations and the transfer into normal operation, but as yet offer no sustainable solutions. The comparison of the first reform pool projects in 2006, the status quo of 2009 and 2011 shows that most of the projects were prolonged (Amler 2006: 399–400; CCIV 2007; Czypionka and Röhrling 2009: 14; BMG 2011). This unsettled long-run funding of the innovation projects may lead to a minimization of actor involvement and process improvement benefits by cooperation in health care service delivery needed to meet the challenges of the ageing society and thus the permanent exclusion of patient-centred quality improvements in health care.

New decision making and funding structures set the scene for working across boundaries in Austria's health care, triggering various types of innovation. We have shown how cross-boundary service delivery has developed out of collaborative decision making and funding structures in a highly fragmented field. An assessment of the emerged reform pool projects' impact upon health system target fields indicates that radical innovations are the instrument of choice for performance enhancement and for soundly bridging the gaps between the fragmented sectors. Interestingly, radical innovations do not seem to depend upon high financial resources, as one might believe. However, a clear picture can be provided only when all projects have been evaluated. From a methodological perspective, future research on this issue could include a Multi-value Qualitative Comparative Analysis (MVQCA) (Cronqvist 2005) as a starting point for international comparison, enhancing our knowledge of if, and how, working across boundaries in this particular policy field really works.

References

Abernathy, W.J. and Utterback, J.M. (1978) 'Patterns of industrial innovations', *Technological Review*, 80(7): 2–29.

Albury, D. (2005) 'Fostering innovation in public services', *Public Money & Management*, 25: 51–56.

Amler, M. (2006) 'Landesgesundheitsplattformen – Reformpoolprojekte', *Soziale Sicherheit*, Okt./2006: 388–402.

Arah, O.A., Klazinga, N.S., Delnoij, D.M.J., Ten Asbroek, A.H.A. and Custers, T. (2003) 'Conceptual frameworks for health systems performance: a quest for effectiveness, quality, and improvement', *International Journal for Quality in Health Care*, 15(5): 377–398.

Berman, P. (1995) 'Health sector reform: making health development sustainable', *Health Policy*, 32(1–3): 13–28.

BGBl I (2005) Nr. 73, Art. 26, Vereinbarung gemäß Art. 15a B-VG über die Organisation und Finanzierung des Gesundheitswesens.

BGBl I (2008) Nr. 105, Art. 31, Vereinbarung gemäß Art. 15a B-VG über die Organisation und Finanzierung des Gesundheitswesens.

BMG (2008), *Die Gesundheitsreform 2005*, Wien, Bundesministerium für Gesundheit.

BMG (2009) *Überblick über Reformpoolprojekte, Stand 23.11.2009*, Online. Available at: www.bmg.gv.at/cms/site/attachments/3/7/2/CH0971/CMS1219052161632/abgestimmte_liste_reformpoolprojekte_stand_november_2009.pdf (accessed 3 January 2010).

BMG (2011) *Übersicht über Reformpoolprojekte: Stand 30.06.2011*, Online. Available at: http://bmg.gv.at/cms/home/attachments/3/7/2/CH1072/CMS1219052161632/liste_reformpoolprojekte_stand_30.06.2011.pdf (accessed 4 July 2011).

Bourque, D. (2005) 'Radical innovation: how established companies must compete', in R. Berndt, *Erfolgsfaktor Innovation*, Berlin, Springer.

Bundesgesundheitsagentur (2008) *Leitlinien für den Kooperationsbereich (Reformpool) gemäß Artikel 31 der Vereinbarung gemäß Artikel 15a B-VG über die Organisation und Finanzierung des Gesundheitswesens*, Wien: Bundesministerium für Gesundheit, Familie und Jugend.

Busse, R. and Schlette, S. (eds) (2003) *Health Policy Developments. International Trends and Analyses*, Gütersloh: Bertelsmann Foundation.

Casebeer, A.L. and Hannah, K.J. (1996) 'The process of change related to health policy shift: reforming a health care system', *International Journal of Public Sector Management*, 11 (7): 566–582.

CCIV (2007) *Survey of Reform Pool Projects of the Competence Center Integrated Care: July 2007*, Vienna: Competence Center Integrated Care of the Austrian Social Insurance.

Chernichovsky, D. (1995) 'Health system reform in industrialized democracies: an emerging paradigm', *The Milbank Quarterly*, 73 (3): 339–372.

Chesbrough, H. and Rosenbloom, R.S. (2002) 'The role of the business model in capturing value from innovation: evidence from Xerox Corporation's technology spin-off companies', *Industrial and Corporate Change*, 11 (3): 530.

Cronqvist, L. (2005) *Introduction to Multi-value Qualitative Comparative Analysis (MVQCA)*, COMPASS didactics paper no. 2005/4, Online. Available at: www.tosmana.net/resources/introduction_to_mvqca.pdf (accessed 15 June 2012).

Czypionka, T. and Röhrling, G. (2009) 'Analyse der Reformpool-Aktivität in Österreich: Wie viel Reform ist im Reformpool?', *Soziale Sicherheit*, II/2009: 1–16.

Czypionka, T. and Röhrling, G. (2010) 'Wie viel Reform ist im Reformpool?', paper presented at the 5th Symposium Integrated Care, Vienna, November 2010.

Damanpour, F. (1987) 'The adoption of technological, administrative, and ancillary innovations: impact of organizational factors', *Journal of Management*, 13 (4): 675–688.

Damanpour, F., Walker, R.M. and Avellaneda, C.N. (2009) 'Combinative effects of innovation types and organizational performance: a longitudinal study of service organizations', *Journal of Management Studies*, 46 (4): 650–675.

Davila, T., Epstein, M.J. and Shelton, R. (2006) *Making Innovation Work: How To Manage It, Measure It and Profit From It*, New Jersey: Pearson.

Dixon, A. and Mossialos, E. (2002) *Health Care Systems in Eight Countries: Trends and Challenges*, London: European Observatory on Health Care Systems.

Do Carmo Caccia-Bava, M., Guimaraes, V.C.K. and Guimaraes, T. (2009) 'Testing some major determinants for hospital innovation success', *International Journal of Health Care Quality Assurance*, 22 (5): 454–470.

Docteur, E. and Oxley, H. (2003) *Health Care Systems: Lessons from the Reform Experience*, OECD Health Working Papers Nr. 9, Paris: Organisation for Economic Cooperation and Development.

Duncan, A.K. and Breslin, M.A. (2009) 'Innovating health care delivery: the design of health services', *Journal of Business Strategy*, 30 (2/3): 13–20.

Evans, D.B., Tandon, A., Murray, C.J.L. and Lauer, J.A. (2001) 'Comparative efficiency of national health system: cross national econometric analysis', *BMJ British Medical Journal*, 323 (11): 307–310.

Evans, I. (2010) 'Follow-on biologics: a new play for big pharma', *Yale Journal of Biology and Medicine*, 83 (2): 97–100.

Figueras, J. and Saltman, R. (1996) *European Health Care Reform: Analysis of Current Strategies*, Geneva: World Health Organization.

Frenk, J. (1994) 'Dimensions of health system reform', *Health Policy*, 27 (1): 19–34.

Garcia, R. and Calantone, R. (2002) 'A critical look at technological innovation typology and innovativeness terminology: a literature review', *The Journal of Product Innovation Management*, 19: 110–132.

Gassmann, O., Reepmeyer, G. and Zedtwitz, M. (2008) *Leading Pharmaceutical Innovation: Trends and Drivers for Growth in the Pharmaceutical Industry*, Heidelberg: Springer.

Glassman, A. and Buse, K. (2008) 'Politics, and public health policy reform', in *International Encyclopedia of Public Health*, Amsterdam; London: Elsevier.

Godoe, H. (2000) 'Innovation regimes, R & D and radical innovations in telecommunications', *Research Policy*, 29: 1033–1046.

Govindarajan, V. and Trimble, C. (2005) *Ten Rules for Strategic Innovators: From Idea to Execution*, Boston: Harvard Business School Publishing.

Granig, P., Gabriel, A., Stadtschreiber, G. and Pertl, M. (2011) 'Wirksames Innovationsmanagement im Gesundheitswesen', in P. Granig and L.A. Nefiodow (eds) *Gesundheitswirtschaft – Wachstumsmotor im 21. Jahrhundert. Mit 'gesunden' Innovationen neue Wege aus der Krise gehen*, Wiesbaden: Gabler.

Habl, C. and Bachner, F. (2010) *Das österreichische Gesundheitswesen 2009*, Wien: Österreichisches Bundesinstitut für Gesundheitswesen.

Hartley, J. (2005) 'Innovation in governance and public services: past and present', *Public Money & Management*, 25: 27–34.

Hauptverband der österreichischen Sozialversicherungsträger (2011a) *Statistisches Handbuch der österreichischen Sozialversicherung 2010*, Wien: Hauptverband der österreichischen Sozialversicherungsträger.

Hauptverband der österreichischen Sozialversicherungsträger (2011b) *Die österreichische Sozialversicherung in Zahlen 2010*, Wien: Hauptverband der österreichischen Sozialversicherungsträger.

Herber, C. (2007) 'Beurteilungsansatz der Umsetzung der Gesundheitsreform 2005. Einrichtung der "Bundesgesundheitsagentur" bzw. der neun "Landesgesundheitsfonds"', in J. Weidenholzer (ed.) *Gesundheitswissenschaften Nr. 14*, Linz: Johannes Kepler Universität Linz.

Herzlinger, R.E. (2006) 'Why Innovation in Health Care is so hard', *Harvard Business Review*, May 2006: 58–66.

Hofmarcher, M.M. (2009) 'Yet to come: health policy response to the crisis', *Health*

Policy Monitor, April 2009, Online. Available at: www.hpm.org/survey/at/b13/1 (accessed 12 June 2011).

Hofmarcher, M. and Rack, H. (2001) *Health Care Systems in Transition. Austria. 2001*, Copenhagen, WHO, European Observatory on Health Systems and Policy.

Hofmarcher, M. and Rack, H. (2006) *Health Care Systems in Transition. Austria. 2006*, Copenhagen, WHO, European Observatory on Health Systems and Policy.

Hussey, P. and Anderson, G.F. (2003) 'A comparison of single- and multi-payer health insurance systems and options for reform', *Health Policy*, 66 (3): 215–228.

Ivansits, H. (2009) 'Krankenkassen in der Finanzkrise und "Finanzierung aus einer Hand"', *WISO* 1/2009: 58–79. Online. Available at: www.image.co.at/themen/dbdocs/LF_Ivansits_01_09.pdf (accessed 1 September 2011).

Kelley, E. and Hurst, J. (2006) *Health Care Quality Indicators Project. Conceptual Framework Paper*, OECD Health Working Papers Nr. 23, Paris: Organisation for Economic Cooperation and Development.

Knopp, A. (2009) 'Erfahrungen zur Evaluation von Projekten integrierter Versorgung in der Steiermark', paper presented at the 4th Symposium Integrated Care, Vienna, November 2009.

Knowles, J.C., Leighton, C. and Stinson, W. (1997) *Measuring Results of Health Sector Reform for System Performance: A Handbook of Indicators*. Special Initiatives Report No. 1, Bethesda: Abt Associates.

Kola, I. (2008) 'The state of innovation in drug development', *Clinical Pharmacology & Therapeutics*, 83 (2): 227–230.

Kruger, C.J. and Johnson, R.D. (2011) 'Is there a correlation between Knowledge Management Maturity and Organizational Performance?', *VINE The Journal of Information and Knowledge Management Systems*, 41 (3), E-publication ahead of print. Online. Available at: www.emeraldinsight.com/journals.htm?articleid=1944393 (accessed 7 September 2011).

Laimböck, M. (2009) *Die Zukunft des Österreichischen Gesundheitssystems. Wettbewerbsorientierte Patientenversorgung im Internationalen Vergleich*, Wien: Springer.

Land Wien (2007) *Wiener Gesundheitsfonds: Tätigkeitsbericht 2007*, Wien: Wiener Gesundheitsfonds.

May, C. (2009) 'Innovation and implementation in health technology: normalizing telemedicine', in J. Gabe and M. Calnan (eds) *The New Sociology of the Health Service*, London; New York, Routledge.

Mayer, H. (2007) *Bundes-Verfassungsrecht, Kurzkommentar*, 4. Auflage, Wien: Manz.

Maynard, A. and Bloor, K. (1995) 'Health care reform: informing difficult choices', *International Journal of Health Planning and Management*, 10 (4): 247–264.

McNulty, T. and Ferlie, E. (2004) *Reengineering Health Care: The Complexities of Organizational Transformation*, Oxford; New York: Oxford University Press.

Merkur, S., Mossialos, E., Ladurner, J. and Lear, J. (2008) *Quality in Health Care Systems: With an Emphasis on Policy Options for Austria*, London; Vienna, LSE Health.

Mulgan, G. (2006) 'The process of social innovation', *Innovations Technology Governance Globalization*, 1 (2): 145–162.

Osborne, S. (1998) 'Naming the beast: defining and classifying service innovations in social policy', *Human Relations*, 51: 1133–1154.

Pavitt, K. (2004) 'Innovation Processes', in J. Fagerberg, D.C. Mowery and R.R Nelson (eds) *The Oxford Handbook of Innovation*, Oxford: Oxford University Press.

Pekkarinen, S., Hennala, L., Harmaakorpi, V. and Tura, T. (2011) 'Clashes as potential for innovation in public service sector reform', *International Journal of Public Sector Management*, 24 (6): 507–532.

Perl, E. (2003) 'Grundlagen des Innovations- und Technologiemanagements', in H. Strebel *Innovations- und Technologiemanagement*, Graz: WUV Universitätsverlag.

Potts, J. (2009) 'The innovation deficit in public services: the curious problem of too much efficiency and not enough waste and failure', *Innovation: Management, Policy & Practice*, 11 (1): 34–43.

Rowley, J., Baregheh, A. and Sambrook, S. (2011) 'Towards an innovation-type mapping tool', *Management Decision*, 49 (1): 73–86.

Sandberg, B. (2008) *Managing and Marketing Radical Innovations: Marketing New Technology*, London: Routledge.

Schultz, C., Zippel-Schultz, B. and Salomo, S. (2011) 'Hospital innovation portfolios: key determinants of size and innovativeness', *Health Care Management Review*, July 2011. Online. Available at: http://journals.lww.com/hcmrjournal/Abstract/publisha-head/Hospital_innovation_portfolios__Key_determinants.99965.aspx (accessed: 13 September 2011).

Segal, L. (1998) 'The importance of patient empowerment in health system reform', *Health Policy*, 44 (1): 31–44.

Spiel, G. and Petscharnig, J. (2009) 'Evaluation im österreichischen Gesundheitswesen: ein Überblick', in T. Widmer, W. Beywl and C. Fabian (eds) *Evaluation: Ein Systematisches Handbuch*, Wiesbaden: VS Verlag.

Statistics Austria (2011) *Current Expenditure on Health by Function of Care, Provider and Source of Funding, 2008*, Online. Available at: www.statistik.at/web_en (accessed 1 September 2011).

Statistik Austria (2010) *Jahrbuch der Gesundheitsstatistik 2009*, Wien: Statistik Austria.

Sturmberg, J.P., O'Halloran, D.M. and Martin, C.M. (2010) 'People at the centre of complex adaptive health systems reform', *Medical Journal of Australia*, 193 (8): 474–478.

Toth, F. (2010) 'Healthcare policies over the last 20 years: reforms and counter-reforms', *Health Policy*, 95 (1): 82–89.

Unger, F. (2007) *Paradigma der Medizin im 21. Jahrhundert*, Heidelberg: Springer.

Walker, R. (2003) 'Evidence on the management of public services innovation', *Public Money & Management*, 23: 93–102.

Walker, R. (2006) 'Innovation type and diffusion: an empirical analysis of local government', *Public Administration*, 84: 311–335.

Walker, R.M., Jeanes, E. and Rowlands, R. (2002) 'Measuring innovation – applying the literature-based innovation output indicator to public services', *Public Administration*, 80: 201–214.

Wendt, C. and Thompson, T. (2004) 'Social austerity versus structural reform in European health systems: a four country comparison of health reforms', *International Journal of Health Services*, 34 (3): 415–433.

WHO (2009) *Environmental Burden of Disease: Austria*, Geneva, World Health Organization, Public Health and the Environment.

Zaltman, G., Duncan, R. and Holbek, J. (1973) *Innovations and Organizations*, New York: Wiley.

16 Community safety

Partnerships across boundaries in England

Joyce Liddle and John Diamond

Introduction

This chapter examines what working across boundaries involves for agencies, organizations and individuals. In particular, the chapter highlights the tensions and the opportunities for professional learning and practice. In addition it identifies the potential benefits for users and beneficiaries of public services.

Collaboration and partnership working in the UK: the New Labour approach

The public policy shift towards partnership or collaborative working in the UK underwent a step change after 1997 and the election of New Labour (Balloch and Taylor 2001). Prior to 1997 there had been a number of policy initiatives seeking to bring together public agencies in shared activities, but they were short-lived and often a reaction to an event or perceived crisis. The primary area of joint work was through regeneration initiatives. The Conservative Government elected in 1979 retained the Urban Programme (launched in the 1960s) and introduced a number of schemes modelled on areas or spatial categorization of need. Through these programs the government developed an approach which brought together different social, economic and community interests in a geographically defined neighbourhood.

After the change in leadership within the Conservative Party, the new Prime Minister and his Deputy adopted a more deliberate and conscious policy of seeking the co-operation of local public bodies (especially local government) as well as key national public and welfare agencies in developing joint work. These programs claimed to be apolitical, but offered an opportunity for the new Conservative Party leadership to position itself as representing a more managerialist, as opposed to ideological, approach to public sector reform (Huxham and Vangen 2000, 2005; McQuaid 2010).

The willingness to support and promote partnership working had positive benefits for agencies as well as for service users and residents. The Major Government established itself as representing an alternative to the New Right politics of the Thatcher years. From 1990 onwards a consensus emerged which saw 'partnership working' as a new orthodoxy for creating a different kind of relationship between users and professionals, with an explicit commitment from service providers to listen to and learn from their users. This practice was neither as new nor as neutral as it was presented, but it did represent a break with the past. In the two key regeneration initiatives – City Challenge and Single Regeneration Budget – programs of activity were developed through a dialogue between local and central government departments, followed by the limited involvement of key individuals drawn from the private, voluntary and community sectors. This dialogue represented an additional commitment to 'partnership working'.

These initiatives were illustrative of the broader policy and practice shift which was emerging at this time – the move to develop specific multi-agency or multi-disciplinary responses to 'wicked issues'. This represented an important change in the way services were managed, funded, structured and valued (Amin and Roberts 2008; Boud and Middleton 2003; Jones and Morris 2008; Karlsson *et al.* 2008; Vangen and Huxham 2003).

Such projects provided rich examples of innovative ways of dealing with structural questions of poverty, poor health, anti-social behaviour, urban decline and poor educational achievement. They highlighted how political leaders and senior civil servants introduced changes to services organization and provision. A shared narrative across the political divide and in the policy and practice literature situated these changes in the following context:

- A recognition that some public health and public service issues were outside the remit and capacity of individual agencies to address;
- A concern that increased public spending would not change the material and social context;
- An acceptance that reforming the structure and organization of state-funded services was not the sole solution to changing practice or behaviours;
- A real concern that the gap between public acceptance and understanding of the role of key agencies (including the police) was growing;
- An expectation that dissatisfaction with all public services, and especially those involved in anti-social behaviour and the criminal justice system, was growing;
- A belief that there was a need to improve the co-ordination, liaison and co-operation between services, and that enhanced co-ordination would lead to an increase in effectiveness.

These changes represented a profound shift in understanding the relationships and negotiations between political leaders, key public service professionals and the public policy community, including administrators and senior civil servants. We suggest that the changes which took place during the 1990s in the UK defined a new approach to the ways in which public services were managed, organized and expected to perform (Mulgan 2007).

The study below examines how the scale and significance of the changes were not anticipated by some of the core interest groups. Indeed, what the data from the case study illustrates is how the idea of working across different boundaries is contested and open to many different meanings and definitions. Often there is an unacknowledged awareness that working in 'collaboration' can be profoundly destabilizing and disruptive for both individuals and organizations. Whilst we can rehearse the different meanings associated with the ideas and concepts of collaborative working, it is important to locate the starting point for the public policy embrace of partnership or collaborative working in the UK (Benneworth 2007; Diamond and Roberts 2006).

We argue that the explicit political commitment to 'partnership' working dates from 1997 and the election of New Labour. We want to distinguish between those initiatives and professionals who deliberately chose to work with others and to promote the idea of cross-boundary working from those who were required to do so after May 1997. There are many examples of the former. During the 1970s and 1980s, through university education and training programs, social work and youth work professionals were prepared to work across different professional boundaries. Indeed, a key part of the practice debates within both professions was the need to recognize the value of a geographic or patch-based approach to their work with the specialist skills and knowledge they needed in other, more user-based contexts.

Community safety: internationally and nationally

Community safety is considered in some definitions to be freedom from crime and violence, and from the fear of crime and violence. Other definitions include safety from accidents. Both understandings of community safety are a subset of 'health and wellbeing' issues integral to a liveable community, and are connected to broader social, environmental and economic sustainability. Community safety broadly includes crime (burglary and hijack) prevention, domestic violence prevention, road safety, alcohol abuse control, natural and social disaster prevention, and other disorder reductions in a community. Community safety also prevents, reduces or contains social, environmental and intermediate factors which affect people's right to live without fear of crime or its impact upon quality of life. This includes preventative measures for reducing crime and anti-social behaviour.

In a UK context, the policy shift over the last decade or so from situational crime prevention to community safety is one which has been interpreted by many as a progressive change, rationally responding to the alleged weaknesses of the situational approach. The Morgan Committee (Home Office 1991) was set up to explore the reasons why crime prevention had failed and why community safety was pushed into the mainstream. Community safety was no longer the sole preserve of criminal justice agencies such as the police, as social problems escalated in inner cities (and later in rural areas). The emphasis during the Conservative administration after 1979 was to make cities attractive places to live, thus 'Action for Cities'. 'Safer Cities Programme' and 'Urban Programmes' were aimed at tackling problems, including high crime rates and race riots. In

1996 the Local Government Management Board, Association of District Councils and Association of Metropolitan Authorities commissioned research into community safety as a legitimate local policy area, and it became a strategic concern of local authorities and their multi-agency institutional milieu (LGMB 1996).

Community safety and crime prevention policies are now firmly near the top of national and local policy agendas. In Canada and Australia, crime prevention polices are considered effective if they integrate activities of all spheres of government and communities (Federal Justice Office 1992). They achieve integration, articulate a vision and motivate individuals and organizations to become actively involved in reducing crime, by establishing agreed measures on reduction. In the UK community safety was absorbed into the broader criminal justice and neighbourhood management agendas as central government attempted to 'join up' local approaches (Joseph Rowntree Foundation 2000). Issues of 'liveability' were addressed through greater localized leadership and participation, increasing community safety and employment opportunities, improving housing stock and working with young people and vulnerable groups in disadvantaged areas (Neighbourhood Renewal Unit 2008).

Leadership of 'place'

Northouse (2004) identified four common themes in current conceptions of leadership: leadership is a process, involves influence, occurs in a group context, and involves the achievement of goals. Interestingly, there is considerable overlap between these four themes and what Grint (1997, 2004) views as the four problems that make consensus around a shared definition of leadership hard to obtain. Is leadership derived from the personal qualities or traits of the leader, or is followership induced through some social process in which leaders and followers are engaged? Does leadership stem from formal authority or informal influence? Is leadership an intentional, causal effort on the part of the leaders, or are followers' actions determined by the situation or context? Is leadership embodied in individuals, or can groups be leaders?

The idea of leadership of 'place' in complex policy environments with individuals working across institutional, thematic, territorial, community and professional boundaries with long term vision-led agendas has been articulated in many statutory instruments in the UK and Europe. The importance of 'place' and 'outcomes' in transforming particular localities illustrated strategic leadership based upon fluid, relational, associational, interactions and collaborations (Gibney and Murie 2008). Whereas Borraz and John (2004) suggested that leadership is crucial to local governance as part of networks and partnerships and observed that central intervention needed creative leaders to direct local policy making, Leach and Wilson (2000) urged caution in an obsession with 'community leadership' because balancing the pressures for transformational change is at odds with existing traditional administrative processes.

Multi-sectoral partnerships are central tenets of contemporary urban and rural regeneration policy and new forms of local participative governance.

Neighbourhood renewal has encouraged a new form of community leadership, one which is in touch with local problems and with local authorities taking the strategic lead in engaging citizens in determining community priorities, and developing the collaborative potential of other local agencies (Hemphill *et al.* 2006). Local authorities, as the 'voice' of a locality, can assert a sense of 'place' as well as having the capacity to bring together agencies to contribute to the aspirations of local communities (ODPM 2005). It is important, however, that collective local leadership develops a full understanding of the communities they serve: what makes them feel safe or unsafe, the causes and complexities of crime, and solutions to local needs and outcome measures (Squires 2008).

Leadership is a central component of good governance in all OECD countries as individuals promote institutional adaptations in the public interest (OECD 2001).

Place, in a criminal justice and community safety context, is not only the specific situational/physical setting and characteristics of where crime occurs, but the wider *social* context too. Social and economic factors influence crime rates in any particular 'place'. Brookes (2009) argued that

> It has long been accepted that police alone cannot combat crime. Wherever you have high levels of crime you will also find poor health, low educational attainment, poor housing, fewer employed people and all of the other 'wicked issues' that are often spoken about.

These wicked social problems are complex, ambiguous and cannot be solved in isolation because many sit outside of traditional bureaucratic hierarchies. There are no right or wrong solutions, and securing collective consent and collaboration is essential (Grint *et al.* 2009). Community safety partnerships are reflective of this wider understanding of crime reduction, and a fuller understanding of place challenges partners to contribute to a collective endeavour. Thus, the shift from a relatively narrow focus on crime prevention to the broader issue of community safety and security as a public good, and a developing consensus about the social and economic conditions that foster crime and victimization have become the dominant orthodoxy (US Department of Justice 2001: 5).

Criminal justice and community safety as part of sustainable communities

Policies for reducing crime levels and maximizing citizen safety are a key part of the UK Government's approach to managing sustainable local areas. Public services have undergone a 'renaissance' since 1997, as a mixture of innovative and, at times, contradictory initiatives have been launched. In 2006 the then Minister for Communities and Local Government (DCLG) argued that 'in a modern world, public services need to be more responsive and that citizens and communities need to be given a bigger say in how the services they use, and the places they live are run' (DCLG 2006). The UK Labour Government's aim for a radical modernization of public services depends upon achieving 'holistic' government, and 'joined-up thinking', as initiatives are managed through networks of state and non-state partnerships.

Multi-agency partnerships created a plethora of arrangements in addition to Crime and Disorder Reduction Partnerships, such as Local Strategic Partnerships, Children's Trusts, Local Resilience Forums, Multi Agency Public Protection Arrangements, Local and Multiple Area Agreements, and many others, with financial 'sweeteners' and promises of more flexibility or freedom from central government controls. Many of the audit and monitoring controls developed by the national Audit Commission since 1983 have changed in nature over the past 25 years, as we shall now discuss.

New performance framework for UK public service delivery, including community safety

Since the passing of the 1999 Local Government (Best Value) Act, the local government performance management regime has been one of the most powerful levers for change within local public services (Martin and Bovaird 2005), including community safety and criminal justice. Between 1998 and 2004 the introduction of national performance indicators, the Best Value regime and the Comprehensive Performance Assessments were very significant drivers of change across local government (Liddle and Murphy 2012). Other changes altered the relationship between central and local government.

Following the election of a Labour Government in 1997, the Local Government Acts of 1999 and 2000 and the Local Government White Paper of 2001 (DTLR 2001) saw the enactment of other initiatives within local government modernization. The intention was to transform local authorities into an outwardly looking, customer-focussed, efficient and effective network of organizations, working in an openly transparent and democratic manner on behalf of communities in order to meet community-defined needs and aspirations. Central Government's 2004 Comprehensive Spending Review (CSR) had included Public Service Agreement (PSA) targets to improve local public service delivery systems, and citizen-centred services took centre stage.

The basis of the modernization agenda of local government had the following key characteristics (Murphy 2010):

1   New legal parameters for continuous improvement and the power of well-being, later enhanced by the duties to inform, co-operate and share information across public services;
2   A long-term vision for localities, articulated through Local Strategic Partnerships and Sustainable Community Strategies, to be agreed by all collaborating agencies, and reflected in Local Area Agreements;
3   Better decision making based on new constitutional and governance arrangements with Councils expected to make continuous improvement in all services;
4   A new performance management regime was introduced.

This audit and inspection regime, promulgated by the Audit Commission, developed into a National Performance Management Framework, as previous Best Value Performance Indicators and Performance Plans complemented, Best Value Service Inspections and Audit Commission Corporate Inspections, Peer Reviews, and Improvement and Development Agency Self-Assessments tools were combined into a Comprehensive Performance Assessment (CPA) regime, which was superseded by Comprehensive Area Assessment (Audit Commission, 2009 a and b) (see Figure 16.1).

Whereas CPA had examined overall performance against national benchmarks, CAA was an annual snapshot of how well all local agencies in an area were working to meet the needs of the people they serve.

In 2001 the UK Government had introduced a number of key initiatives in all local authority areas, culminating in new forms of partnership arrangements, such as Local Strategic Partnerships (LSP) and Local Area Agreements (LAA). Local government managers had a 'duty to involve' citizens and a 'duty to co-operate' with communities, state and non-state agencies to marry social and economic objectives and drive local area transformations. Within a National Performance Framework of 198 national indicators, local areas could, through the LSPs and LAA framework, agree on 35 locally determined targets (see Figure 16.2).

The outcomes–targets–indicators framework

Targets were set through the development of a Sustainable Community Strategy agreed by all partners represented on the LSP in all 360 local areas in England in order to improve co-ordination of public service delivery. LAAs were introduced

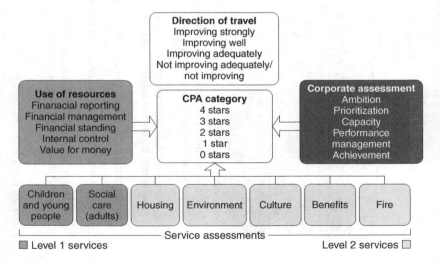

Figure 16.1 CPA framework.

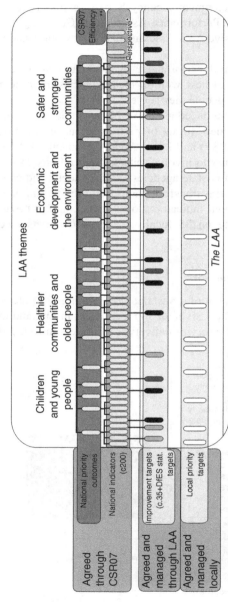

LAA themes

| Agreed through CSR07 | | | | | | | | CSR07 Efficiency** |

National priority outcomes

National indicators (c200)

| Children and young people | Healthier communities and older people | Economic development and the environment | Safer and stronger communities |

Perspective*

Agreed and managed through LAA

Improvement targets (c.35+DfES stat. targets)

The LAA

Agreed and managed locally

Local priority targets

Improvement targets

Non-negotiable target (universal local targets where government determines that an equal level of improvement is required in all areas)

Floor target (where minimum standards are not being met, these targets will specify the amount and/or timescale for improvement up to such standards)

Negotiable target (issues for negotiation will be whether or not to have a target or the level it should be set. The negotiations will be aimed at balancing national requirements and local circumstances, performance and priorities)

Local priority target (set by LAs and partners. Not subject to upward reporting or monitoring by central government)

* A few key national citizen satisfaction and perspective indicators in addition to any used as outcome indicators e.g. satisfaction with place: perception of influence.

** Whether any indicators or local targets are established and what form they would take will be confirmed as part of the CSR07 announcement.

Figure 16.2 National indicator set.

in July 2004 as a three-year agreement, setting out priorities for a local area between central and local government partnerships. The aim was to allow greater flexibility and freedom in finding solutions to local problems and to deliver better outcomes through improved co-ordination. Each LAA has four broad 'blocks', i.e. 'Children and Young People', 'Safer and Stronger Communities', 'Healthier Communities and Local People' and 'Economic Development and Enterprise'. 'Safer and Stronger Communities' led to the creation of CDRPs, as we shall discuss in the next section.

Partnerships within community safety

Crime and Disorder Reduction Partnerships (CDRPs) co-ordinated a local set of programmes to implement crime reduction and community safety, and produced local crime reduction strategies (Home Office 1991). They brought together local authorities, police, fire and rescue, health authorities, probation and community and voluntary sectors as 'Collective Leadership Forums' to align shared leadership across traditional partnerships and strategic alliances (Brookes 2009). The use of such partnerships had been stressed in crime reduction policy for over twenty years. CDRPs, and the county-wide Community Safety Partnerships (CSP), had experienced varied levels of success in bringing together strategic and operational partnerships to achieve national targets. However, the CSP investigated in this case had been recognized as a potential 'red flag' (i.e. in danger) by the Audit Commission, so the Home Office recognized that drastic remedial action was vital if the Partnership was not to fall even further in the national rankings.

Central government intervention: the need for a change programme

In the Community Safety Partnership we explored, the Home Office Police and Crime Standards Directorate (PCSD), in partnership with Government Office (GO), conducted a Partnership Support Programme in August 2007, as part of a wider programme, between PCSD, GO, the County Council and the Community Safety Board, and the District Councils' Chief Executive/Managing Directors in order to review and assess community safety structures and processes across the county. The aims were to improve the overall effectiveness of the partnership so as to meet minimum standards and achieve the six hallmarks of effective partnerships (Home Office 2007a and b).[1] Partnership performance was an essential contribution to the delivery of local priorities.

A change programme was initiated to improve the capacity of the County Council's Team to respond to the Home Office's Review and to build collective leadership, shared definitions, strategic thinking and leadership structure; build a collective approach to performance review, management and shared accountability; build knowledge and skills around delivery of effective interventions; build a shared approach to community engagement and communications; and build a collective use of resources.

The existing Community Safety Board subsequently approved an evaluation of the Programme and appointed the authors as critical friends to the Director of Change and the Change Steering Group in order to facilitate action learning and problem solving activities with key stakeholders, and to produce a report on progress on key achievements, remaining challenges and learning points.

The change programme was aimed at co-ordination, disseminating best practice, and achieving best value. A county-wide Local Strategic Partnership Discussion Paper had already recommended a set of principles, values and relationships, along with specific responsibilities and accountabilities to improve governance (Audit Commission 2009b).

Criminal Justice agencies were required to promote public confidence after the 1998 Comprehensive Spending Review and the introduction of PSAs. The Criminal Justice Boards introduced in 2003 brought together senior executives from agencies in each police force area. Public Confidence was a priority measured by a suite of indicators included in the British Crime Survey (BCS).

The Criminal Justice Business Plan 2009–2010 stated that local areas must develop locally determined indicators for 2010–2011, measurable local improvements in community engagement, and raise public confidence in the fairness and effectiveness of the Criminal Justice System.

The British Crime Survey revealed this county as the poorest performing LCJB for public confidence in the whole criminal justice system. The Local Criminal Justice Board Strategic Plan 2008–2011 suggested that in order to bring about improvements and achieve the vision of 'a confident and engaged public ... criminal justice agencies needed to work together more closely through the LCJB'.

Findings and discussion

In this section we explore the six hallmarks of effective partnerships set out in 2007 by the Home Office, and how they emerged, or did not, in Community Safety.

Hallmark one: collective leadership

The change programme was successful and 'added value' to partnership working as The Community Safety Partnership evolved. The Director of Change established a narrative of collaborative working, raised the profile of community safety at district, county and wider levels, and established a Performance Framework to clearly understand community safety issues. Relationships that had been fragmented were rebuilt and more trusting relationships engendered. The decision to re-brand the Community Safety Partnership and hold a 'launch event' played an important role in altering perceptions of the importance of community safety as a joint venture, not one restricted to the police service only.

In the newly formed Community Safety Board, the Director of Change worked with senior people from contributing agencies in order to integrate and streamline governance structures.

Board members were drawn from community safety agencies, and their ability to 'get things done' and stimulate change processes were critical. The Director of Change was a senior probation professional, and this seniority and professional training were regarded as essential to challenge existing notions of best practice. This level of independence not only allowed a challenge to past practice, but also the instigatation of new activities, processes and procedures.

Hallmark two: intelligence-led business processes

Eventually clarity was achieved at strategic levels, but things were not so clear at district levels with respect to roles, responsibilities and purpose. Much confusion reigned over how the strategic and operational fitted together and there was evidence of duplication.

Members used various measurements to indicate whether or not the partnership had been successful, such as reductions in crime rates, and hitting local priorities through local area agreements.

Data was collected regularly, and was fed in from the Delivery Groups and assessed by the Board. There was a major problem of lack of capacity to assess and interpret the data and align with overall objectives, resource deployment and outcomes achieved.

No sanctions, penalties or mechanisms were in place to identify poor performance. Consequently, the complexity of the reporting structures meant an incapacity to link overall priorities with operational performance and resource deployment. The fact that the Board had no single budget added to the complexities and the lack of ability to link resources with decisions made on priorities.

A key concern remained the extent to which agencies acted 'independently' or in silos. The relative independence of agencies illustrated a broader policy and practice question of how accountability was understood across the Partnership.

Shared learning between the strategic level of the Partnership Board and the districts had developed, but there was room for improvement, as the following quote demonstrates:

> What's not being done is strategic coordination of tactical people on the ground across the County. Sharing best practices is not evident, leading to duplication of effort. There is no resourcing through economies of scale either.

> The dynamics of the partnership increased due to greater level of responsibility created as more community safety indicators were imposed. In a complicated partnership world the integrated framework of statutory bodies meant that members had to consider what they were doing well now, where there were gaps and what should be done in future. It was important to connect them all together.

Hallmark three: effective and responsive structures

The CSP regularly reviewed performance delivery, but 'by exception' only. However, a developing culture of openness and constructive dialogue led to common tasking and pooled intelligence on how well targets were being met and milestones were being achieved. The partnership developed a problem solving approach, with robust information exchange and analysis to tackle crime, disorder and drugs. Existing data was used to establish the existence and extent of problems, their nature and source, to plan interventions and to monitor and evaluate the effectiveness of responses

Other evidence of good practice across the partnership included workshops for cross-agency learning. In particular, the County Acquisitive Crime workshops and county-wide Who's Who on CDRPs were held up as exemplars.

Hallmark four: engaged communities

Community Engagement was one area of Board-working in need of attention. Most of the agencies represented on the Board began individual agency mapping of community engagement across the county. The police distributed a pro forma based on Arnstein's 'Ladder of Citizen Engagement' (Arnstein 1969), and also set up a series of workshops to which district and county level officers were invited. These were well attended, and other criminal justice agencies carried out similar exercises. Few were systematized or 'joined up', as reflected in the need for a County Wide Partnership Comprehensive Engagement Strategy. Each CDRP developed a community safety engagement action plan, in order to integrate neighbourhood policing, criminal justice engagement and community cohesion activities so that local people were involved in identifying community safety issues. The Police Authority agreed to work with the Director of Change and/or the co-ordinator to support CDRPs in these activities.

The scrutiny function of the County Council had not investigated the CSP as a separate entity, but the Chief Constable of Police (who was Vice Chair of the Board) had been called to a scrutiny committee to produce an account of crime figures and other related activities. None of the respondents felt that there was a need to have community/citizen representation on any other parts of the partnership arrangements.

Board members and some of the district-level delivery partnerships were aware of the need to raise the profile of their activities, not least because of the importance of a single confidence measure for the county. At the strategic level, a decision was made to recruit a marketing and communications consultancy company to identify 'good news' stories. Each delivery group developed a marketing and communications strategy, but such activities could have been better aligned between county and districts for cost savings and overall impact.

Hallmark five: visible and constructive accountability mechanisms

As the delivery group reports were submitted to the Board only by 'exception', Board members rarely had a complete overview of all activities or where 'added value' or activities not achieving targets could be recognized. There was no mechanism for Board members to assess variable performance between delivery groups, or to instigate corrective action. It was clear that the mass of data collection presented did not allow a clear link to be made between strategic objectives, resources deployed and outcomes achieved. The quarterly reports were regarded as a welcome mechanism of accountability, but no one was clear on how effective they were.

At both the strategic and the operational/implementation/delivery levels there was little knowledge on commissioning activities on behalf of the partnership. This applied to commissioning research/consultancy or other activities; one example would be the need to commission marketing and communication companies to help to raise the profile, or commissioning research on engagement or confidence levels. The Board and the local delivery groups had different mechanisms for commissioning activities and there was much duplication. In numerous delivery groups, the discussion centred around how effective interventions were going to be, and how those making the decisions could know this without undertaking an 'effectiveness review' of all activities.

Hallmark six: appropriate skills and knowledge

The Director of Change had instigated initiatives to enhance the skills and knowledge base of personnel across the various elements of the partnership.

One key area where skills had developed was in moving towards more collective ownership of problems, improved strategic thinking and implementation. Levels of trust were building up, and 'vertical' and 'horizontal' relationships were improved. A Learning and Development Strategy (2009–2010) was developed, after a Knowledge and Skills Audit, and it recommended skills enhancement across several areas, including induction, individual learning, leadership, performance management, and systemic learning.

Conclusion

This case study provides rich qualitative data that highlights the difficulties of initiating and managing a series of key policy and practice changes across different organizational and professional boundaries and hierarchical structures of (often competing) public agencies. This particular initiative was subject to audit and inspection by central government to evidence its impact upon crime and anti-social behaviour indicators.

Important lessons can be drawn from the study for application to other contexts, but it is important to set the case in its political and economic context. It was one the outcomes of public service reforms introduced by New Labour after 1997, and it represented features of innovation and change associated with the Labour Government until 2010. Additionally, particular issues arose from the intervention of the UK political electoral cycle. It was also embedded in the local government structures present in the area, with competing centres of power and influence. At one level, competing interests were straightforward – one tier of local government was 'won' by the Conservatives while the more geographically local tiers were controlled by Labour. These differences are important because project managers were discussing how to make the initiative sustainable as the Conservatives won power and began to review all initiatives associated with Labour, regardless of their value or impact. Other tensions surfaced between the different tiers of local government, even when both were controlled by Labour. These differences can be understood by the different histories and traditions of the Labour and trade union movement in the localities, the extent to which there were different religious traditions, and the extent to which individuals within the leadership of local Labour groups were identified with New Labour, different factions within the Labour Party, or their perspective on the Iraq War.

Our study, which included interviews with a range of strategic decision makers, points to eight major themes which characterize the potential for learning across different boundaries of practice.

- The necessity and the success of the change process.
- The social and economic context – and the way(s) in which this informed public policy choices and options.
- The apparent 'gap' between the expectation and hope that services/agencies would act in a 'partnership' and the challenge to make it real at street or neighbourhood level. To take 'what works' from a neighbourhood or particular agency and generalize this to actions across the County.
- The importance of locating where 'authority' and decision making sits.
- The capacity of organizations to work with 'blended professionals'.
- The extent to which there was a shared level of understanding and awareness of what the key issues were – the absence or presence of a shared narrative which would open up the discussion within and between agencies.
- The levels of public confidence in those public agencies involved in the criminal justice system and the extent to which officers/politicians share those views (or not).
- How were the objectives defined, measured and reflected upon, and who participated in these processes.
- How resources are allocated/monitored.

These themes were identified as those likely to be present in most initiatives based upon 'collaboration' or 'cross-boundary working'. They captured those elements of cross-boundary working that challenge the status quo or which are perceived as disruptive to existing relationships and structures. The Community Safety Partnership and the Change Programme came at a moment when each of these factors were present or had the potential to be present. The changing national political and economic environment provided pre-conditions for the initiative to be seen as a threat to existing professional interests and the dominant political party.

These contextual factors were identified as part of the processes associated with cross-boundary working, and most of the themes described above might have been anticipated. But, these local (as well as changing national) factors are the ones which provide each initiative with its own particular set of characteristics. In this specific context the changing national and local political environment weakened the potential and the alliances necessary for sustainable change. The Director of Change brokered a complex and fragile alliance to ensure implementation of the core program. This weak alliance model was unlikely to be successful in the implementation of this national initiative. The weaknesses inherent in the steering group responsible for the Change Programme led to sufficient momentum (or authority) to implement the vital changes

The weak brokerage model reflected weaknesses at a strategic level, and so, although there were key public agencies with a track record in collaborative working, this was insufficient. The weakening economy and the damaged credibility of the ruling national party thereby allowed agencies and key personnel to silently resist the initiative. Inter- and intra-organizational conflicts and tensions are hard to manage at the best of times. In this particular context the evidence suggests that successful cross-boundary working required strong and persistent networks and alliances in order to be effective. It is the extent to which we can identify where these pre-conditions exist that we need to reflect upon in our assessments of the degree to which we can provide evidence of the 'potential' or 'capacity' to introduce cross-boundary working or whether to settle for a much more limited and carefully defined practice based upon co-operation or co-ordination.

Note

1 Empowered and Effective Leadership; Effective and Responsive Delivery Structures; Intelligence Led Business Processes; Community Engagement; Visible and Constructive Accountability; and Appropriate Knowledge and Skills.

References

Amin, A. and Roberts, J. (eds) (2008) *Community, Economic Creativity and Organization*, Oxford: Oxford University Press.

Arnstein, S.R. (1969) 'A ladder of citizen participation', *Journal of the American Institute of Planners*, 35(4): 216–224.

Audit Commission (2009a) *Comprehensive Area Assessment: Framework Document*, London: Audit Commission.

Audit Commission (2009b) *CAA News*, Editions 1–13 September 2007 to March 2009. Online. Available at: www.audit-commission.gov.uk/caa/news.asp (accessed 1 June 2011).

Balloch, S. and Taylor, M. (eds) (2001) *Partnership Working: Policy and Practice*, Bristol: The Policy Press.

Benneworth, P. (2007) *Leading Innovation: Building Effective Regional Coalitions for Innovation*, Research Report, London: NESTA. Online. Available at: www.nesta.org. uk/library/documents/Report%20-%20Leading%20Innovation%20v6.pdf (accessed 17 November 2011).

Borraz, O. and John, P. (2004) 'The transformation of urban political leadership in western Europe', *International Journal of Urban and Regional Research*, 28(1): 107–120.

Boud, D. and Middleton, H. (2003) 'Learning from others at work: communities of practice and informal learning', *Journal of Workplace Learning* 15(5): 194–202.

Brookes, S. (2009) Interview: Stephen Brookes. Online. Available at: www.guardianpublic.co.uk/stephen-brookes (accessed 6 December 2011).

Crawford, A. and Jones, M. (1996) 'Kirkholt revisited: some reflections on the transferability of crime prevention initiatives', *Howard Journal*, 35(1): 21–39.

Department for Communities and Local Government (2006) *Reform to Bring 'Devolution to the Doorstep' says Kelly*. Online. Available at: http://webarchive.nationalarchives. gov.uk/20100513032259/http://communities.gov.uk/news/corporate/reformbring (accessed 17 November 2011).

Department of Transport Local Government and Regions (2001) *Strong Local Leadership: Quality Public Services*, Cmnd 5237, London: HMSO.

Diamond, J. and Roberts, S. (2006) 'Intra-organisational collaboration: a story of gains and losses', *Teaching Public Administration*, 26(2): 28–36.

Federal Justice Office (1992) *Creating a Safer Community: Crime Prevention and Community Safety into the 21st Century: Issues Paper*, Canberra: Australian Government Publishing Service.

Gibney, J. and Murie, A.S. (2008) *Towards a 'New' Strategic Leadership of Place for the Knowledge Based Economy: a Report for the Academy of Sustainable Communities*, Birmingham: School of Public Policy, University of Birmingham.

Grint, K., Martin, G., Wensley, R., Doig, B., Gray, P. and Matlew, C. (2009) *Leadership in the Public Sector in Scotland*, ESRC Seminar Series Mapping the Public Policy Landscape, Swindon: Economic and Social Research Council. Online. Available at: www.esrc.ac.uk/_images/Leadership_Scotland_tcm8-2441.pdf (accessed 6 December 2011).

Grint, K. (2004) *What is Leadership? From Hydra to Hybrid*, Oxford: Said Business School and Templeton College, Oxford University.

Grint, K. (1997) *Leadership: Classical, Contemporary and Critical Approaches*, Oxford: Oxford University Press.

Hemphill, L., McGreal, S., Berry, J. and Watson, S. (2006) 'Leadership, power and multi-sectoral urban regeneration partnerships', *Urban Studies*, 43(1): 59–80.

Home Office (2007a) *Cutting Crime: A New Partnership 2008–11*, London: Home Office. Online. Available at: www.homeoffice.gov.uk/documents/crime-strategy-07 (accessed 30 June 2011).

Home Office (2007b) *Delivering Safer Communities: a Guide to Effective Partnership Working: Guidance for Crime and Disorder Reduction Partnerships and Community Safety Partnerships*, The Hallmark Document, London: Police and Crime Standards Directorate, Home Office.

Home Office (1991) *Safer Communities: The Local Delivery of Crime Prevention Through the Partnership Approach*, London: Home Office.

Huxham, C. and Vangen, S. (2000) *Perspectives on Leadership in Collaboration: How Things Happen in a (not quite) Joined Up World,* Urban Leadership Working Paper 8, Bristol: University of the West of England.

Huxham, C. and Vangen, S. (2005) *Managing to Collaborate,* London: Routledge.

Jones, A. and Morris, K. (2008) *Can Collaboration Help Places Respond to the Changing Economy?* London: The Work Foundation.

Joseph Rowntree Foundation (2000) *Tackling Social Exclusion at Local level: Neighbourhood Management.* Online. Available at: www.jrf.org.uk/sites/files/jrf/310.pdf (accessed 18 February 2010).

Karlsson, J., Anderberg, E., Booth, S., Odenrick, P. and Christmansson, M. (2008) 'Reaching beyond disciplines through collaboration', *Journal of Work Place Learning* 20(2): 98–113.

Leach, S. and Wilson, D. (2000) *Local Political Leadership,* Bristol: Policy Press.

Liddle, J. and Murphy, P. (2012) 'Managing the public services in an era of austerity: editorial', *Public Money & Management,* Special Edition, March 2012.

Local Government Management Board (1996) *Survey of Community Safety Activities in Local Government in England and Wales,* Luton: LGMB.

Martin, S. and Bovaird, T. (2005*) Meta-evaluation of the Local Government Modernisation Agenda: progress report on service improvement in Local Government,* London: Office of the Deputy Prime Minister.

McQuaid, R.W. (2010) 'Theory of organisational partnerships: partnerships advantages, disadvantages and success factors', in S. Osborne (ed.) *The New Public Governance,* London: Routledge.

Mulgan, G. (2007) *Ready or Not?: Taking Innovation in the Public Sector Seriously,* Provocation 03, London: NESTA.

Murphy, P. 'The emergence, development and convergence of performance management regimes across locally delivered public services in England', paper presented at PAC Annual Conference, Nottingham Trent University, UK, September 2010.

Neighbourhood Renewal Unit (2008) What is Neighbourhood Management? Online. Available at: www.neighbourhood.gov.uk/page.asp?id=577 (accessed 18 February 2010).

Northouse, P. (2004) *Leadership: Theory and Practice.* London: Sage Publications.

Office of the Deputy Prime Minister (ODPM) (2005) *Vibrant Local Leadership: Local Vision,* London, ODPM.

Organisation for Economic Cooperation and Development (OECD) (2001) *Public Sector Leadership for the 21st Century,* Paris: OECD.

Squires, S. (2008) 'Building collective leadership at local level', paper presented to RSA Research Network on Collective Leadership, Nottingham Trent University, June 2008.

US Department of Justice (2001) *The Role of Local Government in Community Safety,* Crime Prevention Series #2, Washington: Bureau of Justice Assistance. Online. Available at: www.ncjrs.gov/pdffiles1/bja/184218.pdf (accessed 5 May 2009).

Vangen, S. and Huxham, C. (2003) 'Managing trust in inter-organisational collaboration: conceptualisations and tools', in P. Hibbert, (ed.) *Co-creating Emergent Insights,* Glasgow: University of Strathclyde.

17 Airport enclaves

Bridging boundary tensions between airports and cities[1]

Timothy Donnet and Robyn Keast

Introduction

Current approaches to airport development and land use sit at odds with the tradition of airports as spaces for aviation (Stevens *et al.* 2010). While airports remain the primary interface between air transport and society, the functions they include within their boundaries have expanded well beyond the provision of infrastructure for aviation and logistics. Shopping malls, commercial office space, hotels, golf courses and conference facilities are increasingly normal uses of land within airport boundaries (Kasarda 2008), and enhance the role of airports from transport infrastructure to a new form of economic infrastructure (Freestone 2009). However, the expanding role of airports, and the resulting diversification in airport land uses, has not been without opposition.

As regions prosper and cities grow, airports are increasingly less spatially removed from the populations they service. The previous distance between airports and cities meant that neither was required to consider the other's organizational interests or operational requirements. Given their relative isolation (at least initially) from cities, airports created a form of closed space or enclave with special rights or powers because of their importance to strategic and economic agendas at both regional and national levels. Additionally, airports remain dominantly focused towards servicing aviation needs as important nodes within global flight-path networks, so 'today's airport is only partially connected to the environment around it' (Friedman 1999: 14, cited in Graham 2001: 6). This sentiment is supported by Ibelings (1998), who argues that nowhere is the process of enclave formation stronger than the world of airport architecture. The relative isolation of airport decision making, particularly for planning and development, may have been appropriate in the past; however, as the distance between airports and urban environments continues to shrink, the notion of enclaves and the practice of isolated decision making have been challenged. The recent Australian Aviation Policy White Paper (Department of Infrastructure, Transport, Regional Development and Local Government 2009) clearly demonstrates that policy makers, planners and airport operators are increasingly calling for new, more integrated fora to act as conduits between airports and their regions.

Urban encroachment upon airport boundaries has brought city and airport interests and impacts into direct intersection, creating new boundaries and tensions related to decisions of what to build, where, when and how. As several authors have noted, tensions between airports and their neighbouring cities appear to be universal, and planning decisions for airports and cities have rarely been collaborative (Charles *et al.* 2007; Stevens *et al.* 2010). As the proximity of airports and cities has narrowed through urban encroachment, the stakes in planning-related decisions have increased, resulting in planning and development turf wars in which both cities and airports seek to protect their own long-term interests. The privatization of Australia's major airports in 1996, for example, and the resultant outsourcing and decentralization of control, have limited the federal government's authority to directly steer the development of infrastructures. Governments act, instead, in a relationship with their markets in order to achieve long-term regional planning goals, steering and guiding development at arm's length (Stoker 1998). In so doing, the operational and planning control of airports have been divested to private corporatized companies, with the provision of an approved master plan providing the regulatory basis for development. Compounding this, airports are also not subject to local and state planning authority, thus exacerbating tensions. The rise of new airport-centric development forms such as the airport city (Conway 1980, 1993) and Aerotropolis (Kasarda 2001), which position airports as new urban growth nodes, have also contributed to the contested planning space.

The privatization of airports, and the often associated 'inward looking' development ethos, has challenged the stability and order between airport and regional planning regimes by increasing the complexity for airports and cities to plan for future growth in population and aviation capacity. Further, the removal of airport planning from the hierarchical controls of government bodies at local levels requires the creation of new relationships between city and airport planners to negotiate decisions for appropriate and acceptable land uses in and around airports. As separate planning authorities, the need to coordinate their planning is paramount to ensure that future development does not confound the ability of airports and cities to meet their long-term growth objectives.

In effect, the growing trend to privatize airports, and the shift of airport planning regimes to focus on diversified development programmes rather than solely on air transport, begin to explain why working across boundaries has emerged as a central consideration for decision making in the context of airports. However, the isolation of airport planning from local and regional planning agencies, and the resulting power struggles, are not new. Integration of decision making appears to be the next big hurdle for airports and cities to overcome, particularly as airports and cities have grown accustomed to self-directed planning. Despite the tensions and the different interests sets, increasingly all parties are aware of their interdependence: i.e. that they are no longer able to operate as independent silos and require the expertise and resources of others to meet their collective interests. Under current conditions the need to bridge the gap between airports and their urban surrounds through new governance and planning fora has become an increasing, yet under-explored imperative. Drawing on a suite of existing issues and success stories from a suite of national and international airport-city relationships, this chapter contributes to discussions for working across boundaries by responding to the question 'How does it work (or not)?' by providing insights into how cities and airports manage (or don't manage) the integration of their planning and development decisions.

Airports as enclaves

Airports have become decision making enclaves within the planned environments of cities. The development of airports has traditionally been closely geared towards regional and national economic development (Munnell 1992), with governments often providing airports (or their regulators) with special planning and development powers so as to protect the long-term growth of aviation transport nodes. The majority of airports, over time, have become independent decision making entities that sit distinct from their local environments. Graham (2001) discerns airports as a form of logistics enclaves, noting that contemporary airports are essentially concentrations of facilities and services within a defined spatial setting. This perspective matches well with Ezechieli's (1998: 18, cited in Graham 2001: 6) notion that airports are 'similar to that of an island connected with other distant regions only through very selective specialized systems of transportation'.

Cardoso and Falettor's (1979, cited Graham and Marvin 2001) creation of enclaves via direct external control or through relationships with local elites fits closely to the authority typically ceded to airports: airport decision making (or oversight) is often located within non-local governments (at national or regional levels), and the proliferation of privatization is increasingly placing decision making in the hands of private operators/investor consortiums (again, with government oversight).

For planners, the notions of enclaves or segregation are strongly linked to negative aspects of planning (see Caldeira 1999; Luymes 1997) and associated with a separation from the mainstream and potential for limited communication across enclave boundaries. As a consequence, for planners enclaves are more of a threat than an opportunity for society. The relative isolation of enclaves is maintained by the perceived value for residents to remain apart and to somehow protect them from the animosities of outsiders (Caldeira 1999). This is more the view from the urban planning/residential development perspective, but some of the sentiments are apparent for (particularly privatized) airport operators/ decision makers, where the ability to maintain aviation operations may be perceived to be under threat from developments beyond the airport fence.

Enclave airports, with their dominantly internal planning focus (Alexander 1998), challenge networked forms of governance and collaborative planning. However, as a 'space of flows' within the networked society (Castells 1996: 145–147), airports are increasingly seen as channels between places and are reliant upon the ability of external infrastructures to service their operational needs. Airports, therefore, cannot cocoon themselves from their external environment, and must now actively engage with their surrounding jurisdictions in order to survive – that is, the operational nature of airports requires access to be provided both in terms of airspace and in terms of land access (i.e. roads and/ or rail). To maintain air and land access, airports must advocate their interests across boundaries which are jurisdictional, functional and often political in nature.

Airports increasingly recognize that they need to be involved with other decision making actors in their regions in order to protect their own operational requirements and long-term objectives. However, airports must now decide which issues to focus on as cross-cutting and which to retain as internally focused and driven. As to how airports and cities might pursue mutual consideration of their strategic needs – or, in other words, integrate their decisions for planning and development – the governance arrangements underpinning airport and city strategic decision making require careful consideration.

Integrated planning: the way forward?

Planning is defined as the link between ideas and action (Friedmann 1987). There are many approaches to planning, each with complexities so rich that they defy the formulation of a single theory of planning (Rittel and Webber 1973; Mandelbaum 1979). This view of a planning hydra has been challenged by Cooke (1983) and Poulton (1991a, 1991b) who provide compelling logic and theory to the ability of planning to approach planning issues from a positive, normative, rational, linear perspective. While the rationales of Cooke and Poulton for normative planning approaches may appear valid for many cases, the increasing complexity of planning decisions which require the consideration of both airport and city interests means that positive, rational approaches may no longer be sufficient (see Kane and del Mistro 2003). Looking to the literature, the most compelling evaluation of available planning approaches has been forwarded by Alexander (1998), who proposes not to rewrite existing approaches, but to provide a contingent model for planning approaches. This perspective is elaborated further with the acknowledgement that many approaches to planning do not exist in isolation from one another, and that many have overlapping fundamental processes (Alexander 1998).

The spatial planning of airports (mostly) sits in isolation from the spatial planning of their local cities – that is, decisions on what, where, when and how to plan and develop land are subject to different approval laws/requirements, jurisdictions, and agendas from one side of the airport fence to the other. Stakeholder engagement has been pursued as the answer for identifying and appreciating neighbours' needs, and is now considered the norm for many airport and urban planning processes (Farthing 2001; Dempsey 1999). However, stakeholder engagement has taken on a role as an institutional arrangement in the coordination of planning (Alexander 1998), rather than as a truly deliberative process of aligning perspectives and goals (Healey *et al.* 2003).

The disconnect of city and airport interests in planning and development decisions is mirrored in a number of contemporary airport planning models (Blanton 2004; Finavia 2004; Kasarda 2001). While each model attempts to appreciate what happens on the other side of the fence, they all remain focused on meeting the logistics needs of airports, rather than incorporating existing (and future) local/regional societal interests (Stevens *et al.* 2007).

Conventional, rational approaches to planning rely on centrally determined interventions (i.e. land-use plans) to achieve 'a desired overall state of affairs' (Moroni 2010: 138). However, in acknowledging the need to incorporate a range of interests, the practice of planning has moved towards more inclusive and collaborative approaches (Healey 2003). A central feature of these alternative models is the expansion of the actors involved in the development of decision making and planning (Gunton and Day 2003; Innes and Booher 1999). Collaborative planning draws on genuine dialogue and an iterative process of negotiation between members to reach shared agreement on issues and their resolution (Brand and Gaffikin 2007). That is, consensus is established on the rules of engagement and joint fact-finding is used as a way to overcome entrenched opinions and organizational positions (Healey 1998).

Advocates of the collaborative planning approach cite many advantages over other models, including the increased likelihood of developing plans that better reflect the public interest, and the increased likelihood of successful implementation (Gunton and Day 2003; Wondolleck and Yaffee 2000; Susskind *et al.* 2000). Despite these benefits, a number of limitations to collaborative planning have been identified, including the fact that application is often limited to only those cases where all relevant stakeholders are motivated to participate/and or management agencies are willing to delegate power, the high cost in time and resources, an inequality in power that may give some stakeholders an unfair advantage, and a tendency of the consensus approach to produce satisfying rather than optimal outcomes to meet all needs (Yiftachel and Huxley 2000; Brand and Gaffikin 2007).

Identifying pathways for enabling airports and cities to move through these limitations to collaborative planning is clouded by complex puzzles, frustrating barriers and fundamental tensions between decision making actors, and are yet to be well defined (see Healey 2009). The following section details a methodology for identifying the puzzles, barriers and tensions that could be considered normal to efforts to integrate airport and city planning around the world. Additionally, the method provides a means for identifying attributes and arrangements that appear to enable the integration of airport and city planning decisions in the real world.

Method

An explorative approach was applied to this study, drawing upon secondary qualitative data. The data source (Appold *et al.* 2008) was purposefully selected for its broad collection and description of arrangements to overcome problems between airports and cities from around the world. The document provides rich contextual background for six airport cities, and 35 lessons from another 21 major airports spread across Australasia, Europe and North America. The data was thematically coded to identify: (1) *tensions* between airports and cities relating to development and planning decisions; (2) *barriers* that severely hampered the ability of airports and cities to integrate their decisions; and (3) critical success factors acting as *enablers* to city and airport decision making integration. Additionally, while exploring the issues identified within the data, a number of them appeared to be common to a number of airport cases; however, they appear 'hidden', 'unspoken' or under-addressed within current planning and governance literature. These apparently under-explored issues have been identified as (4) *puzzles* for the integration of their development and planning decisions. The result is a range of insights that highlight the steadfast and difficult to manage issues for integrating planning and development for cities and airports. Also, a range of promising pathways and future issues are identified for ensuring that the planning outcomes of both airports and cities do not confound the long-term strategic interests of either.

Findings

Tensions

Analysis of the cases provided by a recent report to the Dutch Commissie Ruimtelijke Ontwikkeling Luchthavens (loosely translated as Commission for Spatial Planning Concerns for Airports; Appold *et al.* 2008), revealed a discourse dominant in spatial and economic planning issues. Foremost is the tension surrounding the limited land resources (available space) to handle increases in population and aviation capacity for a given region. The result of this tension is urban encroachment on airport boundaries, which can be problematic for the long-term sustainability of aviation operations at airports, if poorly managed. Residential developments have the potential to impact upon the safety of airspace, and increasing the number of residents living close to flight operations (including flight paths) results in increased noise complaints. Also, any changes to the volume of aviation operations has an immediate effect upon noise exposure for local residents, so while cities need more space for residents to live, airports want areas under flight paths protected from 'excessive' residential development.

Commercial (non-aviation) developments within airport boundaries appear to be a source of tension, not always for the development opportunities they 'take' from city jurisdictions (as cited in Appold *et al.* 2008), but for the lack of coordinative planning between airport and city. While some tensions arise from the lack of revenue generated through application/approval fees and land taxes, airports are often able to develop land without direct input from local governments and stakeholders. The apparent disconnect of regional stakeholder input from airport development approval has the potential for negative impacts upon local transport and economic infrastructures. These negative impacts stem from increased demands upon transport infrastructure to move workers and consumers to and from the airport. Economic infrastructures, such as local business districts and commercially zoned land, suffer (at least in the short-term) from reduced rents from inflated supplies of office/retail space within the local market.

Tensions do not necessarily have negative impacts upon the decisions made by airports or their surrounding cities. In many of the cases examined, tensions were seen as a constant struggle, of which both airports and cities were well aware, providing common ground from which plans and developments could be negotiated. Tensions appeared to become problematic in decision making processes that had significant barriers to integration of decisions for planning and development, as discussed in the following subsection.

In some of the above instances, the identified tensions appear to stimulate the communicative processes required for implementing a collaborative approach to planning, rather than stifling them. That is, Healey (1998) would argue that debating tensions between city and airport decision makers works towards reaching a common understanding of each others' rationales for planning. In turn, having a common understanding between parties is essential for gaining consensus among participating decision makers (as per Brand and Gaffikin 2007).

Barriers

Barriers to integrating airport and city decisions for planning and development were best defined in cases that lacked finite jurisdictional boundaries and/or well developed horizontal mechanisms for the identification, articulation and consideration of each others' strategic interests. Barriers include issues of physical environment factors and historical planning factors. The physical environment surrounding airports plays an important part in the operational considerations of aviation and in the long-term prospects for both urban and airport development. Natural terrain and the built environment both impose upon operational considerations for aviation; aircraft are required to have a minimum safe distance from obstacles, and aviation regulators often take advantage of terrain (i.e. river systems) to dampen the noise footprints of aircraft. Elements within the spatial environment thus pose natural, and sometimes created, barriers to decision making integration between airports and cities. For example, both airport and city may face limitations in expansion and/or development from environmentally sensitive systems such as wetlands. Additionally, a city desiring high-rise commercial or residential development may face physical limitations in permissible building heights in order to protect airspace, or conversely an airport wanting to build a new runway may be hindered by existing buildings or natural terrain that impose upon the safety of flight operations.

Features within the built environment may also be historically significant to local societies, creating embedded features that mitigate the acceptance of aviation growth for an airport. For example, the citizens of the Municipality of Pratt del Llobregat, located adjacent to Barcelona Airport, traditionally had access to the local beach front, which was located on the far side of the airport from the township. Original proposals to expand the airport with a third runway included the resuming of beachfront and resident beach access; however, the loss of access and way of life for local residents was deemed unacceptable. Accordingly, plans were changed to protect resident access to the beachfront. In this way, elements of societal significance form finite barriers to what is acceptable and what is not in the extent of airport development.

The political impetus driving airport or city development also has a significant influence upon the ability of airports and cities to integrate their planning and development decisions. Centralized governments pursuing grand development schedules to enact large-scale (even system-level) change have been drivers of mega-airport development. While developments at the mega-scale attract top-level support from government, local communities and governments may feel ostracized or circumnavigated in decision making processes to develop such grand infrastructures (such as Dubai's Jebel Ali Airport or South Korea's Incheon Airport). Airport development may be espoused as being in the greater good of a country, however, developments of such a grand scale ultimately result in the demise of other regional assets, or, at a minimum, reduce the attractiveness of existing economic hubs within a region.

The barriers above identify contexts in which there is a revival of the rational comprehensive planning approach, which works against the contemporary shift towards more inclusive models of planning. For example, the centrally planned mega-airports introduced above create interconnected systems within their planned boundaries. While the rational comprehensive approach may coordinate the various private activities at play within the planned sociospatial system (as per Moroni 2010: 138), what of the urban environs at the fringe of these planned mega-airport developments? The development of mega-scale airport-city developments is likely to result in the tacit creation of decision making citadels, where regional economic success so heavily relies on the success of a mega-development as to artificially sway decision making processes and outcomes in its favour.

Enablers

Airport and city decision makers have found interesting ways to leverage their shared tensions and overcome (some) boundaries that otherwise leave their planning and development decisions in isolation from one another. These enabling factors range from formal mechanisms that ensure horizontal communication and consideration of each others' interests, through to informal social networks that enhance information flow between airport and regional planning authorities. Interestingly, in some instances where there were no apparent mechanisms to promote the integration of airport and city planning and development agendas, planning authorities were still able to identify and implement strategies that fostered mutual gains for both airport and city.

While formal mechanisms enabling the integration of airport and city planning and development interests appeared to be custom-made for individual political contexts, each arrangement or mechanism identified as beneficial to integration showed similar traits across cases. These traits include formal, well-defined protocols for the transmission of city interests into airport planning and development decisions, legitimate pathways for the protection of city interests in airport development, and clearly defined limitations to city development to protect aviation safety. Additionally, the inclusion of flight-path planning into the negotiation space for airport and city planning appeared in only one case; however, this inclusion appeared to have significant benefits for the protection of city interests without degrading aviation safety or airport outcomes.

Informal mechanisms fostering the integration of airport and city interests stemmed from social and professional networks linking decision makers from airport and regional planning agencies. Informal mechanisms also included the use of other formal forums between airport and city decision makers that were unrelated to planning and development decisions. These informal communication pathways provided additional feedback for decision makers, giving informal forewarnings of positive or negative responses to formal proposals.

Some cases had limited (sometimes no) evidence of integrated decision making between airport and city. Despite being isolated from airport decision making processes, some cities adapted their plans to best suit and protect the long-term growth of their airports. In very few of these cases, city planning utilized aviation-affected land for industrial and hi-tech commercial parks, effectively protecting residential development from excessive aircraft noise while improving airport access for businesses that benefit from close proximity to air transport. These outcomes suggest that rational comprehensive types of planning can still work for managing the spatial interface of airport and city. Furthermore, the evidence suggests that collaborative planning may not necessarily always be the correct response to urban encroachment on airport boundaries. This finding is consistent with Moroni's advice for rethinking the application of planning theory, namely that the 'the real question, put simply, is "which theory for which kind of practice?"' (2010: 138).

Puzzles

The pursuit of economic/industrial clustering may impact upon the ability of airports and urban environs to coexist, or may conversely facilitate development via putting developments in their appropriate places to make use of land otherwise ill-affected by airports' operational footprints. For example, Incheon Airport is on an island just off the coast of the Incheon region and Seoul. The mass of land available for development around the airport is large enough to support considerable (city size) development. However the possible tension arising from developing this land is the creation of a whole new economic centre away from existing economic and social infrastructures.

The creation of 'mega-airports' or 'airport cities', such as Incheon (Korea) and Jebel Ali (Dubai), has resulted in the emergence of new puzzles and boundaries for integrated city and airport decision making. The development of airports at the mega-scale are often greenfield developments, located spatially discrete of existing urban environs with an apparent 'if you build it, they will come' approach to planning. Jebel Ali and Incheon airports are both developed and overseen by highly centralized governments, which appear to foster the planning and development of the necessary supporting transport and economic infrastructures. However, tensions arise from the coordination of planning with other surrounding cities/urban environs that are not necessarily the focal point of development – old cities left in the shadow of the new.

In many cases, the inclusion of city and regional authorities as investors/ partial owners/overseers of airports is an outright attempt to temper airport decision making with local and regional interests. Airports with at least some government ownership are common around the world; however, they still have troubles integrating planning and development decisions with their surrounding planning agencies. Getting the mix right between structures of airport ownership, planning regulation and horizontal dialogue appears to be the most ambiguous of puzzles drawn from the case data. As an example, Amsterdam Airport Schiphol appears inundated by a myriad of consultative bodies surrounding airport/region coordination; however, they appear to do little to improve relations between the airport and city.

Discussion

The analysis of the case data reveals many tensions and shifting boundaries for the integration of city and airport planning interests, many of which appear to be inescapable (such as spatial and geographical factors). The overarching regional and national economic benefits derived from airports makes them strategic infrastructures that compete with cities for space.

Tensions between airports and cities are not necessarily counterproductive, as evidence from the cases reviewed shows that tensions stimulate debate and may even result in a sense of mutual understanding (albeit somewhat adversarial) between airport and city decision makers. Tensions appear to exist on two levels within the case data: first, as a latent fear that decisions made on the one side of the fence will stymie the long-term needs and objectives of the other; and second, a sense of frustration (or even bewilderment) from previous planning and development decisions on the opposite side of the fence. We theorize that both latent and historical tensions provide stimuli for the discussion and sharing of interests (or points of debate and negotiation) which are critical elements for facilitating horizontal dialogue (Innes and Booher 1999) to underpin communicative processes within collaborative decision making (Gunton and Day 2003). However, should tensions strain relations they will likely become tempering factors to actors' engagement and sharing of critical information, or even preclude actors from engaging with one another, thus becoming barriers to integration. In this way, tensions can be both positive and negative for the integration of planning and development decisions for airports and cities, and are reliant upon the ability of decision makers to manage tensions and barriers from the historical, operational and spatial contexts for each airport and city.

Perhaps the most interesting and significant finding from the study comes from the ability of isolated planning decision makers to provide development strategies that appreciate the needs of both airport and city. The success of Tallinn's zoning of hi-tech business parks under flight paths suggests that airports and cities may grow simultaneously and (somewhat) harmoniously without relying on horizontal forms of governance for mutually beneficial outcomes. At face value the local government appears completely disconnected from airport decision making, except for the consideration of transport needs. However, the mutually beneficial outcome of encouraging hi-tech business parks in noise-affected areas suggests that the city understood both the negative and the positive impacts of the airport. Championing the benefits for hi-tech firms located close to airports, local government provided top-down support for business park development, achieving a 'double win' by encouraging their location in areas affected by aircraft noise. While encouraging non-residential development in noise affected areas appears to be common sense, planning agencies around the world continue to zone and approve residential developments directly under flight paths. Tallinn's planning success suggests that while there is an impetus to collaborate airport and city planning decisions, positive (even innovative) outcomes may still be achieved in isolation when decision makers have sufficient knowledge and legitimacy to leverage tensions for mutual benefit.

As a relatively new phenomenon in planning, mega-projects such as Incheon and Jebel Ali airport cities integrate the needs of cities and airports via highly centralized decision making. While this approach mitigates the apparent need to bridge institutional boundaries for planning for an airport and its local city, follow-on effects into the broader region are likely to be the next significant hurdle for societies neighbouring airport cities (Szyliowicz and Goetz 1995). Placing so much emphasis on a single infrastructure to generate regional economic value will likely lead national and regional governments to favour and protect their airport cities in spatial policy making; likely to the detriment of local governments' ability to sustain their communities.

Conclusions

Airports are, and may always be, to some extent, planning enclaves. There have been significant steps forward in improving horizontal ties between airports and cities; however, planning and development forums between airports and cities typically remain without legitimate and vertically supported influence over decisions made 'on the other side of the fence'. Goetz and Szyliowicz first called for policy makers to transition airport planning processes from rational comprehensive models to more deliberative and collaborative forms in 1997. Since then, however, little has been done to provide substantive legitimate avenues for airport and city interests to be identified, articulated and considered in each others' planning and development decisions. This lack of progress is polarized by the ways in which governments have approached the mega-scale development of airport cities. The political impetus driving the development of airport cities (such as Incheon and Jebel Ali) has the very real possibility of morphing what was an airport enclave into what could best be described as an airport citadel, rejecting Healey's (1998) vision for inclusive and collaborative planning processes in favour of the teleocratic, exclusionary processes of rational comprehensive planning (as per Moroni 2010). We theorize that should governments bias legitimacy and authority in planning and development decisions to airport cities, the planning and development decisions made by the surrounding environs would likely be dominated (without legitimate avenues for redress) by the agendas and interests of the airport citadel.

This chapter has identified a range of tensions, barriers, enablers, and residual puzzles for integrating the planning and development decisions of airports and cities. While not exhaustive, the insights generated present a useful starting point for explaining how working across boundaries can work in the contested space of airport and city planning, while potential limitations in working across the airport-city planning boundary have also been identified. These insights focus future research upon improving the ways in which airports and cities approach the integration of their decisions for planning and development, both inside and outside of airport boundaries. In particular, consideration for the benefits and limitations of the different approaches to planning contested areas in and around airports requires further investigation. Future research should also focus on the role of conjoined airport and city mega-scale developments, particularly for the issues identified in the discussion above. Further investigation is also warranted for identifying and explaining the immutable and negotiable stakeholder interests in planning airports and their surrounds.

Note

1 This work was carried out through the Airport Metropolis Research Project under the Australian Research Council's Linkage Projects funding scheme (LP0775225).

References

Alexander, E.R. (1998) 'Doing the "impossible": notes for a general theory of planning', *Environment and Planning B: Planning and Design*, 25(5): 667–680.
Appold, S., Baker, D., Donnet, T., Kimmet, P., Van de Riet, O. and Van Twist, M. (2008) *TUD – deelrapport Fase 2, Deel C: Internationale Vergelijking*. Delft: Technische Universiteit Delft.
Blanton, W. (2004) 'On the airfront', *Planning*, 70(5): 34–36.
Brand, R. and Gaffikin, F. (2007). 'Collaborative planning in an uncollaborative world', *Planning Theory*, 6(3): 282–313.
Caldeira, T.P.R. (1999) 'Fortified enclaves: the new urban segregation', in S.M. Low

(ed.) *Theorizing the City: The New Urban Anthropology Reader*, New Jersey: Rutgers University Press.

Cardoso, F. and Falettor, E. (1979) *Dependency and Development in Latin America*, Berkley, CA: University of California Press.

Castells, M. (1996) *The Information Age: Economy, Society and Culture: Volume 1 The Rise of the Network Society*, Oxford: Blackwell.

Charles, M., Barnes, P., Ryan, N. and Clayton, J. (2007) 'Airport futures: towards a critique of the aerotropolis model', *Futures*, 39(9): 1009–1028.

Cooke, P. (1983) *Theories of Planning and Spatial Development*. London: Hutchinson Education.

Conway, H.M. (1980) *The Airport City: Development Concepts for the 21st Century*, Atlanta: Conway Publications.

Conway, H.M. (1993) *The Airport Cities 21: The New Global Transport Centers of the 21st Century*, Norcross: Conway Data.

Dempsey, P.S. (1999) *Airport Planning and Development Handbook: A Global Survey*, New York: McGraw Hill Professional.

Department of Infrastructure, Transport, Regional Development and Local Government (2009) *National Aviation Policy: White Paper: Flight Path to the Future*, Canberra: DITRDLG.

Ezechieli, C. (1998) *Shifting Boundaries: Territories, Networks and Cities*, referenced in S. Graham (2001) 'FlowCity: networked mobilities and the contemporary metropolis', *DISP*, 144(4): 4–11.

Farthing, S.M. (2001) 'Local land use plans and the implementation of new urban development', *European Planning Studies*, 9(2): 223–242.

Finavia. (2004) *Civil Aviation Administration Annual Report*. Vantaa: Finavia Corporation.

Freestone, R. (2009) 'Planning, sustainability and airport-led urban development', *International Planning Studies*, 14(2): 161–167.

Friedmann, J. (1987) *Planning in the Public Domain*. Princeton: Princeton University Press.

Friedman, K. (1999) *Restructuring the City: Thoughts on Urban Patterns in the Information Society*, referenced in S. Graham (2001) 'FlowCity: networked mobilities and the contemporary metropolis', *DISP*, 144(4): 4–11.

Goetz, A. and Szyliowicz, J. (1997) 'Revisiting transportation planning and decision making theory: the case of Denver International Airport', *Transportation Research Part A: Policy and Practice*, 31(4): 263–280.

Graham, S. (2001) 'FlowCity: networked mobilities and the contemporary metropolis', *DISP*, 144: 4–11; reprinted in *Journal of Urban Technology*, 9(1): 1–20.

Graham, S. and Marvin, S. (2001) *Splintering Urbanism: Networked Infrastructures, Technological Mobilities and the Urban Condition*, New York, NY: Routledge.

Gunton, T. and Day, J. (2003) 'The theory and practice of collaborative planning in resource and environmental management', *Environments*, 31(2): 5–20.

Healey, P. (1998) 'Building institutional capacity through collaborative approaches to urban planning', *Environment and Planning A*, 30(5): 1531–1556.

Healey, P. (2003) 'Collaborative planning in perspective', *Planning Theory*, 2(2): 101–123.

Healey, P. (2009) 'In search of "strategic" in spatial strategy making', *Planning Theory & Practice*, 10(4): 439–457.

Healey.P., de Magalhaes, C., Madanipour, A. and Pendlebury, J. (2003) 'Place, identity and local politics: analyzing initiatives in deliberative governance', in M.A. Hajer and H. Wagenaar (eds) *Deliberative Policy Analysis: Understanding Governance in the Network Society*, Cambridge: Cambridge University Press.

Ibelings, H. (1998). *Supermodernism: Architecture and Globalization*, Rotterdam: Nai Publishers.

Innes, J. and Booher, D. (1999) 'Consensus building and complex adaptive systems: a framework for evaluating collaborative planning', *Journal of the American Planning Association*, 65(4): 412–424.

Kane, L. and Del Mistro, R. (2003) 'Changes in transportation planning policy: changes in transport planning methodology?', *Transportation*, 30(2): 113–131.

Kasarda, J.D. (2001) 'From Airport City to Aerotropolis', *Airport World*, 6(1): 42–47.

Kasarda, J.D. (2008) 'The evolution of airport cities and the Aerotropolis', in L. Siebert (ed.) *Airport Cities: The Evolution*, London: Insight Media.

Luymes, D. (1997) 'The fortification of suburbia: investigating the rise of enclave communities', *Landscape and Urban Planning*, 39(2–3): 187–203.

Mandelbaum, S.J. (1979) 'A complete general theory of planning is impossible', *Policy Sciences*, 11(1): 59–71.

Moroni, S. (2010) 'Rethinking the theory and practice of land-use regulation: towards nomocracy', *Planning Theory*, 9(2), 137–155.

Munnell, A.H. (1992) 'Policy watch: infrastructure investment and economic growth', *Journal of Economic Perspectives*, 6(4): 189–198.

Poulton, M.C. (1991a) 'The case for a positive theory of planning. Part 1: what is wrong with planning theory?', *Environment and Planning B: Planning and Design*, 18(2): 225–232.

Poulton, M.C. (1991b) 'The case for a positive theory of planning. Part 2: a positive theory of planning', *Environment and Planning B: Planning and Design*, 18(3): 263–275.

Rittel, H.J.W. and Webber, M.M. (1973) 'Dilemmas in a general theory of planning', *Policy Sciences*, 4(2): 155–169.

Stevens, N., Baker, D. and Freestone, R. (2007) 'Understanding the Australian Airport Metropolis', paper presented at State of Australian Cities National Conference (SOAC), Adelaide, November 2007.

Stevens, N., Baker, D. and Freestone, R. (2010). 'Airports and their urban settings: towards a conceptual model of interfaces in the Australian context', *Journal of Transport Geography*, 18(2): 276–284.

Stoker, G. (1998) 'Governance as theory: five propositions', *International Social Science Journal*, 50(1): 17–28.

Susskind, L., van der Wansem, M. and Ciccarelli, A. (2000) *Mediating Land Use Disputes: Pros and Cons*. Cambridge: Lincoln Institute of Land Policy.

Szyliowicz, J. and Goetz, A. (1995) 'Getting realistic about megaproject planning: the case of Denver International Airport', *Policy Sciences*, 28(4): 347–367.

Wondolleck, J.M. and Yaffee, S.L. (2000) *Making Collaboration Work: Lessons from Innovation in Natural Resource Management*, Washington, DC: Island Press.

Yiftachel, O. and Huxley, M. (2000) 'Debating dominance and relevance: notes on the "communicative turn" in planning theory', *International Journal of Urban and Regional Research*, 24(4), 907–913.

Part IV
Conclusion

18 Crossing boundaries in public management and policy

Conclusion and future issues

Janine O'Flynn, Deborah Blackman and John Halligan

Introduction

If the issues of how to work across boundaries are some of the 'most discussed' (Kelman 2007) in terms of achieving public purpose and the performance of government, what have we learnt from all of this discussion? In the conclusion to this book we return to the fundamental questions and use these to draw together the key findings and lessons from the contributions to this volume. In doing so, we point to similarities and differences, and to enduring tensions and puzzles. Following this, we set out future issues and areas for attention for scholars and practitioners.

The fundamental questions

In Chapter 2, O'Flynn set out the fundamental questions that framed the book. These were distilled from various literatures informing our study of cross-boundary activity. Here, we return to these to capture the main themes from across the contributions to this volume.

Question 1: What do we mean by the notion of crossing boundaries?

In Chapter 2, O'Flynn discussed the concept of boundaries. She drew on various ideas from organizational theory, sociology, management theory, and public management and administration. Different forms of boundaries were set out, including constructed, objective, subjective, real, and imagined, and several types were discussed, including organizational, jurisdictional, knowledge, policy, and sectoral boundaries. This provided a basis for understanding the boundary phenomena and enabled the reader to consider the various forms in each chapter and how these often combine to produce challenges in practice.

Contributors focused on these various boundaries in their chapters. Working across boundaries between public sector organizations featured in several of the contributions: Talbot and Talbot, Buick, Eppel *et al.*, Blackman, Paun and Blatchford, Lindquist, Christensen *et al.* all looked at these. Hughes looked at authority boundaries and how these were transforming. Another group of authors considered combinations of these: Korac and Saliterer, Hughes, Head, Le Roux, Liddle and Diamond, Klaster *et al.*, and Donnet and Keast all featured in this group. Korac and Saliterer, for example, analyzed health platforms which involve a range of actors including federal states, social health insurance institutions, ministry representatives, the medical association, patient advocacy groups, and churches. Liddle and Diamond covered the full range in their discussion of community safety which adopted a place-based approach.

Whilst not explicitly referring to them as knowledge boundaries, these emerged in discussions from Liddle and Diamond and Talbot as we delved into the challenges of different professions working together to address complex policy challenges. This also came through in the chapter by Christensen *et al.*, in their discussions of which disciplinary-educated groups dominated cross-boundary forms of working. In Talbot and Talbot's consideration of the clashes between professions and occupations during mergers we also see knowledge boundary issues.

Across the contributions, authors commented on whether these boundaries were rigid, permeable, being shifted, removed, traversed, or whether actors were simply stumbling around them. In sum, the authors provided us with a rich exploration of various forms and types across the range of organizational, jurisdictional, policy and knowledge boundaries.

Question 2: Why has this emerged?

In Chapter 2, O'Flynn set out six 'stories' that have driven cross-boundary activity: the twenty-first century modus operandi story; the coordination story; the disaggregation and fragmentation story; the complexity story; the strategic management story; and the better value story. These manifest differently in various contexts and sometimes emerge in combination as the driving rationales for cross-boundary action.

Eppel *et al.* showed us that shared outcomes and complex problems have driven the cross-boundary agenda in New Zealand and LeRoux argued that boundary spanning has become modus operandi in the United States due to fragmentation, technological innovation, and the American cultural preference for small government. Lindquist noted that coordination and better value have dominated in the Canadian experience. In Australia, both Buick and Blackman showed that complexity and the pursuit of better value have been important drivers. For Donnet and Keast, the strategic management, better value and complexity stories have featured in the experience of airports. Complexity and fragmentation have driven the boundary crossing imperative according to Christensen *et al.* not just in Norway, but also more broadly.

In the United Kingdom various imperatives have been important: Talbot and Talbot highlight the better value story in their chapter on mergers; Paun and Blatchford point to the importance of disaggregation and fragmentation, coordination, and better value as drivers for cross-cutting agreements; Liddle and Diamond highlighted how the coordination, complexity and better value stories influenced community safety developments; and Talbot pointed to coordination, complexity and better value in the equally complex children's services area. For Klaster *et al.*, coordination and complexity have been critical drivers in the cases of education and employment in the Netherlands, and Korac and Saliterer stressed fragmentation in the delivery of health care services and better value as critical in Austria. Head, in his contribution on collaboration, argued that complexity has been a prime driver of the focus on collaborative forms of working across governments.

What does all of this tell us? There are common drivers or imperatives, but these will manifest differently, be that in distinct cases of crossing boundaries, or in specific jurisdictions. There are also unique factors that shape the experiences; the small government preference in the United States is a good example of this.

Question 3: What does cross-boundary working involve?

In Chapter 2, O'Flynn provided an overview of various forms and configurations of crossing boundaries. This included some existing typologies and continua, and some prominent forms, namely collaboration, joined-up government, networks, and whole-of-government. Across the chapters, the authors presented a range of mechanisms and approaches that fitted these categories.

Lindquist provided a comprehensive review of a range of forms that developed in the Canadian experience, and LeRoux set out several that have been prominent in the United States, including contracting, intergovernmental agreements, and formal and informal networks. Talbot and Talbot examined public sector mergers as a structural attempt to solve boundary issues. Korac and Saliterer explored the creation collaborative multi-player health platforms which provided pooled funds for innovation. Buick and Blackman both focused on whole-of-government approaches in Australia. Christensen *et al.* explored collegial bodies, both within and between organizations.

Liddle and Diamond explored experiments with multi-agency, collaborative partnerships based around place. Klaster *et al.* considered a range of approaches, including the creation of specialist directorates, inter-departmental committees, integrated policymaking, and legal reform, which represented very different approaches to crossing boundaries. Talbot examined the creation of trusts as an integrative mechanism for joining up across networks. Finally, Head discussed collaboration in considerable detail, setting out a considered analysis of various types and how patterns of collaboration develop in various domains.

This rich set of forms and configurations allowed us to examine crossing boundaries in various ways, providing us with various lessons on what has worked, or not, in different contexts.

Question 4: What are the critical enablers and barriers?

Our contributors all considered enablers and barriers in some way. In Chapter 2, O'Flynn set out a selection of those that feature in the various literatures informing cross-boundary activity: formal structures; commonality and complexity;

people, culture and leadership; power and politics; and boundary objects. In this section, we focus on various themes that cut across the book.

People, culture and leadership emerged as a major theme, reflecting the relational aspects of working across boundaries. Several contributions pointed to the importance of culture as both enabler and barrier – Buick most extensively, but also Talbot and Talbot, Hughes, Lindquist, and Eppel *et al.* In her chapter, Blackman pointed out the importance of pattern-breaking behaviour, which goes against the status quo and can potentially change cultures. Whether cultures can be managed or changed is a long-standing debate in the literature, but the importance placed on it here reflects the faith that practitioners have in it as a potential panacea to the dilemmas of cross-boundary working. For example, in the United Kingdom, Sir Francis Maude (Minister for the Cabinet Office), argued that structural reform could not solve the challenges of joined-up working. He noted: 'There are things to be done, but this is about behaviour and culture. This is about chemistry, not physics' (Dudman 2012).

Liddle and Diamond emphasized the importance of particular leadership approaches, noting that leaders can develop narratives of collaborative working and emphasize the joint outcomes being pursued in order to facilitate joint working. Blackman argued that central leadership was important to drive whole-of-government models. Relatedly, Eppel *et al.* found that a lack of leadership obstructs collaborative working. Leaders play an important role, then, in demonstrating the importance of cross-boundary working, modelling approaches, and enabling others. Increasingly, however, they need to do this using 'soft power', as Hughes argued, rather than exercising formal authority.

Many of the contributors pointed to particular aspects of cross-boundary skills, echoing those set out by writers such as Williams (2002, 2008, 2010, 2012) and Alford and O'Flynn (2012). Lindquist discussed the emphasis on developing such skills in the Canadian context, Liddle and Diamond commented on this in relation to partnership working, and Klaster *et al.* made the point that cross-boundary skills matter. LeRoux discussed a range of behavioural factors that facilitate cooperation – brokering, negotiating, facilitating and conflict resolution, amongst others, and Hughes echoed many of these, noting that they differed profoundly from the impersonal bases of authority at the centre of Weber's bureaucracy. Buick emphasized the importance of a cooperative mind-set, the development of long-term professional relationships, and high quality communication.

Eppel *et al.* extended the ideas of skills and competencies and looked instead at a set of roles that provide the impetus for the dynamics of collaboration: the public entrepreneur, the fellow traveller and the guardian angel all play a critical role in moving collaborators through important phases. Christensen *et al.* showed that individual demographic factors explain variations in cross-border activity, rather than simply structural factors. In doing so, they allowed us to get some sense of *who* these actors are, providing insight into who gravitates towards, or is selected for, such work. Building cross-boundary competencies is important in a world where cross-boundary working has become more important to the achievement of governmental goals; however, there is little evidence that governments across the board invest in these (Lindquist's discussion of Canada being an exception). For example, Blackman argued that there was little emphasis on recruiting people for their cross-boundary skills, nor was there investment in training and development to sit alongside a major whole-of-government reform program. Talbot expressed similar concerns on the inadequacy of resources to build the capacity for joint work.

Emphasizing the relational aspects of cross-boundary working, trust emerged as an important enabler and barrier. LeRoux pointed to the importance of trust, as did Buick, and both of them discussed how frequent interaction, communication, and information sharing are critical. Liddle and Diamond also emphasized how trust enabled more collaborative approaches to partnerships, and Hughes highlighted trust as important to new ways of working. However, Eppel *et al.* discussed how repeated restructuring has the potential to undermine trust in practice. Trust can also be affected by constant turnover of those working at the boundary, something that Blackman pointed out; frequent changes undermine trust because they require parties to start again and break established norms and relationships.

Commonality and complexity were also important for several contributors. Blackman showed that a shared understanding was a key enabler, and Buick and Eppel *et al.* emphasized the importance of a common commitment to community/client outcomes to enable effective boundary crossing. Interestingly, Donnet and Keast argued that tensions often sparked increased communication between actors with divergent interests, which then enabled more integrated and collaborative processes, and fostered common understanding and goals.

Structures were central to Talbot and Talbot's contribution, which showed how these can clash during mergers, creating challenges that undermine objectives. They argued that even in the so-called 'success' case, the hard boundaries of pre-mergers organization became soft boundaries within the new one, and that, in more problematic cases, the combination of conflicts between task structures and cultural incompatibility created poor results. Blackman also highlighted structure as a critical barrier to cross-boundary working. For Klaster *et al.*, structure can be an important precondition, but cultural awareness of the importance of cross-boundary working must accompany this.

Formal systems such as budgets, accountability and performance shape what Alford and O'Flynn (2012: 251–252) have referred to as the 'enabling environment', and these emerged in various ways across the chapters. Liddle and Diamond commented on how the lack of a single (or shared) budget meant that resources were rarely aligned with joined-up decisions – a point echoed by Paun and Blatchford, who argued that shared budgets were needed to drive shared outcomes. Blackman also noted that funds were too tightly tied to specific programs rather than common goals. Talbot, however, provided another perspective, noting that pooled budgets could leave some parties worse off as dominant actors move more funds into their preferred areas. Korac and Saliterer showed that collaborative funding and decision-making produces mixed results: although it might enable innovation, this was not necessarily the case.

It was commonly argued that governance frameworks needed to adapt to new ways of working. Talbot argued that the existing governance structures were mismatched with the aims of joined-up approaches, stating that the aims were far too ambitious given the *status quo*. Without changes, where clear accountability around joint outcomes is set out, cross-boundary working will remain difficult to embed, according to Paun and Blatchford. Liddle and Diamond showed that complex performance and reporting structures created challenges for cross-boundary working, but that they can be levers for change. A misalignment of evaluation and accountability emerged in Blackman's work, where she noted that the cross-boundary experiments she investigated were over-evaluated and never given sufficient time to deliver the complex outcomes that they were intended to achieve. Interestingly, in their work with those at the front line of cross-boundary working, Eppel *et al.* found these 'hard systems' were not absolute constraints, but rather things to be worked around; in many cases it was 'soft' factors that were more likely to create major barriers.

LeRoux discussed how politics could act as a barrier to effective working across boundaries. She pointed to the potential for conflict between politicians and public managers, arguing that whilst managers may seek to work in more collaborative, multi-organizational modes, political conflict can stymie this. Donnet and Keast highlighted the importance of political actors in driving collaboration, although Talbot noted that this could often be faddish rather than evidence-based. Blackman argued that a political mandate is critical to catalyzing and sustaining cross-boundary working, and that power – exercised by individuals or central agencies – was important in maintaining joined-up approaches. Such notions were echoed by Paun and Blatchford, who argued that when ministers focused exclusively on departmental aims, joined-up objectives were undermined. Central agencies can play a critical role, as they have the power to push strategic aims and monitor and challenge departments; however, this has not been exercised sufficiently to drive more joined-up approaches in the UK, according to Talbot and Paun and Blatchford. Talbot and Talbot discussed how important power was in public sector mergers, with examples of how differential power, often tied to organizational size, has been a barrier to more effective cross-boundary working. Blackman also discussed how a lack of decision-making power stymied cross-boundary working. She argued it was common to find the wrong people at the table so that when it came time to broker, negotiate and deal, these actors did not have the power to make decisions. Hughes, however, gave us a different view, noting that even if public managers could use authority to coerce or force, they do so less and less. Further, their ability to do so is much more constrained in situations where they must try to coordinate the efforts and actions of multiple parties. The answer, he argued, was a 'soft power' approach which is rooted much more in notions of influence than force.

In Chapter 2, O'Flynn discussed how boundary objects act as translation devices across boundaries, facilitating more effective working. Whilst there was not a major emphasis on this in the contributions, some interesting examples emerged. Formalized protocols assisted in cross-boundary working in Donnet and Keast's study, and the discharge reports for patients created a cross-boundary pathway in the health system in Korac and Saliterer's chapter. The failure to develop such objects may help us to explain why, despite, all this effort, many cross-boundary experiments falter because parties cannot speak each other's language.

Whilst many of our contributors looked at these factors as both enablers and barriers, Blackman drew on her findings to put forth a new way of thinking about enablers and barriers, repositioning them as separate continua, and used a force field approach to consider these *in situ*. This provides a basis for rethinking what we consider to be critical enablers and barriers and how to manage for these in practice.

Future issues

Crossing boundaries in public management and policy practice is not a 'trend', but rather a critical capability for government to develop. Whilst there are zealous voices arguing that this is the 'one best way' of operating, our contributors are more pragmatic. Many note that there needs to be more focus on where this type of operating may be most effective, but that it is rarely *the* answer to governmental problems. As we have seen, there are various imperatives to the adoption of cross-boundary approaches, different forms are adopted in practice, and there are a range of factors that can inhibit or facilitate cross-boundary working. Trying to answer the fundamental questions demonstrates that this remains a complex field of study, and a profoundly complicated area of practice.

An important area for future attention is bridging disciplinary differences. There is much to learn from bringing alternative views to bear on these enduring tensions and puzzles, and public management and policy scholars often work within narrow disciplinary boundaries. Those looking to boundary crossing activity exclusively from the political science, organization studies, or public management perspectives will miss key parts of the puzzle. We need to understand organizations as well as politics and, where we are interested in crossing boundaries outside of government, this is even more important. What drives non-profit and for-profit organizations will matter when government organizations seek to engage with them. How to leverage the capabilities of these organizations to pursue governmental goals is critical, but not likely to be successful if we extend our largely bureaucratic modes of operating outward. The practical challenges can be rethought through different theoretical notions, but only where scholars move beyond their own boundaries. Blomgren Bingham and O'Leary, (2006: 161) made a similar point when they edited a special issue of *Public Administration Review* on collaborative governance: 'we tend to play cooperatively each with our own set of blocks ... we do not generally pool our blocks to build a common structure collaboratively'. There are important insights to be gained from across a range of disciplines, and scholars in particular may find that engaging with these different areas provides ways to move the field forward. Exploring the strategic management literature on alliances, mergers, and hybrids can teach us much about how to bring organizations together successfully, or not. Practitioners too can capture benefits from looking to other fields: what does the experience of private firms with mergers and strategic alliances offer them for undertaking public sector mergers, for example?

Contributors in this volume have made some advances in this direction. Talbot and Talbot, for example, used Mintzberg's notion of task structure, combined with cultural perspectives, to analyse the experience of public sector mergers, and showed us that many of these outcomes are highly predictable if we view them through a different lens. Buick draws heavily on the organizational culture literature to explain why the 'culture solution' is not so straightforward. Rather than simply naming culture as the panacea, she explains the various aspects of it and how it develops, and therefore allows us to consider whether or not culture can really be managed in the instrumental way that it is often suggested. Failing to engage with this deep literature means that many scholars and practitioners neither understand the phenomenon, nor its utility in cross-boundary working. Hughes adopts notions of 'soft power' from international relations to inform his discussion of managing without authority. He argues that governments will less frequently exercise 'raw power' or authority in pursuit of goals and will increasingly use the power of influence and preference shaping. Christensen *et al.* bring together structural perspectives from organizational theory with demographic notions and are able to shed new light on how collegial bodies operate in the Norwegian public service. Blackman uses ideas from force field analysis and hygiene factors to re-conceptualize enablers and barriers, providing us with a means to evaluate readiness to work in various cross-boundary ways. In isolation we know a lot about the various parts of this puzzle, but we can make major breakthroughs if we can bring these different strands together in a more problem-solving mode.

Another major issue is around understanding whether or not cross-boundary working has been successful or not. This is a complex notion. Some contributors to this volume put forth arguments for success, failure or mixed outcomes in their chapters, but it is Head who provides us with an analysis of the current understanding of evaluating effectiveness. He argues that many of the claims about the power of multi-sectoral collaborations are not empirically robust and notes that there is still much to be done to develop frameworks for evaluating cross-boundary working, despite this being a topic of discussion for some time (see Huxham and Hibbert 2008, for example). Korac and Saliterer also address the evaluation challenge, and provide us with a means of evaluating innovations driven by cross-boundary working. More comprehensive and more sophisticated evaluation of cross-boundary working is needed to move us forward in theory and practice.

Finally, there is the challenge of austerity. Governments across the world face fiscal challenges of various degrees and this has renewed the focus on cross-boundary working, especially the notion of delivering better value. In the coming years much of the focus for governments and scholars will be on how this will affect the various themes covered in this book. How will austerity affect various types of relationships? Will we see an increased focus on particular forms of cross-boundary working? Will fiscal austerity drive innovation or kill it? Views differ: Paun and Blatchford argue that the focus on cuts in the UK will push joined-up approaches off the agenda, but Lindquist pondered whether fiscal constraint might lead to more long-term collaborative problem-solving, decision-making and experimentation.

In compiling this book we sought to bring together studies of the international experience of crossing boundaries in public management and policy. To do this, however, we sought to set out the fundamental questions of the field and use these to explore a range of issues that cut across countries and forms of cross-boundary activity. In doing so, we have sought to identify enduring tensions and puzzles, draw lessons, and move our thinking forward by connecting to a range of literatures that inform theory and practice in this area. We encourage our colleagues to continue down this path.

References

Alford, J. and O'Flynn, J. (2012) *Rethinking Public Service Delivery: Managing with External Providers*, Palgrave: Basingstoke.

Blomgren Bingham, L. and O'Leary, R. (2006) 'Conclusion: parallel play, not collaboration: missing questions, missing connections', *Public Administration Review*, 66(S1): 161–167.

Dudman, J. (2012) '"Fragile" Whitehall needs chemistry not physics, says Francis Maude', *Guardian Professional*, 14 November 2012. Online. Available at: www.guardian.co.uk/public-leaders-network/2012/nov/14/francis-maude-fragile-whitehall-criticism (accessed 15 November 2012).

Huxham, C. and Hibbert, P. (2008) 'Hit or myth? Stories of collaborative success', in J. O'Flynn and J. Wanna (eds), *Collaborative Governance: A New Era of Public Policy in Australia?*, Canberra: Australia and New Zealand School of Government, The Australian National University, ANU E-Press.

Kelman, S. (2007) 'The transformation of government in the decade ahead', in D. F. Kettl and S. Kelman, *Reflections on 21st Century Government Management*, Washington: IBM Center for the Business of Government.

Williams, P. (2002) 'The competent boundary spanner', *Public Administration*, 80(1): 103–124.

Williams, P. (2008) 'Competencies for collaboration', paper presented to the 2nd Annual Copenhagen Conference on Partnerships: Creating Innovative Solutions through Collaboration, Copenhagen, November 2008.

Williams, P. (2010) 'Special Agents: The nature and role of boundary spanners', paper presented to the ESRC Research Seminar Series 'Collaborative Futures: New Insights from Intra and Inter-Sectoral Collaborations', University of Birmingham, February 2010.

Williams, P. (2012) *Collaboration in Public Policy Practice: Perspectives on Boundary Spanners*, Bristol: The Policy Press.

Index

Page numbers in *italics* denote tables, those in **bold** denote figures.

Department of Justice (US) *see* United
States Department of Justice
Department of National Defense (Canada)
191
Department of the Prime Minister and
Cabinet (Australia) 79, 173
Department of Transportation (US) *see*
United States Department of
Transportation
Department of Work and Pensions (UK)
130
Diamond, J. 9, 265, 298302
Directors for Children's Services (UK)
219, 222
Donahue, J.D. 14, 21, 25
drugs 19, 274; abuse 12; addiction 137;
courts 72; trade 18; treatment
programmes 130

Economic Action Plan 2007 192, 203
Economist Intelligence Unit 15, 25
Edelenbos, J. 73, 148
education 9, 13, 17, 48, 80, 107–8, 118,
121; administrators 95–6; basic 21;
Department for (UK) 137, 222; higher
92, 106, 114, 126, 238; level 39n1;
Ministry initiative 48; policies 126, 232,
234, 236; rule-oriented 115; Service 96,
103, 105; services 102, 221–3; vice-
ministers 238
education 151, 219, 221–2, 225, 229,
232–3, 235, 242, 299; funding 224;
HIV/AIDS 247; medical staff 250;
Minister of Education (the Netherlands)
238; primary 238, 242n2; secondary
238, 242n2; university 265; vocational
232, 238, 242n2
educational 79, 232; attainment 264, 267;
background 115, 118, *119*, 120; law
234, 239; legislation 229, 238; sectors
237
Edwards, M. 36–7, 142
Egeberg, M. 113–14, 117
Eisenhardt, K. 21, 174
Emerson, K. 20, 25, 35, 39n6
employment 9, 13, 79–80, 99–100, 229,
232–5, 242, 299; opportunities 266;
practices 179; rates 127; regional 235–6;
youth 233; *see also* unemployment
Employment Agency 103
Employment Service (UK) 99, 101
England 9, 106, 269; children's services
213–14; governance 220, 224; Local
Government 226n2; urban riots 138;

Whitehall 125, 127–32, 135–9,
139n1–2, 161; *see also* United
Kingdom
English Government departments 129,
131; Business Innovation and Skills
129, 131; Children, Schools and
Families 129, 131, 219–22, 224;
Communities and Local Government
131, 267; Department of Health 129–30;
Education and Schools 213–14, 219,
222; Energy and Climate Change 126,
129; Environment, Food and Rural
Affairs 126; Government Equalities
Office 129; Innovation, Universities and
Skills 126; Work and Pensions 129–30,
133
Eppel, E. 6, 47, 61n1, 297–8, 300–2
Esteve, M. 33, 39n1
Europe 266, 285; European economy 205
Every Child Matters 219, 221–2, 225;
Green Paper 214, 218
Expenditure Management Information
System (Canada) 201

Federated Press 192, 202
Firecone Ventures 47
Foster-Fishman, P. 148
France, A. 223–4
Frederickson, H.G. 3, 18, 26, 64, 68, 74
Frumkin, P. 93–4, 105, 107
Fuerth, L.S. 18, 37

Gerth, H.H. 160–1
Glasby, J. 15, 22–3, 29, 178–9, 184
Goldsmith, S. 64, 142, 145, 154, 168
Good, D. 192, 203, 206n1
Good Governance program (the
Netherlands) 238, 243n5
governance 11, 14, 20, 111, 134, 142,
146, 153, 158, 161–2, 164–5, 170, 201,
203, 213, 224–5, 245, 266, 302;
anticipatory 18; arrangements 127,
150, 268, 283; collaborative 11, 14, 21,
25, 39n6, 111, 303; contemporary 36;
English 220; external environment 204;
fluid 231; framework 216; good 238,
243n5, 267; horizontal 8, 17, 190, 193,
199; innovations 247, 249; integrated
173; joined-up 26–7, 240; market-
based 75; mechanisms 137; network
154; new 64–5, 205, 281; public 143,
202, 242n1; structures 250, 272;
successful 56; tight 163; tools of 70;
weak 219, 225

government 3–4, 7–8, 15, 16–17, 19, 22–3,
26–30, 33, 36, 47–8, 51, 59, 61, 64–9,
70–2, 74–5, 79, 81, 88n2, 93, 99, 102,
104, 108, 111, 123, 126, 128, 131,
133–4, 136, 173, 190, 204, 269; activity
6, 180; agencies 11, 143, 146, 166;
apparatus 115–16; assets 38; Australian
174, 182, 187n1–2; Coalition 107, 137,
215; collaborative 2, 196, 198; cross-
government 34, 192, 202; departments
187n2, 191, 264; Equalities Office 129;
federal 187n3, 201, 281; high-
performing 35; Labour 130, 267–8,
275–6; levels of 21, 150, 233;
manifestos 83; national 206n6;
networked 20, 168, 170, 299; non-local
282; Norwegian 122; organizations 80,
226n1, 303; partners 73; policy 60, 142,
172; political leadership 135; report 18,
37, 134; UK 94, 101, 106, 125, 216,
218; *see also* holistic government;
joined-up government; whole-of-
government
governmental 21; context 148; directorates
233; goals 79, 301, 303; management
168; organizations 149, 169; outcomes
16, 166; power 163; projects 235–6;
reforms 230–1; unit 71
Government Equalities Office (UK) 129
Government Office (UK) 271
Government Urban and Economic
Development Office (NZ) 48
Graham, S. 280, 282
Gray, B. 142, 147
Gregory, R. 104, 111, 122
Grint, K. 266–7
Gulick, L. 13, 113
Gunton, T. 284, 289

Hale, K. 72
Halligan, J. 11, 18, 27, 29, 206n1
Hardy, C. 23, 35
Harlow, E. 220–1
Harrison, R. 94, 96, *97*, 102
Hartley, J. 34, 168, 249
Head, B. 8, 19–20, 25, 30, 142–4, 148–9,
298–9, 304
Healey, P. 283–4, 286, 291
health care 19, 66, 70, 151, 245–51, 253,
257–8, 299; *see also* mental health
Health Maintenance Organizations 217
Heifetz, R.A. 166–7
Heracleous, L. 1213
Her Majesty's Revenue and Customs 92,

100–1, *103*, 104–6, 108, 130; *see also*
Customs and Excise
Her Majesty's Treasury 101, 106, 108,
126, 128, 131, 136–7, 176; Treasury
Select Committee 101, 104
Herzberg, F. 183
Himmelman, A.T. 24–5, 30, 39n5, 143–4
Ho, P. 20
holistic government 11, 14, 29, 111, 215;
local 14, 48, 59, 67–71, 116, 131, 133,
137, 161, 214, 226n2, 233, 263, 266–71,
277, 280, 285, 290; *see also*
government, joined-up government;
whole-of-government
Home Office (UK) 129, 131, 265, 271–2;
Police and Crime Standards Directorate
271
Hood, C. 33, 128
Hopkins, M. 47, 84–5, 191, 196
Horizontal Management Secretariat
(Canada) 199
horizontal working 8, 11, 20, 54, 59–61,
117, 122; challenges 192, 199, 202,
204–5; collaborative 196; coordination
17, 116, 198; development 195;
expenditure rules 57; governance 8, 17,
173, 190, 193, 199, 203; government 14,
26–7, 190, 207n7; initiatives 190–205,
206n2, 206n6, 207n7; interactions 56;
issues 18, 191, 194–5, 197–8, 200–5,
206n3; management 111, 192–3, 196,
198–205; mergers 93, 106; networks 7,
57, 64; policy 190; projects 192, 195–6,
199, 206n3; qualities 195, 205;
specialization 116; strategies 193, 201,
204–5; *see also* across boundaries,
boundary crossing, cross-boundary,
jurisdictional, working across
boundaries
House of Commons Treasury Committee
(UK) 133
Housing and Urban Development (US) 66
Hughes, O.E. 8, 163, 297–8, 300–2, 304
Human Resource Management 32
Huxham, C. 30, 49–51, 55, 144–5, 219,
263–4, 304

Indigenous 79, 88n2; affairs 30, 32;
Australians 79; communities 79–81, 83,
85, 188n4; initiative 173; outcomes 174;
people 83; programs 80; services 13, 83
Indigenous Coordination Centre 79, 87,
87n1, 174, 176–7, 181; Redvale and
Waytown 80–6

Parker, S. 132, 139n1–2
Parston, G. 20, 28, 30, 32–3, 35, 37
performance improvement 15, 21, 127; measures 26, 36, 105; outcome 74; regime 9, 36
Performance and Innovation Unit (UK) 78, 85, 130, 216
performance management 275; framework 136, 269; processes 105; regime 268; systems 18, 31
Personal Responsibility and Work Opportunity Act (US) 67
Peters, B.G. 82, 139n5, 192, 215
Pfeffer, J. 112, 114–15
police 71, 131, 158, 161, 169, 222, 264–7, 271–4; Chief Constable of Police (UK) 274; officers 159–60; policing 192, 274; powers 163
Police Authority (UK) 274
Police and Crime Standards Directorate (UK) 271
Policy Horizons Canada 202
Policy Research Initiative (Canada) 195, 202
Pollitt, C. 13–14, 21–2, 26, 28, 32, 35–7, 78, 111, 122, 215, 240
prime minister: role of 159, 207n7; mandate 175
Prime Minister and Cabinet (Australian) 79, 173, 175–6
Prime Minister (Canadian) 191–2, 195; Office 203
Prime Minister (Norwegian) 116
Prime Minister (UK) 138, 161, 263; Delivery Unit 128, 131, 133–5, 137; Strategy Unit 137
Prison Service (UK) *see* National Offender Management Service
Privacy Act (NZ) 59
Privy Council Office (Canada) 78, 82, 83, 85, 194, 201
Probation Service (UK) *see* National Offender Management Service
Provan, K.G. 64, 71–3, 144, 147, 151, 213–14, 217, 225
public management 3–6, 8, 11–13, 17, 26, 29–30, 36, 39, 47, 50, 64, 67, 72, 111, 158, 161–2, 164–5, 169–70, 230, 297, 303, 305; collaborative 14, 25, 64, 111
Public Policy Forum 202
public safety 65, 71, 75, 192
public sector leadership 33, 59
Public Service Agreement (UK) 126–9, 131–7; targets 139n3–4 268

public services 11, 68, 105, 108, 167, 177, 202–3, 263–4; Australian 15, 20, 27, 29, 37, 47, 78–9, 172–4; Canadian 190–5, 205; contracting out 67; delivery 16, 23, 71, 73, 162, 190, 207n8, 229, 268–9; executives 200, 204–5; fragmentation 14; improvement 249; leaders 193, 196; modernization 130, 267; New Zealand 61; Norwegian 304; organizations 28; reform 131, 223, 275–6; research program 202; spending 219; US 74; UK agreements 7, 126, 133, 268

radical change 9, 136, 241
Rescue Coordination Centre (Canada) 191
Rhodes, R.A.W. 163, 165
Richards, D. 130–1
Rittel, H.W.J. 20, 50, 283
Romzek, B. 71, 73–5
Rosenau, J.N. 163, 165
Rutter, J. 136, 138, 139n1

Sabatier, P.A. 145, 152–3
Salamon, L.M. 64–5, 67, 70
Schein, E.H. 33, 80–1, 84–7
Schraeder, M. 93, 96
Science and Technology MOU for Sustainable Development (Canada) 191
Senior Responsible Owner (UK) 127, 131–3, 135
Serious Case Review (UK) 223
Service Integration Project (Australia) 149–50
Shergold, P. 7880, 85, 173
siloization 7, 117, 122
Simon, H.A. 19, 112–13
Skelcher, C. 20, 111, 145–6, 148–9, 153
Smith, A. 69, 131, 200
spending 37, 58–9, 66, 137; Comprehensive Spending Review (UK) 126, 128, 133, 268, 272; cuts 136–8, 203; on drug-abuse treatment 130; health care 247; public 219, 264; welfare 99
Stake, R.E. 80, 174
stakeholders 22, 33, 143, 146–7, 150–1, 169, 188n4, 194, 197–8, 205, 250, 285; external 192; joint 87; key 21, 145, 147, 152–4, 241, 272; major 153; multiple 39n1, 73, 152, 182; relevant 82, 284
Star, S.L. 32, 38
State Services 59; Authority 28, 231; Commission 47; Development Goals (2008) 59